THE HANDBOOK OF PROFESSIONALLY MANAGED ASSETS

A DEFINITIVE GUIDE TO PROFITING FROM POOLED INVESTMENTS

Keith R. Fevurly

Apress®

The Handbook of Professionally Managed Assets: A Definitive Guide to Profiting from Pooled Investments

ISBN-13 (pbk): 978-1-4302-6019-6

ISBN-13 (electronic): 978-1-4302-6020-2

President and Publisher: Paul Manning
Lead Editor: Robert Hutchinson

Coordinating Editor: Rita Fernando
Copy Editor: Tiffany Taylor
Compositor: SPi Global
Indexer: SPi Global
Cover Designer: Anna Ishchenko

Distributed to the book trade worldwide by Springer Science+Business Media New York, 233 Spring Street, 6th Floor, New York, NY 10013. Phone 1-800-SPRINGER, fax (201) 348-4505, e-mail `orders-ny@springer-sbm.com`, or visit `www.springeronline.com`. Apress Media, LLC is a California LLC and the sole member (owner) is Springer Science + Business Media Finance Inc (SSBM Finance Inc). SSBM Finance Inc is a Delaware corporation.

For information on translations, please e-mail `rights@apress.com`, or visit `www.apress.com`.

Apress and friends of ED books may be purchased in bulk for academic, corporate, or promotional use. eBook versions and licenses are also available for most titles. For more information, reference our Special Bulk Sales–eBook Licensing web page at `www.apress.com/bulk-sales`.

Any source code or other supplementary materials referenced by the author in this text is available to readers at `www.apress.com`. For detailed information about how to locate your book's source code, go to `www.apress.com/source-code/`.

Apress Business: The Unbiased Source of Business Information

Apress business books provide essential information and practical advice, each written for practitioners by recognized experts. Busy managers and professionals in all areas of the business world—and at all levels of technical sophistication—look to our books for the actionable ideas and tools they need to solve problems, update and enhance their professional skills, make their work lives easier, and capitalize on opportunity.

Whatever the topic on the business spectrum—entrepreneurship, finance, sales, marketing, management, regulation, information technology, among others—Apress has been praised for providing the objective information and unbiased advice you need to excel in your daily work life. Our authors have no axes to grind; they understand they have one job only—to deliver up-to-date, accurate information simply, concisely, and with deep insight that addresses the real needs of our readers.

It is increasingly hard to find information—whether in the news media, on the Internet, and now all too often in books—that is even-handed and has your best interests at heart. We therefore hope that you enjoy this book, which has been carefully crafted to meet our standards of quality and unbiased coverage.

We are always interested in your feedback or ideas for new titles. Perhaps you'd even like to write a book yourself. Whatever the case, reach out to us at `editorial@apress.com` and an editor will respond swiftly. Incidentally, at the back of this book, you will find a list of useful related titles. Please visit us at `www.apress.com` to sign up for newsletters and discounts on future purchases.

The Apress Business Team

This book is dedicated to my father,
Dr. James R. Fevurly, who taught me the value of
"earning my first dollar" and then helped provide me
with the education of knowing what to do with it!

Contents

Foreword

Professionally managed assets have been around almost as long as organized financial markets. We will probably never know the name of the very first professional fund manager, but one of the first funds that resembles modern-day managed funds was Eendragt Maakt Magt, managed by Adriaan van Ketwich. It was essentially a closed-end bond fund that was founded in Holland in 1774.[1] Since that time, of course, the number and types of professionally managed investment funds have grown tremendously. Today in the United States there are over 7,000 mutual funds, over 600 exchange-traded funds, about 6,000 unit investments trusts, and about 10,000 hedge funds. Those numbers only hint at the complexity of the managed-funds industry when considering the number of strategies followed, the varieties of legal structures, the ways of reporting and analyzing performance, and so on. What we need is a handbook ... and here we have one.

Whereas in the past investing was primarily for the rich, today most people are investors—whether directly (owning individual stocks, bonds, real estate, and so on) or indirectly through some form of professionally managed investment pool or doubly indirectly through a 401(k), IRA, or other retirement account. As a result, all investors need to ask themselves if they have both the time and expertise to manage their money on their own, or if they should hire a professional. The answer for most is to hire the professional. After all, would you do your own dental work?

In addition to their managers' expertise, professionally managed funds have many features to recommend them, including the following sample of benefits:

- Instant diversification that couldn't be achieved with the size of the average investor's portfolio. Studies have shown that it takes at least 15 to 20 individual stocks to have a well-diversified stock portfolio (some have suggested 80 or more), and that is ignoring other asset classes that are necessary for a truly well-diversified portfolio.

---

[1]Geert Rouwenhorst, "The Origins of Mutual Funds," `http://viking.som.yale.edu/geert/origins.html`.

- The ability to reinvest cash flows automatically, thus removing the incentive for the investor to spend the money instead of investing it.
- Prevention or exploitation for profit of many of the irrational financial decisions that behavioral economists have identified in recent years (such as confirmation bias, hindsight bias, and mental accounting).
- The capacity to invest in asset classes (or geographical areas) that would otherwise be off-limits to a small investor.
- Liquidity in asset classes such as real estate that isn't available with direct investments.

The complete list is a long one and is better explained in Chapter 2 of this book.

Once you decide to invest in professionally managed assets, the next logical question is, "What types of funds are available, and which ones are right for me?" And helping you to answer that question is exactly the purpose of this book. The book describes in detail 12 popular categories of professionally managed assets. Aside from those that cover background information, each chapter generally proceeds along the same very useful path:

1. Definition of the particular category of fund
2. Investment strategies used
3. Advantages and disadvantages
4. The type of investor who should consider investing in this type of fund
5. Criteria for selecting this type of fund
6. How to evaluate performance

In addition, each chapter discusses the fees that are typically charged and the tax consequences of investing in each category of professionally managed asset. Fees and taxes may be some of the most important material discussed in the entire book, because they create a difficult performance hurdle for actively managed funds to overcome. The typical actively managed mutual fund needs to outperform its benchmark by nearly 1.5% each year just to earn its fees—and many other types of funds are even more expensive. Although the book covers some technical terrain, including a few simple mathematical formulas, the average investor should have no trouble following along and can safely skim the technical parts if necessary. Finally, the book also includes a helpful glossary of terms and cross-references the terms included in the glossary by boldfacing those terms in each chapter.

Keith Fevurly has been a friend and colleague of mine at Metropolitan State University of Denver since 2007. We hired Keith because of his unique qualifications and experience in the area of financial planning. His credentials include an MBA in Finance and Accounting, a Juris Doctorate (JD), a Master of Laws (LLM) in Taxation, and Certified Financial Planner (CFP) certification. His expertise is put to good use in this book, and I'm sure that you will benefit by reading it.

Timothy R. Mayes, PhD

About the Author

Keith R. Fevurly is an investment advisor with Integra Financial, Inc., Greenwood Village, Colorado, and a Senior Lecturer in Finance at Metropolitan State University of Denver. He is also an Adjunct Associate Professor of Finance at Webster University, St. Louis, Missouri. He served as the Vice President of Education at the College for Financial Planning, Denver, and as the Executive Director of Kaplan University's financial planning education program. Dr. Fevurly has assisted in the education of over 50,000 financial planners and investment advisors and authored over 20 refereed articles on financial and investment planning. He is the author of *Plan Your Financial Future*, published by Apress in July 2013. He is a member of the Editorial Review Board of the *Journal of Financial Planning* and a former member of the CFP Board's Board of Examiners. He holds an MBA in Finance and Accounting from Regis University of Denver, a JD from Washburn University of Topeka, an LLM degree in Taxation from the University of Denver Graduate Tax Program, and the Certified Financial Planner (CFP) certification.

About the Technical Reviewer

Timothy R. Mayes is Professor of Finance at Metropolitan State University of Denver, and he teaches corporate finance, portfolio management, and financial modeling. His primary research interest is the use of technology in financial education and investments. Dr. Mayes is the author of *Financial Analysis with Microsoft Excel*, 6th ed. (Cengage Learning, 2011). He received his PhD from the College of Business Administration, University of Central Florida.

Acknowledgments

I would like to acknowledge the courtesy of Morningstar, Inc., in permitting me to reproduce the five Morningstar profile or quote pages that appear at the ends of Chapters 5, 6, 8, and 15. I selected the subject funds of these five sample Morningstar quotes exclusively and arbitrarily for the pedagogic purpose of illustrating in pragmatic terms the methods and techniques described in the respective chapters for examining the key metrics and performance history of a given fund as variably afforded by Morningstar. The sample fund or funds reproduced at the end of a given chapter are referenced explicitly and implicitly throughout that chapter. Certain comments in the four chapters with Morningstar quote pages reflecting my analysis of fund information that does not appear in the reproduced Morningstar quote are clearly documented as such. I stress that my selection of specific funds for attention anywhere in this work is motivated solely by educational, illustrative, and informational purposes, and that their mention and examination in this book should in no way be construed by my readers as either an endorsement or rejection of those funds as possible components of their own particular investment portfolios.

I also wish to acknowledge the courtesy of the Investment Company Institute (ICI) in permitting me to reproduce from *2013 Investment Company Fact Book: A Review of Trends and Activity in the U.S. Investment Company Industry* all of the figures and tables appearing in Chapter 3.

I would like to thank Dr. Timothy Mayes, my friend and colleague at Metropolitan State University of Denver, for reviewing the initial draft of this book and for writing the foreword. Dr. Mayes's knowledge of finance and investments is vast and deep, and I thank him for sharing that with me and my readers. I also wish to thank the majority of financial planners and investment advisors who always keep the interests of their clients first and strive to achieve their financial goals.

Finally, thank you to the Apress Business Team for helping me to produce the best possible book to date on the intricacies and planning potential of professionally managed assets!

PART

I

An Overview of Professionally Managed Assets

CHAPTER

1

Understanding Professionally Managed Assets

For as long as individuals have invested, they have sought out the services of someone more experienced than themselves in the buying and selling of assets. In other words, they have turned to the services of a "professional."

Historically, the term *professional* has referred to an individual who is self-employed, is highly educated, and complies with an explicit ethical code of conduct. Among those individuals typically thought of as professionals are physicians, attorneys, accountants, and engineers. Indeed, the IRS classifies those involved in the health, accounting, legal, and engineering professions as subject to a possible penalty for engaging in what is known as a *personal service corporation* in tax law. Currently, however, the term *professional* is used much more broadly to refer to anyone who is a salaried individual and works for someone else, whether that is an individual or a non-manufacturing corporation (in other words, not in a "blue collar" industry).

Among those individuals now considered to be professionals are portfolio money managers, both at the retail and wholesale level. At the retail level, the professional money manager may be either an **investment advisor** or a **broker**. An investment advisor typically works independently or for a Registered Investment Advisor, whereas a broker typically is employed by a wirehouse firm, such as Bank of America Merrill Lynch, or an independent broker-dealer, such as Walnut Street Securities. It is at the wholesale level of investing, however, that most individuals think of professional money managers. An example is a portfolio manager of an open-ended investment company, commonly referred to as a *mutual fund*. This portfolio manager generally is a very experienced individual skilled in investments and investment theory. The manager is able to effectively match the characteristics of the investor to those of the fund investments the investor is making; each fund is then categorized accordingly to specify the types of investments that will be made by the portfolio manager. The manager is paid an annual salary by the investment company, often including a bonus for superior or outstanding investment performance during a given year.

The Definition of a Professionally Managed Asset

Now that we have described the meaning of the term *professional* in today's investment marketplace, what is meant by the term *asset?* In the investment world, an asset is any property of value owned by an individual or individuals. From a corporate balance sheet perspective, assets may be broken down into *current assets*, consisting of cash, accounts receivable, inventory, and short-term marketable securities; and *fixed assets*, consisting primarily of any buildings and land in which the corporation conducts its business, as well as any machinery or equipment used to generate the product or service the business offers.

When translating the term into a statement of personal financial position, assets are commonly delineated into cash and cash equivalents, with the latter including those assets that can be quickly converted into cash without a loss of value, investment assets, and use assets. *Investment assets* include securities, such as stocks and bonds, and are usually further categorized into taxable and tax-deferred accounts. Such assets are sometimes further delineated into financial and real assets, both of which will be discussed in this book. Meanwhile, an example of a *use asset* is an individual's home or personal residence, even though many individuals consider their home to be an investment or a purchase intended to appreciate in value.

A *professionally managed asset* is an investment asset that is managed by someone else, usually a money manager with a level of experience and education that sets them apart from the individual investor (or the investor who invests without the assistance of a manager). As mentioned, most of the time *professional management* refers to management of the investor's assets at the wholesale or fund level, although the term can also be used to refer to an investment advisor working individually with the investor. In this book, we use the term primarily to refer to the manager of a fund or of some type of pooled asset, which may also be held in the form of a trust or insurance-backed investment. Investments in the form of financial assets (stocks or bonds) are also a primary focus, but indirect real estate investments are also considered.

The Ownership and Positioning of Professionally Managed Assets

As we begin our discussion with respect to the investment assets of individuals, it is important to keep in mind two issues: who owns a given asset, and why the asset is owned.

Although the question of ownership may seem elementary, there are several methods of owning or titling assets. For example, an asset can be solely or individually owned. This titling is possible in all states, including those that recognize "property by the community" in the case of married individuals. In those states, such as California and Texas, individual property owned by one spouse and not the other is referred to as *separately owned property*.

An asset can also be owned concurrently or with someone else. Among the concurrent forms of asset ownership are these:

- *Tenants in common:* A form of ownership with the feature of undivided ownership among two or more individuals, typically siblings
- *Tenants by the entirety:* An ownership form available only to married couples and with rights of survivorship
- *Joint tenancy:* An ownership form where each individual owns the entire portion of the property and with rights of survivorship
- *Community property:* a form of ownership featuring an equal one-half interest in all property acquired during the course of the marriage regardless of which spouse contributed any or all the funds used to acquire such property

The second issue involved with investment assets concerns why assets are owned. For example, is an asset owned to meet an individual's short-term financial goals, such as the payment of current or upcoming bills? Or is it owned to meet a longer-term goal, such as saving to purchase a home, start a business, or retire at a planned date in the future? This question underlines the necessity of establishing financial goals for your money; in turn, the establishment of financial goals makes it much easier to discipline yourself to save.

The form in which investment assets are owned depends on the length of the investor's time horizon and the financial goal for which the investor is saving. Most commonly, investment assets may be accumulated in either a taxable or a tax-deferred account, such as a retirement account. There is a longstanding dispute with respect to which individual securities (stocks or bonds) or mutual funds (stock funds or bond funds) to position in which type of account. Conventional wisdom indicates that investments that generate ordinary income, such as interest on bonds and bond funds, are best held in a tax-deferred account, whereas growth investments, such as stocks and stock funds, are best owned in a taxable account. However, there are academic studies, including one by this author, showing that the longer the investment term, the greater the potential benefits from tax deferral. Because this is the case, it may be beneficial to position higher-return growth investments, such as stocks and stock mutual funds, in a tax-deferred account.

Here are three criteria you can use to determine where to position your investment assets:

- What is your marginal income tax bracket? The higher the marginal income tax rate you pay, the more you should pay attention to the *tax-efficiency* of your investment assets. For example, stock mutual funds that pay dividends (income funds) for an individual in a 25 percent or higher marginal tax bracket are best positioned in a tax-deferred account. Conversely, stock mutual funds that pay little or no dividends (growth funds) for a high-bracket taxpayer should likely be owned in a taxable account.
- Do you expect to be in a lower tax bracket during retirement? If you plan to move at the time of retirement to a state with no income tax (such as Florida or Texas), you will experience even greater benefits from investing in tax-deferred accounts. Not only will you benefit from the tax-free compounding of your returns during the retirement accumulation period, but you also will pay lower taxes on the retirement benefits at the time of distribution.
- What is your investment time horizon? As noted, the longer you can keep your assets invested, the greater the potential benefits from tax deferral. In the tax world, to qualify for long-term capital gains treatment, you only need to own an asset for more than one year. However, the time frame for planning for retirement is much longer, in some cases as long as 40 years. As a result, if you are planning to save over such a long time frame, the growth of your assets (capital gain) should be the primary consideration of your investment strategy. This also means the dividend payout on a stock or stock mutual fund probably will be much less important to you. Perhaps consider stocks in a tax-deferred account, which is the opposite of conventional wisdom as it is usually stated.

Self-Directed Investment Accounts

The major type of non-professionally managed account at the retail level is the *self-directed investment account.* These accounts are prevalent in defined-contribution retirement plans (like Section 401(k) plans), where the risk of investment falls on the employee/participant. Although these accounts rely on individual investor expertise (or non-expertise), if individuals invest in one of the many mutual funds offered by their 401(k) plan, they are afforded the advantage of access to a professional money manager at the fund or wholesale level.

Another popular form of self-directed investment account is the self-directed individual retirement account (SDIRA). These come in the form of either a traditional, before-tax, deductible IRA or an after-tax Roth IRA. In either form, certain investments are prohibited, such as investments in life insurance or real estate that is personally used by the investor (such as a vacation home). The majority of investments made in a SDIRA, like the employer-sponsored 401(k) plan, are in mutual funds.

So, what are some considerations to be taken into account by the self-directed investor when selecting mutual funds? I will have more to say about this in Chapter 5, when discussing mutual fund selection criteria, but for now, here are some important tips:

- Many employees/participants in Section 401(k) plans choose one of the preselected funds offered by the employer. This is both good and bad. First the good: because the employer often is worried about potential liability, it chooses only the best funds of each type in which the employee may invest. Now the bad: many employees/participants tend to choose a fund by default or by adopting a "one-size-fits-all" strategy. Thus, they tend not to take into account considerations—such as their age and tolerance for risk—that are important to long-term wealth accumulation.
- Many people who choose a preselected fund ignore the fact that some plans offer a self-directed option that lets them designate a certain portion of their funds to be placed with an outside financial advisor and invested in funds that are not offered on a preselected basis.
- Employees/participants tend to trust the credibility and performance of the mutual fund managers that manage the preselected funds. This is a mistake. Before investing in any fund, including in a self-directed 401(k) plan, investors should investigate the background and tenure of the

mutual fund portfolio manager. The greater their experience with that same mutual fund company or in managing mutual fund investments generally, the more likely the manager has invested throughout any number of market environments, including both upward (bullish) and declining (bearish) markets.

- The one thing employees/participants can control is the fund in which they choose to invest. To avoid a drag on their returns, savvy investors know to limit their selection to funds with lower-than-average operating expenses and management fees. The typical stock mutual fund operating expense, including management and **12b-1 fees**, is approximately 1.4 percent, according to Morningstar, Inc. This means 1.4 percent of the fund's assets are used to pay operational expenses and reduce the amount of return that would otherwise be coming to you. The expenses are even higher for those funds that deal with international securities, where exchange-rate conversions must be made. How do you protect yourself? Choose stock funds that have operational expenses of no more than 1 percent, preferably lower. Moreover, bond funds have lower operational expenses.

All these same considerations also apply to an investor in a self-directed IRA, although the advantages (and disadvantages) of preselected funds by the employer do not apply.

Life Cycle Investing

Before we move on to outlining the types of professionally managed assets that are the focus of this book, I should say a few words about a relatively new form of investing that has been given a significant boost by the Pension Protection Act of 2006: that of life cycle investing and its two representative investments, the target-date retirement fund and the lifestyle mutual fund.

Historically, asset diversification has been used to decrease investor risk while not proportionally reducing the return that can be expected from an investment portfolio. Such a strategy relies on combining assets that have a low positive or slightly negative correlation with each other. (Correlation and correlation coefficients will be discussed in Chapter 5 of this book when we examine mutual fund selection criteria.) Moreover, asset diversification should be accomplished both within and across industries or sectors of the economy to ensure that the strategy's maximum benefit is realized. But is it also possible to diversify across time? The strategy of life cycle investing posits that it is.

A life cycle fund does this by automatically rebalancing the investor's portfolio according to their age and the status of their current lifestyle.

The professional asset mechanisms by which life cycle investing are implemented are the target date retirement fund (target fund) and the lifestyle fund. A **target fund** is a mutual fund that automatically resets or "rebalances" its asset classes, which traditionally include stocks, bonds, and cash equivalents, according to a selected time frame based on the individual investor's projected retirement date. In essence, the fund targets its holdings (and ultimate wealth accumulation) to a specified future date. As such, such a fund is best for meeting the general needs of investors with a similar time horizon. A target fund with an estimated retirement and funding date of the year 2025 may be invested in a proportion of 70 percent bonds, 20 percent stocks, and 10 percent cash. Alternatively, a fund with a target date of 2045 may be allocated to maintain a constant percentage of 80 percent stocks, 15 percent bonds, and 5 percent cash. Market fluctuations may cause the allocation to deviate from its desired percentages, so a computer program will automatically readjust the allocation to the promised mix of assets.

The *lifestyle fund*, on the other hand, maintains a predetermined risk level and generally includes the word *conservative*, *moderate*, or *aggressive* in the fund's name to describe the participants' risk tolerance.

The Pension Protection Act not only encouraged the use of target funds but also authorized the automatic enrollment of employees in Section 401(k) retirement plans unless they opt out. Moreover, target funds are now used as the investment option of choice (the default option) for individuals who never opt out of automatic Section 401(k) enrollment. This leads to many employees/default participants who never know which funds or asset classes their monies are invested in. This is not a good way to invest. Not only have you given complete oversight of your funds to a computer (not a person), but you are likely never to consider factors such as the fund's expense ratio, your own age, and your risk tolerance—all of which are critical to effective investment management. At the very least, you need to understand this old investment maxim: only you are responsible for your investment future, and if you don't invest properly, you will not have much of a future!

Types of Professionally Managed Assets

This book will cover in detail the following types of professionally managed assets:

- Open-end investment companies, commonly referred to as mutual funds
- Closed-end funds
- Unit investment trusts (UITs)

- Exchange-traded funds (ETFs)
- Hedge funds
- Managed futures
- Private equity funds
- Limited partnership investments
- Real estate investment trusts (REITs)
- Individually managed and separately managed accounts
- Variable life insurance
- Variable annuities

Additional types of professionally managed assets (PMAs) are being developed daily, but this list constitutes the best-known and commonly accepted types of PMAs.

Open-End Investment Companies (Mutual Funds)

The defining characteristic of an open-end investment company, or mutual fund, is the continuous offering of new shares to investors and the continuous readiness to buy back outstanding shares of the fund from investors on request. The number of outstanding shares in the fund varies, because shares are constantly being purchased by and redeemed from the company. There is no legal limit on the number of shares that may be issued. The shares are priced daily at the net asset value, which is computed by taking the portfolio's total market value less fund liabilities and dividing the remainder by the number of outstanding shares. Trades do not take place until the end of the market trading day, with shares sold and redeemed at **net asset value (NAV)**. If redemptions requested from the fund exceed purchases, the result is a net cash outflow and fewer dollars that may be invested from the fund. As a consequence, the fund must estimate (and keep in reserve) a certain amount of cash assets at all times to service investor redemptions.

Mutual funds are normally classified by their investment objective, which is specified in the fund prospectus. Although mutual funds can be classified in numerous ways, generally there are four main categories:

- Money market funds
- Stock (or equity) funds
- Bond (or fixed income) funds
- Hybrid funds (a mix of stocks and bonds in the same fund)

According to the 2013 Investment Company Institute (ICI) Fact Book, as of the end of 2012, there were more than 8,700 mutual funds with combined assets of over $13.0 trillion in the United States. Some 45 percent of these funds were stock or equity funds.

Historically, and to date, most mutual funds are actively managed, meaning the fund portfolio manager attempts to earn an annual return in excess of some previously established benchmark. For example, a stock fund investing in large company stocks might attempt to exceed the performance of the Standard & Poor's Index of 500 stocks. But recently, *index funds*—mutual funds that try to replicate the annual performance of a specified index—have increased in popularity. The reasons for this increase in popularity will be explained in Chapters 3 and 4 of this book; but with the increase in index fund investing, there has also been an increasing interest in passive-management investing strategies. *Passive management* simply means the fund seeks to match overall market returns and does not try to outperform a stipulated benchmark index.

Mutual funds are the focus of Chapters 3, 4, and 5 of this book.

Closed-End Funds

Closed-end funds differ from their open-end cousins in that they issue a limited number of shares following their public offering. Therefore, the closed-end fund is structured to neither constantly sell shares nor constantly redeem shares on an ongoing basis. Share prices fluctuate and are determined by market supply and demand. These shares sell at a discount or a premium to the fund's net asset value, a source of continuing (and perplexing) study by academics, who cannot readily state why this phenomenon occurs. Investors cannot sell their shares back to the fund but instead must sell them to another investor on the stock exchange.

Closed-end funds are sold primarily through brokers and tend to be much smaller than open-end mutual funds. Thus they are costlier to operate and have higher operating expenses. Per the 2013 ICI Fact Book, at the end of 2012, there were 602 closed-end funds with total assets of approximately $265 billion.

On a final note, do not be confused by the term *closed* when it is used to describe a mutual fund: closed mutual funds are not the same as closed-end funds. Rather, when a mutual fund is described as *closed*, it means the fund is no longer available to new investors. This occurs when the mutual fund becomes too large, causing market-entry problems for the fund manager. For example, a mutual fund that is very large typically cannot sell one of its holdings without a significant market disruption, forcing the market price of that holding down from where it would otherwise be, given a normal sell order and fund size.

Closed-end funds are discussed in Chapter 6.

Unit Investment Trusts (UITs)

Unit investment trusts (UITs) are similar to closed-end funds in that they make purchases of a fixed amount of securities. Their shares, known as *units*, trade on the stock exchange. However, unlike closed-end funds, UITs never make any changes in the portfolio's holdings. Instead, they keep the same securities until the trust liquidates. This has historically meant that UITs predominately held fixed-income securities, including both taxable and tax-exempt (municipal) bonds. That has changed recently, with stocks and equities now representing more than 50 percent of UIT assets.

UITs are organized by sponsors under *trust indentures*, which are legal agreements specifying the terms of the trust and the obligations of the sponsor to the investors or the trust beneficiaries. The actual assets in the portfolio are placed with trustees, normally banks or trust companies, for safe-keeping and administration of the trust. The portfolio is not actively managed, and the assets purchased by the trust are preselected to meet the trust's investment objectives. As of the end of 2012, there were more than 5,700 UITs with total assets of $72 billion.

UITs are discussed in Chapter 7.

Exchange-Traded Funds (ETFs)

An exchange-traded fund (ETF) may be concisely described as a mutual fund (usually an index fund) that trades like a stock. ETFs are traded throughout the trading day on the stock exchange at a price determined by the market. Unlike investors in mutual funds, ETF investors do not have to wait until the end of the trading day to find out the price at which they bought shares of a fund. Nonetheless, the price of an ETF is typically close to the net asset value (NAV) of a mutual fund, because ETFs normally issue and redeem large blocks of their shares with institutional investors, similar to an index fund. ETFs are usually passively managed, although in recent years the concept and implementation of actively managed ETFs has taken hold.

ETFs evolved from the concept of *warehouse receipts*, which reflect marketable evidence of ownership and facilitate buy and sell transactions of warehoused **commodities**. The underlying concept behind the receipts is that the receipt itself may be bought and sold, but the actual commodity remains in the warehouse. As a result, the term *depositary receipt* has become prevalent in the marketing of ETFs to investors. Note that there are also exchange-traded notes (ETNs). Unlike ETFs, which primarily include stock depositary receipts, ETNs are receipts of company-issued debt.

ETFs are usually structured as hybrid mutual funds or unit trusts and, because they are typically index funds, feature very low fees. ETFs are also very income tax–efficient for investors, as will be explained in Chapter 8. ETNs are also further discussed in Chapter 8. At the end of 2012, there were more than 1,200 ETFs in the United States with total assets of $1.3 trillion. They have grown in both size and assets since then to rival mutual funds as the primary form of professionally managed asset.

ETFs and ETNs are discussed in Chapter 8.

Hedge Funds

There is no precise definition of a hedge fund, but the term has come to mean a loosely regulated, private mutual fund for high net-worth investors. Hedge funds are "loosely regulated" in the sense that they are not subject to nearly as much scrutiny as the mutual fund industry is. In fact, hedge funds were not even envisioned in the Investment Company Act of 1940, the primary legislation governing open-end companies. Hedge funds are "private" in the sense that they employ money managers who usually are not accessible to the general public, as is the case with mutual funds. Next, hedge funds are mutual funds in the sense that they pool investor money much like mutual funds do. Keep in mind that unlike mutual funds, most hedge funds are structured as limited partnerships and not corporations. Finally, the high minimum amount needed to invest in the fund (usually an initial investment of $1.0 million dollars or more) means only high-net-worth or "accredited" investors may participate.

There is no doubt that hedge funds are permitted to, and do, take on more risk than the typical mutual fund. However, there *is* doubt that this increased exposure to risk is rewarded by performance that exceeds that of the typical mutual fund. This irony will be discussed in Chapter 9; for now, just understand that the term *hedge*, which is typically associated with the management of downside risk in any investment, means much more (really, whatever the portfolio manager wants it to mean) when it comes to investing in this type of fund. According to HFR Global Hedge Fund Industry Reports, at the end of 2012, there were estimated to be approximately 8,000 active hedge funds with $2.4 trillion dollars in assets.

Managed Futures

Among the various types of professionally managed assets, managed futures are likely the least well-known and understood. This is because this complex asset combines two alternative investments—commodities and financial instruments—into a derivative- futures- and incorporates professional money managers in an attempt to lower portfolio risk. Moreover, most investment professionals do not practice in the futures market, a standardized market in which futures contracts are traded. A futures contract features an agreed-on price today at a predetermined date in the future (known as the *futures price*, which stands in contrast to the *spot price*, or the price of the commodity if delivered immediately). These contracts trade on the futures market, the primary of which, due to the agricultural history of commodities, is the CME Group in Chicago, Illinois.

The managers who work in the managed futures industry are known as *commodity trading advisors* (CTAs). These managers are required to register with the federal government's Commodity Futures Trading Commission (CFTC), which has regulatory authority over the operations of the futures market. CTAs generally work for a broker-dealer, such as Wells Fargo Advisors, and manage their client's assets using a proprietary trading system. They go *long* (buy a futures contract) or *short* (sell a futures contract) based on their perception (or *bet*) of which direction future prices for that particular commodity or financial instrument will gravitate. Understanding the nomenclature and the various strategies of futures trading is critical to success in the futures market and its private-market counterpart, the forward market. (Note that because forward contracts are not publicly traded, the term *managed futures* does not encompass forward management.)

It is possible for managed futures to outperform (achieve an excess return relative to) the broader overall stock market, but, as mentioned, the focus of the practice is to *hedge*, or minimize the risk of significant portfolio. It attempts to do this by taking advantage of the proven negative correlation of futures contracts and traditional asset classes, such as stocks and bonds. Much more will be said about managed futures mutual funds and proprietary programs in Chapter 10.

Private Equity Funds

A *private equity fund* is a limited partnership formed by a private equity firm (serving as the general partner and investment advisor to the fund) that makes capital available to non-publicly traded, private companies. Typically, the private equity firm manages several funds at once and starts a new fund every three to five years, after the previous fund or funds is fully invested (or *fully subscribed*). The investors in the fund are primarily institutional investors, such as pension funds and university endowments, although depending on the particular institution's investment policy statement, the amount of money that may be invested in private equity funds may be limited. High-net-worth and experienced investors (defined in securities laws as *accredited investors*) may also be interested in private equity investments.

A *fund of funds* may own the shares of mutual funds, which invest in publicly traded securities, or the shares of private equity funds, which invest in private firms. An investor purchasing a fund of funds does so to achieve cost effectiveness and the possibility of greater diversification. In other words, the same amount of money is now spread among many funds, which in turn feature their own diversification potential, because the investment is made in many individual stocks, within and across market sectors, or in many private businesses.

Private equity firms, beyond establishing private equity funds, can also invest directly in a private business. If it chooses to do so, the firm injects capital into the private business in exchange for equity (common stock) or preferred stock that is convertible into equity at a later date. The firm may also loan money to the private business in exchange for convertible debt. This cash infusion can come early in the business's start-up stage, in which case the infusion is known as *venture capital*, or later in the small business's life cycle, when it may be used to improve the efficiency of the business. In either stage, the private equity firm's goal is ultimately to *take the firm public*, meaning to engage in an initial public offering (IPO) of stock. As a result, the private equity firm hopes to recognize its return-on-investment (ROI) goals of a 50 to 70 percent annual compounded rate of return. Private equity firms can also assist in the reverse process of converting a public company back to a privately held business through an investment strategy known as a *leveraged buyout*.

As of the end of 2012, it is estimated that there are 10,000 private equity funds with assets of approximately $1.5 trillion.

Private equity funds and the private equity industry are the focus of Chapter 11.

Limited Partnership Investments

Limited partnerships (LPs) can be either non-publicly traded (in the private equity market) or publicly traded. Regardless of how they are traded, however, state laws dictate that every limited partnership must have a general partner. In a real-estate development, this general partner is the developer, who then *syndicates* the development among investors who assume only limited liability for their investments. *Limited liability* means if the partnership is sued, the investor is liable only to the extent of their capital investment in the fund. This is unlike the general partner, who has unlimited liability for the acts of the partnership—although many general partners limit their liability at the partnership level by forming a limited liability company (LLC) to conduct the partnership's business.

The most common type of publicly traded limited partnership is a master limited partnership (MLP), which combines the tax benefits of a limited partnership with the marketability of common stock by issuing so-called *investment units* that trade on an exchange. In order to qualify as a MLP under existing tax law, the firm organizing the MLP (the general partner) must earn at least 90 percent of its annual income through the partnership's activities, which most commonly involve real estate, commodities, or oil and gas ventures. The MLP entity is not taxed on the profits from the venture until the MLP makes distributions of these profits to the partnership's unit holders (limited partners).

As will be discussed in Chapter 12, LPs have had a long and checkered history. This business form was used heavily prior to the Tax Reform Act of 1986 to provide tax deductions and credits to the limited partner/taxpayer in excess of their actual capital invested. Beginning in 1987, tax limitations like the *at-risk* and *passive activity* rules came into the lexicon to restrict what Congress perceived as an abuse of the tax law. As a result, the economic potential of LPs is now much more of a consideration to a potential investor.

Real Estate Investment Trusts (REITs)

An indirect investment in real estate may be made in the form of a mutual fund, a limited partnership, or a trust. To use the trust form, the investment is made in a *real estate investment trust* (REIT). REITs offer an alternative to direct investment in real estate via the purchase of a home, residential rental property, commercial rental property, or raw land. REITs may be either non-publicly traded (private) or publicly traded.

Regardless of whether REITs are traded on the stock market, they possess even higher risk than stocks or equity. This is because the fund is investing in real-estate assets, and the location of those assets (and the stability of the economy in that location) plays a significant role in determining the assets' value and income-producing potential. For example, in the most recent real-estate recession beginning in 2007, real-estate values declined as much as 50 percent in some parts of the country. Since then, most areas have recovered much if not all of the value lost, but some pockets are still struggling. REIT property is also very sensitive to the effect of rising interest rates and the probability that investors will move into much safer investments, such as Treasury securities. In addition, the effect of leverage or debt may magnify REIT losses.

There are three types of REITs:

- *Equity REITs* invest in and own residential or commercial rental properties.
- *Mortgage REITs* deal in the investment and ownership of property mortgages.
- *Hybrid REITs* combine the merits of equity and mortgage REIT investing.

There is also an alternative form of investing indirectly in real-estate properties: a *real estate limited partnership* (RELP). Both RELPs and REITs will be discussed in more detail in Chapter 12.

As of the end of 2012, approximately 170 publicly traded REITS were registered with the SEC, and these REITs owned combined assets of $650 billion. Keep in mind that there are also non-publicly traded REITs, as well as REITs that are neither publicly traded nor registered with the SEC. Internal Revenue Service records show that approximately 1,100 US REITs in either of those categories have filed tax returns. The asset holdings of these REITs are unknown.

Individually Managed Accounts (IMAs) and Separately Managed Accounts (SMAs)

Individually managed accounts (IMAs) are often confused with separately managed accounts (SMAs). An IMA is a customized money-management service for high-income individuals who want direct, one-on-one access to a private money manager, which is usually provided through a private money-management company. In contrast, a SMA is a funds-management service designed primarily for moderate-income individuals who are seeking an alternative to mutual funds. SMA portfolios are constructed on the basis of a model portfolio, with each investor receiving exactly the same advice from the fund manager. There are also tax-management differences arising from each account. Nevertheless, in the investment world, IMAs and SMAs are often used interchangeably, with IMAs being marketed primarily to higher-income investors.

Like ETFs, IMAs and SMAs are a sign of investor dissatisfaction with the cookie-cutter approach taken by many mutual funds. However, unlike ETFs, IMAs and SMAs are generally only for more affluent investors. The fees charged by private portfolio managers are very high, and the investor's wealth accumulation is directly linked to the money manager's performance. This is not the case with ETFs or mutual funds, where multiple managers and diversification are the norms.

Because IMAs and SMAs are held at the private money-manager level, the number of accounts is not a matter of public record. Nevertheless, it is estimated that, like hedge funds, several trillion dollars are currently held in such a manner.

IMAs and SMAs are discussed in Chapter 13.

Variable Life Insurance

Variable life insurance is a form of permanent (versus temporary or term) insurance that builds cash value and a death benefit by investing in stocks or stock mutual funds. The investor/policyholder can also invest in money market, bond, or hybrid funds, although in this type of insurance's pure variable form, the investor/policyholder generally does not have a great deal of choice in the investments made by the insurance company. This is not the case in the variable universal form of life insurance, where the investment choices are made by the policyholder. In both forms (variable and variable universal life), the policyholder's invested monies are set aside in a separate account for their benefit, an attribute that could be important if financial difficulties occur for the insurance company at a later date.

In variable or variable universal life insurance, the amount of money accumulated as cash value in the policy is completely dependent on the return earned by the separate, mutual fund–like accounts in which the accumulated funds are invested. This may mean an increase in the cash value that the policyholder would otherwise earn in a more traditional whole or ordinary life policy, as well as an increase in the death benefit paid to the policy's beneficiary or beneficiaries. The premiums paid for these advantages are usually greater than in the traditional whole life form of life insurance, because the expenses of maintaining the policy are also greater. Premiums paid for pure variable life insurance are fixed, whereas the premiums allocated to the variable universal form of life insurance are flexible, requiring that only enough premium is paid in the period to ensure that the policy's mortality cost is satisfied.

This book is primarily about assets that are professionally managed by securities professionals or those individuals who are employed independently by an investment company or by a broker-dealer. Nonetheless, the broad subject of PMAs cannot be adequately discussed without considering the forms of insurance products that pool or combine investor assets. Be aware, however, that any insurance product has an added cost: mortality protection, or otherwise insuring against the risk of the policyholder's premature death.

Variable life and variable universal life insurance are discussed in Chapter 14.

Variable Annuities

We conclude this chapter with a brief description of variable annuities. A *variable annuity* is a contract between an individual, referred to as an *annuitant*, and an insurance company, whereby the company agrees to pay the annuitant a periodic payment, either immediately or in the future. If the payment is made in the future, as most payments are (because soon-to-be-retired individuals are the primary purchasers of the product), the annuity is known as a *tax-deferred annuity* (TDA). The annuitant may purchase the contract either in a single payment (a *single-premium deferred annuity* [SPDA]) or over time.

The annuity has two stages: an accumulation phase and a payout phase. In the accumulation phase, the annuitant makes payments that are allocated among various mutual funds to purchase fund shares, referred to in the annuity product as *accumulation units*. The money allocated to each mutual fund increases or decreases over time, depending on the fund's performance. The total number of accumulation units are either distributed to the annuitant over their lifetime in a process known as *annuitizing the annuity* or are paid over a period of installments. Keep in mind that accumulated monies in the annuity may be withdrawn during the policyholder's lifetime in a guaranteed manner, assuming that certain provisions are included in the annuity contract. The contract may also be written (for an additional cost) to provide for a guaranteed minimum income benefit, which generally is tied to a specified annual amount or percentage of income that the annuitant requires throughout their retirement period. The major advantage of any annuity product is that the annuitant is guaranteed never to outlive their money, which is a major fear of any retiree.

A common feature of any variable annuity is the payment of a death benefit to the annuitant's designated beneficiary or beneficiaries at the annuitant's death. At death, the beneficiary typically receives the greater of 1) the account value of the total of the accumulation units in the annuity or 2) a guaranteed minimum amount, such as the total of the purchase payments made during the annuitant's lifetime minus any previous lifetime withdrawals. Unlike variable (or variable universal) life insurance, however, a portion of the death benefit is taxable to the beneficiary. The amount of the death benefit that is taxable depends on the origin of the purchase payments made by the annuitant. In other words, the taxable amount of the death benefit is dependent on whether the payments were made with so-called *before-tax monies* (such as retirement funds) or *after-tax dollars* (such as the annuitant's salary or wages). If before-tax monies were used, all of the death benefit is normally taxable over time. If after-tax dollars were contributed, only the gains on the annuity accumulation units are taxed.

Variable annuities (VAs) are the topic of Chapter 15.

This chapter provided an overview of the predominant types of PMAs in today's investment marketplace. Each of these types of PMAs will be the focus of a subsequent chapter in this book. In the next chapter, we'll address the question of why an individual may wish to include PMAs in their investment portfolio.

CHAPTER

2

Why Professionally Managed Assets?

If you have been thinking about investing in one or more types of professionally managed assets (PMAs), you may have already asked yourself the question, "What is the advantage of investing with professionals instead of selecting my own securities?" The purpose of this chapter is to answer that question, first by examining the pitfalls of investing in individual securities and, subsequently, by evaluating the advantages and disadvantages of PMAs. The chapter concludes with a look at the types of managed money investment vehicles in today's marketplace.

Individual Investing

The potential pitfalls of individual investing include

- The lack of time and expertise that most individuals have to stay abreast of the market
- The inherent lack of diversification in individual securities
- Higher transaction costs associated with the individual purchases of securities
- The outsized difficulty of effective stock picking

We'll discuss each of these hazards in turn in the sections that follow.

Lack of Investor Time and Expertise

Individual investing appears attractive when it is first considered, primarily because of its inherent cost advantages. You save the fees paid to a professional manager, correct? Well, yes, but in the long run, any fees you save are likely to be earned many times over by the possible excess return on investments that a credible professional money manager can generate. Remember, *professional managers oversee the management of portfolios for a living!* That means, unlike you, they have the time and expertise to stay abreast of the market and discern favorable trades. It also means they probably have a level of education that has prepared them for their career that you do not possess.

Where do successful money managers come from, and what skills do they possess? Historically, some individuals became money managers by joining "the family business" and learning skills in market analysis and investment strategies from an older family member, typically their father or grandfather. For example, Abigail Johnson, President of Fidelity Investments, was preceded in the business by her father, Edwin C. Johnson III, and by her grandfather, Edwin C. Johnson II, who founded Fidelity Investments in 1949. Other money managers joined investment firms directly out of college or graduate school and worked their way up. This process involved being mentored by senior persons in the firm, who shared their many years of experience in varying market cycles and conditions with the underling. Currently, major investment management companies are relying more and more on an individual's educational background when deciding who to train as money managers. The optimal educational background for new professional employees is a Master of Science (MS) in Finance, a PhD in Finance, the Chartered Financial Analyst (CFA) designation, or some combination of the three. An individual must pass three rigorous, six-hour examinations over a minimum of three years to receive the CFA designation or charter, and they must also have at least three years of investment experience as a financial analyst. Individuals who pass the CFA exams often already have a graduate degree in finance, because the exam material extends considerably beyond what is taught in any undergraduate degree program in investment or finance.

The likelihood that people with preferable educational and professional backgrounds (experience) will become successful money managers also depends on their ability to retain their existing investing knowledge while remaining current in their field. Thus, continuing education is a practical necessity for money managers. Additionally, the prevailing theory in the securities market today that markets are *efficient* means rational investors outnumber those investors who sometimes act irrationally. As a result, money managers need to think quickly and exhibit rationality on a daily basis to be successful. There is a market maxim that informs money managers that the time to sell is when the inexperienced investor enters the market. Rational money managers were probably responsible for formulating this maxim, because inexperienced investors are more prone to make irrational decisions.

It also seems intuitive that more experienced money managers outperform their less experienced counterparts. But how much experience is enough to ensure success? Unfortunately, there is no quantitative answer to this question. Empirical studies with respect to how much experience is enough have proven inconclusive. The **Marcus study**, which in 1990 analyzed the sterling performance of portfolio manager Peter Lynch and his Fidelity Magellan Fund, determined that the fund's outperformance of the Standard & Poor's 500 market index was probably due to Lynch's personal investment beliefs and *not* his years of experience. A striking aspect of the study was the finding that there was only a 5.9 percent probability that any one of the generally acknowledged 500 best portfolio managers would outperform the index in each of the 13 years studied. So, how much experience is enough? All that can be said with some certainty is that more experience is better than less!

Lack of Diversification in Individual Securities

Diversification is the art of constructing a portfolio (a collection of assets) to reflect less total risk—as measured by the statistical concept of **standard deviation**—without experiencing an equal reduction in expected return. For example, if you put two or more stocks together with an average expected return between the two of them of 20 percent (Stock A has an expected return of 25 percent and Stock B has an expected return of 15 percent) and a total risk of 20 percent (Stock A has a standard deviation of 25 percent and Stock B has a standard deviation of 15 percent), you get an expected return on the portfolio of 20 percent while reducing the total risk of the portfolio to 18 percent. Whether you indeed achieve this reduction in the percentage of total risk depends on what is known as the *correlation* between the two stocks, or the direction—and the degree to which—they move in relation to one another. *Positive* correlation means assets move exactly together (and in the same degree), whereas *negative* correlation means the assets move exactly opposite each other (and in the same degree).

Although some assets exhibit a negative correlation, domestic stocks are *not* among them. (You may get some negative correlation with international stocks, but there you must generally deal with currency fluctuations and exchange-rate conversions.) The best that can be accomplished with domestic stocks is to try to position together two that have low *positive* correlations. Even this is difficult and expensive to do. Most investors simply cannot financially afford to develop a properly diversified portfolio of individual stocks!

Beyond the correlation problem, an investor should hold stock in companies belonging to different sectors of the stock market, as well as in different companies within a given sector, in order to be properly diversified. Note that there are ten generally accepted stock-market sectors:

- Consumer discretionary stocks (example: Ford Motor Company)
- Consumer staples (example: Kellogg's)
- Energy (example: Exxon Mobil)
- Financials (example: Bank of America)
- Health Care (example: Aetna)
- Industrials (example: General Electric)
- Technology (example: Intel)
- Materials (example: Archer Daniels Midland)
- Telecommunications (example: Verizon)
- Utilities (Duke Energy Power)

As we shall see in Chapter 3, which includes a discussion on mutual funds, a *sector* fund is a type of mutual fund that only invests in, for example, energy stocks. Although such funds invest in different companies *within* a given sector, they do not invest in different companies *across* market sectors; thus, sector funds generally are not as diversified as is possible. The Investment Company Act (of 1940) has its own definition of a diversified mutual fund in Section 5 b of that Act: a "diversified company" is one that has at least 75 percent of its portfolio of assets in cash or cash items; not more than 5 percent in government debt; and not more than 10 percent in the voting stock of companies.

Most stock purchases are made in what is called a *round lot*, or 100 shares of stock. An investor investing in individual stocks would need to purchase 100 shares in each of the 10 sectors—or a minimum of 1,000 shares—before addressing the "different companies within a given sector" prerequisite to proper diversification. As an example, the share price of Exxon Mobil was $90.11 per share at the date of this writing, so the investor's initial investment in the energy sector would be $9,011.00. This is much more than most individual investors can afford in either an initial or subsequent purchase of individual stocks. Moreover, this is just the purchase of *one* stock, when many more are needed in order for an individual investor to be properly diversified.

Higher Transaction Costs in Individual Securities

An investor can buy individual securities either directly (usually over the Internet) or by using a broker. We have already seen from our discussion in the previous section that if an investor wants to buy individual securities, they should buy a number of different companies and different shares to be properly diversified. This takes time and money. The alternative is to use a broker to make the purchases.

There are three types of brokers: those who work for a full-service brokerage firm, a discount brokerage firm, or a deep-discount broker. The third of these types of firms—the deep-discount brokerage firm—is designed for the direct investor who really only needs a trading platform. The difference between a full-service firm and a discount brokerage firm has historically been the amount of stock-market research and analysis that is offered the investor; but that distinction has become more blurred in recent years. Stock brokers are paid primarily on the basis of a charge against the amount of sales they make in a given month. The commission paid by an investor for the purchase of an individual security can be as low as 5 percent or as high as 30 percent, depending on the broker's contract with the firm. Regardless, that money does *not* go to work immediately for you, the investor. A discount broker costs less, but you still pay out of your own pocket for the service!

You may be *required* to use a broker if you want to purchase individual stocks using *margin*. Borrowing from the broker to purchase additional shares—also known as *buying on margin*—is a feature of a brokerage account. The margin requirement, currently 50 percent of the initial purchase price, is established by the Federal Reserve Board. The requirement actually specifies how much of the initial purchase price of a transaction must be contributed by the *investor*, but right now, that also means you may borrow 50 percent of the purchase price and buy twice as many shares as you otherwise could. For example, if you want to purchase 200 shares of a stock that has a current market price of $50 per share (a total of $10,000), you would contribute $5,000 of your own money and borrow the other $5,000 from the broker to complete the transaction. The interest paid on this loan is potentially income-tax deductible, but borrowing on margin is a type of **leverage** and increases your portfolio risk. If the stock price declines to below a specified amount, you will receive a margin call from the broker and will be forced to either sell some other stocks from your account or add cash to the account to cover possible losses. If you do not "meet" the margin call, the broker will likely terminate your margin privileges and close out your margin account.

Difficulty of Effective Stock Picking

Empirical studies have shown that professional money managers who practice active management techniques can select stocks that outperform the market in the short run, defined as one year or less. However, very few can select stocks that outperform the market over a period of 20 years or more. One of the few who can is mega-investor Warren Buffett, who earned an average compounded annual return of approximately 22.5 percent for investors in his Berkshire-Hathaway mutual fund from 1956–2006. (An annual return of this magnitude means if an investor had invested $1,000 with Mr. Buffett in 1956, this same $1,000 would be worth over $25.5 million dollars at the end of 2006!) All this, coupled with the previously discussed lack of time and expertise that most investors face, means your chances of achieving economic success when picking your own stocks are quite low!

If you do decide to pick your own stocks, one of the metrics you should know up front (before you buy) is the correct or proper price of the stock. In other words, what *should* the market price of the stock be at that particular point of time? There are various ways to determine this figure, but ultimately you must use either a *relative* or an *intrinsic* method of valuation.

The first, or *relative*, method of valuation relies on multiplying the company's quarterly earnings by an accepted price–earnings (PE) ratio. For example, let's say the annual earnings of Stock A are $5 per share. If the PE ratio for that particular stock was determined to be 12, you would conclude that the proper price of Stock A was $60 per share ($5 per share times 12). A style of investing known as *value investing* partly relies on identifying stocks that have an average PE ratio lower than that of the overall market. Historically, the average PE ratio of the Standard & Poor's Index of 500 stocks has been about 16; multiplying the $5 earnings per share of Stock A by 16 means the current stock price of $60 per share should grow to a price of $80 per share, resulting in a $20 per share profit to the investor. However, this average PE ratio of 16 may not be a good average for the stock you are considering buying. In addition, 16 is the *market* average PE ratio, which includes a lot of factors (unexpected and expected) that may or may not be relevant to Stock A.

The second method of valuing stocks, the *intrinsic* method, removes market factors from its price analysis, although it is still imperfect in some ways. The intrinsic method relies on a financial technique known as the *discounted cash flow* (DCF) approach, which discounts the future cash flows expected from a particular stock back to a present value in order to determine the stock's proper price. This cash flow is then used as the numerator of a formula, with the denominator reflecting a so-called *capitalization rate* for the stock, as determined by subtracting the growth rate of the cash flow from the investor's required rate of return. The entire formula is known as the *constant dividend growth model* and is written as follows:

$$V \text{ or } P_0 = \frac{D_1}{r-g}$$

where V or P_0 is equal to the present value price of the stock, D_1 is equal to the next year's estimated dividend paid by the stock, r is the investor's required rate of return, and g is the constant growth rate of the dividend:

Let's look at an example using this formula. Stock A is estimated to pay a dividend of $5 per share next year ($D_1$). The investor's required rate of return (r) is 12 percent, and the constant growth rate of the dividends (g) is 3.70 percent, for a total capitalization rate of 8.33 percent. When dividing $5 by 8.33 percent, we derive a proper stock price of $60 per share, or the same price we arrived at when using the relative method of valuation.

Under the intrinsic model of valuation, what could change and therefore result in a stock price of $80 per share for Stock A, as in the relative method of valuation example? Assuming the dividend amount of $5 per share did not change, we would want to drive the capitalization rate down to 6.25 percent from 8.33 percent. This could happen in one of two ways: the investor's required rate of return could *decrease*, say, from 12 percent to 11 percent; or the constant dividend growth rate could *increase*, say, from 3.70 percent to 4.75 percent. These changes could result either from factors unique to the particular stock under consideration (Stock A) or from macroeconomic factors impacting the market as a whole or both.

Still, the intrinsic model has problems. First, it can only be used if the stock under consideration is expected to pay a dividend or has paid a dividend in the past. What happens, as is the case with many technology stocks, when the stock has never paid a dividend and never will? In those cases, another model known as the "residual income model" (not discussed here) must be used. Second, in the denominator of the intrinsic model, the required rate of return (r) must exceed the constant growth rate of the dividends (g), or the stock price will be calculated as negative (or below zero) in the model, which is a practical non-event. Finally, the model requires that the user have some understanding of what might change: either the investor's required rate of return or the dividend growth rate. This is beyond the expertise of most investors and is yet another reason individual stock picking is not a good idea for most of us!

The Advantages of Professionally Managed Assets

Among the major advantages of PMAs are the following:

- Increased diversification
- The ability to access professional management at relatively low cost
- The ability to participate in investments that would otherwise be available only to more affluent investors (preferred investments)
- Owner liquidity
- Government oversight of the asset and asset structure

We'll discuss each of these advantages in turn in the sections that follow.

Increased Diversification

As has been previously discussed, it is difficult to achieve proper diversification when purchasing individual securities, and it remains a challenge to do so when using PMAs. Nevertheless, the goal of reducing the risk of an investor's portfolio is greatly improved with the use of PMAs.

To take a quick step back, *diversification* is defined in most investment textbooks as the process of adding securities to a portfolio for the purpose of greatly reducing their unique or firm-specific security risk (referred to in investment terminology as their *unsystematic* or *diversifiable risk*), which thereby also reduces the *total* risk of the portfolio. The basic idea of diversification is to position together securities that exhibit negative correlation or, in other words, do *not* move in concert with each other. For example, let's say you find two stocks that move directly opposite one another (one moves up while the other moves down). These stocks are said to have a *correlation coefficient* of −1.0, which statistically means you have eliminated all total risk of both stocks.

Unfortunately, as has been mentioned previously, this is impossible to do! Taken together, all securities still possess what is known as *systematic* or *market risk*, and this type of risk cannot be reduced as greatly as unsystematic risk. Systematic risk is sometimes called *nondiversifiable risk* for this very reason. As a result, the goal of diversification is to position together securities with the *lowest* possible systematic risk without significantly reducing the future, expected return of the portfolio. Because the measure of systematic risk is an investment's *beta coefficient* (or *beta*), the professional manager tries to position together two securities—one with a low beta and the other with a somewhat higher beta—to achieve diversification.

Ultimately, beta is a measure of the relative movement or *volatility* of the security with the overall market. The problem is, securities with the highest beta also feature the highest reward or expected return, which is consistent with the risk-reward principle that characterizes proper investing. *The greater the risk or beta of the investment, the greater the investment's potential reward or expected return.* For example, a stock with a beta of 2.0 would be expected to require an investor risk premium that was twice that of the market as a whole while also possessing twice as much systematic risk. An investment's *risk premium* is the investment's expected return less the risk-free rate of assets in the marketplace, typically measured by the rate of a US Treasury security with a similar maturity. Professional portfolio managers run a series of computer projections using the betas of various securities and arrive at the optimal risk-reward scenario for a planned portfolio.

Harry Markowitz developed the core model for constructing a portfolio with an optimal risk-reward scenario, also known as an *optimal portfolio.* His model later became the cornerstone of "modern portfolio theory" (MPT), the precepts of which almost every budding portfolio manager learns in collegiate investment and finance courses. The Markowitz model demonstrates precisely how diversification reduces portfolio risk by applying a risk measure to portfolios with various asset mixes in order to derive the specific risk-return characteristics of those portfolios. Markowitz measured risk by the statistical metric of standard deviation; William Sharpe of Stanford University later developed the metric of **beta** when expanding on Markowitz's work. The optimal portfolio, as defined by Markowitz, consists of a set of all *efficient* portfolios (defined as those portfolios with the least amount of total risk that achieve the same expected returns) lying on a curvilinear line known as the *efficient frontier.* The investor constructs an optimal portfolio consisting of one of these efficient portfolios while considering the investor's own risk tolerance, as graphically demonstrated by what is known as an *indifference curve.* Finally, in the practical implementation of Markowitz's theory, the investor or investment advisor chooses the portfolio that best matches the possible maximum expected return with the amount of possible minimum risk inherent in the selected portfolio.

The Ability to Access Professional Management at a Relatively Low Cost

The best way to describe the second advantage of PMAs is to consider, again, how difficult it is for the average investor in individual securities to construct a diversified portfolio in a cost-efficient manner. Professionals are better at it—although those who are really good tend to be very expensive. (Think of trial lawyers who are very good at their craft; their hourly court fee may be as high as $1,000.)

PMAs spread the cost of the professional fee among many investors. For example, when analyzing the management fee charged by a mutual fund, you can anticipate that the smaller the assets managed by the fund, the greater the percentage fee will be. (There is a smaller amount of assets over which to spread the dollar amount of the fee), Keep in mind, though, that the management cost of smaller funds needs to be balanced against the fact that larger funds are not able to trade their assets as efficiently without potentially dragging down their net asset value (which is known as *blockage*). In tax law, a valuation discount is given for the price impact that occurs when a large number of fund shares are sold in any given day. Still, economies of scale are evident in any large company; the same holds for large mutual funds and can be an advantage for the small investor.

You will notice that this section's heading uses the term *relatively*. Here, the "relative" relationship is paying the professional manager directly versus sharing the cost. If you contrast a cost-efficient mutual-fund management fee (1 percent or less of total assets managed) to the normal hedge-fund manager fee (2 percent or more of total assets managed *plus* a 20 percent share of the profits made by the fund), you can begin to appreciate how much a good professional money manager can cost! Then again, hedge funds are really only for affluent investors anyway.

Although low cost is the norm for most PMAs, there are exceptions. This is why it is important to understand up front how the professional manager will be paid and where the money will come from.

The Ability to Participate in Preferred Investments

It has already been mentioned that diversification in investments is very difficult for most investors. Without access to PMAs, it is even more difficult—especially for investors who wish to invest according to a personal preference, such as in securities issued by companies that are considered to be "socially responsible." Put another way, diversification is a monumental challenge when investment selection and performance are evaluated primarily by subjective (qualitative) rather than objective (quantitative) criteria.

An example of a socially responsible investing strategy is to avoid investing in "sin" companies, such as those that sell tobacco or alcohol products. However, historically these companies have performed very well, regardless of economic conditions. We could argue that tobacco and alcohol stocks are "recession proof"—not to mention that they also advance strongly when the economy is accelerating. There is also the problem of deciding which stocks are socially responsible: some companies have recognized the preferences of the socially responsible crowd and diversified *as a company* into other businesses. For example, R.J. Reynolds, a major cigarette manufacturer, once bought Nabisco, a company noted for cookies. (Cookies have very little in common with cigarettes). Expansion into other non-core businesses also is a key characteristic of **conglomerate** companies, the most notable of which has been General Electric throughout American history.

If you are truly an investor in the traditional sense, in that you try to maximize investment return while minimizing investment risk, socially responsible investing (or any other type of personal investing preference) may work *against* you—not to your benefit. If you choose to pursue an investing strategy based on a personal preference, PMAs at least will allow you to participate in a fund or limited partnership of like-minded investors and give you access to a manager who will attempt to diversify within the limitations of the fund or limited partnership investment objectives.

Owner Liquidity

The term *liquidity* is often used interchangeably with *marketability* in the investment world. But liquidity often builds on marketability. For example, if you have a fund or security that you want to sell to another individual, and there is a forum in which to sell it, that fund or security has marketability. However, you may *not* be able to sell the fund or security to someone else without a (sometimes substantial) loss. If you can convert the fund or security to cash relatively quickly and without fear of a significant loss, that fund or security is said to have liquidity.

PMAs help ensure the liquidity of funds or securities by reducing the length of time it takes for owners to access their accounts and convert them into spendable bank balances. An example is a wire redemption of funds, which usually is offered free of charge to owners. The more quickly owners can access fund balances, the less likely it is that they will suffer a significant loss in the value of those balances. Still to be considered, of course, is the asset class in which the PMA is invested (for example, real estate is usually thought to be less liquid—or more *illiquid*—than stocks or bonds). Nevertheless, the fact that most PMAs can be quickly converted to cash is definitely advantageous. And because professional managers oversee the administration of PMAs, they will often advise you when a particular asset class is likely to experience a future decline in value so that you can quickly convert to cash and minimize your losses.

Government Oversight

The Investment Company Act of 1940 (ICA) assigns primary regulatory authority over mutual funds, closed-end investment companies, and unit-investment trusts (broadly categorized as investment companies) to the Securities and Exchange Commission (SEC). The requirements are as follows:

- Investment companies must register with the SEC by filing notifications that include investment policies, annual reports, and other required information.
- To protect the assets of shareholders, all securities must be held with a **custodian**, such as a bank or securities firm, and all persons with access to those assets must be bonded.
- Capital structure limitations on the companies ensure that they do not issue preferred stock or bonds other than notes payable to banks.
- The companies must distribute shareholder dividends equal to at least 90 percent of the fund's taxable ordinary income to avoid taxation at the entity level.
- The companies may not purchase securities on margin, sell securities short, or participate in joint trading accounts. (As you will see when we discuss hedge funds in Chapter 9, this particular limitation has been relaxed for that form of PMA.)
- No investment company may invest more than 10 percent of its assets in another investment company. This limitation essentially mandates that a fund of funds must invest in a number of other funds and not just two.

The corollary legislation to the ICA is the Investment Advisors Act of 1940 (IAA). This law regulates the activities of investment advisors, including retail money managers and financial planners. It also requires professionals who are compensated for providing investment advice to register with the SEC, although the SEC has delegated this function to a self-regulatory organization of brokers and dealers known as the Financial Industry Regulatory Authority (FINRA). According to its web site, `www.finra.org/`, an equally important role of FINRA is "to protect investors by maintaining the fairness of the U.S. capital markets."

Among the most significant of the provisions of the IAA is the act's broad prohibition of fraudulent conduct by investment advisors. Although the term *fraud* would appear to be self-evident, it has been interpreted by the US Supreme Court as it pertains to the investment world to mean the advisor owes a *fiduciary duty* to the client. In practical application, this duty requires the advisor to disclose to clients any material facts that may constitute a conflict of interest with the client, refrain from taking advantage of the relationship of trust placed in the advisor by the client, and act at all times in the exclusive interest of the client. If the advisor breaches this duty, the SEC (through FINRA) may deny, suspend, or revoke the license of the investment advisor and impose various forms of sanctions, including fines, on the advisor.

Other forms of PMAs may be regulated by other agencies or regulatory bodies, at both the federal and state levels.

The Disadvantages of Professionally Managed Assets

Among the disadvantages of PMAs are the following:

- Fees
- Less control over the tax recognition of gains and income
- The inability to customize your own portfolio

As we did with the advantages of PMAs, we'll discuss each of these disadvantages in turn in the sections that follow.

Fees

When dealing with PMAs, fees are charged at both the asset and the asset-manager level. At the asset level, fees must be charged in order to operate the PMA. For the average mutual fund, these operating fees amount to approximately 1 percent of the fund assets or size. The operating fees of funds that deal with international assets are higher, and the fees of funds that are composed primarily of bonds are somewhat lower. Lowest of all are the fees of passively managed funds, such as index or exchange-traded funds (ETFs).

The operating expenses of funds include three components:

- Management fees
- Rule 12b-1 fees
- Other expenses

While the first type of fee (a management fee) is self-explanatory and the third type of fee is a catch-all charge to essentially add fees at the discretion of the fund or investment company, so-called Rule 12b-1 fees are more mysterious.

Rule 12b-1 of the SEC regulations allows investment advisors to use mutual-fund assets to pay distribution expenses, including sales commissions, administrative services, and marketing costs. Sales commissions are by far the largest component of these expenditures, making up some 65 percent of the total. In addition, under the regulation, Rule 12b-1 fees may not exceed 1 percent, including a maximum 0.25 percent annual servicing fee that is paid to the advisor for providing continuing customer service to investors. Investment advisors contend that Rule 12b-1 fees are necessary to compensate them for services, such as responding to phone calls and e-mail inquiries about the state of the fund or investment markets generally, for which they cannot otherwise charge.

In recent years, Rule 12b-1 fees have become controversial, and some investment advisors and broker-dealers have done away with them. Meanwhile, the SEC is studying the need for 12b-1 fees and whether they have fulfilled their intended purpose. It is likely that although investment advisors have benefited from the additional fees, the same cannot be said for shareholder/investors. This is particularly true for shareholders who were charged at the time of purchasing the fund in the form of a sale charge, known in the industry as a *front-end load*, and who continue to be charged the ongoing 12b-1 marketing fee.

Fees at the asset level should certainly be a concern for investors, and fees at the investment-advisor level should also be a focus. After all, most advisors charge a percentage fee based on the amount of assets they manage for the client (you). Typically, this fee is an additional 1 percent on top of the fund operating expenses of 1 percent, which means investors with an average account size (usually defined as ranging from $250,000 to $500,000) are charged a total of 2 percent in fees (or more for some funds). Some advisors charge a much higher percentage fee: sometimes as high as 2-1/2 percent of assets managed, for a total of at least3-1/2 percent of all asset and asset-management expenses. Most advisors charge a lower percentage amount if they manage a greater sum of money (say, above $500,000 or $1.0 million dollars) on your behalf. You should ask for the lowest percentage amount possible and negotiate with the advisor. Better yet, some advisors charge by the hour, although these advisors also tend to be financial planners, which is a service that you may not need or may wish to complete on your own.

As you can appreciate, the fees associated with PMAs mean the asset and asset manager need to outperform the market index on an after-fee basis. For example, if the market index (say, the Standard & Poor's Index of 500 stocks) reflects a 16 percent percentage gain in a given year, and you are being charged a total fee of 3 percent between the fund and investment advisor, you must outperform the index by 3 percent in that year. If you don't, you would have been better off investing without a PMA and retail investment advisor.

Less Control Over the Recognition of Taxable Income

As mentioned in the previous discussion on ICA requirements, mutual funds must distribute at least 90 percent of their taxable income annually at the entity or fund level in order to avoid taxation. But just because the mutual fund does not pay taxes on the distribution does not mean the distribution is not subject to taxation. The income is "passed through" to the fund's shareholders, who must then pay taxes on their portion of the distribution. As a result, shareholders who want to minimize their taxable income should look for mutual funds with a low *turnover* of stocks or bonds. A fund with a low turnover ratio of assets earns less taxable income than one with a high turnover ratio, which in turn results in a lower income-tax liability for the fund's shareholders/investors. As you are shopping for mutual funds, keep in mind, however, that shareholders/investors have no say as to when the fund engages in taxable transactions at the entity level.

Three major types of taxable distributions are made by mutual funds and, by extension, most types of PMAs:

- Total ordinary dividends
- Qualified dividends
- Total capital gain distributions

Ordinary dividends, or *nonqualified dividends*, are taxable to the shareholder/investor at the taxpayer's highest marginal income-tax rate, which currently range from 10 percent to 39.6 percent. Moreover, as of 2013, the Patient Protection and Affordable Care Act of 2010 (also known as *Obamacare*) has begun to impose an additional 3.8 percent surcharge on these dividends.

A *qualified dividend* is defined in the tax law as an ordinary dividend paid by an American company or a qualifying foreign company that meets a requisite dividend holding period before the dividend is paid. The benefit of payments constituting a qualified dividend is that they are taxed at a lower rate than the taxpayer's income. This rate is generally only 15 percent for a taxpayer who would otherwise pay 25 percent or higher if the dividend was paid in the form of an ordinary or nonqualified dividend, although a taxpayer in the highest 39.6 percent bracket must pay a rate of 20 percent. (Note that no tax whatsoever is paid on payments from a qualified dividend if the taxpayer's ordinary tax rate is 15 percent or less.)

Finally, the taxation rate of capital gain distributions depends on how long the asset generating the tax has been owned by the fund before the gain (or loss) is distributed to the investor/shareholder. All this will be examined in more detail later, during Chapter 5's discussion of how to evaluate and select a mutual fund based on its tax efficiency.

The point right now is that the investor in a mutual fund or any type of PMA loses or has significantly less control over their tax planning when turning over money to a professional asset manager.

The Inability to Customize a Portfolio

Some individuals refer to themselves as *do-it-yourself investors*. If you consider yourself as such, you are unlikely to find any type of PMA that is suitable for you. Indeed, turning over the responsibility of managing your investments to someone else will be a significant *disadvantage* for you, because you will not be able to customize your portfolio (someone else will do it for you).

If you consider yourself a do-it-yourself investor, ask yourself, "Why is this the case?" Do you really believe you are a better investor than a highly educated and experienced professional asset manager? Also, can you really remove yourself from the day-to-day emotions that befall all-human investors? An entire branch of finance—*behavioral finance*—has been developed in recent years to explore the emotional and sometimes *irrational* method in which many people invest. For example, many investors do not practice the tried-and-true maxim of "buy low and sell high;" instead, they tend to do the opposite, which means they buy high and sell low. Why? Because they succumb to the natural human emotions of greed and fear. A professional asset manager, at both the entity and retail level, can help you avoid this tendency.

One of the underlying principles of behavioral finance is known as *prospect theory*, which posits that typical individuals fear losses about twice as much as they value gains. This means a $2 decline in the value of a stock or fund affects an individual twice as much emotionally than does a $1 increase in the value of the asset. As a result, the typical investor is much more likely to *sell* in the event of a decline in stock value, even if the long-term future of the company issuing that stock is favorable. The same reaction happens in reverse on the upside, when a stock experiences an increase in value: the herd effect of not getting in on a good thing (for example, a hot stock) causes the typical investor to *buy* the asset at a financially unsupportable high price. For most investors, it is far better to transfer the responsibility of making investment decisions to the professionals. You will find that they are much less likely to succumb to such non-fundamental market factors as greed and fear.

Managed-Money Investment Vehicles in Today's Marketplace

The normal compensation arrangement for managed-money investment vehicles in today's marketplace is a fee-based investing account. When investors participate in a fee-based account, they receive the advice of a professional investment advisor for a stated percentage fee. The advisor is responsible for assessing an investor's risk tolerance, matching that tolerance to a portfolio of individual securities or PMAs, selecting the portfolio assets, and monitoring the performance of those assets. The advisor has traditionally fulfilled these responsibilities in one of two investment vehicles, but a third vehicle has also recently come into play for high-net-worth clients.

Historically, investment advisors managed their clients' money in a *wrap account*. This term was created to refer to a variety of services bundled or wrapped into one account for which the client was charged a single fee. Among these services was the availability of unlimited trading, with no commission charged on any of those trades. The stated percentage fee covered the expenses of the professional financial advisor's ongoing guidance and eliminated the concern that many investors have with a traditional brokerage account, wherein they are charged a commission for every trade that is made.

Wrap accounts evolved into more-descriptive *fee-based brokerage accounts*. However, there was a problem with fee-based brokerage accounts. Such accounts reversed the incentive for brokers working at traditional brokerages to encourage investors to trade; instead, these types of accounts led brokers to emphasize advice-for-a-fee. Regulators became concerned that investors in fee-based brokerage accounts were not trading enough and were paying higher fees than they would have paid in traditional commissions. As a result, regulators banned the implementation of fee-based brokerage accounts as of October 1, 2007, which led to the next evolution of managed money: the *advisory account*.

Most firms have now introduced this type of account to replace the historical wrap account. Advisory accounts may be either *nondiscretionary*, meaning the investment advisor cannot exercise discretion in the selection of account assets without the consent of the investment client, or *discretionary*. In a discretionary account, which is the more popular of the two types of advisory accounts, the client employs a registered investment advisor (RIA)—or an advisor who works for the RIA—for management purposes. This individual is separately registered with the SEC to provide investment advice to clients and is not employed by a broker-dealer to manage the account.

In a nondiscretionary advisory account, a portfolio of PMAs is selected to match a preset, computer-generated asset-allocation model that is appropriate for the investor's financial goals. This account may be either taxable (for example, to meet a short-term financial goal, such as saving for an overseas vacation) or tax-deferred (for longer-term goals, such as saving for a child's education or the investor's retirement). One of the responsibilities of the investment advisor of a nondiscretionary account is to rebalance the portfolio to keep it consistent with the asset-allocation model, which is often specified in a separate document known as an *investment policy statement*. This asset-allocation model should change over time as the investor ages; for example, most investors become more conservative as they approach retirement age and prefer a higher allocation of fixed-income investments than do younger investors. Sometimes the investment advisor tiers the advisory account and seeks the advice of another investment advisor with whom the percentage fee charged for the account is shared.

Recently, high-net-worth clients have been given access to yet another type of managed-money account: an *individually managed account*. In this account, the client contracts a professional money manager to manage an account that is separate and distinct from the accounts of other investors. The services the professional money manager provides to their client in this type of account include the customization of a portfolio specific only to that client, as well as significant tax management. Investment decisions are based on the investor's individual goals, and not on the basis of a previously announced investment objective, as is the case with a pooled investment such as a mutual fund or ETF.

We have now considered the different types of PMAs and why an investor may wish to consider using the services of a professional money manager, both at the wholesale and retail levels. The next section of this book looks at the most popular type of PMA: the open-end investment company, more popularly known as a mutual fund. Subsequent chapters and sections address other types of PMAs, including those managed by insurance companies.

PART

II

Mutual Funds

CHAPTER

3

The Growth of Mutual Funds

When the term *mutual fund* is used in the investment marketplace, most people think of *open-end funds* (funds that offer an unlimited number of shares and redemption privileges at any time). In addition to open-end investment company funds, however, there are three other primary types of pooled funds in the United States: *closed-end* investment company *funds* (CEFs), *unit investment trusts* (UITs), and *exchange-traded funds* (ETFs), which are the subjects of Chapters 6 through 8, respectively. The present chapter reviews the tremendous growth of mutual funds, including recent trends in mutual fund investing. Then it discusses who owns mutual funds, why they own them, and where they own them. The chapter concludes with a description of the normal classification of mutual funds by their principal investments.

Trends in Mutual Fund Investing

The total number of open-end investment company funds ("Mutual Funds" column, Table 3-1) in the United States has increased by 52% over the period 1995–2012. This growth occurred at the same time that the number of CEFs fluctuated but grew 21%, and the number of UITs declined 55%. Over the same interval, the number of) ETFs—index mutual funds that trade like stocks—exploded by 619%. The growth in the number of ETFs is projected to continue, owing to the low cost and tax efficiency associated with this type of *professionally managed asset* (PMA).

Table 3-1. Number of Investment Companies in US by Type, 1995–2012 (Year-End)[1]

Year	Mutual Funds*	CEFs	ETFs**	UITs	Total
1995	5,761	499	2	12,979	19,241
1996	6,293	496	19	11,764	18,572
1997	6,778	486	19	11,593	18,876
1998	7,489	491	29	10,966	18,975
1999	8,003	511	30	10,414	18,958
2000	8,370	481	80	10,072	19,003
2001	8,518	491	102	9,295	18,406
2002	8,511	544	113	8,303	17,471
2003	8,426	583	119	7,233	16,361
2004	8,415	619	152	6,499	15,685
2005	8,449	635	204	6,019	15,307
2006	8,721	646	359	5,907	15,633
2007	8,746	663	629	6,030	16,068
2008	8,880	642	743	5,984	16,249
2009	8,612	627	820	6,049	16,108
2010	8,540	624	950	5,971	16,085
2011	8,678	632	1,166	6,043	16,519
2012	8,752	602	1,239	5,787	16,380

**Data for open-end funds, including mutual funds that invest primarily in other mutual funds.*
***ETF data includes investment companies not registered under the Investment Company Act of 1940 and ETFs that invest primarily in other ETFs.*
Note: Investment company data includes only investment companies that report statistical information to the Investment Company Institute.

Although the total number of investment companies rebounded 5% in the five years after its low point in 2005, the number in 2012 was still 15% below its peak in 1995, owing almost solely to the decline in the UIT form of pooled investment.

[1]Sources: ETF data prior to 2001 courtesy of Strategic Insight Simfund. All other data courtesy of Investment Company Institute from 2013 Investment Company Fact Book: A Review of Trends and Activity in the U.S. Investment Company Industry. Washington, DC: Investment Company Institute (2013). Available at www.icifactbook.org.

The total worldwide assets owned in mutual fund form at the end of 2012 amounted to $26.8 trillion, with the United States constituting the single largest market, $13.0 trillion. The number of US households owning mutual funds was 53.8 million, and the number of individuals owning funds was 92.4 million (Figure 3-1)—constituting 39% of the adult population of the United States. In households owning mutual funds, the median amount invested in mutual funds was $100,000, and the majority of those assets were held in tax-deferred or retirement fund investment vehicles.

2012 Facts at a Glance

Total worldwide assets invested in mutual funds	**$26.8 trillion**
U.S. investment company total net assets*	**$14.7 trillion**
Mutual funds	$13.0 trillion
Exchange-traded funds	$1.3 trillion
Closed-end funds	$265 billion
Unit investment trusts	$72 billion
U.S. investment companies' share of:	
U.S. corporate equity	28%
U.S. municipal securities	28%
Commercial paper	42%
U.S. government securities	12%
U.S. household ownership of mutual funds	
Number of households owning mutual funds	53.8 million
Number of individuals owning mutual funds	92.4 million
Percentage of households owning mutual funds	44.4%
Median mutual fund assets of fund-owning households	$100,000
Median number of mutual funds owned	4
U.S. retirement market	
Total retirement market assets	$19.5 trillion
Percentage of households with tax-advantaged retirement savings	68%
IRA and DC plan assets invested in mutual funds	$5.3 trillion

***Components do not add to the total because of rounding.**

Figure 3-1. Mutual fund and other fund ownership as of 2012. [Source: Investment Company Institute. *2013 Investment Company Fact Book:A Review of Trends and Activity in the U.S. Investment Company Industry*. Washington, DC: Investment Company Institute (2013). Available at www.icifactbook.org.]

At the end of 2012, 753 sponsors or open-end investment companies managed mutual funds. No one mutual fund sponsor or company ruled as predominant, although market leaders are emerging in the ETF market (see Chapter 8). Nonetheless, the share of mutual fund assets managed by the 25 largest companies increased from 68% in the year 2000 to 75% in 2012.[2] Most of these gains were captured by companies offering a **fund family** (a number of funds offered across a broad range of investment objectives and fund categories).

Consistently with the lackluster performance of the financial markets since the onset of the economic recovery in mid-2009, the cash outflow from equity-type mutual funds has been considerable from 2009–2012. However, a longer-term factor is causing this development as well. *Baby boomers* (Americans born between 1946 and 1964) are approaching their retirement years, and as investors grow older, their willingness to assume investment risk typically declines while their interest in safety of principal increases. This tendency to become more conservative in respect of tolerance for risk has been strengthened, of course, by the severe market decline of late 2007 to mid-2009. (The Standard & Poor's Index of 500 stocks declined almost 37% from the previous year in 2008 alone.) Once adult investors live through a severe bear market for the first time, they generally become more conservative in practice. I expect this tendency to continue, particularly among aging baby boomers, as they shift more of their equity mutual fund assets into bond and hybrid funds.

Figure 3-2 shows the level of risk that all US households were willing to assume as of the year 2012 and breaks out the risk profile into households that own and do not own mutual funds. Although the figure and the data generally show an increase in the willingness to assume risk among mutual fund households, the most striking conclusion is that these households are willing to take any risk at all. After all, almost half of all US households report that they are unwilling to take any risk or are willing to take below-average risk for below-average gain, a metric that increases to some 65% for those households not owing mutual funds. These results can be attributed partly to the fact that some households lack the money with which to invest. However, a portion of the results is probably due to the lack of information about mutual funds and misunderstandings about this investment vehicle's risk-reward relationship. History has shown that investing, and investing in equities in particular, is one of only three ways (the others being owning your own business and investing in real estate) in which the average American can grow wealthy.

[2]Figure 2.2 in *2013 Investment Company Fact Book: A Review of Trends and Activity in the U.S. Investment Company Industry*. Washington, DC: Investment Company Institute (2013). Available at `www.icifactbook.org/fb_ch2.html`.

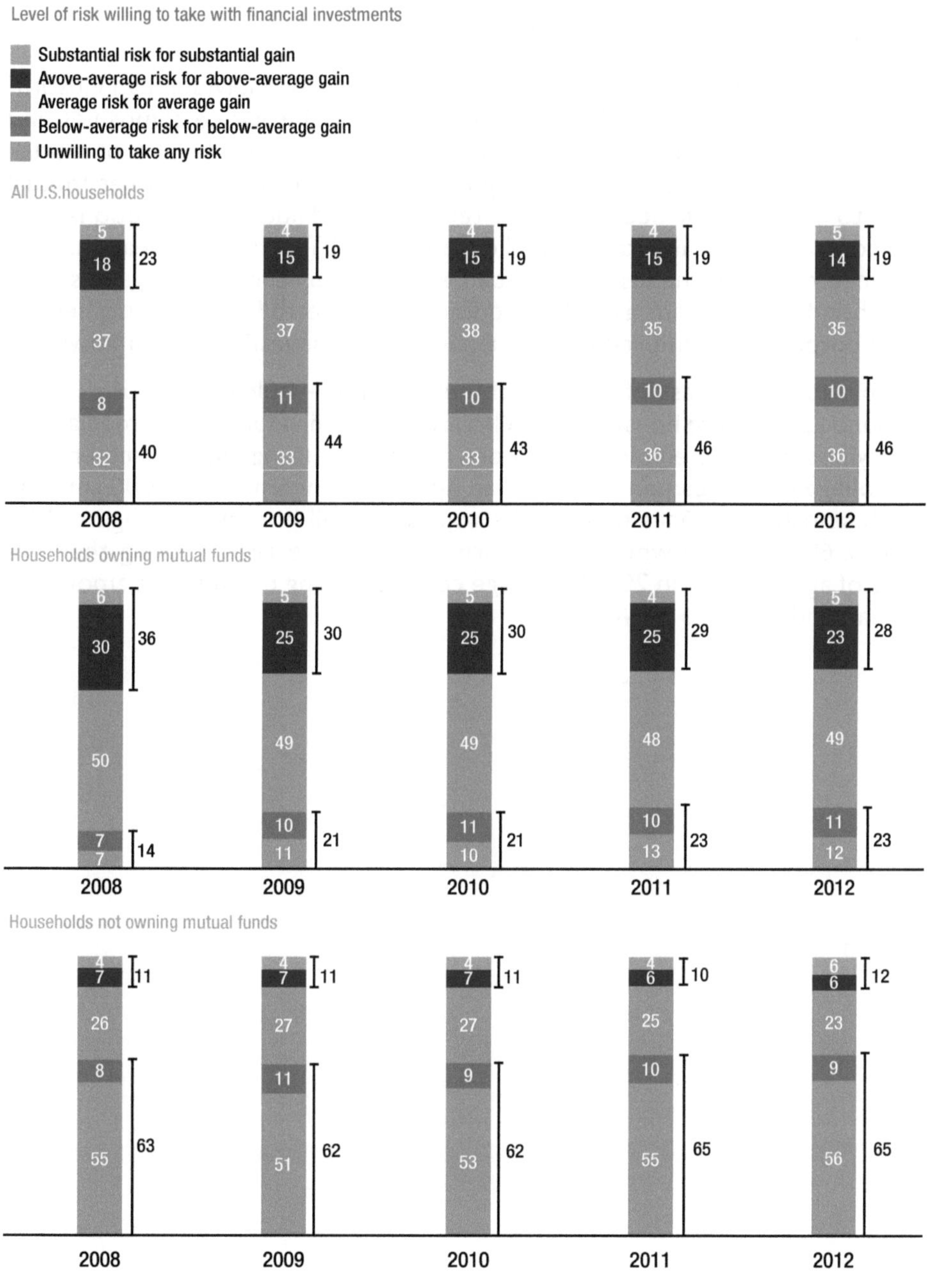

Figure 3-2. Household's willingness to assume investment risk. [Source: Investment Company Institute. *2013 Investment Company Fact Book: A Review of Trends and Activity in the U.S. Investment Company Industry*. Washington, DC: Investment Company Institute (2013). Available at `www.icifactbook.org`.]

Who Owns Mutual Funds?

There are two broad classes of owners of mutual funds: individuals and institutions. The latter class includes pension funds, banks, insurance companies, and university endowments. In addition to owning approximately 11% of mutual funds for investment purposes, many institutions use money market mutual funds to manage their need for short-term cash and liquidity. Institutions have also contributed greatly to the rapid expansion of ETFs in recent years, and it's not uncommon for the institutional balance sheet to reflect holdings of short-term bond mutual funds as well. In addition, short-term funds are also held by some corporations and reflected as a part of their investment cash flows.

The predominant class of owners of mutual funds—holding 89% of all funds and fund assets—are households. Who are these individuals? Their median age is 51 years; 72% are employed; 75% are married or living with a partner; 48% are college graduates; and their median household income is $80,000 annually, which statistically places them in the top 20% of all households (Figure 3-3). Almost 60% of the owners were born in 1964 or earlier (making them 49 years of age or older in 2013). The age cohort owning the greatest amount of mutual funds is 35 to 64 years old.

How many people own mutual funds?
92.4 million individuals
53.8 million U.S. households

Who are they?
51 is the median age of the head of household
75 percent are married or living with a partner
48 percent are college graduates
72 percent are employed (full- or part-time)
14 percent are Silent or GI Generation
44 percent are Baby Boomers
25 percent are Generation X
17 percent are Generation Y
$80,000 is the median household income

What do they own?
$190,000 is the median household financial assets
68 percent hold more than half of their financial assets in mutual funds
68 percent own IRAs
80 percent own DC retirement plan accounts
4 mutual funds is the median number owned
$100,000 is the median mutual fund assets
79 percent own equity funds

When and how did they make their first mutual fund purchase?
52 percent bought their first mutual fund before 1995
63 percent purchased their first mutual fund through an employer-sponsored retirement plan

Why do they invest?
93 percent are saving for retirement
50 percent hold mutual funds to reduce taxable income
48 percent are saving for emergencies
27 percent are saving for education

Figure 3-3. Characteristics of mutual fund investors, May 2012. [Source: Investment Company Institute. *2013 Investment Company Fact Book: A Review of Trends and Activity in the U.S. Investment Company Industry*. Washington, DC: Investment Company Institute (2013). Available at `www.icifactbook.org`.]

Why Own Mutual Funds?

In descending order, the primary reasons Americans own mutual funds are the following:

1. To save for retirement
2. To manage their income tax liability
3. To save for financial emergencies
4. To save for higher education

As of the end of 2012, 73% of mutual fund–owning households indicated that saving for retirement was their primary financial goal, with 93% of these households indicating that retirement planning was one of several financial goals.[3] Half of these households used mutual funds to manage their income tax liability—specifically, to reduce the amount of taxable income on which taxes were paid. Meanwhile, 48% of households included financial emergencies among their goals, and 27% listed saving for higher education as a priority.

In categorizing financial goals by broad investment vehicles, those individuals who are using mutual funds to save for retirement are taking advantage of **tax-deferred accounts**, such as employer-sponsored Section 401(k) plans or traditional and Roth *individual retirement accounts* (IRAs). A Section 401(k) plan, named after the section of the Internal Revenue Code that gave rise to the plan, is a defined-contribution type of retirement plan where the employer's contribution is limited by law but the amount of ultimate retirement benefit is unknown. The plan also permits the employee/participant to make salary-reduction contributions to his or her individual account, typically with the employer "matching" those contributions with a specified percentage. A traditional IRA, meanwhile, permits individual contributions (usually outside of an employer-sponsored plan) to be made to an account, either on a deductible or nondeductible basis. Finally, a Roth IRA permits individual contributions to be made to an account, but only on a nondeductible or after-tax basis, assuming that the individual's adjusted gross income (AGI) does not exceed a specified amount in a given year.

Individuals who are using mutual funds to manage their income tax liability are investing in **tax-exempt accounts**, which typically are made up of municipal bonds. Why? Most municipal bonds and municipal bond funds feature an exemption from income tax on interest paid from that account. (Note that this does not mean there is an exemption from tax on the sale of such funds; a sale of a municipal bond or municipal bond fund generates a capital gain—or loss—that is similar to most other investments.) The interest from certain municipal bonds or municipal bond funds, known as *private activity bonds*, generates income for **individual alternative minimum tax (AMT)** purposes. However, if the owner is not in an otherwise-taxable AMT situation, the purchase of even these bonds is nontaxable.

Individuals who are saving for financial emergencies are most interested in *liquidity*: the ability to turn their mutual fund proceeds into cash quickly and with no loss in dollar value. As a result, they are most likely to use a money market mutual fund as a substitute for cash, or what is referred to in the investment marketplace as a *cash equivalent*. Money market mutual funds can

[3]Figure 6.2 in *2013 Investment Company Fact Book: A Review of Trends and Activity in the U.S. Investment Company Industry*. Washington, DC: Investment Company Institute (2013). Available at `www.icifactbook.org/fb_ch6.html`.

generate either taxable or tax-exempt income, depending on the assets that constitute the portfolio of the fund. If the fund is classified as a *taxable* money market fund, it is investing in short-term (and relatively safe) securities, such as US Treasury bills, negotiable certificates of deposit, banker's acceptances, promissory notes, and commercial paper. If the fund is classified as a *tax-exempt* money market fund, it is investing primarily in municipal bonds issued either by a city, a state, or a territory of the United States.

Investors using a tax-exempt money market fund are typically in a higher marginal income tax bracket, because these individuals derive the most benefit from their investment. For example, say an individual in a 35% marginal income tax bracket wishes to invest in a tax-exempt money market fund with a yield of 2%. This individual's *equivalent taxable yield*—that is, the yield that he or she would earn in an alternative taxable money market fund—is 3.08% (derived by dividing the nominal yield of 2% on the tax-exempt fund by the denominator of 1 minus the marginal tax rate of the taxpayer or, here, 35%). Alternatively, an individual in a 15% bracket only needs to find a taxable money market fund yielding 2.35% (0.02 divided by the denominator of 1 minus 0.15).

The other issue individuals saving for a financial emergency must consider is what amount of funds they should keep in their taxable or tax-exempt **money market mutual fund**. The answer to this question varies, depending on whether one or two incomes are currently supporting the investor's lifestyle. However, there is general agreement among financial planners that an investor with only his or her own income supporting his or her desired lifestyle should keep an amount equal to six months of expenses in his or her money market mutual fund. A married investor or an investor with another income supporting his or her desired lifestyle, meanwhile, should only keep an amount equal to three months of expenses.

Finally, investors saving for higher education are most likely using a private Section 529 savings plan (named after the Internal Revenue Code section that gave birth to the vehicle). The advantage of this type of plan is that it gives investors the ability to pay for higher-education expenses on a tax-free basis while, depending on the state, also receiving a tax deduction for contributions made to the account. Each state then offers a mutual fund alternative (sometimes two) in which to invest, usually in conjunction with a well-known mutual fund family. Other education savings vehicles that make use of mutual funds include the Coverdell Education Savings Account and custodial accounts, which are permitted under either the Uniform Gifts to Minors Act (UGMA) or the Uniform Transfers to Minors Act (UTMA), depending on the state in which the investor lives.

Where Are Mutual Funds Owned?

The amount of assets held in employer-sponsored defined-contribution plans, including Section 401(k) plans, equaled approximately $5.1 trillion at the end of 2012.[4] Long-term mutual funds accounted for approximately $2.72 trillion of this amount. In addition, $1.8 trillion in annuities were held outside of retirement plans at this same date, with a portion of that amount held in variable annuities, an insurance product using mutual funds as its primary investment (see Chapter 15). Approximately $1.05 trillion of mutual funds were invested in variable annuities as of the end of 2012.

The composition of 401(k) plan accounts was predominated by the inclusion of equity mutual funds as of the end of 2012. Although the asset allocation of 401(k) accounts varied slightly by age, with younger participants being more heavily invested in equity funds (Figure 3-4), the preference for growth-of-capital funds was strong. As would be expected, given baby boomers' changing risk tolerance and growing preference for more conservative allocations, bond funds, **stable value funds**, and **guaranteed investment contracts (GICs)**[5] were more prevalent in the 401(k) accounts of older participants. Interestingly, however, the allocation of participants in their 60s to target date retirement funds was *less than* that of participants in their 20s, likely due to the relative newness of this type of fund.

---

[4]Figure 7.7 in *2013 Investment Company Fact Book: A Review of Trends and Activity in the U.S. Investment Company Industry*. Washington, DC: Investment Company Institute (2013). Available at `www.icifactbook.org/fb_ch6.html`.

[5]A *guaranteed investment contract* (GIC) is an insurance product offering a guaranteed interest rate for some period of time as well as a protection of principal. It is similar to a bank certificate of deposit, but without federal insurance protection up to $250,000 per deposit. A *synthetic GIC* that combines an asset owned directly by a retirement plan trust and a wrap contract providing book-value protection for participant withdrawals prior to the maturity of the contract.

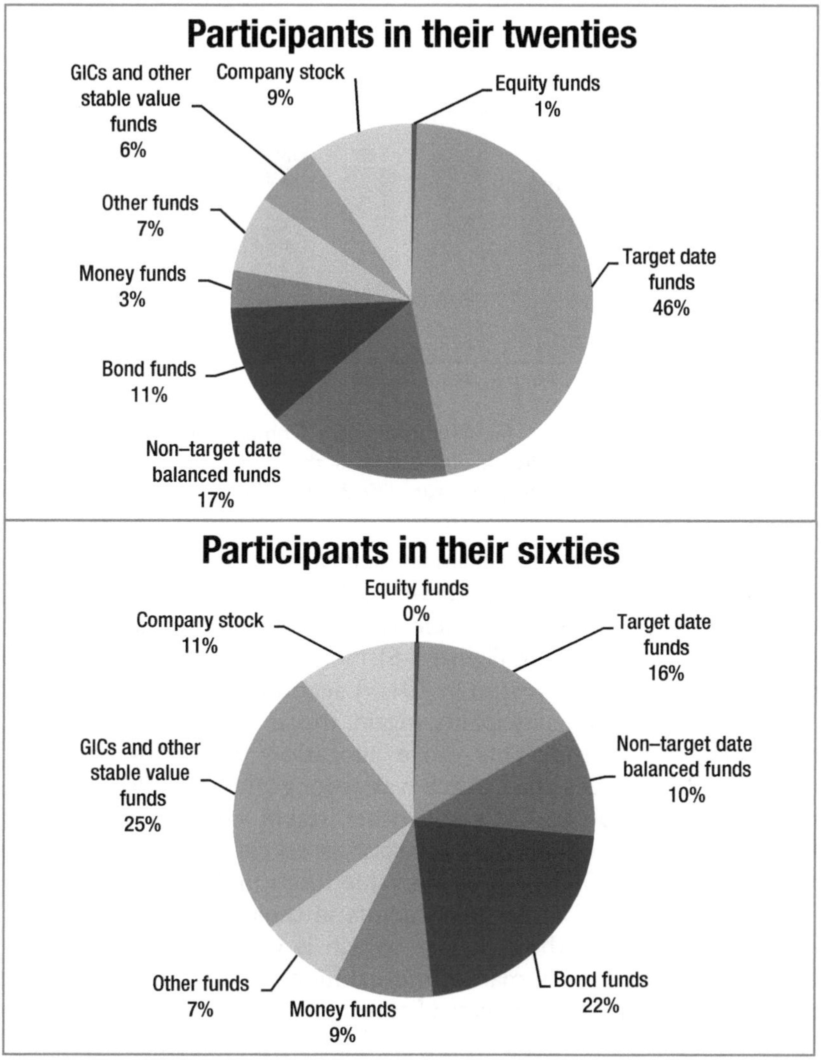

Figure 3-4. 401(k) asset allocations for participants in their sixties and twenties. [Source: Investment Company Institute. *2013 Investment Company Fact Book: A Review of Trends and Activity in the U.S. Investment Company Industry*. Washington, DC: Investment Company Institute (2013). Available at `www.icifactbook.org`.]

The amount of assets held in IRAs, among them traditional and Roth IRAs, equaled $5.407 trillion at the end of 2012 (see Figure 3-5). Mutual fund investments, including both long-term funds and money market funds, made up an estimated $2.473 trillion of this amount. The Investment Company Institute (ICI) separately reported that, similar to the composition of 401(k) accounts, equity mutual funds predominated in households that invested their funds in several assets, with 54% of total households relying on growth investments.

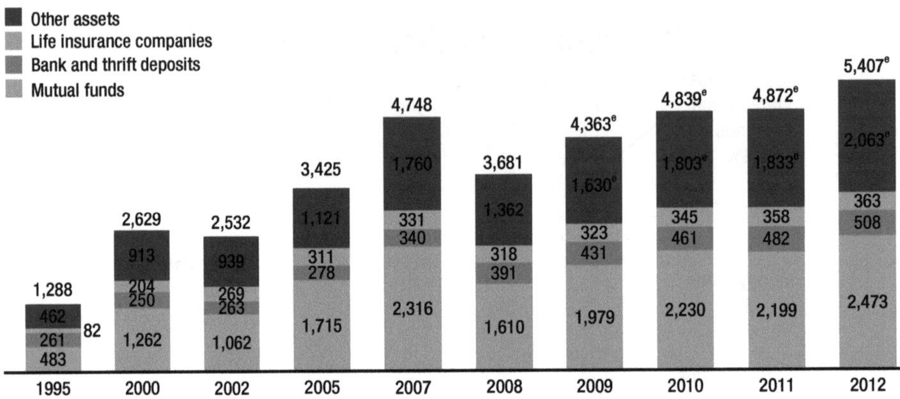

Figure 3-5. IRA asset allocations. [Source: Investment Company Institute. *2013 Investment Company Fact Book: A Review of Trends and Activity in the U.S. Investment Company Industry*. Washington, DC: Investment Company Institute (2013). Available at `www.icifactbook.org`.]

Just as younger 401(k) account holders demonstrated a stronger preference for equities than older account holders did, younger IRA owners preferred equities and equity funds over their older counterparts by almost a 6% difference (51.5% cf 45.7%: see Figure 3-6). Meanwhile, the overall composition and percentage of assets invested in 401(k) accounts and IRAs was amazingly consistent among older participants (again, those in their 60s). Interestingly, though, there was considerably more allocation to money market funds among older IRA owners than there was among older 401(k) holders—and there was no allocation to GICs and other stable value funds, an insurance product that is only used in employer-sponsored retirement plans. However, adding the amount of GICs and stable value funds in 401(k) plans (16.5%) to that in money funds (6.2%) for participants in their 60s, the result is a total percentage of 22.7% for these funds—which is very close to the total percentage of 24.5% for money market mutual funds in IRAs. This speaks to the senior investor's desire for stability of asset principal.

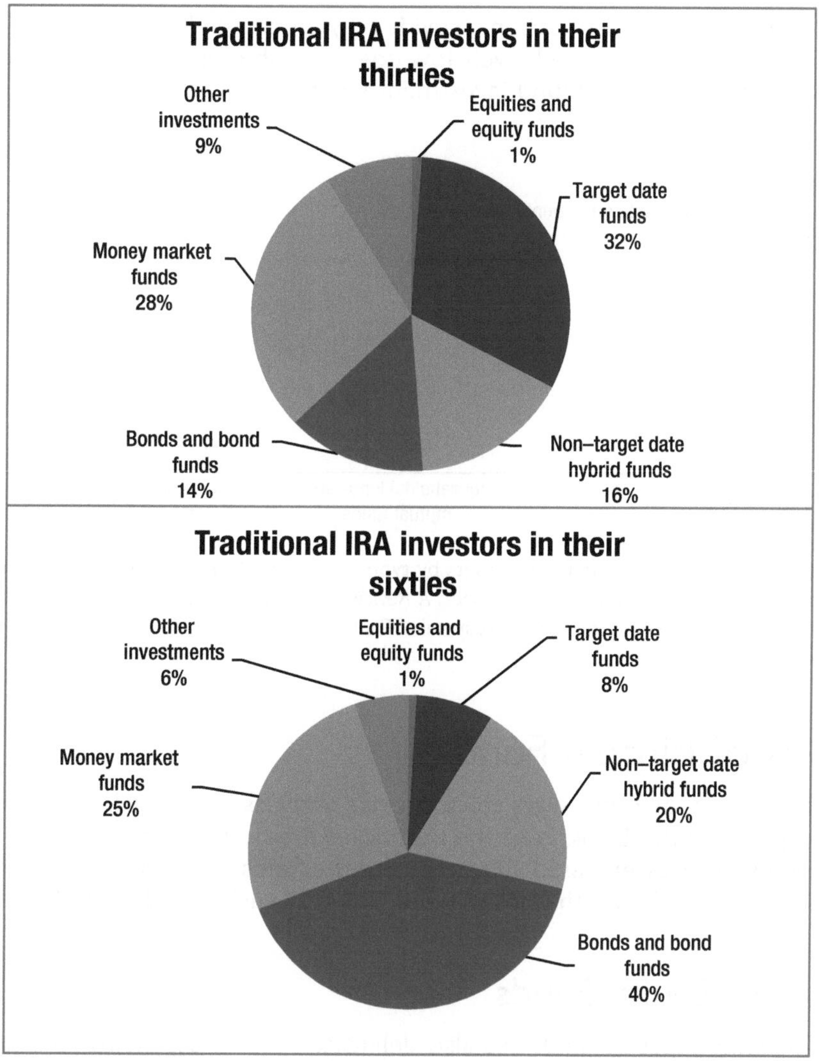

Figure 3-6. IRA asset allocations for investors in their sixties and twenties. [Source: Investment Company Institute. *2013 Investment Company Fact Book: A Review of Trends and Activity in the U.S. Investment Company Industry*. Washington, DC: Investment Company Institute (2013). Available at `www.icifactbook.org`.]

The amount of long-term mutual funds held in other household accounts, including taxable, tax-exempt, and education savings accounts, totaled $3.8 trillion as of the end of 2012. Money market mutual funds that were held for these same reasons totaled $1.388 trillion as of the same date (Figure 3-7). From this data, it is clear that investor preference for mutual funds as a primary method of reaching financial goals is strong. Part of this is likely due to the automatic diversification provided by most funds, with access to a professional manager at a relatively low cost contributing as another practical reason to use the mutual fund investment vehicle.

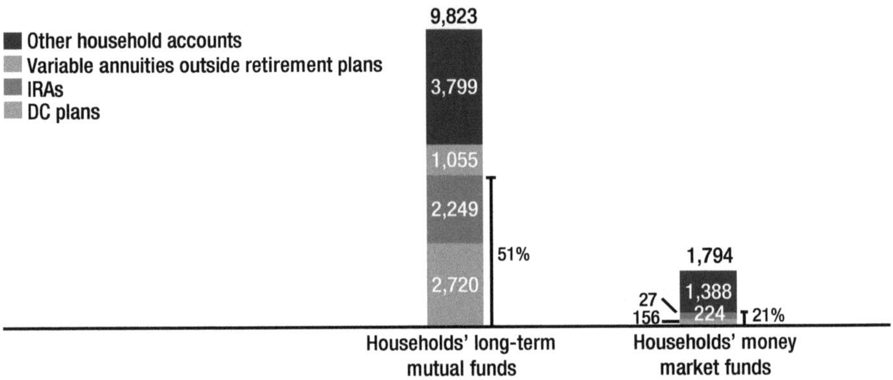

Figure 3-7. Household mutual fund assets by type of account. [Source: Investment Company Institute. *2013 Investment Company Fact Book: A Review of Trends and Activity in the U.S. Investment Company Industry*. Washington, DC: Investment Company Institute (2013). Available at www.icifactbook.org.]

Types of Mutual Funds

There are many different ways to categorize and classify mutual funds, but for the purposes of this book, I use the traditional method and categorize by type of investment or asset class. I subcategorize the funds by the fund's investment objective. I then discuss the broad types of funds, such as index funds.

Types of Equity Funds

The following types of funds are also delineated into those funds investing in large-capitalization (large-cap) stocks, typically defined as stocks with a **market capitalization** of $10.0 billion or more; middle-capitalization stocks, defined as stocks with a market capitalization of between $2.0 billion and $10.0 billion: and small-capitalization stocks, defined as stocks with a market capitalization of less than $2.0 billion. Sometimes, a fourth size-of-stock category, micro-cap, is also used. Micro-cap stocks are stocks with a market capitalization of less than $300 million.[6]

[6]The *market capitalization* of a stock is its current price per share times the number of outstanding shares. The following definitions are widely accepted in the investment community, as reflected at Investopedia.com.

Aggressive Growth

This type of equity mutual fund invests in small- and micro-cap stocks, with the investment objective of the fund emphasizing the capital appreciation or growth of the stocks. The risk of this type of fund is relatively high compared with the rest of the market. The turnover of such funds is also unusually high.

Growth

This type of (mostly) equity fund invests in small-cap stocks and emphasizes growth of capital, but with less overall risk than an aggressive growth fund. Some bonds may be held in this fund, but the amount is usually very small; and, if held, the focus is on those bonds with the highest **duration** and the most opportunity for capital or price appreciation in the face of declining interest rates.

Growth and Income

This type of (mostly) equity fund invests in stocks that generate both capital appreciation and current income through the payment of dividends. As such, the stocks in which the fund invests are so-called *blue chip stocks*, or stocks of mature, established companies with predictable or increasing cash flow. If bonds are held, the focus is on high-quality, investment-grade bonds with low default risk. A corresponding term for a type of bond fund stressing both capital appreciation and a relatively safe yield is a *total return* fund. The total return of a fund includes interest or dividends (if used in the context of an equity fund), capital gain distributions, and capital appreciation.

Equity Income

This type of equity mutual fund invests in dividend-paying stocks, including blue chip stocks. The fund attempts to invest only in stocks with a relatively high dividend yield, historically in the range of 4% to 6% annually.

International Equity

These funds may be further broken down into international developed countries funds, global or world funds, and emerging market funds. An *international developed countries* or diversified fund invests in equities outside of the United States, usually in European countries, Australia, or Japan. A *global or world* fund invests in equities of companies throughout the developed world, including the United States. An *emerging market fund* invests in equities from companies in the developing world, including the so-called BRIC countries: Brazil, Russia, India, and China. Stock in Mexican companies is also becoming a popular component of emerging market funds.

Sector

These funds usually have narrow investment objectives, such as investing only in the equities of a particular market sector: for example, energy. (Chapter 1 enumerates the ten commonly accepted sectors of the stock market.) By definition, therefore, these funds do not provide the same degree of diversification as other equity mutual funds.

Specialty

These funds invest only in the stocks of companies of a specific industry or according to a particular investment preference. For example, the "socially responsible" funds, discussed in Chapter 2, fall into the category of specialty funds. A "green fund" that invests only in the stocks of environmentally friendly companies is also an example of a specialty equity fund.

Types of Bond Funds

Note that the term *income fund* is often used interchangeably with *bond fund*, but with an emphasis on the interest paid from a bond and not that of dividends from stock.

High-Yield

These funds invest in lower-quality or non-investment-grade corporate bonds that generate a higher yield or income payment to the mutual fund owner and have a greater risk of default by the bond issuer. The bonds in which such funds invest are sometimes referred to pejoratively as *junk bonds*, although in recent years the bonds' probability of default (default risk) has improved dramatically.

US Government

As the name implies, these funds invest in US Treasury securities, including both notes and bonds. A *note* is a shorter-term debt obligation of the US government, with a maturity date of two to ten years. A *bond*, per government terminology, is a debt obligation of the US government, with a maturity date of more than ten years. Meanwhile, the *long bond*, which is also issued by the US government, possesses a maturity of 30 years. The two primary features of a US government bond fund are the lack of default risk and an exemption of bond interest from state income tax.

Ginnie Mae

These funds invest in government agency securities issued by the Government National Mortgage Association, commonly shortened to the name Ginnie Mae. The yield on these funds is slightly higher than it is on a US government bond fund, owing to the additional agency risk characterizing an issue that is not directly issued by the US Treasury.

Convertible Bond

These funds invest in convertible bonds or bonds that are convertible at a later time into the common stock of the issuing corporation. Convertible securities, which also include convertible preferred stock, are sometimes components of hybrid mutual funds or funds having some characteristics of both equity funds and bond funds.

International Bond

These funds are similar to international equity funds, except that debt or bonds issued by corporations and countries (sovereign governments) are the focus. The bonds may be issued by foreign companies or governments, as part of a global community including the United States, or by emerging market countries. A feature of an international bond fund, like its international equity cousin, is the relatively low correlation of the security with the US market, thus making any type of international fund an effective fund diversifier.

Municipal Bond

These funds invest in bonds issued by municipalities, such as state and local governments. The types of bonds in which the fund invests are primarily so-called *general obligation bonds*, which are backed by the taxing authority of the municipality to pay the bond principal and interest, and *revenue bonds*, which are repaid only by revenues generated from the particular project for which the bond is issued. The primary feature of a municipal bond fund is the exemption of bond interest from federal income tax.

Strategic Income

This is a relatively new category of bond mutual fund that uses alternative strategies to generate a positive total return even when interest rates rise—a situation that generally results in the traditional type of bond fund suffering a reduction in value. Such funds invest in corporate bonds, international corporate or government bonds, or mortgage-backed bonds (such as a Ginnie Mae bond fund). Convertible securities are also used to diversify and hedge investor risk. In addition, these funds trade international currencies.

Types of Money Market Funds

The types of equity and bond funds reviewed in the preceding section invest in the *capital* or long-term investment market. The capital market is defined as that market wherein the maturity date of the debt obligation is more than one year or there is no maturity date on the obligation. Alternatively, the *money market* is defined as that market wherein the maturity date of any obligation is one year or less.

Taxable

A taxable money market fund invests in short-term, fixed-income investments that are liquid. As mentioned in the "Why Own Mutual Funds?" section of this chapter, a taxable money market fund frequently is used to position assets for emergency use by the owner. Such funds are also used as a temporary mechanism to safeguard liquid assets before the assets are invested in the capital market. The fund returns little to no income, but it does not suffer from the loss of principal in its net asset value, which is currently tied to a constant $1.00 of value.

Tax-Exempt

A tax-exempt money market fund invests in short-term securities that do not produce currently taxable income to the fund owner. Such funds accomplish this objective by investing primarily in municipal securities. They are used heavily by high-income taxpayers to manage their income tax liability.

Types of Hybrid Funds

The term *hybrid* is typically used by investment professionals to mean anything that is neither an equity fund, bond fund, nor money market fund. Here, the term is used in its traditional sense to mean a fund that includes a mix of equities, bonds, and money market financial instruments.

Balanced

These funds feature a mixture of equities and bonds in a proportionate allocation determined by the fund portfolio managers. The focus of these funds is on lower growth of capital while also providing interest income to the mutual fund owner. Given the inclusion of bonds in the portfolio of assets, such funds have lower risk than equity funds, but they carry slightly higher risk than investment grade bond funds.

Asset Allocation

This is a catch-all category of funds that includes *target-date*, *stable-value*, *lifestyle*, and *absolute-return funds* (discussed in Chapter 1). Stable-value funds, which are available only in retirement plans, offer higher returns along with guaranteed principal by investing in bonds and synthetic GICs. Absolute-return funds, meanwhile, are managed with an investment objective of a positive annual return, regardless of market conditions. Asset-allocation mutual funds invest in a mixture of equities, bonds and other fixed-income securities, and money market instruments. They generally maintain a specific weighting in each asset class that is tied to the owner's projected retirement date.

Commodity Funds

A *commodity* is an asset whose value is determined primarily by supply and demand and is not significantly impacted by the quality of the asset. Examples of commodities include agricultural products, oil and gas, and natural resources. The term *commodity fund* encompasses funds that invest directly in commodities, as well as those that invest in the commodity futures market. (Futures and the futures markets are discussed in Chapter 10, which considers managed futures as a type of PMA.) There are also *combination commodity funds*, which invest directly in commodities and participate in the commodity futures market.

Commodity funds offer portfolio diversification but are subject to extreme price volatility. This is because of the price risk associated with commodity assets, which suffer from the "fear and greed" mentality of most investors. An example of a commodity fund investing directly in commodities is a gold fund that holds gold bullion among its assets, thus necessitating the payment of an additional expense by the fund owner because the bullion must be separately warehoused by the fund.

Real Estate Funds

There are two ways to invest in real estate: directly or indirectly. A real estate mutual fund is an indirect investment in real estate that focuses on *real estate investment trusts* (REITs) and real estate companies. REITS are corporations that own and manage a portfolio of real estate properties and mortgages with funds collected from investors or trust beneficiaries. Real estate companies, meanwhile, directly sell real estate to individuals and support real estate ventures through property management services. The purchase of a primary or secondary residence is another example of a direct investment in real estate.

REITs are the partial focus of Chapter 12, which compares the advantages and disadvantages of REITs to those of a *real estate limited partnership* (RELP), a commonly used alternative indirect investment in real estate. However, a REIT may also be compared to a real estate mutual fund. A major advantage of a real estate mutual fund is that it allows an investment to grow and generate sizeable capital gains without having to distribute profits to investors each year. In contrast, a REIT is required by law to return most of its income (90% or more) annually to its investors, resulting in current taxation of the income.

Collective Funds

A *collective fund* is operated by a bank or trust company and includes pooled accounts of bank customers. It is not a mutual fund in the sense of an open-ended investment company. The pooled accounts are combined into a single trust, known as a *master trust account*, under the control of the bank or trust company. Often, the trust account consists of an A1 Fund, which is a fund of grouped assets contributed by the bank for reinvestment purposes, and an A2 Fund of assets contributed by pension and profit-sharing plans exempt from federal income tax.

Index Funds

All of the types of mutual funds that have been described in this chapter are **actively managed**—meaning that the portfolio manager attempts to outperform a specified market index, also known as a *benchmark*, through superior security selection. Index funds, however, are **passively managed**, and their portfolios require little oversight by the fund manager. The manager of an index fund purchases each security in the index that is modeled (for example, the S&P 500) and then attempts to replicate the performance of that index. Very little trading or "turnover" of the fund then takes place. As a result of their management strategy, index funds have lower expenses, which is one of their major advantages. In addition, an index fund investor benefits from the low turnover ratio of the fund, meaning appreciation of the fund's portfolio of assets is not recognized for income tax purposes by the investor.

An (ETF) is often structured similarly to an index mutual fund, but instead of being priced at the end of each trading day at its net asset value (NAV), an ETF share trades like a stock and is priced throughout the market trading day (Chapter 8).

I have just considered the growth in mutual funds and their primary place as the investment vehicle of choice of many ordinary Americans—particularly people who are saving for retirement. Now, let's look at long-term investment strategies carried out through the various types mutual funds, including the investment styles of growth versus value investing followed by some individual investors and many fund portfolio managers.

CHAPTER

4

Long-Term Investing in Mutual Funds

The efficacy of any investment should be evaluated on the basis of a risk-reward analysis, which is why, in this chapter, we examine the relationship between risk and reward as it applies to mutual-fund investing. The chapter begins with a look at the principle of diversification, which is a major advantage afforded to mutual fund investors. It then offers an example of a typical mutual-fund investment objective and explains that objective by delineating its various parts, with special emphasis placed on the concept of *investor constraint*. The chapter concludes with an explanation of some of the common investment strategies that are used in long-term mutual-fund investing and how to determine which mutual fund shares have been redeemed.

The Principle of Diversification

In investing, *diversification* is the process of trying to achieve a portfolio's maximum expected return while assuming the least amount of total risk. The expected return of a portfolio, one type of which is the prototypical mutual fund, may be determined by first calculating the weighted average of the expected returns for each individual security contained within the portfolio

(w_i). To do so, divide the amount invested in the individual security (i) by the total amount invested in the portfolio (t):

$$w_i = \frac{Amount\,invested\ (i)}{Total\,amount\,invested\ (t)}$$

The respective weights are then multiplied by the individual security's expected return and summed to derive the portfolio's total expected return.

For example, let's say that an investor purchases 100 shares of Stock A at a current market price per share of $23.75 (an amount invested of $2,375). The investor then adds those shares to a portfolio including 100 shares of Stock B, which has a current market price per share of $45.00 ($4,500), for a total amount invested of $6,875. The expected return of Stock A is 25.20 percent, and the expected return of Stock B is 30.55 percent. Thus, the portfolio's expected return is (.3455 times .2520) + (.6545 times .3055), or 28.70 percent.

Now that we know the portfolio's expected return, how do we determine how much risk the investor needs to assume in order to achieve this expected return? We do this by referencing the **standard deviation** associated with each stock. As anticipated, Stock A has a *lower* standard deviation (20 percent) than Stock B (25 percent) because of Stock A's lower expected return. However, in order to determine the portfolio's total risk—also known as the portfolio's *standard deviation*—it is not enough to merely take the weights of Stock A and Stock B by their individual standard deviations. This is because the expected returns of Stock A and B are *correlated*, meaning there is a predictable relationship between their respective movements.

When two returns are perfectly positively correlated (or exhibit a correlation coefficient of +1.0), they move in exactly the same direction—and in the same degree—at all times. Stocks specifically and securities generally exhibit some degree of positive correlation, meaning not all total risk can be eliminated, or *diversified away*. Nonetheless, investors can reduce the total risk of their portfolios by combining stocks that are less than perfectly positively correlated. Stated another way, investors can hold several risky investments in one portfolio and carry less risk than they would if any of these investments were held in isolation.

What risk is left after we diversify a portfolio, and how do we measure—or, even more important, manage—this left-over risk to obtain the maximum benefits of diversification? The answer to these questions is found in *modern portfolio theory (MPT)*, which has been the predominant rationale for explaining portfolio risk and returns since its introduction by Professor Harry Markowitz in the early 1950s.

Modern Portfolio Theory

In MPT, Markowitz identified two distinct components that make up the total risk of a portfolio: *diversifiable* and *nondiversifiable risk*. Diversifiable risk, also known as *unsystematic* risk, is micro in nature and includes only those types of risk that affect an individual firm, such as the threat of a labor strike or loss of a major customer. Alternatively, nondiversifiable risk, also known as *systematic* or *market* risk, is macro in nature and includes those types of risk that impact all firms, such as the annual rate of inflation or changes in gross domestic product. As may be anticipated from the terms themselves, only diversifiable risk can be totally eliminated by the diversification process; nondiversifiable risk can only be managed by the investor. Put another way, *diversification reduces risk, but only to a point.*

Markowitz viewed portfolio construction as a *mean-optimization* problem. In other words, he wanted to know how an investor could best achieve (optimize) a particular expected return on a portfolio while minimizing that portfolio's total risk to the greatest extent possible. To address that quandary, Markowitz generated the portfolio weights of individual assets for the highest mean expected return at each gradation of standard deviation, resulting in a set of portfolios known as the *efficient frontier*. He then suggested that investors choose an optimal portfolio by matching their risk tolerance for any given mixture of assets (as graphically measured by the investor's indifference curve) with one or more of these efficient sets of portfolios.

Sharpe Additions to Modern Portfolio Theory

Although Markowitz pioneered the concept of MPT, Professor William Sharpe of Stanford University significantly contributed to the theory by positing the addition of a risk-free asset to Markowitz's efficient set of portfolios. Sharpe's concept of an asset that pays a risk-free rate of return was meant to be hypothetical; in practice, the closest approximation to a risk-free asset in today's investment marketplace is a short-term government security, specifically a US Treasury Bill. Nevertheless, investors today might consider purchasing a Separate Trading of Registered Interest and Principal (STRIP) bond to fulfill the purpose of Sharpe's hypothetical risk-free asset. Such bonds carry no default risk, because they are issued by the US Treasury. Moreover, these bonds pay a fixed rate of return, which is set once the price of the bond is established and issued to the investing public. The certainty of this return, with no variability, results in a standard deviation of *zero* for a STRIP bond.

Sharpe's work on MPT was important because it showed that investors may choose one of two ways to minimize their portfolio risk: they can construct an optimal portfolio consisting entirely of risky assets from Markowitz's efficient frontier, or they can invest in risk-free assets. Sharpe analogized Markowitz's optimal portfolio to the overall market. In other words, because the overall market is very large and exceedingly well diversified (in fact, it cannot be any more diversified, because the market includes all assets), it has *no diversifiable risk*. Meanwhile, Sharpe used his concept of the risk-free asset as a component in his famous formula for determining the expected return of a portfolio: the *capital asset pricing model* (CAPM), which uses a stock's *beta coefficient* (or beta) with the market as a measure of nondiversifiable or systematic risk.

The Concept of Beta

The *systematic risk principle* states that an investor's reward for assuming risk depends only on the investment's systematic risk. The underlying rationale for this principle follows from the assertion made in the previous section that the portfolio of the overall market includes no diversifiable or unsystematic risk; that type of risk has been entirely diversified away by rational investors. The predominance of rational investors outnumbering irrational investors is a major precept of MPT. As a result, there is no reward (in the form of an investment's expected return) for an investor who assumes any amount of unnecessary, diversifiable risk. Stated another way, the *expected return of an asset depends only on its systematic risk*. This is referred to as the "systematic risk principle" in investments and finance.

Because systematic risk is the sole determinant of an asset's expected risk premium (and, by extension, a portfolio's expected return), there was a need to develop a way to measure the amount of systematic risk assumed by investors when they purchase that asset. Accordingly, Sharpe developed the metric of an investment's *beta coefficient*, a term that is commonly shortened to *beta* in the investment world. Beta is the key measure of risk for large portfolio holders, such as investors who use mutual funds as their primary investment choice. It reflects an individual asset's marginal contribution to the overall risk of the fully diversified market portfolio.

A beta coefficient of 1 is used to identify the market's systematic risk. Assets (or portfolios) with a beta of greater than 1 carry more systematic risk than the overall market does, but with a proportional increase in the asset's (or portfolio's) expected return. For example, say Stock A has a beta of 1.25. It thus exhibits 25 percent more systematic risk than the overall market does. Assuming the market portfolio increases in value by 10 percent in the current year, Stock A should increase in value by 12.5 percent, or a multiple of (.10 times 1.25). Keep in mind, though, that the value of Stock A should also decline by 12.5 percent when the market portfolio decreases by 10 percent, making Stock A more aggressive than the typical stock traded on the market.

The formula for beta reflects the correlation in movement between the individual asset and the overall market portfolio:

$$\beta_i = \text{Corr}\ (R_i\ R_m) \times SD_i\ /\ SD_m$$

In other words, beta (β_i) is equal to the correlation coefficient (Corr) between the return on the individual asset (R_i) and that of the market portfolio (R_m) multiplied by the ratio of the standard deviations between the individual asset (SD_i) and the market portfolio (SD_m).

The beta of each individual asset (stock) is reported by various financial services, as is the beta for each mutual fund (portfolio). But a word of caution is in order at this point: *not all betas are created equal.* Various financial services use different procedures to compute the beta they report for an individual asset or portfolio. For example, some publications use monthly historical data to derive beta, others use quarterly data, and still others use annual data. Regardless, there should not be a statistically significant variation in the beta index number reported for a given asset or portfolio across financial services.

Portfolio Betas

Similar to the computation of the expected return of a portfolio, the beta of a portfolio (β_P) is a weighted average of the betas of the individual securities:

$$\beta_p = \sum w_i\ b_i$$

As such, the beta of a portfolio consisting of two stocks, each with the same beta, would equal the beta of each of the two stocks. However, what happens if we add a third stock with a low beta (and thus a low amount of systematic risk)? As we would expect, the portfolio's overall systematic risk *declines*.

For example, imagine a portfolio comprising three equally weighted stocks: Stock A (33.3 percent), Stock B (33.3 percent), and Stock C (33.3 percent). Stock A and Stock B both have a beta of 1.10. If Stock C also has a beta of 1.10, the portfolio beta amounts to 1.10 as well. But let's say that Stock C features a beta of .60. As a result, the portfolio beta declines from 1.10 to .93, computed as (.3333)(1.10) + (.3333)(1.10) + (.3333)(.60). In selecting a third stock with a beta that is lower than that of the overall market, we have succeeded in constructing a portfolio with less systematic risk than that of the overall market portfolio.

As the previous example demonstrates, it is possible to add new stocks to a portfolio (such as a mutual fund) and change the systematic risk of that portfolio. Systematic risk is one of two components of *total* risk (the other being unsystematic, or diversifiable, risk), so we have also reduced the portfolio's total risk. Therefore, because a stock's beta coefficient determines how the stock impacts the risk of a diversified portfolio, beta is a most useful predictor of the effectiveness of the diversification process.

The Capital Asset Pricing Model (CAPM)

Sharpe encapsulated his extension of MPT by deriving the famous CAPM to compute the expected return of any asset or portfolio. The CAPM proved that the expected return of any asset or portfolio is related to systematic risk. Specifically, the expected return is derived by the interrelation of three factors:

- The current risk-free rate, which usually is approximated by using the proxy of the 13-week Treasury Bill for short-term rates and the proxy of the 10-year Treasury Note yield for long-term rates (note that I have suggested the use of a STRIP bond as a proxy)
- The so-called *market risk premium* for any asset that is part of the overall market portfolio
- The amount of systematic risk assumed by the investor as measured by the asset's beta coefficient

The broad implication of the model is that a security's expected return should be related to the portion of its risk that cannot be eliminated by diversification, which is consistent with the systematic risk principle. Under one of the model's assumptions, an investor should expect to receive the CAPM return when the market is in equilibrium or is reasonably *efficient*. Thus, the CAPM asset return is the investor's fair or *required* return, insofar that the return compensates them for the amount of risk that they have taken.

The formula for the CAPM is

$$E(r_i) = R_{rf} + (R_m - R_{rf})\beta_i$$

where $E(r_i)$ is the expected return on the investment, R_{rf} is the current risk-free rate, $(R_m - R_{rf})$ is the market risk premium, and β_i is the beta coefficient of the investment.

The formula is easy to use and generates not only the investment's expected return, assuming an efficient market, but also the investor's required rate. However, in the real world of market practice, the investor's required rate of return is usually *different* than the investment's expected return. This difference between the investment's expected return and the investor's required rate serves as the basis for an investment decision. For example, let's say an investor is considering the purchase of ABC mutual fund, which has a beta of 1.25. The next year's return of ABC fund is projected to be 14 percent. Meanwhile, the risk-free rate is 3 percent, and the expected return on the market is 12 percent. Should the investor purchase the fund? The answer is no, because the expected return for ABC fund using the CAPM is 14.25 percent, or .03 + (.12 – .03) times 1.25. Because the investor requires a return of 14.25 percent to be fairly compensated for the systematic risk they are assuming with the investment, and the projected return of the fund is only 14 percent, the investor should *not* make the purchase.

In the previous example, ABC fund is currently mispriced to the investor's detriment. But what if the fund's beta was 1.15 instead of 1.25? This would result in a required return of only 13.35 percent for the investor, with the fund projected to return 14 percent over the next year. Accordingly, the fund would now be mispriced *in favor* of the investor, and as a result, the investor should buy it.

Academics have long studied whether a security's beta is indeed the primary factor in predicting an investment's expected return. For the most part, the empirical studies have supported the CAPM's accuracy and the importance of beta in explaining the expected return of a portfolio such as a mutual fund. But one famous study by Professor Burton Malkiel of Princeton University found that mutual-fund companies, despite all their resources, cannot generate returns on a long-term basis that are in excess of what the CAPM predicts. Thus, most investors should allocate at least part, if not all, of their mutual-fund contributions to an index mutual fund or a stock market index exchange-traded fund (ETF).

Index Mutual Funds

An *index mutual fund* (also known as an *index fund*) is a passively managed fund that seeks to match the performance of a preselected market index, such as the Standard & Poor's index of 500 stocks. In an index fund, the fund manager typically attempts to reproduce or replicate the composition of the preselected index in as exact a manner as possible. The manager buys the same securities that form the index, in the same proportions as in the index, and subsequently alters those positions only as the composition of the index changes. Because such changes are infrequent, an index fund tends to generate very low trading and management expense ratios.

An index fund, because it is passively managed, stands in marked contrast to most mutual funds, which generally are **actively managed**. Nevertheless, academic studies have shown that passive management, or *indexing*, is appropriate for all types of equity mutual-fund investing, with the notable exception of small capitalization funds. International stock mutual funds will also likely outperform the index if they are actively managed. Taxable bond funds provide a mixed preference for indexing. Finally, Treasury and municipal bond funds that are actively managed have *not*, historically, outperformed passively managed funds, whereas corporate bond funds, particularly those holding bonds of intermediate-term maturity, may benefit from an active management approach.

The Investment Company Institute reported in its 2013 Handbook that, of households owning mutual funds, 33 percent owned at least one index fund. About 50 percent of the money contributed to index funds in the year 2012 went to bond funds, with 31 percent going into domestic stock index funds and the remaining 19 to 20 percent going into funds indexed to global and international stock indexes. The total amount invested in index funds rose to $1.3 trillion in 2012, up significantly from an amount of $837 billion only three years earlier. If nothing else, these statistics reflect a growing understanding of the importance of paying as low a management fee as possible when investing in mutual funds. Indeed, the management expense ratio is one of the only factors in mutual-fund investing that an investor can control. Although investors also cannot directly control the trading expenses incurred by the fund, they can manage those expenses by investing in funds that trade only infrequently, such as index funds.

Practical Considerations in Mutual-Fund Investing

Suppose you are considering investing in a mutual fund that describes itself as follows:

> ABC Mutual Fund is an actively managed growth fund investing in small, domestic equities, with the portfolio manager using fundamental analysis to construct the fund portfolio, which may be purchased by the investor at no sales charge, and with the fund having a lower-than-average management expense ratio.

Of course, this description provides much more detail than a typical mutual-fund description would: it informs the investor of the fund's investment objective (such as growth or growth and income) and the securities in which the fund is investing (such as equities, bonds, or alternative investments). This description provides an illustration of the considerations and constraints an investor should keep in mind when deciding whether to purchase shares of a particular mutual fund. Let's break down the description into its individual considerations and discuss each separately:

ABC Mutual Fund is: 1) an actively managed; 2) growth fund investing in; 3) small, domestic equities, with the portfolio manager; 4) using fundamental analysis to construct the fund portfolio; 5) which may be purchased by the investor at no sales charge, and; 6) with the fund having a lower-than-average management expense ratio.

Active Management of Fund

MPT, described at length earlier in this chapter, is the prevailing theory used to explain market behavior today. Although this was not mentioned explicitly in our previous discussion on MPT, the theory is based on the belief that the overall market is at least reasonably efficient, if not perfectly efficient. Note that *efficient* in this context means the number of rational investors outnumbers those behaving irrationally—that is, trading based on their emotions and not on company and market fundamentals. Active management strategies, then, can be described as those wherein investors effectively bet *against* the efficiency of the overall market.

Generally, active managers use three strategies to add value to a mutual fund in excess of a preselected benchmark index:

- They may try to *time the market* by shifting funds into and out of stocks, corporate bonds, and US Treasury securities, depending on broad market forecasts.
- They may practice what is known as *sector rotation* by shifting the fund's asset holdings among different equity sectors and industries.
- They may practice *stock picking* by analyzing individual stocks in an attempt to find stocks that either are generating higher-than-average growth or are currently undervalued by the market. If they select higher-than-average growth stocks, active fund managers are said to be *growth investors*, whereas if they select currently undervalued stocks, they are said to be practicing a *value investing* strategy. Active managers who include both growth and value stocks in their fund are said to be constructing a *blended* fund.

Active managers can select securities based on the philosophy of either fundamental analysis or technical analysis, both of which will be discussed in further detail later in this chapter. As a primer, managers who proceed from the perspective of *fundamental analysis* rely on the financial statements provided by the company that is issuing the security when deriving what they believe to be the proper or intrinsic value of that security. Thus, fundamental analysts are primarily *inward-looking* and focus on individual securities. They make an investment decision to buy or not buy the stock by comparing this proper price to the price placed by the market on the stock.

Managers who proceed from a *technical analysis* perspective, on the other hand, study broad trends in the overall market, primarily focusing on the supply of and demand for the security in the past to determine its proper value today. Technical analysts are primarily *outward-looking* and reference the overall market in trying to predict the future price of a security.

One disadvantage of the active-management approach is that investors incur higher fund-management fees. The total fees charged by an actively managed fund average 1.4 percent (.014) of the total assets included in the fund, which is much higher than the average .20 percent (.002) charged by a passively managed index fund. Another disadvantage is that this higher fee, which is charged to compensate for the active-management strategies, may result in some active managers underperforming their preselected benchmark index. If the active-management fee is analyzed not in terms of the assets managed but as a percentage of the fund's incremental returns, the disadvantage becomes even more pronounced. For example, if index fund expenses are contrasted to those of an actively managed fund, and both funds earn a total annual return of 8 percent, the index fund has to outperform the benchmark index by only 2.5 percent (.002 divided by .08). The same fund, if actively managed, must beat the index by 17.5 percent (.014 divided by .08). This is not easy for some active fund managers to accomplish, particularly on a longer-term basis of ten or more years of market performance. According to S&P Indices Versus Active (SPIVA), 66.08 percent of all domestic mutual funds underperformed when matched against the benchmark of the S&P 1500, an index that includes more than 90 percent of all exchange-traded stocks. In 2011, their performance was even worse, with 84.07 percent of all domestic mutual funds underperforming the S&P 1500.

Growth Fund

A *growth fund* was described in Chapter 2 as a type of equity fund that primarily invests in small-capitalization stocks emphasizing growth of capital. Which type of investor will most benefit from a fund that is focused on the stock value's capital appreciation and not any dividends that might be paid from the stock? Generally, the answer to this question is any individual who wishes to accumulate wealth by taking advantage of capital gains (and not salaries or wages). This individual tends to be younger, with a considerable amount of time to let the compounding effect of annual returns work in their favor. Such an individual will also rely on their future earning power to generate needed income. The possibility of increased future earning power is not as significant for retired individuals or those individuals approaching retirement, thus necessitating a greater reliance on dividend-paying stocks or bonds as a more reliable source of income.

There is also a tax advantage for investors who use mutual funds to generate wealth in the form of capital gains: the investor may choose (up to a point) when to pay taxes on, or *recognize*, the value of these capital gains. They may choose *not* to sell the appreciated mutual fund shares in a given year, thus enabling them to avoid accruing taxable income for that year. (Note, however, that this advantage may be somewhat offset by the capital gains distributions paid by a mutual fund with *high turnover*, or frequent sales of securities held within the fund.) Finally, even when the investor does decide to sell the mutual fund shares, currently the maximum capital gains tax rate incurred is 20 percent, which is almost 20 percentage points lower than the maximum rate of 39.6 percent on salaried income.

Small Domestic Equities

Some mutual funds invest only in small domestic equities. In other words, they invest exclusively in small-capitalization equities or stocks, or those securities with **market capitalizations** below $2.0 billion in value. Further, these funds invest only in stocks issued by US-based companies whose base currency is the US dollar. Of course, the fact that some mutual funds invest only in domestic stocks prompts the alternative geographical approaches of international and emerging-market funds. An international fund tends to invest in diversified and well-developed international markets and companies, whereas an emerging market fund concentrates on markets and companies evidencing a significant future growth rate.

Investing in domestic market equities does not involve as much investment risk as is inherent in international and emerging-market equities. The types of risk associated with an international investment, for example, include currency risk, political risk, and potentially different accounting standards. *Currency risk* is the risk of processing transactions in and converting to a currency denomination other than the US dollar. In the individual stock context, a security known as an *American Depositary Receipt* (ADR), which translates all foreign stock company purchases automatically into the US dollar, helps minimize currency risk. But there is no corresponding ADR in the mutual-fund world. *Political risk*, meanwhile, refers to the possibility of the nationalization of a multinational company by the foreign country where it does business (witness the American petroleum companies conducting business in Venezuela) and the unanticipated restriction of cash flows to the multinational company by the foreign government. Finally, US companies prepare and file financial statements in accordance with Generally Accepted Accounting Principles (GAAP), which are promulgated by the Financial Accounting Standards Board (FASB). In contrast, companies incorporated outside the United States prepare statements based on internationally accepted accounting standards, which are not fully consistent with GAAP. Thus, financial statements vary based on the location of the company issuing the securities, which makes it difficult to analyze and compare the proper or intrinsic stock value between domestic and international companies.

Fundamental Analysis

As previously discussed, there are two methods by which a mutual-fund manager may make the decision to add a particular security to the fund portfolio: by practicing a fundamental analysis approach or a technical analysis approach. To recap, *fundamental analysis* involves making investment decisions based on an examination of the economy, an industry, or other company financial statement factors that lead to an estimate of the security's proper or intrinsic value, which is then compared to the investment's current market price. In a perfectly efficient market, these two values (the market value and the intrinsic value of the stock) should be the same. However, the overall market is not perfectly efficient, and, thus, credible fundamental analysis under past empirical studies has proven to be a worthwhile exercise. *Technical analysis*, on the other hand, involves the examination of past market data to predict future price trends, which then help to inform the investment decision. If an investor believes in any form of a widely understood efficient-market hypothesis, it is unlikely that they will find a technical analysis technique to be of value when attempting to outperform the overall market.

At its core, fundamental analysis is the quantitative search for a stock's proper price. This price is also referred to as the stock's *intrinsic value*, because the process of its determination takes advantage of a discounted cash-flow analysis using time-value-of-money concepts. The stock's intrinsic value may be correctly computed by discounting the future value of the cash flow from the stock, as represented by the growth rate of its dividend payments, back to a present value. Assuming this growth rate of dividends is constant—which is a realistic assumption, given that most companies prefer never to cut the dividend's growth rate or miss a dividend if at all possible—we can calculate it using the *constant dividend growth model*, which also is known as the *Gordon model* after its chief proponent. If we know the investor's required rate of return for purchasing the stock (for example, as previously determined using the CAPM), we may, in turn, find the stock's proper value (or mutual fund net asset value [NAV]) at any point in time.

The following is the constant growth formula and a subsequent example of its application:

$$r = (D_1/P_0) + g$$

For example, let's say we have previously determined that, using the CAPM, the investor has a required rate of return (r) of 14.25 percent to purchase ABC mutual fund. We have also determined that ABC mutual fund has stocks in its portfolio with a constant dividend growth rate (g) of 4 percent. Finally, the fund is expected to return a dividend of $2.00 per share to its shareholders next year (D_1). What is the fund's proper or intrinsic NAV? The answer is

\$19.51 per share (P_0), which is computed using the algebraic equivalent of the constant dividend growth model:

$$.1425 = (\$2.00/P_0) + .04$$

$$.1425 - .04 = (\$2.00/P_0)$$

$$.1025 = (\$2.00/P_0)$$

$$\$2.00/.1025 = P_0$$

$$\$19.51 = P_0$$

As a result, if \$19.51 is in excess of the actual NAV of ABC mutual fund, the investor should purchase shares of the fund. On the other hand, if the actual NAV of ABC mutual fund exceeds \$19.51, the investor should avoid the fund.

A fundamental analyst does not typically limit their analysis to the search for an intrinsic value. The analyst also searches for the *relative value* of the stock or mutual fund by using one or more of the following techniques:

- Price/earnings ratio (P/E)
- Price/cash flow ratio (P/C)
- Price/book value ratio (P/B)
- Price/sales ratio (P/S)

All these ratios derive a price for the stock or mutual fund shares by relating or comparing the price to another metric—usually another company in the same sector of the market.

The *price to earnings ratio (P/E)* is the most widely applied ratio and reflects how much investors are willing to pay for a dollar of reported profits or earnings by the company. For example, if Stock A sells for \$30.00 per share and reports earnings of \$2.50 per share in a given quarter, its P/E ratio is 12. This means an investor is willing to pay \$12.00 for a dollar of reported earnings by the company issuing Stock A.

The *price to cash flow ratio (P/C)* reflects how much investors are willing to pay for a dollar of reported cash flow by the company. P/C indicates a company's ability to generate cash and acts as a measure of the company's level of liquidity. In using the ratio, *cash flow* is defined as the company's net income plus any depreciation or amortization expenses claimed by the company for the quarter.

The *price to book value ratio (P/B)* reflects how much investors are willing to pay for a dollar of the company's *book value*, which is a record of the past that shows the cumulative amount that stockholders have invested in the company either directly (by purchasing newly issued shares) or indirectly (by the company retaining earnings). In company balance sheet terms, a company's book value is the stockholder's equity in the company or the historical cost of assets purchased minus company liabilities. Companies with relatively high rates of expected return on equity generally sell at higher multiples of book value than do companies with lower rates of expected return.

The *price to sales ratio (P/S)* reflects how much investors are willing to pay for a dollar of the company's quarterly or annual sales. This ratio has not been commonly used by fundamental analysts in the past, given the volatility of sales compared to other metrics. However, it is important to point out that the growth in a company's sales drives all its future earnings and cash flow. Sales growth also is not as easily manipulated by the company's accountants using the discretion given to them under the GAAP convention.

Mutual Fund Sales Charges

Some mutual funds impose sales charges at the time the investor purchases shares. This type of fund, known as a *load fund*, stands in contrast to a fund that does not impose a sales charge, known as a *no-load fund*. The *sales load*, consisting of one of three charges, is used to compensate investment advisors and brokers for their services and may be imposed separately or in addition to 12b-1 marketing fees.

There are three types of sales load classes—front-end load, back-end load, and level load—with each corresponding to a particular type of share purchased by the investor. A *front-end load*, corresponding to a Class A mutual fund share, is the traditional method of paying for securities-related assistance. The actual sales charge imposed may range from the low end of 1 percent to a high-end charge of 5.75 percent of the fund's offering price, not its net asset value. This computation results in a slightly *higher* charge than that quoted to the investor. For example, if the front-end sales charge on a mutual fund is $2.00 and the offering price of the fund is $100.00 per share, a 2 percent load has been imposed. But the investor has only $98.00 of their initial $100.00 purchase going to work for them, so the actual percentage charge is 2.04 percent, or $2.00 divided by $98.00. Meanwhile, if the mutual fund shares are purchased as part of an advisory fee, where a separate, asset-based percentage (*assets-under-management percentage*) is charged, the front-end load is typically waived by the investment company. Note, also, that front-end load fees often decline as the size of an investor's initial purchase increases.

Back-end load charges, corresponding to a Class B mutual fund share, are imposed at the time the investor redeems their shares. For this reason, Class B shares are often said to include a *contingent deferred sales charge* (CDSC). However, this sales charge often declines over the time that the investor owns the mutual fund shares. For example, the charge may start out at 6 percent for shares held for less than one year, then drop to 5 percent for shares held for less than two years, and decline by a percentage point per year until the redemption charge reaches zero and is phased out. An annual 12b-1 marketing fee is also charged on Class B shares. After six to eight years, back-end load shares usually convert to a share class with a lower 12b-1 fee. Generally speaking, investment companies (mutual funds) have not been transparent in the sales of shares that include a back-end load charge. As a result, a considerable consumer outcry has taken place, so much so that some mutual-fund companies have stopped offering Class B shares. Some securities firms have also prohibited their representatives from selling this class of shares to clients.

Level-load charges, corresponding to a Class C mutual fund share, generally are not accompanied by a front-end load. Instead, in the sale of a Class C share, advisors and brokers are compensated with a combination of an annual 12b-1 fee, typically 1 percent of the fund's assets per year, plus a CDSC, also typically 1 percent, but on the value of the shares redeemed with the fund within a specific period of time after purchase.

Note that 12b-1 fees frequently are used in conjunction with a CDSC (Class B or Class C mutual fund shares). This may also be the case with a fund that advertises itself as a no-load fund. Although such funds do not charge a front-end load, they may increase other fees, like their 12b-1 fees, to encourage their advisors or brokers to sell the fund to clients. This type of fund is really a disguised load fund and should be evaluated carefully, given that *all funds* (no-load and load funds) must also charge separately for the management expenses associated with the fund.

Finally, some funds have what is known as an *exit fee* or fee for early withdrawals. Such fee is designed to discourage frequent redemptions by investors seeking only short-term gains from the fund. Typically, there is a time limit on the imposition of this fee, with 90 days (three months) to six months standard. The exit fee can be as high as 2.00 percent of the amount of withdrawal in some funds.

Management Fees

According to the ICI, mutual-fund management fees for a domestic equity fund averaged .77 percent (commonly referred to as 77 *basis points*) in the year 2012. (A basis point is 1/100 of a percent.) This was a decline of almost 30 percent from only 22 years prior, when investors on average paid 99 basis points in management fees. Therefore, management fees are declining, primarily due to competition among funds. But remember that such fees are only one of three primary types of fees paid by mutual-fund investors; the other types are sales loads and, sometimes, 12b-1 fees.

A number of factors account for or drive the amount of management fees charged by a fund:

- Expense ratios often vary inversely with the amount of fund assets. Certain fund costs, such as directors' fees, remain fixed, no matter how many assets the fund manages. However, when fund assets increase, these fixed fund costs become smaller relative to the total cost of operating the fund.
- There has been a sharp increase in the demand for mutual funds over the years (thus forcing up expense ratios), but economies of scale achieved from the growth in fund assets have more than offset this trend.
- Funds' investment objectives result in varying expenses. Equity funds are more expensive to manage than bond or money market funds, and international equity funds are more expensive still. In addition, expense ratios tend to be higher for sector funds.
- Shareholder demand for lower-cost funds (and greater knowledge about no-load funds) tends to drive management expenses ratios down.

So, what is a reasonable management fee to pay for an actively managed mutual fund? There is no simple answer to this question. But unlike the remainder of the professional world, where the maxim "you get what you pay for" normally holds in practice, it is possible to pay a *lower* relative management fee for an excellent fund and fund manager. This possibility underscores the need to review the number of years the fund has been in existence and how many of those years the fund has been managed by the same manager or team of managers. In the previous example, we did not specify the number of years ABC mutual fund was in existence and managed by the same manager; but the general rule to follow is that the longer the fund has been in existence and the longer the manager's tenure with the fund, the more appropriate the fund may be to consider as a potential investment.

Mutual-Fund Investment Strategies

There are certain investment strategies that are particularly appropriate in mutual fund investing. We discuss four of the most popular strategies in this section of the chapter.

Buy and Hold

The most fundamental long-term mutual-fund investment strategy is that of purchasing shares at as low a market price as possible and then waiting for the price of the shares to increase. This is known simply as a *buy-and-hold strategy*. Historically, if the investor is disciplined enough to follow it resolutely through bull and bear markets, this strategy has generated significant gains. Passive portfolio management, including investing in index funds, is really an extension of the buy-and-hold investment strategy as pursued by the portfolio manager.

The buy-and-hold strategy has several advantages. First, investors minimize their transaction costs in the acquisition and trading of mutual fund shares. Over a long period of time, this can add up to substantial savings. Second, the strategy may assist in managing an investor's potential income tax liability. If appreciated mutual fund shares are owned for more than one year from their date of purchase, they are entitled to preferential long-term capital gain rates at sale. Moreover, no tax is incurred on the shares' appreciation until the shares are sold. Finally, a buy-and-hold strategy ensures that an investor is not out of the market during an upturn in share prices. Empirical studies have shown that the majority of an investor's price gains in mutual fund shares occur over only approximately ten market days per year. Of course, no one can accurately predict when these ten days will take place. Thus, a constant investment position in the market has proven important.

Strategic Asset Allocation

Strategic asset allocation is designed to maintain the long-term asset class weights in a portfolio. Typically, long-term historical average rates of return, along with risk measures, are used as estimates of the portfolio's future or expected performance. For example, a constant mix of 60 percent equities and 40 percent bonds may be used for an investor with moderate risk tolerance that is under the age of 55. This predetermined mix or allocation, consistent with the investor's long-term financial goals, is used as the standard for any adjustment to the portfolio (or *rebalancing*), as based on the actual performance of the composite securities.

For an example of a fund that is rebalanced to achieve a strategic asset allocation, look no further than a target-date mutual fund. In such fund, the portfolio manager varies the initial asset allocation based on the client's advancing age or changing risk tolerance (for example, safety of principal becomes more important as the client approaches retirement). Meanwhile, changing market conditions, which are a hallmark of the competing form of asset allocation known as *tactical* asset allocation, do *not* play a significant role in the rebalancing decision.

Dollar Cost Averaging (DCA)

Dollar cost averaging (DCA) is a type of **formula investing** wherein the investor purchases additional mutual fund shares at regular intervals and, usually, in equal dollar amounts, regardless of current market conditions. Even in a declining market, as long as the market eventually reverses course and turns upward, the investor will benefit. This is because more shares are acquired when the price of the mutual fund declines, which in turn reduces the average cost of an individual share. Subsequently, if the mutual fund share price increases, the investor will earn more profits on the lower-priced shares.

DCA is frequently used in the purchase of mutual fund shares via a retirement plan, such as a Section 401(k) plan. As mentioned, the strategy works best when markets are declining in price or are fluctuating up or down. The strategy does not work well, however, when the market is steadily increasing in price, because in that event, the investor would be better off buying as many shares as possible initially, when the fund's price per share is much lower. The investor should be careful not to assume that the market will eventually increase in value. "Eventually" can be a very long time indeed—sometimes even longer than the current life span of an elderly investor.

Short Selling

Short selling or *selling short* is an investment strategy used by many hedge-fund managers and will be discussed in Chapter 9. An investor who owns (purchases) a security or mutual fund is said to be *long* as it relates to that security. Alternatively, an investor who does not own the security but borrows it from a third party (usually, a securities firm) is said to be *short* as it relates to that security. The investor who *shorts* a stock is hoping that the stock price declines and they can subsequently buy it back (or *cover the sale*) from the securities firm at a lower price.

For example, say an investor sells short a stock with a current market price of $25.00 per share. The investor does this by borrowing the stock from a securities firm and another investor's account. Assuming that the stock price decreases to $20.00 per share, the investor then covers the sale by buying the stock at the lower per share price, thus generating a profit of $5.00 per share.

The Determination of Which Mutual Fund Shares are Redeemed

At the end of the calendar year, a mutual fund will report the sale of shares by remitting a Form 1099-B to the investor. However, this form does not indicate *which* mutual fund shares were redeemed! Naturally, the investor wants those appreciated shares in which they have the highest cost basis to be considered as sold, thus limiting the amount of capital gains that is taxed. Distributions are taxed even though they may be reinvested and added to a investor's cost basis, but the investor needs to prove the actual cost basis. This underscores the need for the investor to retain all mutual fund monthly or quarterly statements. Failure to do so increases the probability that the investor will not be able to prove the cost basis and, thus, carry out a potentially favorable tax consequence on sale of the shares.

In the absence of adequate records, the general rule is that the first mutual fund shares purchased (and reinvested distributions) are considered to be the first shares sold. Of course, in an appreciating market over time, this rule can operate to the investor's considerable detriment by resulting in additional capital gains taxes paid. An alternative technique lets the investor determine the average cost of all the shares sold and use that for the cost basis. However, this averaging process precludes the investor's ability to select which shares have been sold. The preferable way of proceeding is for the investor to retain all mutual fund statements (maintain adequate records) and to write to the mutual fund sponsor or broker and instructing them that only the shares with the highest cost basis on the date of sale are to be sold. Typically, the mutual fund sponsor or broker will then confirm this direction in writing, which documentation can then be shown to the IRS in the event of an audit of the investor's tax return for the year of sale.

This chapter has discussed the very important process of diversifying a portfolio and the basic theory proving the beneficial effects of the diversification process. It also looked at investment strategies to use in long-term mutual-fund investing. We now proceed to two essential exercises in mutual fund investing: deciding whether to invest in a particular mutual fund, and determining how the mutual fund (in which you have invested) has performed over time.

CHAPTER

5

Mutual Fund Performance Measures and Selection Criteria

There are two main ways to evaluate the performance of an open-end investment company or mutual fund. The first is to read the *prospectus* that every fund is required to issue. The performance history of the fund, along with the fund's investment objective and expenses, are included in the first several pages of the prospectus. The second is to use a *professional reference service*.

Several services track mutual fund performance (and provide other important data), but the most frequently used is Chicago-based Morningstar, Inc. Morningstar's web site (`www.morningstar.com`) hosts a wealth of data, some of which is available only by enrolling in the company's premium subscriber service. Other important information that is typically used by an investor or investment advisor is available on the web site without charge. This information includes the following subcategories:

- The category, investment style, and portfolio of the fund
- Performance measures
- Ratings and risk measures
- Management of the fund
- Expenses and fee level of the fund
- Tax efficiency of the fund

These subcategories are used as headings in this chapter (and whenever relevant in subsequent chapters) to assist you in the proper selection of mutual funds for your portfolio. Sample fund profile pages (known in Morningstar terminology as *quotes*) for both an equity (stock) fund and a bond fund appended to this chapter are likewise organized into these six subcategories.

For each mutual fund with at least a three-year history, Morningstar awards a rating based on a proprietary risk-adjusted return measure that accounts for variation in a fund's adjusted monthly performance and places more emphasis on the declines in the fund's net asset value. The top 10% of funds in each category are awarded a 5 star rating, the next 22.5% receive 4 stars, the next 35% receive 3 stars, the next 22.5% receive 2 stars, and the bottom 10% of category funds receive 1 star. A Morningstar analyst rating is also awarded based on five key pillars:

- Process
- Performance
- People
- Parent
- Price

The analyst rating scale ranges from *Gold* to *Negative*, with Gold corresponding to the highest rating and Negative the lowest. A fund with a Gold rating excels across all five pillars, whereas a fund with a Negative rating is flawed in at least one analyst pillar.

Category, Investment Style, and Portfolio of Sample Funds

The sample stock fund used is the **Fairholme Fund**, which has a market identification or *ticker symbol* of FAIRX. The sample bond fund analyzed is **Harbor Bond Institutional**, or HABDX. The quote pages for both of the sample funds are reproduced at the end of this chapter as Figures 5-1 and 5-2, respectively, and are implicitly referenced throughout the chapter. Owing to the contrasting nature of these two sample funds (stock fund versus bond fund), some of the data provided by Morningstar is different for each subcategory of information. Accordingly, I do a separate breakdown of each broad type of fund. Also note that only the Morningstar quote pages are reproduced and that some comments made in this chapter may include analysis of fund information that is not reproduced at the back of the chapter.

These funds are used for informational purposes only, and their use in this book should not be viewed as either an endorsement or rejection of the funds as possible components of your investment portfolio.

Fairholme Fund

Morningstar categorizes the Fairholme Fund (henceforward *Fairholme*) as a U.S. open-end (OE), large value fund. Accordingly, the investment style of the fund is *large value*. As discussed in Chapter 4, mutual funds typically employ one of two fundamental investment styles: *value* or *growth*. Morningstar uses a third investment style classification of *blend* to describe a fund that pursues both value and growth strategies. The company also includes among its stock funds the separate classification of *foreign large blend*, which reflects a mutual fund consisting only of international stocks where the manager pursues both value and growth strategies.

When these broad investment styles are employed to purchase a certain market capitalization of stocks—for example, large-, mid-, or small-capitalization stocks—Morningstar compartmentalizes the style and size of stock fund into a *style box*. Fairholme fits in the style box of *Large Cap Value*. Entire books have been written on value investing, but the underlying principles of the strategy were laid out by Benjamin Graham in his 1934 treatise, *Security Analysis*. Those principles were then put into practice by many successful investors—most notably, by mega-investor Warren Buffett in the management and operation of his fund, Berkshire Hathaway.

At its core, value investing is the search for underpriced quality stocks that sell in the market at a substantial discount from their intrinsic value. Further, a value investing strategy implements the adoption of a buy-and-hold mentality, as encapsulated in the belief that "good things happen to cheap stocks." Finally, because value investors believe that the value of a stock is more important than (or at least as important as) the earnings generated by the stock, they are focused on the *numerator* of the P/E ratio, or price. This is in notable contrast to *growth* investors, who place more emphasis on the *denominator* of the P/E ratio, or earnings.

The current portfolio of assets held by Fairholme reflects the adoption of value investing principles. For example, an approximately 75% concentration of stocks in the financial services sector illustrates Fairholme's belief in a relatively cheap and recently beaten-down market sector—that of banks, securities firms, and insurance companies. In addition, consumer cyclical stocks, which represent some 12% of the fund's assets, also have declined in price in recent years and fallen out of favor due to the Great Recession of 2007–2009. The same comment also holds with respect to real estate, which makes up approximately 9% of the portfolio and ranks as the third largest sector of the fund. Overall, Fairholme's value investing principles are most notably exemplified by the fact that the stock fund portfolio features a P/E ratio of only 3.75, compared to a benchmark P/E ratio of 13.23 and a category average of 12.73. This margin of safety leaves plenty of room for the fund's net asset value to grow before achieving a price indicative of an average fund in the category of U.S. large value funds.

Harbor Bond Institutional

The Harbor Bond Institutional Fund (henceforward *Harbor*) is an intermediate-term taxable bond fund that invests in debt securities issued by the U.S. Treasury Department, governmental agencies, and corporations. Morningstar classifies bonds that are intermediate- or medium-term as those debt securities having a maturity of 3.5 to 6 years, although some financial publications will extend the intermediate term classification to a bond with a maturity date of 10 years. This categorization is evident from a review of the fund's bond holdings, which have an average effective maturity of 7 years. Morningstar also has established short-term and long-term bond categories, which have a maturity of 0 to 3.5 years and more than 6 years, respectively. All the bond terms are lengthened by one year each in the Morningstar classifications that are assigned to municipal or tax-exempt bond funds.

Harbor is a bond fund that consists of individual bonds. Thus, it offers the advantages of diversification and professional management—hallmarks of any mutual fund. But a bond fund offers several distinct disadvantages as compared to individual bonds. First, bond mutual funds do not generally hold bonds until the maturity date of the bonds—meaning that investors cannot eliminate any interest-rate risk associated with the bonds. In contrast, if an investor purchased an individual bond and held it until its maturity date, interest-rate risk would be eliminated. Second—and probably of more importance to an income investor—as a bond fund changes (trades) its bond portfolio, the fund's interest payments change. This results in an unpredictable income stream to the fund investor. In contrast, when an investor purchases an individual bond with a fixed coupon payment, the investor knows exactly how much interest payment he or she will receive on a monthly or quarterly basis and when he or she is going to receive it. Thus, the income stream generated by the individual bond is known with much more certainty. There are also income tax disadvantages associated with a bond fund such as Harbor, which are discussed in the "Fund Tax Efficiency" section of this chapter.

No investment style classification is assigned to Harbor. This is consistent with the fact that the fund's assets are concentrated in bonds and not in stocks, to which Morningstar's value, growth, and blended investment styles pertain. However, in place of the investment style classification, Morningstar includes a category entitled Credit Quality/Interest Rate Sensitivity for all bond funds. *Credit quality* is self-reported to Morningstar by each bond fund and combined with an average default-rate calculation of all corporate bond funds to derive a weighted-average credit quality for the fund. Standard & Poor's rating letters are used as a standard, with the familiar BBB- and above used to identify investment-grade bonds; BB+ and lower are used to describe high-yield or non-investment-grade bonds. Specifically, funds with a *low* credit quality are those whose weighted-average credit quality is determined to be less than BBB-; funds earning a *medium* or *mid* quality rating are those with bonds rated as less than AA- but greater than or equal to BBB-; and funds rated as *high* are those with bonds with an average credit quality of AA- or higher. Here, Harbor is rated with a mid quality rating, meaning the weighted-average credit quality of bonds included in its portfolio is between AA- and BBB-.

The following list provides the general bond credit ratings of Standard & Poor's and their explanation.

AAA Extremely strong capacity (of issuer) to meet financial commitments.

AA Very strong capacity to meet financial commitments.

A Strong capacity to meet financial commitments, but somewhat susceptible to adverse economic conditions and changes in circumstances.

BBB Adequate capacity to meet financial commitments, but more subject to adverse economic conditions.

BBB- Considered lowest investment grade by market participants.

BB+ Considered highest speculative grade by market participants.

BB Less vulnerable in the near term, but faces major ongoing uncertainties to adverse business, financial, and economic conditions.

B More vulnerable to adverse business, financial, and economic conditions, but currently has the capacity to meet financial commitments.

CCC Currently vulnerable and dependent on favorable business, financial, and economic conditions to meet financial commitments.

CC Currently highly vulnerable.

C Currently highly vulnerable obligations and other defined circumstances.

D Payment default on financial commitments.

Bond prices move inversely with changes in market interest rates: if interest rates increase, the price of a bond decreases. This occurs because the bond is now yielding a lower interest rate (as reflected in the bond's **coupon rate**) than is currently available in the market. Investors are unwilling to purchase the lower-yielding bond, so its price declines. Conversely, bond prices increase if interest rates decline. The interest-rate sensitivity of a bond is measured by a concept known as *bond duration*, which is the weighted-average number of years until the present value of the bond's interest and principal payments is recovered; it reflects the approximate percentage change in the price of a bond for a 1% change in the bond's yield. Like the relationship of bond price to interest rates, a bond's duration has an inverse relationship to its yield. Therefore, *bonds with a lower yield have a greater duration and are more price-sensitive to a change in market interest rates.*

For example, a bond with a duration of 8 (for 8 years) will be twice as sensitive to interest-rate changes as a bond with a duration of 4. If interest rates increase by one percentage point, the price of the bond with a duration of 8 may be expected to decline in price by approximately 8% (versus only half that amount—or 4%—for the bond with a duration of 4).

A bond fund's interest-rate sensitivity is measured by the weighted average of the individual durations of the bonds in the portfolio. As is the case with credit quality, a bond fund self-reports the average effective duration of its holdings to Morningstar. The reference service then classifies the particular bond fund based on the effective duration of the Morningstar Core Bond Index (MCBI), which is currently (as of 2013) three years. Funds whose average effective duration is between 25% and 75% of MCBI's average effective duration are classified as Limited; funds whose average effective duration is between 75% and 125% of the MCBI are classified as Moderate; and funds whose average effective duration is 125% or greater of the MCBI are classified as Extensive. Here, Harbor is classified with a Moderate interest-rate sensitivity rating, which is consistent with its average effective duration of 5.95 years, as shown in Figure 5-2. This also means that if market interest rates increase by one percentage point, the net asset value of Harbor can be expected to decline by approximately 5.95 %.

Performance Measures

Morningstar's performance numbers are of course subject to almost daily change, but its performance measures are not. For both stock and bond funds, Morningstar provides five years of past performance data, in addition to year-to-date performance data for the current year. This data reports the growth in before-tax ***annualized return*** of a sample $10,000 portfolio. A portfolio's annualized return is also known as its *compounded annual growth rate* and may be computed on either a geometric or an arithmetic average. Because it takes compounding into account, the geometric average will be slightly less than the arithmetic average. For example, a return of 40% over four years would result in an annualized arithmetic return of 10% and an annualized geometric return of only 8.78%. This is because the geometric return takes into consideration the effect of interest compounding.

To calculate the annualized return, the investor needs to know the initial value of the investment, its final value, and the number of years (or months) the investment was owned before it was sold. An ***effective annual rate*** (EAR) computation then needs to be performed. Consider the following example:

> An investor buys 100 shares of Mutual Fund A at $18 per share. Three months later, the investor sells the shares for $19 per share and had not received the payment of a dividend during this time period. To compute the investor's annualized return, first observe that there are 4 holding periods in this example (12 divided by 3). The holding period percentage return of the investor is 5.56% [($19-$18)/$18]. The effective annual rate is $(1+.0556)^4 = 1.2416$. Subtract 1 and multiply by 100 to derive the annualized return percentage. The investor's annualized return is therefore 24.16%.

Fairholme Fund

Morningstar also provides the relevant benchmark and category performance data against which a given stock or bond fund is compared, and then reports the difference (plus or minus differential) of the fund against both the benchmark and category averages. For example, Fairholme is compared against the most notable of the total return (TR) indices, the Standard & Poor's (S&P) 500 index of large-cap stocks, and the large value (LV) category of funds. (Note that total return assumes reinvestment of all dividends and capital gains paid by the 500 stocks on the S&P index back into the fund and not distribution to the individual investor.) Finally, Morningstar assigns the fund a percentage rank, from a top 1% to a bottom 100%, to differentiate it from other funds in its category. Some investment advisors rely on the annual percentage rank more than others do, but the important takeaways for investors are the fund's percentage ranking over time and the direction in which that ranking is trending. Most investment advisors will tell a client that any fund can have either one good year or one bad year, in terms of performance (and category ranking), but an excellent portfolio manager generates a consistently superior ranking of the fund over a longer period of time, such as five to ten years.

Information on the Morningstar performance page(s) then reflects the trailing total return of the fund on a daily, monthly, and quarterly basis. As Morningstar explains in its mutual fund detail report and disclosure statement (which are only available to premium subscribers), a fund's "total return" and "quarterly return" reflect its performance without adjusting for any sales charges imposed at the time of purchase or for the effects of income taxation. (Morningstar's percentage rank within the Morningstar category also does not account for a fund's sales charge, if any.) But the metric *is* adjusted to reflect all ongoing fund expenses, such as maintenance or 12b-1 fees, if applicable. The trailing total returns are provided for most funds for the greater of 15 years or the fund's lifespan, again along with a comparison of the total return annualized percentage against the benchmark and category averages.

Two important performance measures are also included on the Quote page of any fund: the *trailing twelve months* (TTM) yield and the SEC yield (the yield metric required for all funds by the Securities and Exchange Commission). The TTM yield is the percentage income the fund returned over the previous 12 months and is computed by taking the weighted average of the yields of the securities that make up the fund. For a stock fund, then, the TTM yield is the average of the ***dividend* yield** on the stocks within the fund; for a bond fund, it is the average of the ***interest* yield** returned by the bonds within the fund. The SEC yield, also known as the *standardized yield*, is based on the most recent 30-day period covered by the fund's required filings with the SEC. The yield figure reflects the dividends and interest earned during this period, after the deduction of fund expenses. Because it captures the effective rate of interest that an investor can expect to receive in the future, the SEC yield is much more relevant as a comparison metric for bond funds.

An investor purchasing a growth stock or equity mutual fund should expect to see a very low TTM or SEC yield due to the fund's emphasis on capital appreciation (capital gains) rather than income (dividends). A growth-and-income fund, however, reflects a higher yield; and an income fund shows an even greater yield. In contrast, the TTM and SEC yield metrics are much more important for bond funds, particularly for so-called *high-yield* or *junk bond* funds (see the next section).

Harbor Bond Institutional

As of September 13, 2013, Harbor was showing a TTM yield of 2.38% and an SEC yield of 1.41%. Keep in mind, though, that there are several types of yield on a bond or bond fund, the most important of which is the bond's ***yield to***

maturity (YTM), or the rate required by the market. The YTM is also what is meant by the term *yield* in the Morningstar quote. As noted in the opening section on Harbor Bond Institutional, there is an inverse relationship between the price of bonds or a bond fund and the direction of interest rates. This is also the case with bond prices and bond yields: if bond prices *increase*, the yield *decreases*. Bond prices may increase as a function of the economic factors of supply and demand. As a result, if there is more demand for bonds, the yield on the bonds or bond fund declines. For example, since the Great Recession of 2007-2009, the increased demand for U.S. Treasury debt securities, such as Treasury bonds, has resulted in historically low yields. Bond prices are also a function of risk: the greater the default risk of a bond, the *lower* the price, and the greater the *yield*. Corporate bonds, which partially constitute the portfolio of Harbor, carry a default risk that U.S. Treasury securities do not; thus, corporate bonds or bond funds have a higher yield than that of a U.S. government bond fund.

The degree of default risk inherent in a corporate bond or bond fund is measured by a bond rating service. As discussed in the opening section on Harbor Bond Institutional, bond rating services, such as S&P, rate bonds either as investment grade or non–investment grade. A non–investment grade bond or bond fund is also referred to as a *high-yield* fund—which is logical, because the yield is much higher, given the perceived risk of the fund. High-yield bonds are unmistakably bonds, but they behave much more like stocks or stock funds. Indeed, since 1999, empirical studies have shown that high-yield bonds have been *positively correlated* with stocks. As of the year 2013, this correlation is approximately 0.70, meaning that 70% of the movement of high-yield bonds mirrors that of stocks. Moreover, typically, the *lower* the rating of a bond, the *greater is* its correlation to the S&P 500 index of large-cap stocks. Investors should consider this fact as they continue to invest in high-yield bond funds, not only to achieve a higher income yield, but also because of the perceived safety of a bond as compared to a stock.

Harbor's portfolio of assets is over-weighted in U.S. Treasury and agency securities, including mortgage-backed securities and collateralized mortgage obligations. Thus, unlike a high-yield or speculative fund, Harbor is investing primarily in safer government securities and secured obligations. The annual performance of Harbor is compared against both the benchmark of Barclay's U.S. Aggregate Bond Index and the *comprehensive intermediate-term* (CI) bond category. The difference in Harbor's performance vis-à-vis the index and category for both the past five years and the most recent year is then provided by Morningstar's quote, as is the applicable category rank. A potential investor should note that the annualized return of a bond fund consists of not only the fund's YTM but also its capital gain yield, which is generated by the sales of bonds that are selling at a premium (or above the par value of the bond). Typically, the YTM constitutes a greater portion of the bond fund's annualized total return than does the capital gains yield. This is in contrast to a stock or equity fund, where the capital appreciation (or gains in stock value) constitutes a greater portion of the fund's total return than does the dividend yield of the stocks in the portfolio.

Ratings and Risk Measures

In the ratings and risk section of its report, Morningstar provides *modern portfolio theory* (MPT) statistics. As discussed in Chapter 4, MPT is an approach to portfolio construction that uses expected returns and *total risk* as measured by a portfolio's standard deviation. MPT subsequently led to the development of capital market theory and the famous ***capital asset pricing model*** (CAPM), the latter of which extended the concept of an *optimal portfolio* to the market in general and to the valuation of individual securities by specifying the relationship between expected returns and a portfolio or asset's ***systematic risk***. With the advent of CAPM, a new measure of risk was needed to measure the amount of systematic risk inherent in a portfolio or asset. This new measure of risk, known as *beta* or the *beta coefficient* between the market and the portfolio or asset, is an index of the volatility of the individual asset relative to the volatility of the market and assumes that the investor has constructed a well-diversified portfolio. The *more variable* the asset's return is relative to the variability of the market—both as measured by the standard deviation of returns—the *greater the risk* is that is associated with the individual asset.

In the context of a portfolio, yet another measure of systematic risk was needed in MPT analysis to account for, among other factors, the investment skill or expertise of the portfolio manager. This risk, known as *alpha*, is derived by subtracting the expected return of the portfolio using the CAPM formula from the actual, realized return of the portfolio. In practice, an investor should view beta as the market asset allocation of a portfolio and alpha as the residual component of the portfolio's expected returns that cannot be attributed to the market asset allocation (beta). For example, if the investor's portfolio returns 10% annually and the beta-relevant portion of the portfolio returns 14%, the alpha, or the residual return not explained by beta, would be -4% (or 10% less 14%).

As you may anticipate from the preceding explanation, an investor purchasing an actively managed mutual fund (the classical well-diversified portfolio) should seek a fund that is exhibiting a *positive alpha*. This means the portfolio manager has outperformed both the expected return of the fund (as predicted by CAPM) and the beta-relevant portion of the portfolio. In other words, the manager is "earning their money" that is charged back to the investor in the form of management expenses. Meanwhile, an investment advisor who is assisting investors at the retail level should be earning their fee by selecting only funds that have exhibited a positive alpha over a longer period of time or over several market cycles (bull and bear markets). As will be discussed in Chapter 9, providing a *diversified positive alpha* is a major selling point for a hedge fund manager.

Fairholme Fund

The MPT statistics for Fairholme reveal that the alpha for both the fund and the manager have been *negative* over a three-year period but *positive* over a ten-year period. Thus, we should anticipate one or more years of poor performance in the three-year period—and this is indeed the case, given that the performance of the fund in 2011 was a negative -32.42%, which also resulted in a category percentile performance of the lowest 100%. Only a few funds in the large-capitalization value fund category performed as poorly as or worse than Fairholme did in 2011. But we should also anticipate very good fund performances over a ten-year period—and very positive performance is indeed reported for that time frame.

Morningstar also provides a third alternative measure of portfolio (mutual fund) performance known as the *Treynor ratio* (also known as the *Treynor index number*), originally formulated by Jack L. Treynor. The formula for the Treynor ratio is

$$T_i = \frac{r_i - r_f}{\beta_i}$$

where

$T_i \equiv$ Treynor ratio of portfolio *i*

$r_i \equiv$ Actual return on portfolio *i*

$r_f \equiv$ Risk-free rate

$\beta_i \equiv$ Beta coefficient of portfolio *i*

Example: The Treynor ratio of a fund portfolio with an annual return of 15%, a risk-free rate of 5%, and a beta of 1.1 is

$$\frac{(.15 - .05)}{1.1} = 0.0909$$

To determine if the fund portfolio manager has underperformed or outperformed the overall market, a Treynor ratio must be computed for the market. The numerical value of the beta coefficient for the market is by definition 1.0. If during the time period under review the market return was 14%, the Treynor ratio for the market is

$$\frac{(.14 - .05)}{1.0} = 0.0900$$

In this example, then, the fund portfolio manager outperformed the market on a risk-adjusted basis.

The Treynor index may also be used to compare the performance of one mutual fund portfolio manager to another, with the higher index number indicating superior performance. For example, over a ten-year period, Fairholme's Treynor ratio indexed to the S&P 500 market ratio was higher than to those of its peers in the large-capitalization value fund category. This means the fund has outperformed its category peers when compared to the market on a risk-adjusted basis.

Morningstar also uses an MPT statistic of ***R-squared*** in its ratings and risk section. R-squared reflects the percentage of a mutual fund's movement that is explained by a benchmark market index. Moreover, the statistic assists in determining the statistical validity of alpha and beta. As such, the *higher* the R-squared coefficient, the *greater* is the validity or reliability of alpha and beta in assessing both manager performance and the systematic risk of the fund.

Morningstar employs two indexes when presenting the alpha, beta, and R-squared statistics: a standard market index and *best-fit index*. The latter is determined by calculating the R-squared statistic for the fund against the approximately 100 indexes that Morningstar tracks. The index representing the highest R-squared is then used as the best-fit index. For the Fairholme Fund, Morningstar uses the Morningstar SEC/Financial Services index as the best-fit index—which is understandable, given the preponderance of financial services stocks in the fund's portfolio. Notice, too, that the standard index that Morningstar uses for comparison purposes is the S&P 500—which is also understandable, given that Fairholme is categorized as a large-capitalization value fund.

The term *volatility* is a broader risk measure and compares the fund against all risky assets, including those assets that would not be part of a well-diversified portfolio as assumed by the MPT statistics. Morningstar presents *volatility measures* for all funds in its ratings and risk section. They include the following measures for each fund as compared to the standard index and its fund category and are discussed in turn next:

- *Standard deviation*
- *Mean or average return*
- *Sharpe ratio*
- *Sortino ratio*
- *Bear market percentile rank*

Standard deviation is a statistical measure of the volatility or dispersion from the mean return of the fund. It may be thought of as a weighted average of the deviations from the expected return of the fund and provides a measure of how far above or below the expected return the actual, realized return is likely to be. The *larger* the dispersion of deviations from the expected return, the *greater* is the amount of total risk of a given fund. Conversely, the *smaller* the standard deviation, the *less* is the total risk of the investment. The average standard deviation of the market, as represented by the S&P 500 stocks for a ten-year period, is approximately 15%, with the large value category slightly higher than 15%. Fairholme's ten-year standard deviation of approximately 20% means that the fund has assumed more total risk than the market as a whole. This may be good or bad, depending on the risk tolerance of the individual investor. If the investor tends toward a more aggressive stance with respect to risk, he or she should like the fund, because it will likely generate a greater return than its category peers. However, if the investor is more conservative, Fairholme may exhibit too much risk for him or her to actually purchase shares in the fund. Nonetheless, Fairholme's standard deviation of 20% is only half that of the average stock, with a standard deviation of 40%—owing to the risk-mitigating effect of diversification in mutual funds.

The *mean or average return* of the fund represents the annualized geometric return for the period of time shown in the ratings and risk section of the Morningstar report. The geometric average return gives the investor's average compound return per year over a particular period and, as shown in the "Performance Measures" section of this chapter, yields a slightly lower percentage than the arithmetic return. Because the geometric average return takes compounding into account, it is more likely than the arithmetic average to generate the true return of a fund, but it is still only an estimate of the actual return. As a practical matter, if an investor wants to forecast an average return over a period of longer than ten years, then the *arithmetic* average, which gives the return in an average year over a particular period, is probably better. The choice between geometric or arithmetic average return varies among reference services; Morningstar prefers the geometric mean in its reporting.

The *Sharpe ratio*, named after William Sharpe of CAPM fame, is a risk-adjusted measure of performance that standardizes the return to determine the reward per unit of risk. It does this by stating the return in excess of the risk-free rate divided by the standard deviation of the portfolio's return.

The Sharpe ratio formula is

$$S_i = \frac{r_i - r_f}{\sigma_i}$$

where

$S_i \equiv$ Sharpe ratio of portfolio *i*

$r_i \equiv$ Actual return on portfolio *i*

$r_f \equiv$ Risk-free rate

$\sigma_i \equiv$ Standard deviation of portfolio *i*

Example: The Sharpe ratio of a fund portfolio with an annual return of 15%, a risk-free rate of 5%, and a standard deviation of 30% is

$$\frac{(.15-.05)}{.30}=0.3333$$

The *higher* the Sharpe index number, the *better* is the performance of the fund and its manager in terms of percentage units of return (reward) per unit of total risk (standard deviation). The Sharpe metric does not, however, tell the investor whether the fund manager is outperforming the broader market. For this purpose, Morningstar provides the Sharpe ratios for the standard market index and the category of the fund. Over the previous ten-year period, Fairholme's Sharpe index number is higher than those of the standard index (the S&P 500) and the large-capitalization value fund category. Yet over the previous three-year period, it is lower than both. These relative Sharpe ratios predict a poorer risk-adjusted performance for Fairholme over the previous three-year period and a more favorable risk-adjusted performance over the previous ten-year period. The relative performance results bear out the expectation.

The *Sortino ratio*, developed by Brian M. Rom and popularized by Frank A. Sortino, differentiates the downside volatility of a fund from the overall volatility of the fund as measured in the Sharpe ratio. It is computed by dividing the excess return of the fund over the risk free rate by the ***semivariance*** of the fund. The semivariance of any fund or individual asset is the standard deviation of the negative asset returns.

Why is the Sortino ratio important to a potential investor? The answer is based on a premise of behavioral finance known as *prospect theory*: individual investors fear potential losses from an investment about twice as much as they value a potential gain. By contrasting how often the fund returns are positive with how often they are negative, the Sortino ratio assists investors in meaningfully assessing total risk, rather than simply measuring excess returns to overall volatility, as the Sharpe ratio does.

The formula for the Sortino ratio is

$$SR_i=\frac{r_i-r_f}{\sigma_d}$$

where

$SR_i \equiv$ Sortino ratio of portfolio *i*

$r_i \equiv$ Actual return on portfolio *i*

$r_f \equiv$ Risk-free rate

$\sigma_d \equiv$ Semivariance of portfolio *i*

Like the Sharpe ratio, the *higher* the Sortino ratio, the *better* is the performance of the fund and its manager. A high Sortino ratio indicates that there is a relatively low risk of significantly large losses occurring from the fund. In most cases, the relative direction of the Sharpe and Sortino ratios (up or down) are the same. In examining the relative direction of the respective ratios for Fairholme, this rule holds.

The *bear market percentile rank* is the percentile rank of the fund in a steadily declining market. A *bear market* is conventionally defined as a decline of at least 20% in the value of a broad market index, such as the S&P 500, over a two-month period. (The Morningstar report on Fairholme does not include this volatility measure.)

The third and final section of Morningstar's ratings and risk section for any fund, including Fairholme, is the "Upside and Downside Capture Ratio." This ratio shows the investor whether a given fund has outperformed a broad market index during periods of market strength and market weakness and, if so, by how much. *Upside capture ratios* are determined by dividing the fund's monthly return during the months in which the index had a positive return by the index return during that same month(s). *Downside capture ratios* are computed similarly, except it uses months where the fund and index exhibited negative performance. An upside ratio greater than 100 indicates that a fund has generally outperformed the index in a market of strength (a *bull market*), and a downside ratio of less than 100 indicates that a fund has lost less than the index over the same time period. All stock fund ratios are calculated against the S&P 500.

An investor might intuit that it is prudent to purchase only funds with low downside capture ratios. But some funds achieve low downside capture ratios simply by keeping a greater amount of fund investments in cash or cash-equivalents. When markets rebound, those cash holdings will cause a drag on returns, and the investor will miss out on the significant upside returns of a bull market. A thoughtful investor will accordingly ascertain the robustness of a low downside capture ratio.

Harbor Bond Institutional

Morningstar employs the same MPT statistics metrics and volatility measures in analyzing the performance of Harbor as it does for Fairholme. But because Harbor is a bond fund, Morningstar uses different benchmark indexes for it: the Barclays U.S. Credit index as its best-fit index and the Barclays U.S. Aggregate Bond Index as the standard index. The Barclays U.S. Aggregate Bond Index is also used as the benchmark index in computing the upside/downside capture ratios of all bond funds, including Harbor. Similarly, the category that Morningstar uses for comparison against Harbor— *comprehensive intermediate* (CI)—is the relevant one for bond-only analysis.

As was the case with Fairholme, the performance metrics applied to Harbor are not as favorable against the indexes and category over a previous three-year time period as they were over the previous ten years. Unlike Fairholme, however, Harbor does not exhibit any negative ratios or metrics in the three-year period, indicating better portfolio and management performance for Harbor overall and a long-term bull market in bonds over that period.

Fund Management

Both the Fairholme Fund and Harbor Bond Institutional are actively managed funds. As such, the performance objective of each is to achieve an annualized return in excess of a benchmark index. The implementation of this objective is the responsibility of fund management. Indeed, achieving an excess return is how the fund managers earn their pay.

Fairholme Fund

Fairholme, like most actively managed mutual funds, is managed by a fund advisor—in this case, Fairholme Capital Management LLC. A fund's advisor is primarily responsible for the investment performance of the fund, and the management fee it charges the fund (open-end investment company) constitutes the largest percentage of the management expenses passed on to the investor by the fund. Operationally, the fund advisor company assigns one or more advisors to make the daily investment decisions in accordance with the stated investment objectives of the fund prospectus. Thus, for a potential fund investor, judging the quality and length of experience of the advisors assigned to the fund is a very important practical consideration.

Fairholme Capital Management LLC has historically assigned a team of advisors to manage Fairholme, although after its reopening to new investors in August 2013 only one advisor, Bruce Berkowitz, was managing the fund. A team approach is in contrast to some funds that assign only one advisor—usually referred to as a *star manager*—to manage the fund. Which is the better approach? Unfortunately, there is no definitive answer to this question. Under SEC regulations, team-managed funds are required to list each portfolio manager or advisor assigned to the fund, as well as the team leader. Additionally, funds are required to disclose a manager's personal percentage ownership of fund assets in the fund prospectus, as well as any other funds the manager may manage. The major advantage of the team concept is continuity or the fact that, if one or more managers leaves the fund for any reason, another experienced manager is "on the bench" to assume the management responsibilities. Another advantage is the fact that more than one opinion is rendered with respect to a potential fund investment.

This last advantage of the team-managed approach can, however, shade into the offsetting disadvantage of *group think*. Group think occurs when individuals begin to let the group consensus shape their own individual conclusions. This tendency can be especially dangerous in the investment world, where behavioral finance studies have proven the existence of a *herd effect* in market behavior. This effect is evidenced daily in the stock market as investors "chase performance" and purchase a stock primarily because everyone else is doing the same. Mutual fund companies exacerbate this effect by typically advertising to potential investors only their fund *winners* (the best-performing stocks within a fund). A knowledgeable and rational investor needs to beware of this irrational tendency in some team-managed funds.

Accountability and marketability are the primary advantages of the star-manager approach. If fund performance is extremely favorable (or unfavorable), an investor can credit (or blame) only one person rather than not knowing which particular managers of a team are responsible. The fund can also trumpet the stock-picking ability of only one individual and market the manager as well as the fund. These advantages, however, may be more than offset by the disadvantages of the approach. If the portfolio manager leaves, there is often a loss of continuity and the potential for a shareholder exodus from the fund. In the wake of Peter Lynch's retirement and departure from the Fidelity Magellan fund in 1990, shareholders sold shares of Magellan in great quantities, driving down the fund's net asset value in the following years. Such an exodus may be minimized in part by the reputation of the fund family or company, but even the strong name of Fidelity Funds could not completely limit the damage in the case of Magellan and the departure of its star manager.

There is a surprising dearth of academic studies comparing the performance results of team-managed versus star-managed funds. One study in 2008 did conclude that there was no significant difference in the risk-adjusted performance of team-managed and individually managed funds over the longer term, but it also found that funds managed by teams exhibited lower turnover of assets and were significantly less risky than funds managed by individuals.[1] The study also showed that team-managed funds attracted significantly greater investor flows than individually managed funds, after controlling for performance, risk, and expenses. Finally, the study showed that team-managed funds had lower expenses than individually managed funds by about 50 basis points at the time of the study.

---

[1]R. T. Bliss, M. E. Potter, and C. Schwarz, "Performance Characteristics of Individually-Managed versus Team-Managed Mutual Funds," *The Journal of Portfolio Management*, 34, no. 3 (2008): 110-119.

Harbor Bond Institutional

Like Fidelity Magellan under Peter Lynch, Harbor is an example of the star manager approach. Harbor is managed by William H. Gross, likely the most famous bond or fixed-income portfolio manager in the world. Gross is the founder and co-CIO of Pacific Investment Management Company, LLC (PIMCO), headquartered in Newport Beach, California, and is the first portfolio manager inducted into the Fixed Income Analyst Society's Hall of Fame in 1996. He also is the manager (and has been since 1987) of the largest bond fund in the world: the PIMCO Total Return Fund. Gross started Harbor as an alternative for investors who believe that the PIMCO Total Return Fund has grown much too large in size and cannot easily trade its holdings without significantly impacting its net asset value.

Gross's long tenure with PIMCO and Harbor is noteworthy for any prospective investor. The longer the tenure of a manager with a company and fund, the more likely it is that their investment style and strategies have proven to be profitable. The performance of Harbor should be analyzed—as should any actively managed fund—on a *net-of-fees* basis. That is, the annualized, actual performances of an actively managed fund and a passively managed fund should not be compared unless the management expenses of both fund are taken into account. If the performance of an actively traded fund does not measure up to its passively managed counterpart on a net-of-fees long-term basis, the potential investor likely should purchase shares in the much less expensive index mutual fund or exchange traded fund, which Chapter 8 discusses.

Fund Expenses and Fee Level

The factors to consider in evaluating the expenses and fee level of any mutual fund are discussed in detail in Chapter 4. To recap in brief, there are usually three expense components for any fund:

- Initial sales charges, referred to as a *front-end load*
- 12b-1 marketing expense charges
- Management expenses

Fairholme Fund

Fairholme levies no initial sales charge and is categorized as a *no-load fund*. Fairholme does, however, impose a charge of 2% of the amount redeemed if redemption occurs within 60 days of the purchase of the shares. Redemption charges have become more common in a volatile market where investors are increasingly short-term-oriented in their thinking. To plan and manage its cash flow effectively, the fund requires assurance that cash proceeds sufficient to redeem an investor's shares will not be necessary for at least a short period of time.

The expense section of Morningstar's Fairholme report characterizes the fund's *management net expense ratio* (fee level) of 1% of average net assets accrued on a daily basis as being "average" in comparison to Fairholme's category group of *large-cap no-load* funds. There is also a comparison to the Morningstar category average that includes both load and no-load U.S. *large value funds* (a slightly different category group). Here you can observe the steadily declining fee level of most mutual funds today. For example, the Morningstar category average for large value funds was 1.25% of assets managed in the year 2009; four years later it was down to 0.94% of assets managed.. The reasons for this reduction include not only competition among funds for investor contributions, but also extremely negative press reports questioning why fund fee levels are so high. You should expect to see this trend continue in the future.

Finally, as reported in the Other Fees/Expenses section of its Morningstar report, Fairholme does not charge 12b-1 fees. This again is consistent with current trends, and even more funds will likely abandon these types of fees in the future. On the other hand, no *expense waiver* is associated with the fund, meaning that Fairholme has elected not to waive any portion of the expenses that otherwise make up its overall expense ratio.

Harbor Bond Institutional

Harbor is a bond fund, so an investor would expect to see a lower expense ratio than that of a stock fund, in which the portfolio of assets is traded much more frequently. But Harbor's ***turnover ratio*** of 473% would seem to imply an extremely high level of trading activity and hence higher expense charges. So why is Harbor's expense ratio only 0.54% of average net assets managed by the fund, categorized as only "average" for its fund group category of *intermediate-term bond institutional*? There are likely two reasons for this. First, a turnover ratio of more than 100% does not necessarily mean that all securities in the fund portfolio have been traded over the course of the last year. Rather, the ratio may reflect the percentage of the fund's holdings that have changed over the last year.

Believing that market interest rates would increase, resulting in a decline in the net asset value of the fund shares, Harbor's manager Bill Gross made a premature decision in 2011 to change over a large part of its portfolio from U.S. Treasury securities to almost any other type of debt security. After recognizing his error in judgment, Gross switched course back to more Treasury securities again in the years 2012 and 2013. The second reason for the relatively low expense ratio is that trading costs represent only a small percentage of the net expenses charged by any mutual fund. As discussed in Chapter 4, a much larger percentage of the expense ratio consists of fees charged to the fund by the fund advisory company—in this case, Harbor Capital Advisors, Inc. Therefore, a high turnover ratio does not automatically lead to a higher-cost fund. Alternatively, as discussed in the next section, a high turnover ratio may indicate a *tax-inefficient fund*, because frequent trading may increase a fund's taxable distributions to its shareholders.

Fund Tax Efficiency

The more tax-inefficient an investment is, the more tax is paid on its assets at the shareholder level. By law, to avoid double taxation of income, a regulated investment company (such as a mutual fund) must distribute at least net 90% of interest and dividends earned on the company's investments and 90% of the company's capital gains net income. However, capital gains income is only recognized when the company (mutual fund) sells its holdings; dividends are not recognized for tax purposes unless and until the issuer of the stock's board of directors actually declares a dividend. This makes stock funds generally tax-efficient, because stocks may or may not ever pay a dividend to shareholders; and, if there is a sale of the fund's holdings after a year, any gain is taxable at long-term capital gains rates. (Note that these sales were taxed in 2013 at a top rate of 23.8%, consisting of a top long-term capital gains rate of 20% plus a 3.8% Medicare surtax on net investment income.) In contrast, bond funds are generally less tax-efficient than stock funds, because interest on bonds is taxed as ordinary income, at the same rate as an investor's salary and wages (in 2013, this top rate was 43.4%, including the Obamacare tax surcharge). Real estate investment trusts (REITs), discussed in Chapter 12 of this book, are also less tax-efficient than stock funds.

In its tax analysis section, Morningstar provides for each fund its *tax cost ratio* and *potential capital gains exposure*. The *tax cost ratio* measures how much a fund's annualized return is reduced by the taxes investors pay on fund distributions. This ratio is typically concentrated in the range of 0–5%, with zero indicating that the fund had no taxable distributions and ranged in tax inefficiency (loss of shareholder return due to taxes) from 1-5% thereafter. For example, if a fund had a 3% tax cost ratio and achieved a 13% annualized return, an investor in the fund earned approximately a 10% annualized return on an after-tax basis. (The annualized return would actually be slightly less because the return is compounded.)

The *potential capital gains exposure* measures any gains in the fund that have not yet been distributed to shareholders. A relatively high, positive metric can indicate the potential for upcoming capital gains distributions and a higher tax bill for a new purchaser of the fund. This can be a particularly important consideration for an investor making an initial fund purchase late in the year, because such an investor may incur a larger-than-expected tax liability as a result of the fund distributing gains. Alternatively, a negative metric means that future capital losses may be distributed to the shareholder, although the fund may be able to minimize this result to some extent by using the losses to offset any future capital gains. Therefore, as a fund's total amount of assets grows, the tax impact of previous gains to shareholders is likely diminished.

Fairholme Fund

The tax cost ratio of Fairholme over the ten previous years is 0.51, meaning that, of its reported pre-tax return of 11.80%, only 0.51% has been lost to taxes at the shareholder level. This ratio increased to 0.70 over the previous three years. These ratios indicate Fairholme's tax efficiency and relatively consistent holdings over a long time period. The implication that the manager is practicing the buy-and-hold strategy of a value investor is supported by the fund's very low turnover ratio of 2.0%. The fund does, however, exhibit a relatively high potential capital gains exposure of 12.42%, indicating a multiplicity of appreciated securities in its portfolio.

Harbor Bond Institutional

Compared to Fairholme, Harbor has a much higher tax cost ratio of 2.01 over a ten-year period, reflecting the fixed-income, pass-through orientation of the bond fund. Harbor's higher tax cost ratio results from the dual constraints that the interest on bonds is taxed at a higher rate than that of dividends on stocks and that the issuing debtor has no discretion as to when to pay the interest on bonds. An issuing company has a legal obligation to pay interest on bonds at the time specified in the bond indenture agreement with the bondholder. If it does not, the issuing company can be sued for non-compliance and ultimately forced into bankruptcy if it does not resume payment.

In contrast, Harbor's potential capital gains exposure of 4.10% is much lower than Fairholme's, reflecting the much lower capital appreciation of its bond holdings compared to the appreciation of the securities in the stock fund. An investor should buy bonds and bond mutual funds for their income potential, while purchasing stocks and stock mutual funds for their growth or capital appreciation potential.

This chapter concludes our detailed look at mutual funds as a professionally managed asset. We now proceed to the other two generally recognized types of investment companies as provided for in the Investment Company Act of 1940: closed-end funds and unit investment trusts (UITs).

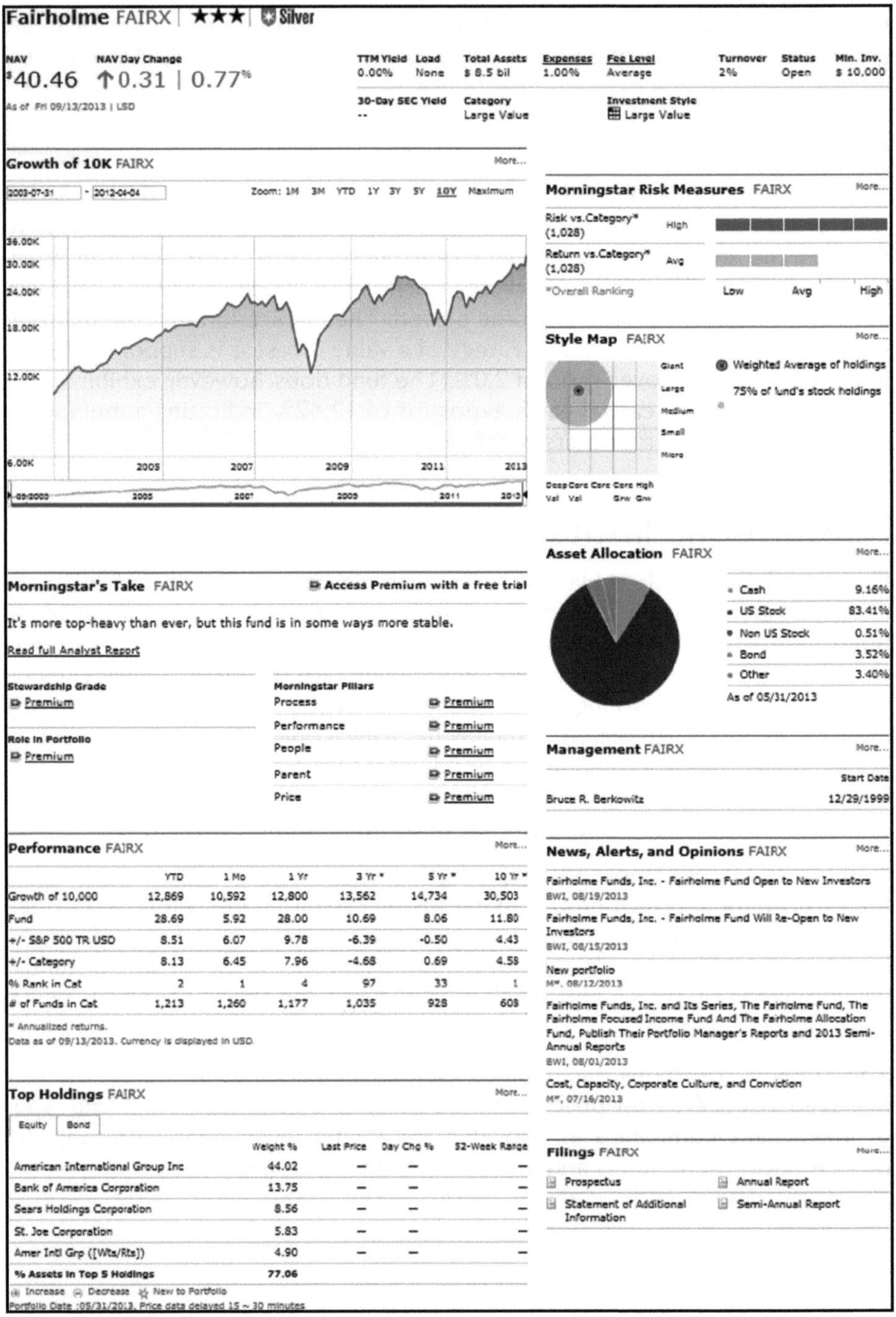

Fairholme FAIRX | ★★★ | Silver

NAV	NAV Day Change	TTM Yield	Load	Total Assets	Expenses	Fee Level	Turnover	Status	Min. Inv.
$40.46	↑0.31 | 0.77%	0.00%	None	$ 8.5 bil	1.00%	Average	2%	Open	$ 10,000

As of Fri 09/13/2013 | USD

30-Day SEC Yield: -- Category: Large Value Investment Style: Large Value

Growth of 10K FAIRX More...

2003-07-31 - 2012-04-04 Zoom: 1M 3M YTD 1Y 3Y 5Y 10Y Maximum

Morningstar Risk Measures FAIRX More...

Risk vs.Category* (1,028) High

Return vs.Category* (1,028) Avg

*Overall Ranking Low Avg High

Style Map FAIRX More...

Weighted Average of holdings

75% of fund's stock holdings

Asset Allocation FAIRX More...

Cash	9.16%
US Stock	83.41%
Non US Stock	0.51%
Bond	3.52%
Other	3.40%

As of 05/31/2013

Morningstar's Take FAIRX Access Premium with a free trial

It's more top-heavy than ever, but this fund is in some ways more stable.

Read full Analyst Report

Stewardship Grade: Premium

Role in Portfolio: Premium

Morningstar Pillars

Process	Premium
Performance	Premium
People	Premium
Parent	Premium
Price	Premium

Management FAIRX More...

	Start Date
Bruce R. Berkowitz	12/29/1999

Performance FAIRX More...

	YTD	1 Mo	1 Yr	3 Yr *	5 Yr *	10 Yr *
Growth of 10,000	12,869	10,592	12,800	13,562	14,734	30,503
Fund	28.69	5.92	28.00	10.69	8.06	11.80
+/- S&P 500 TR USD	8.51	6.07	9.78	-6.39	-0.50	4.43
+/- Category	8.13	6.45	7.96	-4.68	0.69	4.58
% Rank in Cat	2	1	4	97	33	1
# of Funds in Cat	1,213	1,260	1,177	1,035	928	608

* Annualized returns.
Data as of 09/13/2013. Currency is displayed in USD.

News, Alerts, and Opinions FAIRX More...

Fairholme Funds, Inc. - Fairholme Fund Open to New Investors
BWI, 08/19/2013

Fairholme Funds, Inc. - Fairholme Fund Will Re-Open to New Investors
BWI, 08/15/2013

New portfolio
M*, 08/12/2013

Fairholme Funds, Inc. and Its Series, The Fairholme Fund, The Fairholme Focused Income Fund And The Fairholme Allocation Fund, Publish Their Portfolio Manager's Reports and 2013 Semi-Annual Reports
BWI, 08/01/2013

Cost, Capacity, Corporate Culture, and Conviction
M*, 07/16/2013

Top Holdings FAIRX More...

Equity | Bond

	Weight %	Last Price	Day Chg %	52-Week Range
American International Group Inc	44.02	—	—	—
Bank of America Corporation	13.75	—	—	—
Sears Holdings Corporation	8.56	—	—	—
St. Joe Corporation	5.83	—	—	—
Amer Intl Grp ([Wts/Rts])	4.90	—	—	—
% Assets in Top 5 Holdings	77.06			

Increase Decrease New to Portfolio
Portfolio Date :05/31/2013. Price data delayed 15 ~ 30 minutes

Filings FAIRX More...

Prospectus Annual Report
Statement of Additional Information Semi-Annual Report

Figure 5-1. (continued)

Top Sectors FAIRX

More...

	Fund	3 Yr High	3 Yr Low	Cat Avg
Financial Services	75.58	78.67	74.60	20.94
Consumer Cyclical	10.81	12.48	10.81	7.74
Real Estate	6.94	8.58	4.70	1.44
Consumer Defensive	5.64	5.64	0.00	10.56
Energy	1.03	1.03	0.00	12.49

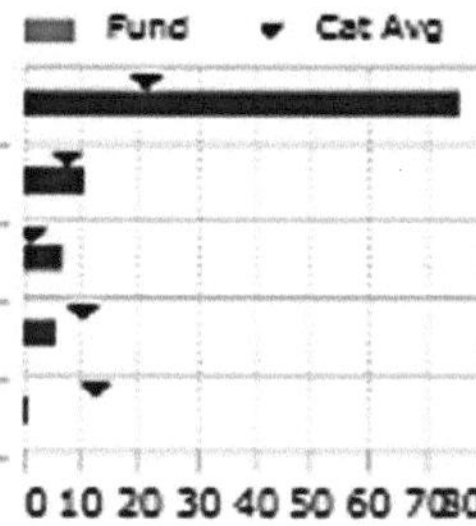

Portfolio Date: 05/31/2013

Dividend and Capital Gains Distributions FAIRX

Distribution Date	Distribution NAV	Long-Term Capital Gain	Short-Term Capital Gain	Return of Capital	Dividend Income	Distribution Total
12/16/2011	23.48	0.0000	0.0000	0.2089	0.6995	0.9084
12/31/2010	35.58	0.0000	0.0000	0.0000	0.0753	0.0753
12/16/2010	34.04	1.6903	0.0000	0.0000	0.3131	2.0034
12/16/2009	29.72	0.0000	0.0000	0.0000	0.2674	0.2674
12/17/2008	21.12	0.4347	0.0000	0.0000	0.1057	0.5404

Currency: USD

Figure 5-1. Morningstar Quote for Fairholme Fund FAIRX, September 13, 2013[2]

[2]Reproduced with the permission of Morningstar, Inc., from `http://quotes.morningstar.com/fund/f?ops=p&t=FAIRX&region=USA&culture=en-US`.

Harbor Bond Instl HABDX | ★★★★ | Gold

NAV	NAV Day Change
$11.94	↑0.01 | 0.08%

As of Fri 09/13/2013 | USD

TTM Yield	Load	Total Assets	Expenses	Fee Level	Turnover	Status	Min. Inv.
2.38%	None	$ 6.8 bil	0.54%	Average	473%	Open	$ 1,000

30-Day SEC Yield	Category	Credit Quality/Interest Rate Sensitivity
1.41%	Intermediate-Term Bond	Mid/Moderate

Growth of 10K HABDX

More...

2003-07-31 - 2012-04-04 Zoom: 1M 3M YTD 1Y 3Y 5Y 10Y Maximum

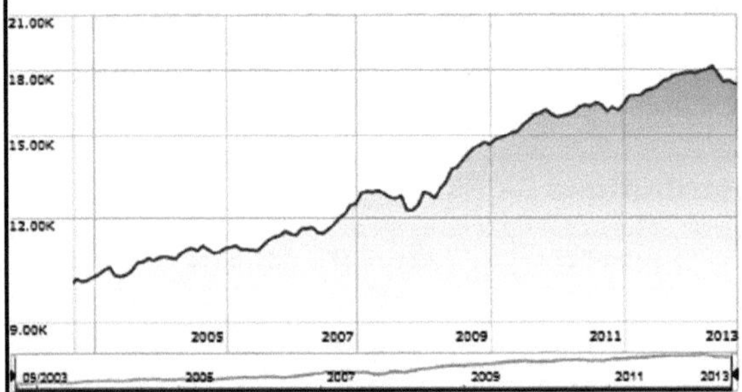

Morningstar Risk Measures HABDX

More...

Risk vs.Category* (1,011)	Avg
Return vs.Category* (1,011)	+Avg

*Overall Ranking — Low / Avg / High

Style Map HABDX

More...

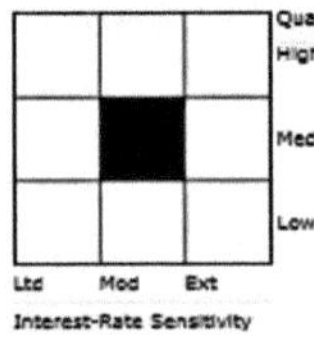

Avg Eff Duration	5.95 Yrs
Avg Eff Maturity	7.00 Yrs
Avg Credit Quality	BBB

Asset Allocation HABDX

More...

Type	% Net	% Short	% Long
Cash	-54.46	64.58	10.12
US Stocks	0.00	0.00	0.00
Non US Stocks	0.00	0.00	0.00
Bonds	153.84	30.40	184.24
Other	0.62	0.03	0.65

Note: Contains derivatives or short positions

As of 06/30/2013

Morningstar's Take HABDX

Access Premium with a free trial

Nobody's perfect.

Read full Analyst Report

Stewardship Grade
Premium

Role in Portfolio
Premium

Morningstar Pillars	
Process	Premium
Performance	Premium
People	Premium
Parent	Premium
Price	Premium

Management HABDX

More...

	Start Date
William H. Gross	12/29/1987

Performance HABDX

More...

	YTD	1 Mo	1 Yr	3 Yr *	5 Yr *	10 Yr *
Growth of 10,000	9,667	9,917	9,808	10,926	13,515	17,283
Fund	-3.33	-0.83	-1.92	3.00	6.21	5.62
+/- Barclays US Agg Bond TR USD	0.00	-0.18	0.69	0.39	1.58	1.03
+/- Category	-0.34	-0.20	-0.30	-0.26	0.78	1.16
% Rank in Cat	56	84	49	55	28	13
# of Funds in Cat	1,205	1,236	1,164	1,009	871	617

* Annualized returns.
Data as of 09/13/2013. Currency is displayed in USD.

News, Alerts, and Opinions HABDX

More...

A Bucket Portfolio Stress Test
M*, 08/01/2013

New portfolio
M*, 07/26/2013

New Morningstar.com Analyst Report or Note
M*, 07/16/2013

What Investors Were Researching in June
M*, 07/07/2013

New 3rd Quarter Model Portfolios
M*, 07/02/2013

Top Holdings HABDX

More...

	Weight %	Maturity Date	Amount	Value
☆ 90day Eurodollar Futures Cme Jun15 Xcme	16.68	06/15/2015	1238.25 Mil	1225.68 Mil
Swu0566v5 Irs Usd R F 1.50000 Cme Vanilla	13.19	03/18/2016	965.80 Mil	969.17 Mil
Swu0566v5 Irs Usd P V 03mlibor Cme Vanilla	- 13.14	03/18/2016	965.80 Mil	-965.80 Mil
⊕ 90day Eurodollar Futures Cme Dec15 Xcme	10.65	12/14/2015	794.50 Mil	782.58 Mil
☆ Us 10yr Note (Cbt)sep13 Xcbt 20130919	5.95	09/19/2013	345.70 Mil	437.53 Mil
% Assets in Top 5 Holdings	**33.32**			

⊕ Increase ⊖ Decrease ☆ New to Portfolio
Portfolio Date : 06/30/2013

Filings HABDX

More...

Prospectus
Annual Report
Statement of Additional Information
Semi-Annual Report

Figure 5-2. (continued)

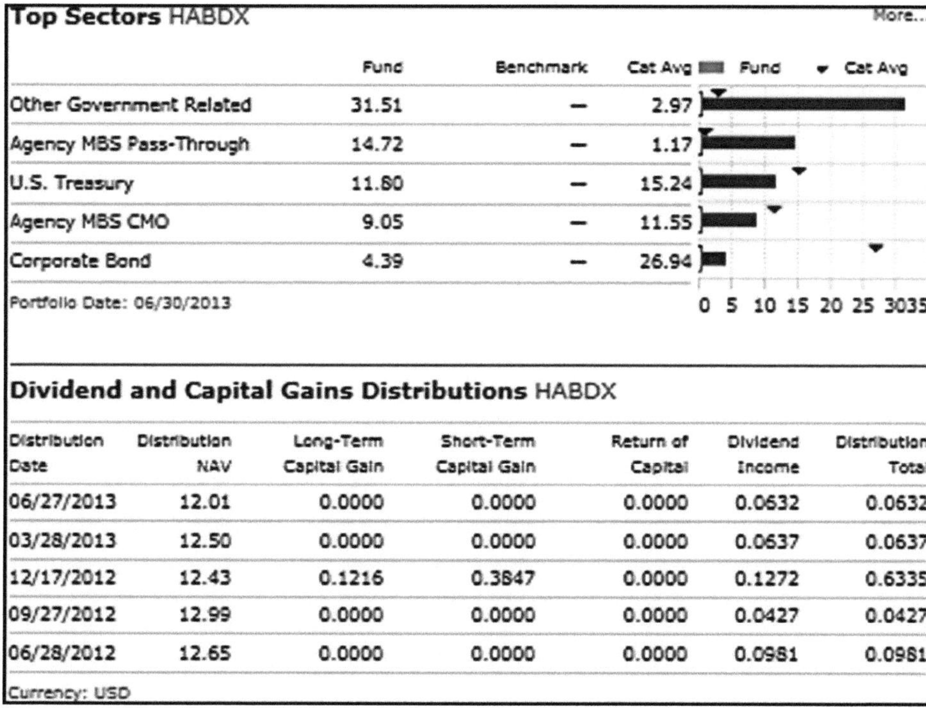

Top Sectors HABDX

More...

	Fund	Benchmark	Cat Avg
Other Government Related	31.51	—	2.97
Agency MBS Pass-Through	14.72	—	1.17
U.S. Treasury	11.80	—	15.24
Agency MBS CMO	9.05	—	11.55
Corporate Bond	4.39	—	26.94

Portfolio Date: 06/30/2013

Dividend and Capital Gains Distributions HABDX

Distribution Date	Distribution NAV	Long-Term Capital Gain	Short-Term Capital Gain	Return of Capital	Dividend Income	Distribution Total
06/27/2013	12.01	0.0000	0.0000	0.0000	0.0632	0.0632
03/28/2013	12.50	0.0000	0.0000	0.0000	0.0637	0.0637
12/17/2012	12.43	0.1216	0.3847	0.0000	0.1272	0.6335
09/27/2012	12.99	0.0000	0.0000	0.0000	0.0427	0.0427
06/28/2012	12.65	0.0000	0.0000	0.0000	0.0981	0.0981

Currency: USD

Figure 5-2. Morningstar Quote for Harbor Bond Institutional Fund HABDX, September 13, 2013[3]

[3]Reproduced with the permission of Morningstar, Inc., from `http://quotes.morningstar.com/fund/f?ops=p&t=HABDX&region=USA&culture=en-US`.

PART

III

Other Professionally Managed Assets under the 1940 Act

CHAPTER

6

Closed-End Funds

This chapter begins this part of the book on other pooled assets in the lexicon of *professionally managed assets* (PMAs) with a "backwater" (less well-known) asset: *closed-end funds (CEFs)*. The next chapter then takes up another backwater asset: the *unit investment trust* (UIT). Chapter 8 closes Part 3 with a type of PMA that is burgeoning in popularity: *exchange-traded funds* (ETFs).

This chapter introduces the pattern I will follow in the next three parts of this book for discussing each successive form of PMA, call it *X*:

- What is *X*?
- Advantages of *X*
- Disadvantages of *X*
- Who should purchase *X*?
- What selection criteria should be used before purchasing *X*?
- How to evaluate the performance of *X*

What Is a Closed-End Fund?

In contrast to an open-end investment company (mutual fund), where an unlimited number of shares may be issued, a CEF is created with only a limited number of shares. If any new investors wish to purchase shares of a CEF, they must buy shares from the current or existing investors. Moreover, current investors cannot sell their shares back to the CEF; rather, new investors are the market for current investors' shares, in turn meaning that CEF shares are not redeemed (like mutual funds) but are marketable just like a stock. A CEF raises money just like a stock—that is, via an **initial public offering** (IPO)—but it subsequently uses the money it receives from the IPO to buy and sell individual stocks and bonds and then *pools* them into a single fund.

The unique way in which a CEF is structured leads to another interesting characteristic of the fund: the fund shares often trade at a discount or premium to their *net asset value* (NAV). This never happens with an open-end company (mutual fund) and, as discussed in Chapter 8, rarely happens with an ETF. So why does this phenomenon occur with a CEF? The answer to this question is a bit of a mystery, but here are several theories:

- A discount in share price might reflect the risk that a reduction in the price of a fund's shares could result from the immediate selling pressure if a closed-end fund had to be terminated and liquidated with its assets converted to cash distributed to shareholders, given the large holdings of the fund's assets.
- A discount price might reflect the expectations of buyers and sellers of the fund that even if a fund were not liquidated and the shareholders of the fund could potentially receive the NAV of the shares, the probability of total return of initial capital invested was unlikely.
- A premium price for the fund shares might reflect investor expectations that the assets of a given fund portfolio will perform well in the future. Unless the investor values the quality of the management of the closed-end fund, however, he or she will likely just go purchase individually the stocks or bonds held by the fund.

Usually, the shares of a closed-end fund trade at a discount, thereby permitting investors to comply with a basic investing rule of "buy low and sell high."

At the end of 2012, there were 602 CEFs in the United States with total assets of $265 billion. Bond funds were the most popular type of CEF, accounting for about 65% of the total number of CEFs, with municipal bond funds constituting 37% of the total number of CEFs in 2012.[1]

[1]Investment Company Institute. *2013 Investment Company Fact Book: A Review of Trends and Activity in the U.S. Investment Company Industry*. Washington, DC: Investment Company Institute (2013). Available at `www.icifactbook.org`.

Advantages of a Closed-End Fund

Like a mutual fund, a CEF offers the PMA's advantages of professional management and instant diversification. CEFs offer four additional advantages discussed in this section: convenience; a known, periodic distribution of income; flexibility of investments; and the ability to buy fund shares at a sometimes sizeable discount to NAV.

Convenience

Proponents of CEFs point to the convenience provided to the investor after purchasing fund shares. Specifically, the fund trades like a stock, so an investor may buy and sell shares easily during the trading day from a fixed number of shares offered initially by the fund. Unlike in a mutual fund, where the investor must wait until the end of the trading day to determine the price at which they traded the fund shares, in a closed-end fund, a positive movement in market price may be taken advantage of much more quickly. Alternatively, an investor can sell his or her shares much more rapidly if the market moves downward quickly, as happened frequently throughout calendar year 2008.

Some individuals also like the convenience and expertise of brokerage firms in the investing process. Unlike most mutual funds, CEFs must be purchased from a broker-dealer, such as Bank of America Merrill Lynch or Morgan Stanley. The reputation of the firm can be a positive factor in deciding whether to buy a specific CEF or whether to invest in the closed-end form of PMA. For example, a particular broker-dealer may specialize in a specific sector of the economy, such as energy, and offer a number of CEFs in that sector. Although the investor may be sacrificing diversification when purchasing a closed-end energy fund, the additional return may more than compensate for the increased risk.

Periodic Distribution of Income

Like a mutual fund, a CEF is taxed as a *conduit*—meaning that it passes through income to the shareholders annually to be taxed at the shareholder level. In doing so, the fund avoids taxation at the entity level, and, because the fund is a legal corporation, double taxation of income is not imposed.

Unlike a mutual fund, however, a CEF typically offers a predetermined schedule for the distribution of current income and capital gains. This allows for some tax planning on the part of the shareholder/taxpayer. For example, assume that the taxpayer is a self-employed individual paying estimated taxes for which there is not only a late-payment penalty, but also a penalty if the amount of taxes paid in for any given quarter are not attributable to that quarter's actual earned amount of income. Knowing when taxable income and capital gains will be paid may assist in proper income recognition at the proper time. A CEF can provide that certainty to the shareholder/taxpayer.

Flexibility of Investments

A major feature of a CEF is that the number of shares typically remains at a fixed number with additional shares seldom issued. As a result, the manager of the fund has a great deal of flexibility in managing the fund assets. Moreover, unlike in a mutual fund, where shares may be redeemed at any time, the CEF manager has no need to maintain a cash reserve on hand at all times to fund payment of redeemed shares. This single advantage of the structure of the fund allows the manager to invest in less liquid securities that may have higher expected returns, such as stocks. It also means the bond assets that may constitute all or part of the fund's portfolio may be longer-term in nature, because there is no need to match a shorter-term investor time horizon. The overall duration of the bond fund may be longer as well.

Ability to Buy Shares at a Discount

As noted in the opening section of this chapter, a unique characteristic of a CEF is its pricing. If the fund shares are selling at a discount, it means those shares are selling at a price lower than the fund's NAV. In 2013, for example, many closed-end bond funds sold for above-average discounts—some as high as 50% from NAV. Why was this occurring? The answer is that shareholders in the funds believed that the price of bonds was likely to decline in the future, given an expected increase in market interest rates, and so they wanted to sell the fund shares, creating an excess supply of the shares compared to the demand for them. Thus, the funds' shares dropped below their NAV. Did that mean that such shares should have been bought at that point? Not necessarily, because there may have been an additional discount on the shares coming in the future months. Nevertheless, purchasing any asset at a discount from its market price is a plausible consideration for a knowledgeable investor.

Some funds achieve an even greater discount on their shares by leveraging the purchase of assets within the funds. Borrowing by a closed-end bond fund boosts the yield of the fund and makes it even more attractive than a non-leveraged fund selling at a discount. But remember the basic rule of leverage: borrowing boosts returns, but it also magnifies losses! Leveraged assets are more sensitive to changes in downward market conditions, so if interest rates increase, the price of a leveraged closed-end share will suffer proportionally more than the equivalent non-leveraged closed-end share. As a rule, CEF managers are more likely to use leverage than their mutual fund counterparts, making the purchase of shares on the whole a riskier proposition.

One additional pointer with respect to the purchase of CEF shares: do not buy the fund at the time of its initial offering to the public. Fund shares are most often priced at a discount several months after the initial offering—in other words, the price of the fund shares will be lower than what you paid for them. Therefore, it is preferable to wait to buy the shares until after the price decline has taken place; and even then, you should purchase only if you believe the fund shares have "hit bottom" and will not decline in price further. Pinpointing when the market will not decline any further is beyond the expertise of most investors and even of many investment advisors assisting individual investors.

Disadvantages of a Closed-End Fund

Offsetting the advantages of CEFs are the following four disadvantages to investors discussed in this section: higher-than-average management expenses, trading costs, lower relative transparency than ETFs, and the purchase of fund shares at a premium to NAV.

Higher-Than-Average Management Expenses

The imputation of higher management expenses to CEFs is disputed by some CEF advocates, who make the valid point that CEFs do not incur ongoing costs associated with the buying and selling of fund shares, as is the case with mutual funds. Remember that CEF shares are marketable and not redeemable by the fund itself. Thus, the internal management expenses of a CEF may actually be less than those of a comparable mutual fund.

Nonetheless, a CEF certainly does have higher sales and management expenses than a no-load mutual fund or an index mutual fund. When contrasting the CEF purchase to that of a *no-load fund* (in the sense of a mutual fund that does not impose a sales charge on the purchase of shares), you need to remember that CEFs are sold only by brokerage firms, which impose a sales charge in the form a commission. In turn, this charge reduces the potential percentage return on investment (more expense, less capital invested). Moreover, the majority of CEFs are actively managed—in contrast to index mutual funds, which are passively managed.

Figure 6-1 at the end of this chapter shows the profile or "quote page" of Eaton Vance Tax-Managed Global Dividend Equity Income Fund (ticker symbol: EXG). The fund had a total expense ratio reported for 2012 of 1.06% of assets. This is a ratio comparable to that of an actively managed mutual fund in the same category, but consider comparing EXG to that the Vanguard Developed Market Index (ticker symbol: VDMIX), a passively managed index mutual fund also investing in dividend-paying stocks of the United States and abroad. VDMIX has an expense ratio of only 0.20% of assets managed. (Of course, the next step is to look further at both funds and take into account the expected return for the amount of risk that is assumed.)

CEFs tend to be smaller than mutual funds, and, therefore, the expense charges must be distributed over a lesser amount of assets managed, raising the expense ratio. However, as with mutual funds, the NAV of a CEF is calculated daily after expenses, making the actual amount of expense charges less transparent.

Trading Costs

Like ETFs (Chapter 8), CEFs are traded throughout the market day at a price determined by the market. Therefore, trading costs are incurred on the buying and selling of the shares. This includes the payment of brokerage commissions, which are typically about 5% of the trade. Again, similar to up-front load charges on the initial purchase of the shares, less of the investor's money is put to work.

In addition, thinly traded CEFs can have a substantial difference or **spread** in the price of their shares. A *thinly traded* fund is one with a lower-than-average volume of shares traded each market day. In the case of some CEFs, an investor may be the only trader that particular day (other than the offsetting position), so that he or she is the "market maker" for the stock. Because a CEF trades like a stock, it must be purchased from a broker-dealer at an "ask" price or sold at the "bid" price for the fund shares. If the investor is selling all or some of the closed-end shares and the shares are not frequently traded, the dealer will offer a lower bid price to buy them from the investor, thus exacerbating the spread that the investor must incur and/or the cost of trading the shares. There is now also a lower return to the investor.

Lower Relative Transparency

By law, CEFs are only required to disclose their portfolios on a quarterly or semi-annual basis. The same is true of mutual funds. In contrast, ETFs typically disclose their portfolio holdings on a daily basis. The practical effect of greater disclosure (or transparency) by ETFs is that investors in those funds may engage in **arbitrage**, which tends to keep the price of the ETF shares very close to the underlying market value of their holdings. The lack of transparency of CEF positions may be another reason contributing to the divergence in share price from portfolio holdings, resulting in the discount/premium characteristic of CEFs.

Another point is relevant to transparency: before purchasing a closed-end or mutual fund, an investor should verify that the disclosed holdings match up to the fund's stated objective. For example, a growth and income stock fund should be investing in both capital appreciation and dividend-paying stocks. Given the latitude provided to closed-end and mutual fund managers not to be transparent on a daily basis, *style drift* is likely to occur. Although monitoring of this drift may occur at the fund level, there is no legal requirement to do so. Thus, to be a knowledgeable investor in this regard is also to be a diligent investor.

Purchase of Fund Shares at a Premium to NAV

Ideally, an investor should avoid incurring excessive risk by buying CEFs at large premiums. These premiums typically occur when either the fund features a much-sought-after professional manager or the holdings of the fund have over-performed relative to their fund category. It is likely that this premium will either widen or continue for a period of time before reverting to the mean, making the fund a candidate for losses while owned by the investor.

To make matters worse, some investors pay premium prices for CEFs that return in the form of dividends more than the fund earns. This of course means the fund is returning principal or capital invested by the shareholder. Like an operating corporation or "going concern" dipping into retained earnings to pay shareholders an income return on funds invested, ultimately there may be no additional capital remaining to remit. Thus, a fund that is paying out more than it earns can only cut its future dividends to substitute for the declining cash flow. When it does so, investors will react by driving down the market price of the fund shares.[2]

Who Should Purchase a Closed-End Fund?

Particularly since the advent of ETFs, the popularity of CEFs has declined. However, CEFs do offer benefits that (most) ETFs do not. First, a CEF often trades at a discount to its NAV; therefore, it is possible for an investor to "buy low" in the hope of profiting from the purchase when the gap between the share price and the NAV narrows over time. Moreover, if a CEF persistently trades at a sizeable discount to its NAV, the manager will sometimes liquidate the fund, returning to the investor the higher NAV price.

[2]To determine whether a fund is returning principal, check the *return of capital* (ROC) column on the Closed End Funds Association website, `www.cefconnect.com`.

Second, CEFs are actively managed, whereas the majority of ETFs are passively managed. If, as an investor, you believe in the merits of active managers practicing credible fundamental analysis to outperform the index (as encapsulated in the *semi-strong* form of the **efficient market hypothesis**), a CEF may be a worthwhile purchase.

Also, as mentioned, the majority of CEFs are bond funds, and a majority of the bonds are municipal bond funds. Therefore, if you need higher levels of interest income, you may wish to invest in CEFs. Who needs higher levels of interest income? Predominately, individuals who no longer can generate income through earning power, such as retirees, are candidates for a CEF purchase. Moreover, higher-income retirees can benefit by a purchase of a municipal bond CEF and achieve a greater after-tax yield than with a taxable fund.

Still, the real comparison to be made when considering the purchase of a CEF is between such a fund and a traditional mutual fund. Unless, as a prospective purchaser, you are willing to commit to researching CEFs selling at a sizeable discount and then anticipate profiting from a future reduction in that discount, mutual funds offer you the same advantages as a CEF for typically a much lower overall cost.

What Selection Criteria Should Be Used before Purchasing a Closed-End Fund?

An investor considering the purchase of a CEF should weigh the following selection criteria:

- Performance, including the tenure of the fund manager
- Expenses
- Amount of leverage
- Income yield
- Tax considerations
- Comparison to mutual funds and ETFs

Performance

The historical performance and length of tenure of the fund manager are as important to the decision whether to purchase a specific CEF as they are to the decision whether to purchase a specific actively-managed mutual fund. How long the fund should have been in existence is a separate consideration for which there is no definitive answer, other than that the longer the fund has been in existence, the better. A common rule of thumb is that an investor should not consider purchasing shares of a CEF unless the fund has been operating for at least five years, but the better rule is to consider a fund that has performed through several market cycles or, in recent years, probably since 2003. (The time period of 2003–2013 includes bullish cycles from 2003–2007, a severe bear market from 2007–2009, and a recovering market from 2009–2013). A fund that has had the same manager throughout this time period (and preferably before) and has outperformed its peers is the best option for an investor.

Because a unique characteristic of a CEF is the fact that it may sell at a discount or premium to its NAV, it is interesting when analyzing the performance of EXG (Figure 6-1) to compare the last actual discount to NAV of 10.27% to the 3-year average discount of 11.17%. This means that the current discount percentage is below that of the fund's 3-year average, indicating that now may not be the best time to purchase the fund: the discount is likely to widen over time, resulting in a loss in investor value. However, the real answer to the question of whether to buy is based on what may happen to the fund's underlying holdings. If those holdings outperform the broader market, the share price of EXG will increase regardless of any movements in the discount percentages.

CEFs have *distribution rates* instead of yields or dividends. The distribution can be composed of the same items as mutual funds, such as dividends, interest income, and realized capital gains, but it is not reported in the same manner as dividend yield or capital gains yield for mutual funds. Rather, the *total distribution rate* on a CEF's share price may be thought of as a performance measure tracking the rate of return an investor receives as a percentage of the total share price. The total distribution rate as a percentage of NAV reflects the yield that the fund's holdings must achieve in order to provide the current distribution amount.

Expenses

The expense ratio of EXG for the year 2013 is reported as 1.06%. This percentage is relevant only as a comparison to that of the fund's peers. However, remember that CEFs are actively managed, so by process of management, a CEF is more expensive to operate than an ETF. Whether the expense ratio of the CEF is greater than that of an alternatively actively managed mutual fund is the real question to be answered by the investor before a possible purchase.

Another consideration is what broad category of CEF is being analyzed for possible purchase. As discussed in Chapter 4, bond funds are the least expensive funds to manage, then stock funds, and finally international stock funds. EXG is a global stock fund, so it includes some international stocks. Comparing EXG to an actively managed world-allocation mutual fund, First Eagle Global (ticker symbol: SGENX) reveals that First Eagle carries an expense ratio of 1.15% of assets managed, not too far above EXG's reported expense percentage. But remember, the trading costs of a CEF are typically more than those of a mutual fund, and an upfront sales charge (*load*) is also charged. Finally, EXG is the largest CEF available in the market today and thus can spread its expenses over a large volume of assets managed. This is not the case with the majority of CEFs, which necessarily have to impose a greater expense ratio than mutual funds.

Amount of Leverage

The concept of leverage is simple. The amount of leverage or *leverage rate* is the asset value divided by the cash required of the investor at the time of purchase. The most familiar example of the concept of leverage is a home purchase. If a house costs $100,000, and the purchaser's down payment is $20,000, he or she is said to be "leveraged 4 to 1" or leveraged to the extent of 80%. The greater the leverage, the greater is the investment risk. This is because as underlying asset value declines, a borrower's ability to continue borrowing rapidly decreases, potentially resulting in a forced sale of the asset at a below-market price. Therefore, it is preferable to be less leveraged when making an investment, to guard against the negative effects of a market downturn.

Under the Investment Company Act of 1940, a CEF is required to report its total leverage ratio. This ratio is computed as the total leverage used by the fund divided by the sum of the total leverage and the net assets of the fund. When computing the ratio, total leverage includes both 1940 Act leverage, such as loans, lines of credit, and notes payable, and non-1940 Act leverage, such as reverse repurchase lending and securities lending.

In considering whether to purchase shares of a CEF, what constitutes a safe total leverage ratio? The general answer is a ratio that is as small as possible. The specific answer is that an investor should be wary of any fund carrying a total leverage ratio of more than 40% of debt to total assets. At this level, the fund value and fund share price become extremely susceptible to the effects of a market downturn, and percentage losses can multiply quickly.

Income Yield

Most CEFs are bond funds, with a sizeable percentage of those constituting municipal bond funds. Investors typically buy bond funds for income (they buy stock funds for growth or capital appreciation), and higher-income investors buy municipal bond funds for tax-free income. Therefore, the income yield is very important to potential CEF investors.

There are several types of income yield, but the most common are *current yield* and *yield to maturity*. Current yield is the annual interest paid by the bond or bond fund divided by the bond's current price. Yield to maturity (YTM) is the rate of return expected for a bond or bond fund if the bond is held until its maturity date. YTM is a better measure of the income yield of a bond or bond fund because it takes into account the current price of the bond as it is constantly changing in the marketplace. A bond selling at a discount to its par value has a higher YTM than a bond selling at par or a bond selling at a premium. Similarly, a CEF whose shares are selling at a discount to the fund's NAV has a greater YTM or income yield. This is a reason why closed-end bond funds are preferentially purchased in markets in which bond yields (and particularly Treasury bond yields) are very low. Remember, bond yields move in inverse direction to bond prices. Treasury bond prices are high when the Federal Reserve stimulates demand for them, driving up the price.

A heuristic when investing in CEFs is to buy only funds that are selling at a discount. But at what discount percentage should an investor start to think about the purchase of a CEF? The accepted wisdom is to buy when the discount approaches 10% off the NAV of the fund. In this manner, the investor benefits from a higher income yield on the fund. Moreover, when comparing yields to Treasury securities, an investor should typically look for an income yield at least two percentage points higher than U.S. Treasuries, a yield that also depends on the term to maturity of the security. Note that a closed-end stock fund also has an income yield, but there it is referred to as a *dividend yield* (computed as the next year's expected stock dividend divided by the beginning price of the stock—that is, what you purchased it for). An investor considering the purchase of a closed-end stock fund should look for a fund selling at a discount to its NAV as well as an underlying portfolio of blue-chip stocks, known historically for paying reliable and growing dividends.

Tax Considerations

As discussed in the "Periodic Distribution of Income" section of this chapter, CEFs (like mutual funds) serve as conduits through which income and capital gains are distributed to investors. Income from the fund's holdings is taxable as ordinary income to the investor, whereas capital gains, assuming the position has been held longer than one year by the fund, are taxed as preferential long-term capital gain income to the investor. This raises the question of whether an investor should position a given CEF in a taxable or tax-deferred account. This question can only be answered by identifying whether the type of CEF that the investor purchases is a closed-end bond fund or a closed-end stock fund.

A bond fund (whether closed or open-ended) should normally be positioned in a tax-deferred account so that it is not taxed currently at the higher ordinary income tax rates. The only usual exception to this rule is a municipal bond fund, which generates tax-free or tax-sheltered income. It generally is not good tax planning to position a tax-sheltered asset (such as a municipal bond fund) in a tax-sheltered savings vehicle (such as a tax-deferred account). When, as in recent years, municipal bond funds have a relatively favorable income yield, the tax disadvantage historically associated with tax-deferred positioning is somewhat lessened. Add to this the growth element resulting from a purchase of a CEF at a lower discount, with the discount ultimately widening, and there may be a very good argument to position a closed-end bond fund in a tax-deferred account.

Alternatively, stock funds (whether closed or open-ended) should be positioned in a taxable account because dividend payments are generally low, if made at all. Nevertheless, if you are "stretching for yield" by means of higher-than-average dividend payments from the fund, the argument for positioning where those payments may be taxed at ordinary income rates goes away, and the attractiveness of a tax-deferred account titling increases.

Comparison of CEFs to Mutual Funds and ETFs

Although authorized as part of the same 1940 Act that regulates mutual funds, CEFs technically are not mutual funds. Neither are ETFs, although they may arguably be thought of as a broad type of index mutual fund. These statements may be made because all three types of investment choices—CEFs, mutual funds, and ETFs—differ greatly in criteria to be considered before purchasing each and, once purchased, in operation of the investment choice.

Table 6-1 compares the three types of investments. In the next chapter, Table 7-1 compares CEFs with their close cousin, UITs—the third type of PMA permitted under the 1940 Act. Table 8-1 compares ETFs with mutual funds. You can use all three of these tables to assist in making an investment decision.

Table 6-1. Comparing Closed-End Funds, Mutual Funds, and ETFs

CHARACTERISTIC	CLOSED-END	MUTUAL FUND	ETFs
Diversification	Yes	Yes	Yes
Expenses	Relatively high	Depends	Low
Leverage	Depends	Rarely	Sometimes
Sells at discount to NAV	Yes	No	Slightly
Tax efficiency	Some	No (unless index fund)	Yes
Ability to issue new shares	Generally not	Yes	Maybe
Trades like a stock	Yes	No	Yes
Income yield	Yes	Depends	Depends

How to Evaluate the Performance of a Closed-End Fund

As I did with open-end funds (mutual funds), I will refer to an actual Morningstar profile (namely, that of EXG in Figure 6-1) to exemplify the key metrics and past performance of a CEF.

The reporting data used to evaluate the performance of a CEF are similar in many respects to those used for evaluating open-end funds. Evaluating a CEF also involves the following distinctive metrics:

- Last closing share price and last actual NAV
- 1-year Z-statistic
- Total leverage ratio
- Total distribution rate (share price)

Last Closing Share Price and Last Actual NAV

In Figure 6-1, the last closing share price of EXG ($9.52) is at a discount to its last actual NAV ($10.61). The percentage discount of shares to NAV was hovering around the minimum 10% discount that is generally recommended before considering a purchase of the fund. However, observe the last actual disc/prem percentage of -10.27% as quoted by Morningstar compared to the 6-month avg disc/prem of -9.18% and the 3-year avg disc/prem of -11.17%. This indicates that the share price discount still had some room to move, meaning that an even greater discount was possible, so that an investor might accordingly wish to postpone a possible purchase.

Of course, whether the discount becomes even greater in a given case depends on why the phenomenon is taking place. The investment objective summary indicates that the objective of the sample fund is "current income with capital appreciation through investment in global common stock and through utilizing an options strategy." There are two primary reasons to engage in option trading: **speculation** and **hedging**. However, there is sometimes a third: to generate income by the sale of covered calls. It is likely that the managers of EXG are engaged in options trading to generate income for investors, but you would want to investigate further. Regardless, options trading increases the risk of the fund and constitutes operating leverage. It is likely that the amount of operating leverage is the reason the fund shares are selling at a discount from the fund's NAV. Morningstar notes that Eaton Vance has been "moderately successful with its suite of covered call funds," but it also states that it has engaged in the "extensive use of destructive return of capital in this fund." So, a decision whether to purchase EXG at this time, or at all, is a very close call. The discount percentage may grow, meaning you should wait before purchasing; moreover, the fund has been distributing the investors' return of capital as part of its distribution rate, meaning you may not want to purchase the fund in the first instance.

1-Year Z-Statistic

According to the Morningstar definition, the *Z-statistic* is a metric designed to assist the investor in assessing whether a CEF is relatively inexpensive or expensive at its current discount level. The metric shows whether the current discount percentage is close to its mean or average for a given period—here one year of investment performance. A positive Z score indicates that the current discount percentage is higher than its mean, and a negative Z score reflects that the current discount percentage is lower than its mean. The metric is computed by dividing the current discount less the mean by the standard deviation of the discount or the extent to which the discount has varied from the mean.

For example, assume that a fund has a mean discount over last year of -10% with a standard deviation of 4% and a current discount of -6%. The Z-statistic is [(-6) - (-10)] or +4 divided by 4 or 1. This means that the fund is relatively expensive at its current discount percentage, although not inordinately so, because the greater the Z-statistic, the greater the relative cost of the fund at its current discount percentage.

EXG has a 1-year Z-statistic of 0.28, indicating that the current discount percentage is 0.28 standard deviations higher than its mean. As an investor, you want this Z-statistic to be less positive—so this is an indication that the price of EXG is moving in the direction of a possible buy, although probably not yet. As a rule, any Z-statistic with an absolute value greater than 2 indicates a fairly extreme departure from the historical average discount or premium. In the case of a negative Z score, an investor would want the Z-statistic to be at least a negative 1 (and a negative 2 would be even better), because it would be a relatively inexpensive fund and the investor might buy in hopes that the discount would revert to its mean. As an alternative strategy using the Z-statistic, if the CEF were liquidated and the investor purchased the fund at an extreme discount, he or she would profit from the distribution of the fund assets at their higher NAV.

Total Leverage Ratio

The concept of leverage is discussed in the "Amount of Leverage" section of this chapter. This section considers leverage specifically in the sense of *financial leverage*—that is, using borrowed money to "juice" investor returns. The corollary type of leverage is *operating leverage*—defined in corporate finance as the extent to which fixed costs are used in a firm's operations. If a high percentage of a firm's total costs are fixed costs, then the firm is said to have a high degree of operating leverage. EXG is a not a corporation in the sense of operating leverage just defined, but it is nonetheless a corporation (investment company) in terms of legal structure. When engaging in options trading, EXG is employing operating leverage for the purpose of increasing the percentage return to the fund investor with a minimal use of cash that is actually invested.

The total leverage ratio of 0.00% shown for EXG, although true to what needs to be reported for the fund under 1940 Act requirements, is nevertheless a bit tendentious. The fund does use leverage, just not leverage that needs to be disclosed. Thus, an argument could be made that the fund is nontransparent in information provided to prospective investors. An investor is left with two alternatives: either educate yourself on the intricacies of CEF analysis, or engage the services of a professional investment advisor or registered investment advisory firm.

Total Distribution Rate (Share Price)

As discussed in the "Performance" section of this chapter, CEFs use the metric of total distribution rate instead of the metric of total return that is common with mutual funds. As you will recall, total return is the sum of the mutual fund's dividend (or income) yield plus its capital gains yield annualized over time; or the share price at the end of the period divided by the share price at the beginning of the period minus 1. Total distribution rate, on the other hand, may be computed on the basis of either share price or net asset value, but it can be distorted by the return of the shareholder's own investment or capital in the fund. It can also be manipulated by the amount of leverage used by the CEF.

Consider the following example of the total distribution rate on a CEF as computed on the basis of its share price. Assume that the share price of the fund is $10.00 per share and that the most recent monthly distribution is 12 cents per share. Therefore, the annual distribution is $1.44 share (or 12 times 0.12). The total distribution rate per share price is 14.4%, or $1.44 divided by $10.00.

The average CEF features a distribution rate of around 6%—an extremely favorable rate of return, particularly for a closed-end bond fund. The distribution rate per share price indicated in Figure 6-1 for EXG as of 10/31/12 was 10.25%—which was relatively high and therefore potentially attractive to income-seeking investors. However, remember the discomfort of Morningstar on its profile page when discussing EXG: it is concerned about the "extensive use of destructive return of capital in this fund."

Over time, a distribution consistently paid from a return of capital will result in an erosion of the fund's NAV. To prevent this, the only strategy that a fund can follow is to reduce its distribution amount in the future. When it does this, the fund's share price will fall. Depending on the amount of the discount or premium at which a fund's shares are selling, shareholders are left with a declining fund NAV, assets in the fund's portfolio that are not generating a sufficient rate of return, and a declining distribution. Like mutual fund investors who chase total return, CEF investors who chase distribution return risk setting themselves up for a loss in shareholder value.

Chapter 7 will analyze the third type of investment company or structure permitted under the Investment Company Act of 1940: the UIT investment vehicle.

EV Tax-Mgd Gbl Div Equity Income Common EXG | ★★★ | Neutral

Last Price $9.48 | Day Change ↓-0.04|-0.42%

As of Mon 09/23/2013 1:57 PM EST | USD

Last Closing Share Price	Day Range	52-WK Range	1-Year Z-Statistic	Market Value	Total Leverage Ratio
9.52	9.45-9.57	8.29-10.00	0.28	2,907.8 mil	0.00 %

Last Actual NAV	Last Actual NAV Date	Last Actual Disc/Prem	6-Month Avg Disc/Prem	3-Year Avg Disc/Prem	Total Dist. Rate (Share Price)
10.61	09/20/2013	-10.27 %	-9.18 %	-11.17 %	10.25 %

As of 09/20/2013

CEF Price EXG More...

09/17/2013 - 09/23/2013 Zoom: 1D 5D 1M 3M YTD 1Y 3Y 5Y 10Y Maximum

XNYS:EXG:-0.05|-0.47%

9.70
9.60
9.50
9.40
Volume
Sep 17 Sep 18 Sep 19 Sep 20 Sep 23
Jun Sep

News, Alerts, and Opinions More...

Eaton Vance Announces Updated Results Of Equity Option Closed-End Fund Share Repurchase Program
PRN, 09/19/2013

Eaton Vance Closed-End Equity Option Funds Declare Monthly Distributions
PRN, 09/13/2013

Eaton Vance Tax-Managed Global Diversified Equity Income Fund August 2013 Distribution
PRN, 08/30/2013

Eaton Vance Closed-End Equity Option Funds Declare Monthly Distributions
PRN, 08/13/2013

Eaton Vance Tax-Managed Global Diversified Equity Income Fund July 2013 Distribution
PRN, 07/31/2013

Morningstar Category EXG

World Stock

▶ View Other Funds in this Category

Morningstar's Take EXG Premium Content

Eaton Vance has been moderately successful with its suite of covered-call funds, especially when it comes to limiting volatility of total returns. Though absolute returns are not stellar, risk-adjusted returns have been better. This fund's record has been helped by smaller-than-average losses in 2008 and 2011 as well as a strong 2012. We've noted our discomfort with the extensive use of destructive return of capital in this fund (and its sister funds). Eaton Vance has lowered payouts over the last few years and, for the first time in its history, this fund used no destructive return of capital in fiscal 2012. We welcome this improvement, but overall, the fund has earned a Morningstar Analyst Rating of Neutral.

Read full Analyst Report

Benchmark EXG

Fund Benchmark	S&P 500 TR USD
Morningstar Benchmark	MSCI EAFE NR USD

Investment Objective Summary EXG

The Fund seeks current income with capital appreciation through investment in global common stock and through utilizing an options strategy

Role in Portfolio
Premium

Monthly Premium/Discount EXG

More...

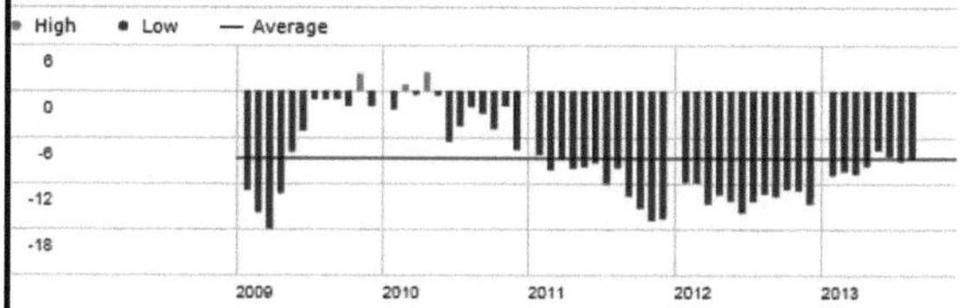

Top Holdings EXG

More...

	Weight %	Last Price	Day Chg %	52-Week Range
Royal Dutch Shell PLC Class B	3.42	—	—	—
Nestle SA	3.15	—	—	—
Roche Holding AG	2.56	—	—	—
HSBC Holdings PLC	2.54	—	—	—
Sanofi	2.21	—	—	—
% Assets in Top 5 Holdings	13.89			

Increase Decrease New to Portfolio
Portfolio Date :07/31/2013, Price data delayed 15 ~ 30 minutes

Key Statistics EXG

Assets

Total Assets USD	3,240.8 mil
Net Assets USD	3,241.0 mil
Market Value USD	2,907.8 mil

Leverage

1940 Act Leverage Ratio	0.00 %
Non-1940 Act Leverage Ratio	0.00 %

Frequency

NAV Update Frequency	DAY
Distribution Payment Frequency	M

Expenses

Total Expense Ratio Reported 2012	1.06 %
Total Expense Ratio Adjusted 2012	1.06 %

Liquidity

Daily Shares Traded As of data not available	—
Average Daily Shares Traded 3 Month	0.87 mil
Average Daily Value Traded USD 3 Month	8.24 mil
Number of Outstanding Common Shares	305.44 mil

Valuation Statistics EXG

	09-20-2013	3-Year Low	3-Year High
Price USD	9.52	7.45	11.55

Style Map EXG

More...

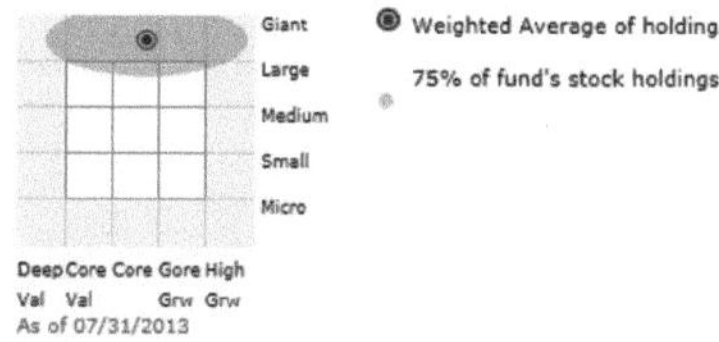

Asset Allocation EXG

More...

Type	% Net	% Short	% Long
Cash	0.14	0.00	0.14
US Stock	42.39	0.00	42.39
Non US Stock	55.49	0.00	55.49
Bond	0.00	0.00	0.00
Other	1.99	0.25	2.23

As of 07/31/2013

Management EXG

More...

Fund Family	Eaton Vance
Manager(s)	Eaton Vance

Distribution EXG

More...

Total Distribution Rate (Share Price)	10.25 %
Total Distribution Rate (NAV)	9.20 %
Current Distribution (Per Share) USD	0.0813
Undistributed Net Investment Income (UNII) per share As of 10/31/2012	$ 0.0004

Policy

Commencing with the Funds first distribution, the Fund intends to make regular quarterly distributions to Common Shareholders sourced from the Funds cash available for distribution. This will consist of the Funds dividends and interest income after payment of Fund expenses, net option premiums, and net realized and unrealized gains on stock investments. The Funds distribution rate may be adjusted from time to time. The Board may modify this distribution policy at any time without obtaining the approval of Common Shareholders. The Fund has applied for an order from the SEC to permit the Fund to include realised long-term capital gains as a part of its regular distributions to Common Shareholders more frequently than would otherwise be permitted. If such an order is obtained, the Fund will consider increasing the frequency of its regular distributions from quarterly to monthly.

Valuation Statistics EXG

	09-20-2013	3-Year Low	3-Year High
Price USD	9.52	7.45	11.55
NAV* USD	10.66	9.03	12.24
Discount/Premium	-10.27%	-17.68%	-1.36%
Z-Statistic (6 Mo)	-1.20	—	—
Z-Statistic (3 Yr)	0.26	—	—

The NAV is-at best-previous day's NAV, but check below to see frequency.

Total Returns EXG More...

	Total Return
Price	-1.65%
NAV	-0.47%
Category Price	-1.09%
Category NAV	-0.51%
Morningstar Benchmark	-0.42%

Time Period: 1D 1M 3M 1Y 3Y 5Y 10Y

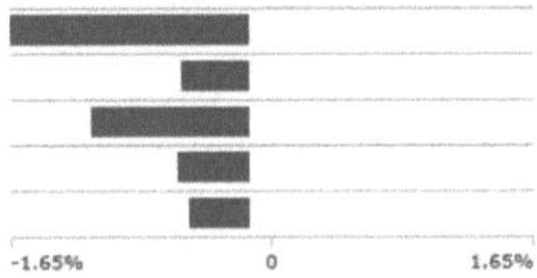

Latest Distributions EXG More...

Ex Date	Income	S/T Cap Gain	L/T Cap Gain	Return Cap	Total
09/19/2013	0.0115	0.0000	0.0000	0.0698	0.0813
08/21/2013	0.0115	0.0000	0.0000	0.0698	0.0813
07/22/2013	0.0115	0.0000	0.0000	0.0698	0.0813
06/19/2013	0.0115	0.0000	0.0000	0.0698	0.0813
05/22/2013	0.0143	0.0000	0.0000	0.0670	0.0813
04/19/2013	0.0144	0.0000	0.0000	0.0669	0.0813
03/19/2013	0.0113	0.0000	0.0000	0.0700	0.0813
02/19/2013	0.0107	0.0000	0.0000	0.0706	0.0813
01/22/2013	0.0120	0.0000	0.0000	0.0693	0.0813
11/20/2012	0.0383	0.0000	0.0000	0.2057	0.2440
08/22/2012	0.0695	0.0000	0.0000	0.1745	0.2440
05/22/2012	0.0503	0.0000	0.0000	0.1937	0.2440

Currency: USD

S&P 500 index data: S&P 500 Copyright © 2013

All data supplied by Morningstar Real-Time Data. U.S. intraday real-time exchange quotes are sourced from BATS when available. End-of-day quotes for Nasdaq, NYSE, and Amex securities will appear 15 minutes after close. Graph times are Eastern Standard. © Copyright 2013 Morningstar, Inc

the SEC to permit the Fund to include realised long-term capital gains as a part of its regular distributions to Common Shareholders more frequently than would otherwise be permitted. If such an order is obtained, the Fund will consider increasing the frequency of its regular distributions from quarterly to monthly.

Operations Information EXG

Domicile	USA
Exchange	ARCA
Launch Date	February 23,2007
IPO PriceUSD	20.00
Financial Year-End	October 31,2013

Figure 6-1. The Morningstar profile of Eaton Vance Tax-Managed Global Dividend Equity Income Fund (ticker symbol: EXG), 9/20/2013[3]. Reprinted with permission of Morningstar Inc.

[3]http://cef.morningstar.com/quote?ops=clear&t=EXG&region=USA&culture=en-US

CHAPTER

7

Unit Investment Trusts

The number of unit investment trusts (UITs) has decreased by over 55% from 1995 to 2012.[1] In 2012, there were a total of 5,787 UITs with assets of $72 billion—paltry in comparison with assets of over $13 trillion in mutual funds, $1.3 trillion in exchange-traded funds (ETFs), and $265 billion in closed-end funds (CEFs). Yet UITs were formerly among the most important of PMAs and even today are appropriate for some investors—particularly retiree investors.

What Is a Unit Investment Trust?

A UIT is a hybrid type of PMA combining some characteristics of mutual funds (Chapters 3–5) and CEFs (Chapter 6). Similarly to mutual funds, UITs issue *redeemable* shares, meaning that these shares (*units* in UIT terminology) are repurchased by the trust and subsequently resold to other investors through a secondary market. Similarly to most CEFs, UITs issue only a *specific and fixed number of shares priced once a day.*

The UIT may be structured either as a **regulated investment company** (RIC) or a grantor trust. Most UITs are RICs in which investors have voting rights but do not have a direct interest in the investments of the trust. A grantor trust provides investors with a proportional ownership of the

[1]*2012 Investment Company Fact Book: A Review of Trends and Activity in the U.S. Investment Company Industry.* Washington, DC: Investment Company Institute (2012). Available at www.ici.org/pdf/2012_factbook.pdf.

underlying securities. (As discussed in Chapter 8, some ETFs are structured in the UIT form, whereas others are structured in the mutual fund form.)

In addition to these characteristics shared with mutual funds and CEFs, UITs feature a sui generis characteristic. A UIT is *self-liquidating*—meaning that the fund (in the form of a trust) terminates at a varying predetermined date based on the assets in the trust. Most UITs terminate after 15 or 24 months in existence. This feature is most observable in a UIT bond fund in which the maturity dates of the bond holdings are known at the time the UIT is established. At the time of *liquidation* (when the fund assets are converted to cash), the proceeds from the assets or securities within the trust are either paid to the trust *unitholders* or reinvested in another trust. The ongoing trend is to distribute the proceeds to the trust unitholders.[2]

There are two primary categories of UITs: bond trusts and equity trusts. *Bond trusts* are further divided into *taxable trusts*, consisting primarily of corporate bonds, and *tax-exempt trusts*, consisting primarily of municipal bonds. The municipal bonds may be insured, thereby decreasing their risk of default. Corporate bonds, however, carry default risk in addition to the other types of investment risks discussed in Chapter 2 and typically are not insured. *Equity trusts*, like stock mutual funds generally, are segregated into domestic and international or global trusts. Many hold bundles of high-yielding assets such as dividend-paying common stocks, preferred stocks, REITs, or *master limited partnerships* (MLPs). (REITs and MLPs are discussed in Chapter 12 of this book.) Beginning in the bull market of the 1990s, equity trust assets have far exceeded those of bond trusts, with equity trusts making up $52 billion of the total $72 billion invested in UITs as of August 2012.[3]

UITs are not as transparent as either mutual funds or ETFs. Investors must obtain UIT price quotes from their broker, and not all UITs even list their prices. For those that do list prices, an investor can typically find a price quote on NASDAQ's Mutual Fund Quotation Service.[4] Most UITs must be purchased through a broker or registered representative of a brokerage firm, although investors may now also purchase units from representatives of firms selling third-party trusts.

---

[2] *2012 Investment Company Fact Book: A Review of Trends and Activity in the U.S. Investment Company Industry*. Washington, DC: Investment Company Institute (2012). Available at www.ici.org/pdf/2012_factbook.pdf.

[3] *2012 Investment Company Fact Book: A Review of Trends and Activity in the U.S. Investment Company Industry*. Washington, DC: Investment Company Institute (2012). Available at www.ici.org/pdf/2012_factbook.pdf.

[4] www.nasdaqtrader.com/.

Advantages of a Unit Investment Trust

Because a UIT is a hybrid investment with some of the characteristics of mutual funds and CEFs, the following six advantages of UITs include some of the advantages of mutual funds and CEFs:

- Professional management of assets
- Diversification
- Economies of scale/reduced transaction costs
- Easy access to assets, not otherwise available to the small investor, with no minimum investment period
- A fixed portfolio with a more stable income stream
- Possibility of purchase of units at a discount

Professional Management

Like other types of PMAs, a UIT offers the small investor access to a professional manager of invested funds, which the investor probably would otherwise not be able to afford. (In contrast, hedge funds are designed for high-income investors who can afford well-known professional managers.) The investment funds are also selected to meet the stated investment objective of the trust—for example, whether it is an equity or bond trust.

As ever, with professional management comes the need for the investor to select a good fund manager. This is not easy, particularly with the multiplicity of funds and fund managers. The choice of management is usually not quite as important with a UIT as with other types of PMAs, because the UIT fund is passively managed and the assets are self-liquidating; but it might be argued that the management choice is *more* critical with a UIT, because changing positive market conditions may not be as easily leveraged as with an actively managed fund. Whatever the relative importance of fund managers, a potential investor in a UIT should be aware of the investment limitations imposed on the trust's manager.

Diversification

Like professional management, diversification is an advantage that UITs have in common with all PMAs. Diversification is designed to minimize risk through the investment of securities both within and across asset classes, such as equities (stocks) and debt (bonds). This advantage is inherent in a UIT and is multiplied by the wide range of UITs that are offered to a potential investor. For example, UIT sponsors typically offer stock or equity UITs in four broad categories—asset allocation, sector, target strategies, and "theme" portfolios—as well as taxable fixed income (bond) and tax-free fixed income (municipal bond) UITs.

These equity and bond portfolios are diversified very similarly to their mutual fund counterparts, except that the UITs are not actively managed and the asset mix is not changed.

Economies of Scale/Reduced Transaction Costs

A UIT is a pooled investment, taking the collective invested monies of many unitholders and managing the total as one trust. With this approach comes the ability to spread the costs of managing the trust among many investors and many assets. These economies of scale may incentivize an investor to purchase PMAs rather than individual stocks or bonds.

The economies of scale of UITs must be balanced against their somewhat higher fees. Although the transaction costs are reduced for all unitholders in a UIT, this same advantage occurs with an index mutual fund or ETF but with much lower overall fees. It is not surprising then that as index funds and ETFs have increased in popularity since the 1990s, the number of UITs has declined. Some of this decrease has occurred because of the self-liquidating nature of UITs and the fact that a number of trusts have now terminated, but the low rate of replacement by new trusts reflects the competitive advantage of index funds and ETFs in providing a low-cost investment vehicle to the small investor.

Easy Access to Assets/No Minimum Investment Period

UITs can invest in a broad array of assets, some of which may not be easily accessible to the small investor. For example, historically, the bond market has been dominated by large institutional investors, such as pension funds, that have the capital necessary to purchase large bond issues. Moreover, bond holdings are traded in large amounts, further restricting the entry of the individual (small) investor into the market. UITs solve these problems by making bonds and fixed-income type products available to the individual investor, usually for only a minimal initial investment. Most trusts also offer the possibility of a systematic or periodic investment program, whereby investors can add to their initial investments through **dollar-cost averaging** (DCA). They then infrequently trade, or do not trade at all, the bond holdings constituting the trust portfolio.

A UIT has no minimum investment period. If an investor/unitholder needs to access his investment in the trust before its scheduled termination, he may do so by selling his units to other investors. But, depending on the market demand for those units, the units may need to be sold at a discount to the fund's NAV. Of course, this is an advantage to the purchaser but a *disadvantage* to the seller. Therefore, like the previous comparison to index mutual funds and ETFs, which also have no minimum investment period, this stated advantage of UITs may not really separate it from its peers.

Fixed Portfolio with a More Stable Income Stream

The funds invested in a UIT are used to purchase a fixed portfolio of assets, either stocks or bonds. As in the case of a CEF, the fixed portfolio of a UIT permits the fund's managers to better adhere to the trust's stated investment objective. Also like CEFs, UITs do not have to manage fund liquidity (maintain a sizeable allocation to cash) to meet potentially large investor redemptions. The principal of a fixed-income portfolio may also be safer because investors know what the values of their units will be at termination of the UIT. Finally, managers of the UIT generally are not subject to changing market conditions and pressures. For example, a bond trust manager does not have to sell the UIT holdings if market pressures otherwise dictate a sale. Maintaining a fixed portfolio is in effect a type of forced buy-and-hold investment strategy for the investor.

Like CEFs, UITs are structured to provide a more stable income stream than other managed products. In the case of an equity trust, it is not subjected to constant cash inflows and outflows over time, which may impact future dividend payments from the underlying assets. This is also why an investor is much more likely to be offered the possibility of a UIT holding preferred stock among its holdings than a mutual fund with the same portfolio. One of the overriding features of a preferred stock is a fixed dividend income right, which amount may be compromised in the event of significant cash outflows from the fund or trust. In the case of a bond trust, however, and particularly one consisting primarily of corporate bonds, the possibility of bond calls by the issuer can threaten the stability and consistency of the fund's income payments.

Possibility of a Discount Purchase of Units

Depending on market conditions as driven by supply and demand for the trust's individual units, the NAV of the trust assets may exceed the cost of buying in to the trust. Thus, there is the possibility of a discount purchase of the trust's individual units. Like any investment asset, if the demand for units of the UIT is weak, the price of those units will be driven down (a similar result occurs if there is an oversupply of the units). This phenomenon may also appear in reverse; that is, if there is a strong demand for the units, the unit price may increase to the point of a premium being necessary to purchase the shares. But as with the possible purchase of CEF shares discussed in Chapter 6, a premium on the units does not present an opportunity to profit unless the investor is anticipating an eventual narrowing of the premium and reversion to the mean price of the units.

If the unit is redeemed, the trust sponsor is required to buy back (redeem) the unit from the investor at the unit's current NAV without any additional fees or commissions. This is in marked contrast to a CEF, which can trade at a significant discount to the fund's NAV in the secondary market. Moreover, CEFs are much more likely than UITs to engage in leverage when purchasing the holdings of the fund, thus potentially increasing the size of the discount in relation to the fund's NAV.

Disadvantages

The major disadvantage of a UIT is the self-liquidating nature of the investment—although this may also be accounted an advantage, depending on the investor's perspective. When the assets in the trust mature, the investment is terminated and the investor has the following choices:

> *Option #1: Roll over the units into another trust at a reduced sales charge*. The investor may roll over their units into a new series of units in the same trust (if it continues) or into other UITs from the same sponsor in the primary or IPO market. Note, however, that the term *roll over* here is really a misnomer because the term usually implies a tax-free exchange of the investment from one fund or plan to another. This is not the case with a UIT because at the time of transfer or re-investment, a taxable event occurs.
>
> *Option #2: Do nothing*. In this case, the unitholder allows the portfolio units to mature and receives a cash distribution from the trust proceeds.
>
> *Option #3: Receive an in-kind distribution*. Unitholders may generally request an in-kind distribution of securities in the trust if they own at least 2,500 units at the time of purchase or maturity. This is similar to the distribution possible with an ETF (see Chapter 8) and generally results in a tax advantage to the unitholder.

In addition to the self-liquidating disadvantage (or advantage, depending on the investor's goals), UITs have other disadvantages such as

- High cost base
- Restriction on the purchase of additional units
- A fixed portfolio that is not responsive to changing market conditions

High Cost Base

A UIT is sold by a broker who earns a *commission* (sales charge) on the sale of units to an investor, similar to a load charge on a mutual fund. This is the first of three fees charged by a UIT. The other two are a *repurchase fee* (deferred sales charge) when the units of the fund are redeemed and a *creation and development fee*. The initial service charge (load) on a UIT can be as high as 3.95% of the NAV. The deferred sales charge is a percentage charge typically based on the trust's *public offering price* (POP), which is higher than the trust's NAV. The creation and development fee is a dollar charge per unit collected at the end of the initial offering period associated with the trust and can be as much as much as 1% of the POP. Add all these expenses together, and a UIT can be an expensive vehicle in which to invest.

The good news is that annual management expenses charged by the UIT are typically lower than those charged by a mutual fund. The annual UIT expenses are often just 0.25% to 0.30% of assets managed by the trust, as compared to the 1.4% average of mutual funds. In addition, because there is generally no trading by a UIT manager, few if any transaction costs are incurred by the trust. As for some mutual funds, there is also a reduction in the sales charges if the investor contributes more than $50,000 initially to the trust.

Remember also that a UIT is a passively managed (not actively managed) fund. Therefore, an additional *opportunity cost* is incurred in not pursuing cheaper passively managed alternatives, such as an index mutual fund or ETF.

Restriction on the Purchase of Additional Units

As with a CEF, the units of a UIT are first offered to investors through an initial public offering (IPO). Subsequent to the IPO, a UIT sponsor may offer additional units to investors but is not required to by law. Given that the purpose of the trust is to issue only a certain number of units, many UIT sponsors do not offer investors the opportunity to purchase more units. Thus, an investor who wants to make multiple investments in a trust can sometimes end up owning more than one UIT, also increasing the cost of ownership.

If an investor is allowed to purchase more units of a UIT, he or she must typically purchase those units from a broker and pay a commission. In addition, across all UITs, the purchase price is not competitive; rather, a more standardized pricing approach is adopted in the industry.

Fixed Portfolio Not Responsive to Changing Market Conditions

The fixed portfolio characteristic of a UIT has already been considered in its advantageous light to an income investor—that is, an investor who desires a predictable (and hopefully higher) income stream, such as bond trusts and equity trusts generating a steady stream of dividends. However, the fixed portfolio characteristic may also impose a disadvantage because the same stocks or bonds are held by the trust until the trust's termination or liquidation. If the company issuing the stocks or bonds encounters financial problems, the trust usually has no way to dispose of the troubled asset, leading to a decline in the trust's NAV (and probably a reduction in the unit price). The same disadvantage results at the market or *macro* level when the UIT's portfolio cannot be modified because of changing market conditions.

As a rule, an investor should not consider the purchase of a UIT unless he or she believes in the fundamental validity of passive management techniques. Such management, which can be followed in the case of either equities or bonds, attempts to design a portfolio that *replicates* the performance of a specific index or investment strategy. A passive manager earns his or her fee by constructing a portfolio that closely tracks a *benchmark index*. Given the multiplicity of UITs, and their investment objectives, a passive manager must choose a replicating index. The use of the proper index is also very important when attempting to evaluate the performance of a UIT, as discussed later in this chapter. Fortunately, as investors have embraced passive management techniques, portfolio managers have created an index or investment strategy for virtually every market category of assets.

The techniques of constructing a passive portfolio for an equity trust are inherently complex and require the use of sophisticated technology. The most basic technique, however, is that of *full replication*, whereby all the securities in the benchmark index are purchased by the trust portfolio manager in proportion to the weights in the index. Other techniques, such as sampling or quadratic programming, can also be used. Bond trust techniques are simpler to implement, such as *indexing*, where a bond portfolio is created that attempts to equal the performance of a specified bond index. In both types of trust, the fixed nature of the UIT portfolio often proves to be an advantage in terms of reducing transaction costs when constructing the portfolio but also a potential disadvantage because changing market or company conditions cannot be easily accommodated by the portfolio manager.

Who Should Purchase a Unit Investment Trust?

The profile of a suitable candidate to purchase a UIT is a long-term investor who is interested in a steady income stream and who believes in the effectiveness of passive portfolio-management techniques. Gains from an investment in UITs are not realized immediately but are deferred until the fund liquidates. During the term of the investment, an investor can sell the units to another investor but usually would do so only if the price of the units increased from their purchase price. This could happen, although the movement of the share price is typically dependent on supply and demand factors separate from market movements. Operationally, this means that any movement in unit prices lags that of market prices, particularly in a bullish market. The investor may also sell units to the trust at their current NAV before the trust's termination, although this value may be lower than the investor's initial cost.

What type of investor fits the profile of a long-term investor interested in a steady income stream? A retiree or an investor approaching his or her retirement years is the most obvious candidate to purchase a UIT. The type of UIT in which the retiree is most likely to be interested is a bond trust or, perhaps, an equity trust consisting of high-dividend-paying common stock, preferred stock, or REITs. A bond trust is best purchased by a retiree if there is a low risk of bond default, possibly suggesting either an insured municipal bond trust or a corporate bond trust consisting only of investment-grade bonds. However, given the risk-return tradeoff, a retiree purchasing such a trust sacrifices possible yield or income return. The alternative of a preferred stock UIT offers the possibility of a greater yield, but preferred stock suffers from more extreme volatility in price than bonds. Finally, an investor considering the possible purchase of a UIT should compare the advantages and disadvantages of that type of PMA to those of index mutual funds and ETFs. But for the self-liquidating feature of UITs (and the possibility of a discount purchase of the trust units), index mutual funds and ETFs may accomplish the same financial objectives of the investor at a lower overall cost.

What Selection Criteria Should Be Used before Purchasing a Unit Investment Trust?

An investor considering the purchase of a UIT should weight the following selection criteria:

- Loss of control
- Length of investment or investment time horizon
- A belief in passive management theory and strategies
- Selection of investment objective
- Comparison to index mutual fund and ETFs

Loss of Control

The loss of control that occurs with a UIT investment is a characteristic common to all PMAs. If you are a do-it-yourself investor, a UIT or any other type of PMA is, therefore, probably not for you! However, ask yourself why you believe that you are best able to make investment decisions and then manage those investments, when you are likely not educated or trained to do so. Do you really believe that you are a better investor than professional portfolio managers who study the market every day and have the education and credentials to specialize in just such a discipline? Many portfolio managers devote every waking minute of the day to making and managing investments and monitoring international markets. Can you, or do you want to, do the same?

A characteristic that better warrants an investor's scrutiny for purposes of comparing different types of PMAs and different funds of a given type is the total amount of expenses charged by the trust and portfolio manager to manage your investment. A UIT sometimes has a higher expense ratio than either an index mutual fund or ETF, but the advantages of self-liquidation, a predictable income stream, and knowing when you will receive the proceeds from a UIT may be worth this additional cost. If so, you should then be comparing the expense ratio of one UIT as compared to another. The rule that bond funds are less expensive to manage than equity funds holds for UITs: bond trusts are usually less expensive to operate than equity trusts. Therefore, you also want to know the UIT's investment objective before you consider a purchase of its respective units. Of course, the tradeoff for the loss of control in a UIT is that the broker and brokerage firm offering the UIT now do all the work that the investor would otherwise have to do.

Length of Investment and Investor Time Horizon

A UIT's length of investment—that is, how long the trust lasts before it self-liquidates—should match the investor's time horizon. This is why bond trusts potentially have such appeal to retirees and pre-retirees. Such individuals can budget for a significant cash inflow (receipt of principal) at some point in the future, while enjoying the income return during the term of the trust. There is, of course, some possibility that the bond trust's NAV will decline if market interest rates increase in the interim; but if the bonds feature a low duration, the bond price decline may not be significant. Moreover, the volatility of the bond trust should not be as extreme as that experienced by an equity trust where the NAV rises or falls based on market prices of the individual stocks making up the equity trust's portfolio. If the value of the stocks were to rise at the time of liquidation of the trust, the investor would earn a profit. However, if stock prices were to decline, a disadvantage of the equity trust is that trust management cannot wait beyond the liquidation date to recover the lost NAV.

As with any potential investment plan, the investor should prepare an **investment policy statement** (IPS) with the assistance of a professional advisor. The investor's time horizon and asset allocations should be included in the IPS, and the UIT portfolio should be rebalanced in accordance with the specified asset allocations. Fortunately, rebalancing in a UIT is relatively simple: when the portfolio of assets in the trust terminates, the investor has the option to reinvest the proceeds into a new, rebalanced UIT, typically at a reduced sales expense charged by the broker. Still, it is important to emphasize again that this rebalancing constitutes a taxable event unless units of the trust are purchased using a tax-deferred investment vehicle, such as an IRA or 401(k) retirement plan.

Belief in Passive Management and Passive Management Strategies

The techniques or strategies of passive management were discussed in the "Fixed Portfolio Not Responsive to Changing Market Conditions" section of this chapter. An investor considering the purchase of a UIT should understand the underlying principles of passive management and believe in the efficacy of those principles before proceeding. As discussed in Chapter 4, at the heart of passive management theory is a belief that the market is "reasonably efficient"—meaning that if it is possible to outperform the market on a long-term basis, the method of doing so is not immediately apparent. A purchase of units in a UIT is a demonstrated acceptance of this belief, because the trust portfolio manager does not attempt to outperform the market index, only to replicate it. This same approach is taken by portfolio managers of an index mutual fund and ETF, although how the approach is put into practice does vary somewhat from that of the UIT.

The alternative to passive management is, of course, active management, as practiced by the majority of mutual fund portfolio managers. A potential investor in UITs, index mutual funds, or ETFs (Chapter 8) should review Chapters 3 and 4 to appreciate how few active managers are able to outperform the market on an after-tax and after-expense fee basis over time.

Selection of Investment Objective

A further consideration in the selection of an appropriate UIT is the trust's investment objective. Equity trusts invest in the common stock of companies and pass along applicable voting rights to the unitholder. But as for mutual funds, the investment objective of such trusts can vary from aggressive growth to equity income (dividend-paying stocks). Moreover, an investor needs to decide whether to invest only in domestic equity trusts or also in those that feature international or global holdings.

In contrast, bond trusts break down into taxable and tax-free offerings. The decision between these two subtypes has historically been driven by income-tax considerations—for example, an individual in a higher tax bracket would prefer a tax-free UIT. In recent years, however, income yield considerations have played an increasingly larger role in the decision-making process of investors.

How does a potential investor know the investment objective of the UIT? Under the 1940 Act, all unit trust sponsors, like all mutual funds, are required to issue a **prospectus** to prospective investors. This is part of the IPO process. At the time of purchasing units, the investor is required to be provided with this prospectus. Prior to purchase, the prospective investor should consult the portfolio objective in the fact sheet usually provided by the trust sponsor. This fact sheet is a brief summary of the trust prospectus that otherwise must be provided under law. In addition, if considering an existing UIT, the investor should review the current holdings of the trust to ensure that it is actually complying with the investment objective. One of the cited advantages of a fixed portfolio and a potential UIT investment is that style drift of the portfolio manager is prevented, unlike what may occur in an actively managed mutual fund. However, before purchasing units in an existing UIT, a prospective investor should compare the actual trust holdings to its investment objective to ensure that style drift is not in fact taking place.

Comparison to Index Mutual Funds and ETFs

UITs are the third of the three investment company types authorized and regulated by the 1940 Act. A UIT resembles a CEF in structure and an index mutual fund or ETF in operation. Thus, for purposes of evaluating your opportunity cost of investment, it is useful to tabulate the characteristics of UITs in comparison to those of mutual funds (bearing in mind that an index mutual fund is a type of mutual fund) and ETFs (Table 7-1).

Table 7-1. Comparison of UITs, Closed-End Funds, Mutual Funds, and ETFs

CHARACTERISTIC	UITs	CLOSED-END	MUTUAL FUND	ETFs
Diversification	Yes	Yes	Yes	Yes
Expenses	Relatively high	Relatively high	Depends (index fund low)	Low
Sell at discount to NAV	Yes	Yes	No	Depends (slightly)
Self-liquidating	Yes	No	No	No

(continued)

Table 7-1. (*continued*)

CHARACTERISTIC	UITs	CLOSED-END	MUTUAL FUND	ETFs
Fixed number of shares	Yes	Yes	No	No
Passive management	Yes	No	No (unless index fund)	Yes (usually)
Predictable income stream	Yes (if bond trust)	Yes (if bond fund)	No (generally)	No (generally)
Trades like a stock	No	Yes	No	Yes

How to Evaluate the Performance of a Unit Investment Trust

In a word, evaluating the past performance of a UIT is difficult! Neither *Morningstar* nor *Thomson Reuters* tracks or reports the performance of UITs as they do for mutual funds, CEFs, and ETFs. The UIT sponsor may provide performance tracking for the trusts it offers, but those are only a small fraction of the total number of UITs. For the most part, the real performance history of UITs is beset by a lack of transparency. This is a major disadvantage in deciding, first, whether to invest in *any* UIT and, second, in which *particular* UIT to invest. UIT sponsors frequently use *back tests* to substitute for the actual performance of trust holdings. Back tests use "what-if" analysis—that is, if the UIT had existed in the past, "this" (insert an annualized return here) is how the UIT would have performed. Moreover, the UIT's actual composition may be manipulated so that a high performance record may be constructed. The beginning and end dates for this historical performance may also be uniquely chosen to maximize the reported gains of the trust.

With this caveat in mind, if you trust the annual performance returns reported for the particular UIT, you should compare this performance number against that of a relevant benchmark index (and preferably two indexes). Whatever index is used should match the investment objective of the given UIT and the general composition of its portfolio holdings.

Notwithstanding the possible lack of reliable performance information for the typical UIT, let's look at some important metrics that may be used to differentiate among UIT choices, such as distribution per unit amounts, dividend and income yields, and volume discounts.

Estimated Net First-Year Distribution and Subsequent-Year Distribution per Unit

It is typically a fact that the first-year distribution amount per unit of any UIT will be *more* than that of subsequent years per unit. Why is this so? The reason for this disparity is because a portion of the securities or holdings of the UIT portfolio must be sold during the first year to pay for organizational and other costs associated with offering the UIT to investors. This is analogous to a surrender charge being imposed for early redemptions from a mutual fund. Moreover, every UIT fact sheet and subsequent prospectus includes a disclaimer that there is no guarantee that the issuers of the securities included in the portfolio will declare distributions in the future.

Thus, the distribution amount per unit in subsequent years will always be *less* than the first-year distribution amount—meaning in the case of a bond fund that the investor's realized income yield will be less than that paid out initially. Subsequent distributions may not even be paid. Finally, a prospective UIT investor should compare the first-year distribution amount to the maximum sales charge imposed by the trust. This distribution amount should be compared net of charge—typically consisting of a separate initial transaction fee, a deferred percentage sales charge, and the previously mentioned creation and development fee. Although the maximum sales charge is sometimes reduced if the UIT is positioned as part of an investor's advisory or wrap account, the investor still will not receive the full amount of first-year distribution amount paid by the trust.

Dividend and Income Yields

When using a discounted-cash-flow approach to valuation of the holdings in a UIT, the present value of the trust is determined by its future cash flows discounted at the investor's appropriate required rate of return. The cash flows generated by a UIT depend on whether the holdings consist of stocks, corporate bonds, or municipal bonds. If stocks reflect the concentration of holdings in the trust, the future cash flows consist of a dividend yield and a potential capital gains yield (or loss). Alternatively, corporate and municipal bonds generate an income or interest yield as well as a possible capital gains yield if, among other factors, market interest rates decline from the date of purchase. A distinguishing factor between corporate and municipal bonds is the tax-free nature of the income yield of municipal bonds under federal tax law.

Many UITs are invested in municipal bonds generating an income or interest yield. As such, the use of a conversion table in equating tax-free yields to taxable equivalent yield is very helpful and illustrates the benefit to a higher-income investor of purchasing units of the trust. (The higher the taxpayer's marginal income-tax bracket, the more advantageous is a purchase of the units.) The proper comparison is then between a UIT purchasing municipal bonds and an ETF investing in the same asset class and the corresponding income yield (and expenses) of the respective investment choices.

There is one other important point with respect to a trust's holdings of municipal bonds. Sometimes the portfolio objective of a UIT states that "certain distributions paid by certain funds may be subject to federal income taxes *and alternative minimum tax (AMT).*" As a result, when evaluating the performance of the fund, the more relevant benchmark index to be used may be a municipal bond index that also includes so-called *AMT bonds* (bonds whose interest is considered as a tax-preference item for purposes of individual alternative minimum tax), such as the Barclay's Municipal Bond Index. Of course, if an investor does not want to see his income yield reduced by the imposition of the individual AMT, he should check the underlying holdings of the trust to ensure that such bonds are not part of the portfolio.

Finally, what are you to expect as a realistic future annualized return on the portfolio holdings in the trust? The answer to this question depends on an understanding of those factors that impact bond prices generally, such as the interest-rate sensitivity of the bonds and the price risk inherent in bonds. *Micro* or company-specific factors, such as business and financial risk, also impact the price of bonds and the trust's future NAV. (Chapter 5 discusses the factors that impact bond prices and the NAV of a bond fund.)

Volume Discounts

Most UITs, like mutual funds and CEFs, offer a reduction in the maximum sales charge with a greater initial purchase. For example, if an investor makes an initial purchase of at least $100,000 but less than $250,000, he or she receives a discount of 50 basis points (0.50%) from the standard maximum sales charge of 3.95%. The decision whether to take advantage of such a discount may be viewed from two opposing perspectives. From the positive perspective, any volume discount achieved redounds to the investor's benefit because that discount amount does not have to be overcome by the fund's or trust's investment performance. From the negative perspective, the investor incurs the opportunity cost of not investing a rather sizeable amount of funds (here, at least $100,000) in a lower-cost vehicle. The opportunity cost may be recovered if the UIT outperforms an alternative investment choice, but remember that this may be difficult to determine, given that the actual performance of any UIT is not readily observable and may be open to question when merely reported.

This concludes the discussion of the UIT investment vehicle. Chapter 3 showed the inverse correlation since 1996 between the decline in the number of UITs and the explosion in the number of ETFs. The next chapter examines the considerations involved in choosing whether to invest in the most rapidly growing PMA type: the ETF.

CHAPTER

8

Exchange-Traded Funds

Exchange-traded funds (ETFs) are currently the most rapidly growing type of professionally managed asset, According to the Investment Company Institute (ICI) statistics presented in Chapter 3., total net assets invested in ETFs have exploded from approximately $83 billion in 2001 to over $1.3 trillion in 2012. The number of ETFs has also increased from 359 to over 1,200 by the end of 2012.

In this chapter, I deviate slightly from the method of discussion for each PMA outlined in Chapter 6. After defining an ETF, I distinguish it from its close cousins—*exchange-traded notes* (ETNs) and *holding company depository receipts* (HOLDRs)—as well as from mutual funds more broadly.

What Is an Exchange-Traded Fund?

An *exchange-traded fund* is a security that represents ownership in a basket of stocks. The fund typically tracks an index, such as the S&P 500 index of large capitalization stocks. However, unlike an index fund priced at its NAV at the end of the day, an ETF trades like a stock, meaning that it trades throughout the day and is priced at that moment in time. Also, like a stock, an ETF experiences price changes throughout the day, permitting traders to take advantage of daily market fluctuations. ETF shares trading at a price *above* their NAV are said to be trading *at a premium*, whereas shares trading at a price *below* their NAV are said to be trading *at a discount*. This is consistent with the terminology applied to closed-end funds (Chapter 6), although the NAV of a CEF (like that of an index mutual fund) is determined only once at the end of the trading day. Like other investment company offerings, however, ETFs must comply with the provisions of the Investment Company Act of 1940.

Originally, ETFs were passively managed, meaning there was no attempt to outperform the tracked index. In 2008, the now-defunct Bear Stearns Investments introduced the first actively managed ETF. In 2012 there were 61 actively managed ETFs. In addition, more ETFs are now *leveraged*, meaning the fund is making purchases of the basket of stocks with borrowed money (using debt). A specific type of leveraged fund is known as an *inverse fund*. This type of leveraged fund is structured to perform inversely or opposite to the direction of the index that the fund is tracking, although there are also leveraged funds that move in the same direction as the tracked index. Leveraged funds are often designed in multiples of the percentage movement, depending on whether the market index increases or decreases. In investment terminology, *going long* means you own the security and are hoping market prices increase. A *double long inverse fund* means the investor will receive a percentage return of twice the actual annualized return of a market increasing in price. *Going short* means you want to own the security and are hoping market prices decrease. A *double short inverse fund* means a return of twice the percentage of a market declining in price will be theoretically received by the investor.

In practice, however, the percentage return received by the investor is less than 200% (in the double short inverse fund) because compounding applies. For example, SPXL is a 3 times positive leveraged fund tracking the S&P 500 index of 500 large-capitalization stocks. Over the 3 years 2011–2013 to date, SPXL has returned a total of 43.59 % as compared to 17.40% for the index. Thus, the investor would expect a total NAV return of 52.20% (0.1740 times 3) if the fund actually returned 3 times the index return.

As of 2013, the three largest issuers of ETFs were BlackRock, Inc., State Street Global Advisors, and Vanguard Funds. Respectively, the brand names of the ETFs issued by each company are iShares, SPDRs (for Standard & Poor's Depository Receipts), and Vanguard ETFs. ETFs also offer an alternative to mutual funds and closed-end investment companies that offer foreign securities. Initially, iShares were issued by Barclays Bank of Scotland and tracked a specific foreign index, such as the European, Asia, and Far East (EAFE) index. The largest ETF by asset size is currently SPDR S&P 500, ticker symbol SPY, a type of stock index-based ETF. Figure 8-1 at the end of this chapter is a profile of this fund.

Exchange-Traded Funds vs. Exchange-Traded Notes

An **exchange-traded note** (ETN) is so similar to an ETF that commonly they are lumped together under the heading of *exchange-traded products*. Nevertheless, there is one huge difference between an ETN and an ETF. An ETN is a *debt* security, whereas an ETF is a *stock* or equity security. Therefore, an ETN behaves more like a bond or bond fund than a stock or stock fund, with metrics such as yield to maturity and duration much more important than is typically the case with a stock-based security such as the traditional ETF.

Like a bond holder, the purchaser of an ETN is in the position of a creditor, meaning he or she can enforce payment should the issuer default. But unlike a bond holder, who is paid the fixed rate of interest (coupon rate) specified in the bond indenture, the owner of an ETN is paid according to a different measure, usually the rate of return commensurate with the underlying index. For example, Barclays Bank—which issues a series of commodity ETNs known as *iPath* (one of which is the iPath Pure Beta Crude Oil ETN)—promises to pay the owner according to how much the price of the commodity (such as crude oil) goes up or down, less fund expenses. Therefore, as emphasized in the discussion in Chapters 4 and 5 of the characteristics of bonds and bond funds, the financial stability of the ETN's issuer (like that of a bond issuer) is critical. As a potential owner of an ETN, buy only from solid companies and, even then, practice good diversification strategies.

True to its exchange-traded form and tracking of indexes, ETNs are often segregated into commodity ETNs, currency ETNs, fixed-income ETNs, and alternative (investments) ETNs. They also may practice leverage strategies, permitting you to double or triple your invested monies by going either long (and, therefore, profiting in a bull market) or short (profiting in a bear market). But be careful. Remember: leverage permits investors to dramatically increase their return, but they also suffer equally if the market index declines.

Exchange-Traded Funds vs. Holding Company Depository Receipts

Holding company depository receipts (HOLDRs) are very similar to ETFs but focus only on narrow industry groups. Moreover, unlike ETFs, HOLDRs do not track indexes, but consist of baskets of only about 20 or more stocks to represent a sector or industry in the overall market. Although HOLDRs trade like stocks or ETFs, they may only be bought in *round lots* (unit groups of 100 shares), versus an ETF, where as little as 1 share may be purchased. Finally, HOLDRs do not have to calculate their daily NAVs, making it very difficult for investors to determine whether the securities are trading at a discount or premium relative to their underlying portfolio of stocks.

HOLDRs were made popular by Merrill Lynch Securities (now Bank of America Merrill Lynch) and are organized not as mutual funds or ETFs, but as grantor trusts. Thus, HOLDRs are exempt from the requirements of the Investment Company Act of 1940 that apply to mutual funds and ETFs. This means that HOLDRs can and do become very concentrated, with potentially only a very small number of portfolio stocks after any mergers or acquisitions of originally owned stocks. Merrill Lynch also does not sell HOLDR stocks after they appreciate in value, meaning that only a couple of stocks can dominate the portfolio. Any diversification advantage inherent with either a mutual fund or an ETF is therefore minimized with a HOLDR.

Two major advantages are associated with a HOLDR as compared to the typical ETF: there is no management fee, and investors can obtain direct ownership of approximately 20 stocks for only one brokerage commission (or "20 stocks for the price of one"). An investor may also take delivery of the individual securities making up the HOLDR, thereby leading to potential arbitrage opportunities. HOLDRs are also relatively tax-efficient because they rarely make capital gains distributions to owner/investors. Nevertheless, the extremely low management fee of a passively managed ETF and its diversification advantage over a HOLDR have led to a dying out of this latter form of security. In addition, as discussed in the "Advantages of an Exchange-Traded Fund" section of this chapter, ETFs are more tax-efficient than HOLDRs.

Exchange-Traded Funds vs. Mutual Funds

Table 8-1 lists the differences between an ETF and its major alternative PMA investment, an open-ended investment company (mutual fund). The fundamental difference between ETFs and mutual funds comes down to passive versus active management and the fees incurred by these alternative management strategies. As discussed in Chapter 4, the higher fees typically associated with mutual funds may be minimized by investing in index mutual funds. ETFs use indexing while simultaneously affording investors the flexibility of stock trading and tax-efficiency. It is therefore not surprising that ETFs are rapidly growing in popularity among the investing public.

Table 8-1. Comparison of ETFs and Mutual Funds

Characteristic	ETFs	Mutual Funds
Diversification	Yes	Yes
Trades like a stock	Yes	No
Minimum investment	No	Yes
Load fees	No	Yes
Tax efficiency	Yes	No (unless index fund)
Passive management	Yes	No (unless index fund)

Advantages of an Exchange-Traded Fund

The advantages of ETFs are many. In addition to the advantages of diversification, indexing and its associated low cost, and flexibility of trading like a stock (enhanced liquidity), there are two significant tax advantages:

- Redemption of ETF shares
- Ability to avoid distributing capital gains to investors

Redemption of ETF Shares

ETF shares are typically redeemed for the shares of the underlying stocks making up the ETF portfolio (*in-kind redemption*). This does not create a taxable event because the ETF does not need to sell its share holdings. In practical effect, the in-kind redemption is the equivalent of a *tax-free exchange* of shares. Therefore, the only time a shareholder pays capital gains tax on the appreciation of stocks in the ETF portfolio is when the portfolio sells any stocks, which is a rare event. Low to nonexistent turnover is a hallmark of most ETFs. Moreover, daily market pressures generally keep ETFs trading at very close to their NAVs. (This is in marked contrast to closed-end funds, as discussed in Chapter 6.) If turnover of ETF shares does take place, and the share price is in excess of the index's underlying NAV, the ETF's ability to redeem the shares for the stocks in the index typically negates the payment of any capital gains tax at the shareholder level.

There is one notable exception to the favorable tax redemption of most ETFs. Those ETFs that invest in actual commodities instead of commodity index funds, and distribute those commodities, tax the investor at a flat rate of 28%. However, this is not unique to actual commodity ETFs, because if an investor directly purchases commodities, such as gold or silver bullion, and then sells the bullion at a profit, the same 28% flat tax is incurred. This is yet another reason why, absent a fetish for bullion, the typical investor should purchase only gold index ETFs or mutual funds and not the metal itself.

Finally, fixed-income-type ETFs investing only in bonds and then distributing the interest from the bonds to the ETF shareholders are not nearly as tax-efficient as stock-index-type ETFs. This is because bond interest is taxed at the shareholder level as ordinary income and does not qualify for the more favorable long-term capital gains tax rate as do stock appreciation and certain dividends declared on stock.

Avoidance of Capital Gains to Shareholders

As discussed in the preceding section, the legal structure of ETFs allows them to avoid distributing capital gains to shareholders who are not selling their shares at the shareholder level. Both ETFs and index mutual funds typically have a very low turnover of stocks, but when an ETF does sell a stock, the redemption feature can be used. This is not possible with an index mutual fund that must sometimes sell stocks to cover redemption requests by shareholders in the form of cash. For example, consider an ETF shareholder owning 100 shares of SPY, whose NAV has increased from $25/share to $35/share for a total capital gain of $1,000 (100 shares times $10 per-share gain). The ETF can redeem the shares for stocks in the SPY portfolio and avoid distributing the capital gains to the shareholder. In contrast, an index mutual fund holding the same stocks that are part of the SPY portfolio must sell enough stock to convert the gain into $1,000 cash in order to satisfy any shareholder redemption request.

Lower Expenses

It should be reiterated that lower expenses are a primary advantage of ETFs as compared to the typical mutual fund. As noted, the typical mutual fund is actively managed, resulting in a higher average expense ratio of 1.4% of fund assets. From the investor standpoint, this means you pay $14 in annual fees for every $1,000 invested. In contrast, the average expense ratio of an ETF is approximately a full percentage point *lower* than that of a mutual fund, or 0.4%. This results in a saving of $10 for every $1,000 invested ($1,000 times 0.004 = $4).

This advantage cannot be overstated, because the cost of investing in any professionally managed asset is the one expense that is in the control of the investor and not the fund. There is an immediate savings of 1% in purchasing an ETF rather than a non-index-type mutual fund—a savings that is compounded over time if the performance of the ETF is equal to that of the mutual fund.

Disadvantages of an Exchange-Traded Fund

The disadvantages of ETFs include the following:

- Payment of commissions on the purchase of ETF shares
- Disparity between the bid and ask prices of ETF shares, and the possible trading of the ETF shares at a premium or discount to the NAV of the ETF
- Lack of automatic reinvestment of ETF shares

Commissions on ETF shares

Because ETFs trade like stocks, investors who purchase ETFs must pay commissions just as if they purchased an individual stock. This causes problems for investors who make systematic contributions to retirement plans, like a 401(k) plan. In addition, the low fees and expenses associated with an ETF may result in an overtrading of the shares in a non-retirement (taxable) account. In other words, the attractiveness of ETFs as an investment choice may result in "churning" of the investor's account, thereby incurring higher commissions. Of course, if the investor is disciplined and not speculating in the market with excessive trading, this disadvantage may be minimized.

The good news is that, as for mutual fund expenses generally, competition has been driving down the cost of trading commissions for both ETFs and stocks. In some instances, the cost of an online trade may be as little as $10, and commission-free ETFs are becoming more prevalent. Still, an investor who is engaged in systematic investing, such as dollar-cost averaging, should be careful not to overdo the amount of trading in an ETF.

Disparity between Bid and Ask Prices and Possible Discount/Premium to NAV

ETFs are sold at their market price. This is in contrast to a mutual fund sold at its NAV. As discussed in the "Redemption of ETF Shares" section of this chapter, market competition usually keeps the market price of an ETF very close to the fund's NAV. At times, however, the two prices may diverge, resulting in the ETF's market price exceeding its NAV; in this case, as mentioned earlier, the fund shares are said to be trading at a premium to the fund value. An investor needs to be aware of this possibility and try not to purchase ETFs shares that are trading at a premium if at all possible.

Like any individual stock, ETFs are sold at the bid price and bought at the ask price. Because the bid-ask price is determined from the standpoint of the broker/dealer (and not the investor), the bid price is always *lower* than the ask price. The bid price is below the market price, and the ask price is above the market price. This permits the broker/dealer to profit from the spread between the two prices. From the standpoint of the investor purchasing ETF shares, the disparity in bid and ask prices (known in investment terminology as *the spread*) represents a trading cost in addition to the normal trading fee. Can ETF shares sell at a discount or premium to NAV? I have already hinted that the answer to this question is yes, but any discount or premium should be relatively small. An ETF typically permits large financial institution shareholders to exchange shares in the companies that make up the ETF's portfolio (see the redemption of shares tax advantage discussed earlier). As a result of increased demand for the ETF shares, they could be selling for a premium. However, when they do, a financial institution should buy the underlying shares of the existing ETF and create new ETF shares. They then profit on the difference between the cost of the underlying stock in the existing ETF (after exchanging the stock shares for the ETF shares) and the proceeds from the sale of the new ETF shares. If the ETF shares are selling at a discount, the financial institutions simply reverses the process. As a result, these actions by the financial institutions eventually return the price of ETF shares to the NAV of the ETF securities in the portfolio.

Lack of Automatic Reinvestment

Most mutual funds permit automatic reinvestment of the fund's annual capital gains and income dividends to purchase additional shares under a *dividend reinvestment program* (DRIP). Historically, ETFs have not offered this option. Although this is not a significant issue with respect to capital gains distribution from an ETF (as mentioned, ETFs are usually very tax-efficient in this regard), it can be a problem with income dividend payments. Currently, the dividend income received from the underlying stocks or bonds in an ETF is distributed to the shareholder. The frequency of such payments depends on the ETF, but the ability to purchase additional shares with the dividend income is thereby limited. This may be a reason for a potential investor to consider an index mutual fund instead of an ETF: the ability to reinvest with the index fund may outweigh the slightly lower expenses of the ETF.

Who Should Purchase an Exchange-Traded Fund?

ETFs are attractive to investors who are interested in the advantages of indexing: low cost, no minimum investment, and tax-efficiency. They are also attractive to investors who want an alternative to managing a large number of individual stocks, bonds, or commodities as part of their portfolio. ETFs can also be an effective method of rebalancing a portfolio and making it more concentrated with respect to a specific sector of the market or international markets. They can also be leveraged, potentially magnifying the potential return of the investor.

A leveraged ETF should, however, only be purchased by an investor with a short-term time horizon. In a flat market in which prices essentially move sideways (no discernible direction up or down), a leveraged ETF generates losses for investors because of the mathematical reality of how much any asset that has previously lost value must recover to return to the previous price. For example, suppose the S&P 500 index that is tracked by a particular ETF declines by 4 percentage points from 1500 to 1440. To recover the number loss of 60 (1500 – 1440), there must be a percentage gain of 4.17% (60 divided by 1440). If the ETF is leveraged and generates a return twice the daily performance of the S& P 500, this means a realized percentage loss of 8 percentage points with a percentage gain of almost 8.7% (120 divided by 1380) to recover.

From a theoretical viewpoint, investors who purchase ETFs are implicitly demonstrating a belief in the efficiency of the market and the effectiveness of passive versus active portfolio management. There are exceptions, inasmuch as more ETFs are now being actively managed.

Investors who are concerned about risk should avoid ETFs that practice leveraging (using borrowed money and derivatives to make fund purchases), because the extent of potential losses from that type of fund is magnified.

What Selection Criteria Should Be Used before Purchasing an Exchange-Traded Fund?

The major selection criteria that should be used by an investor considering the purchase of an ETF include the following, which are discussed in turn:

- Diversification
- Trading volume
- Product and legal structure
- Valuation
- Cost

Diversification

Like index mutual funds, ETFs provide an efficient way to invest in the broader stock or bond market. They also may be used to invest in a specific part of the market, such as small-capitalization stocks, or a sector of the market, such as energy or health care. However, an investor must be careful: a considerable number of ETFs are not broadly diversified (such as an ETF that tracks a certain sector of the market), and thus the investor may not minimize total risk as much as with a broader-based index mutual fund. When in doubt, the investor should select only the type of ETF that matches his or her financial objectives. As discussed in Chapter 1, that means first adopting an investment policy statement and then purchasing investments in accordance with the specified financial objectives listed therein.

For a much broader discussion of diversification and its role in PMA investing, review the principles of diversification in Chapter 4.

Trading Volume

It has become conventional wisdom that, when considering a purchase of an ETF, an investor should *avoid* an ETF with low trading volume. The reasoning is that if any investment is thinly traded, a sizeable buy or sell trading order from any one fund or institution will cause an artificial decline or increase in the price of the shares.

This is a myth. Conventional wisdom in this case ignores how an ETF is structured and operates. Specifically, ETF shares can be created and redeemed every day, unlike traditional stocks, where only so many shares are issued and outstanding at any period of time. So, unlike with a thinly traded individual stock (of which there are many in today's market), a securities firm can soften the impact of a sudden increase in ETF buying or selling pressures by creating or redeeming ETF shares.

Instead, the important factor to consider is the amount of trading in the ETF's portfolio, be it in stocks, bonds, commodities, or currencies. A potential investor should review the top ten holdings of any ETF and track how frequently they are traded each day. In the larger ETFs tracking a broad market index (such as SPY investing in S&P 500 large-cap stocks), trading frequency is not usually a concern. But in the smaller ETFs with a very low trading volume, the frequency of trading of the largest holdings may be telling. If the underlying stock-trading frequency of the largest holdings is significant in proportion to all fund holdings, the popular myth of avoiding ETFs with low trading volume is debunked.

Product and Legal Structure

There are two product structures for an ETF: physical and swap-based. Most ETFs adopt a *physical* structure, meaning that the fund holds the underlying index shares. Alternatively, some funds are *swap-based* and strive to generate the return of a benchmark index by purchasing derivatives underwritten by a third party (*counterparty*). As a result, investors purchasing a swap-based ETF open themselves up to counterparty risk or the risk that the firm underwriting the derivative will become financially unstable. A recent example of counterparty risk was the financial trouble that American International Group (AIG) incurred when it underwrote credit-default swap derivatives before the Great Recession of 2007–2009. Leveraged ETFs are examples of swap-based funds.

There are also two legal structures for an ETF: the unit investment trust (UIT) structure and the mutual fund structure. Many older ETFs are structured as UITs, as discussed in Chapter 7. If an ETF is structured as a UIT, all securities forming an index are required to be included in the fund's portfolio. The provider of the ETF does not have the discretion to pick and choose which securities to include or, in investment terminology, does not have the opportunity to *sample and optimize* specifically chosen securities to track the index. This structure does not usually prove problematic for a broad-based ETF, such as the SPDR S&P 500, but it may prove restrictive for ETFs that target a particular market sector or international region. Alternatively, most newer ETFs have adopted the mutual fund legal structure. In this form, the ETF's provider may use sampling and optimization techniques when constructing its portfolio of securities.

Before purchasing an ETF, investors should check the physical and legal structure of the fund. As stated, most ETFs are structured as physical funds, but broader-based funds have adopted the UIT legal structure. Thus, the investor is exposed to the actual risk of the underlying index but no counterparty or *synthetic* risk. The investor also owns a share of the percentage of all securities in the tracking index. If the ETF is structured as a swap-based fund, the investor is taking on additional risk for which he or she is likely not receiving a commensurate amount of return. There should be no greater concern for an investor than assuming the high risk of derivative investments when there is a simultaneous lack of awareness that the fund is even investing in such financial instruments.

Valuation

The share price of most ETFs is set at a percentage of the index on which the ETF is based. For example, SPDRs are priced at an approximate relationship of 1 to 10 (10%) of the daily level of the S&P 500 index of large-capitalization stocks. Therefore, if the S&P 500 index number for a given trading day were 1,300, the price of a share of SPDRs should be $130 (1,300 times .10).

But this does not always happen. As mentioned, the value of securities held by the ETF may trade above or below the index it tracks. This situation is referred to as *tracking error* and may be indicative of a poorly managed fund. It is common that foreign-stock or bond ETFs experience tracking error because of currency fluctuations. They must offer redemption of the underlying stocks or bonds in a different currency and sometimes at outdated quotes, thus inviting **arbitrage**. As a rule, the shares of most domestic ETFs should trade very close to the true underlying securities in the fund and experience only *minimal tracking error*.

Cost

Cost efficiency is widely touted as a major advantage of ETFs. But not all ETFs, particularly those that are actively managed, have a cost advantage over index mutual funds. In practice, the stock-trading nature of the ETF often increases the cost of investing in an ETF. Investors in an ETF also have to pay a broker's commission when they make a trade. Thus, adopting a buy-and-hold mentality should be an attribute of any ETF investor. Alternatively, investors who wish to dollar-cost average should likely invest in an index mutual fund to avoid the payment-of-commission disadvantage.

The expense ratio quoted by all ETFs is its *total expense ratio* (TER), which covers the management expenses and other administrative costs incurred in operating the fund. When evaluating the cost of an ETF, investors should consider other expenses such as brokerage commissions, rebalancing of portfolio costs, and trading spreads. The TER plus these additional costs may be summed up in a concept known as the *total cost of ownership* (TCO), an average ratio that is not easily found in online or printed reference services because it is so investor-specific.

How to Evaluate the Performance of an Exchange-Traded Fund

As with open-end and closed-end funds, I use here a Morningstar profile or quote page to examine the key metrics of an ETF, including its past performance. The fund I review here is SPDR S&P 500, which has ticker symbol SPY (Figure 8-1).

As is apparent in Figure 8-1, there is great similarity between the reporting data used to evaluate the performance of an open-end fund and that for an ETF. However, the following performance metrics are specific to evaluating an ETF and are discussed in turn:

- Reference to a standard and category index
- Average premium/discount percentage to the NAV of the ETF portfolio
- Market total return percentage versus NAV total return percentage
- Risk and return profile
- Legal structure

Reference to a Standard and Category Index

Because an ETF is essentially an index fund that trades like a stock, evaluating the performance of an ETF requires information about the index that the fund tracks. In the case of SPY, the standard index is the S&P index of 500 large-capitalization stocks. Because the subject index includes both growth and value stocks, the Morningstar category is Large Blend. A blended fund represents a marriage of the growth and value investing styles in an effort to generate the maximum expected return for the commensurate risk assumed by the investor, including here that of institutional investors. Among the top ten holdings in the S&P 500 index are such companies as Exxon Mobil, Microsoft, General Electric, and Johnson & Johnson, all of which also appear as the top holdings of SPY. Therefore, there is significant correlation between the index and the ETF.

Average Premium/Discount Percentage to the NAV of the ETF portfolio

The "What Is an Exchange-Traded Fund?" section of this chapter discussed the possible tendency of ETF shares to trade at either a premium or a discount to the NAV of the underlying securities owned as the fund portfolio. In the words of the Morningstar ETF Detail Report Disclosure Statement:

> *ETFs trading on a secondary market may trade at, above, or below their net asset value (NAV). If an ETF's shares trade at a price above their NAV, they are said to be trading at a "premium." Conversely, if they are trading at a price below their NAV, they are said to be trading at a "discount."*

In the case of SPY and its history of performance, the ETF shares have been trading at a slight discount from the NAV of the ETF portfolio of securities. For example, as of October 2013, the shares traded at a percentage discount of 0.09 (nine basis points) from the overall NAV. This is very close to the actual NAV; but from a practical standpoint, if you are an investor concerned about the disparity in prices, consider using a limit order instead of a market order when a trade for an ETF share is executed. A *limit order* is an order to buy or sell a stock (or an ETF share) at a specific price or better. If the share price does not reach the limit price, the order is never executed. Alternatively, a *market order* is an order to buy or sell at the best available price. Generally, a market order is executed immediately. Although a market order is the type of order executed by most investors, it offers no protection against dramatic price swings in the price of a stock or an ETF share. On the buy side, this means that the investor may pay more than expected, whereas on the sell side it means that the investor does not receive as great a price as expected. Over a considerable period of time, this could add up to a significant amount of money!

The fact that the shares of SPY are selling at a discount to the fund's NAV can also be appreciated by observing the market price of SPY shares relative to the NAV price. The market price is slightly lower than that of the NAV price per share of the fund.

Market Total Return Percentage vs. NAV Total Return Percentage

Because an ETF is basically an index fund and an index fund tracks the broader market, it is appropriate to compare the ETF's total return to the broader market. For example, the broader market as reflected by the S&P 500 index shows a total annualized return in 2012 of positive 15.99%.

The NAV annualized return of the SPY ETF was 15.84% in 2012. The Morningstar ETF Detail Report notes:

> *For ETFs, standardized total return depicts performance without adjusting for brokerage commissions and the effects of taxation, but is adjusted to reflect all actual ongoing ETF expenses and assumes reinvestment of dividends and capital gains. If adjusted, the effects of brokerage commissions and taxation would reduce the performance quoted.*

Because the market's total return also does not consider the effects of brokerage commissions and taxation at the shareholder level, the comparison between the two measures is appropriate. The slightly lower total return of SPY relative to the broader market is likely attributable to fund expenses—State Street Global Advisor charges a management fee of 0.09% or 9 basis points—and trading costs incurred in SPY.

Risk and Return Profile

The *modern portfolio theory* (MPT) statistics used to report the historical performance of the SPY ETF are the same as those for an open-end mutual fund, such as the Fairholme Fund (Chapter 5). The beta of the standard index (S&P 500) is 1.0 and the R^2 of the index is 100%, for the index is the market (which has a beta under MPT of 1.0) and it is fully diversified such that 100% of the movement of the index number is explained by the stocks in the index. Because SPY tracks the S&P 500 index, you should therefore expect the same metrics.

The separate risk and return profile for SPY likewise indicates that it is not leveraged. *Leverage* as defined by the Morningstar glossary is "seeking profit by using borrowed funds, margin accounts, or by buying securities through rights, warrants, or options." (The terms *rights*, *warrants*, and *options* are well understood by investment professionals as referring to types of derivative that increase the risk of a fund, just as do borrowed funds.) Thus, SPY has a *lesser* amount of total risk than a leveraged ETF. SPY also tends to be more tax-efficient than a leveraged ETF. Why? Leveraged ETFs do not use a portfolio of physical securities to track their benchmark index. Rather, they keep assets in a pool of cash and use *custom swap agreements* (derivatives) to generate annualized percentage returns. This means that when an investor's ETF shares are redeemed, cash is exchanged by the fund for their shares. Normally, this does not result in a problem. However, if the fund has more redemption requests than available cash, the ETF portfolio managers must sell some of the derivatives used to replicate the benchmark index instead of distributing them to investors. This can sometimes lead to sizeable capital gains distributions for the shareholders remaining in the ETF.

Legal Structure

As an older type of ETF, SPY (with a separately cited inception date of January 22, 1993) is structured as a UIT. The significance of this form, along with the newer mutual fund structure, is discussed in the "Product and Legal Structure" section of this chapter. There is also a third type of legal structure, as embodied in HOLDRs: the publicly traded grantor trust structure. As discussed in the "ETFs vs. HOLDRs" section, HOLDRs are sometimes considered to be ETFs, even though they lack many of the characteristics of ETFs—most notably an absence of restrictions imposed by the ICA of 1940.

Summary

The following list of the major types of ETFs available in today's marketplace may be expected to grow, given the burgeoning popularity of this investment vehicle:

- Index ETFs
- Stock ETFs (both domestic and international)
- Bond ETFs (both domestic and international)
- Commodity ETFs
- Currency ETFs
- Leveraged ETFs
- Inverse ETFs
- Actively managed ETFs

This chapter concludes Part 3, "Other Professionally Managed Assets under the 1940 Act," which discussed pooled assets other than mutual funds—among them CEFs, UITs, and ETFs. Like open-end funds (mutual funds), all are governed by the provisions of Investment Company Act of 1940. Although ETFs did not exist in 1940, they are nevertheless subject to the 1940 Act because they are a type of open-end fund that trades on an exchange.

Part 4, "Professionally Managed Assets for High-Net-Worth Investors," treats those types of professionally managed assets used primarily by high-net-worth clients who employ investment advisors and companies to customize their holdings. They include hedge funds, managed futures, and private equity funds, which are the respective subjects of the next three chapters.

Figure 8-1. *(continued)*

Monthly Premium/Discount SPY More...

New portfolio
M*, 10/03/2013

Five Downsides to ETFs
M*, 08/12/2013

Should You Allocate to Allocation Funds?
M*, 08/09/2013

A Phantom Menace?
M*, 08/07/2013

Charting a slow-motion rally to record territory
MW, 07/23/2013

Top Holdings SPY More...

	Weight %	Last Price	Day Chg %	52-Week Range
⊖ Apple Inc	2.91	488.32 USD	1.10 ↑	385.10 - 666.00
⊖ Exxon Mobil Corporation	2.51	86.10 USD	-0.25 ↓	84.70 - 95.49
⊖ Microsoft Corporation	1.70	33.29 USD	-1.73 ↓	26.26 - 36.43
⊖ Johnson & Johnson	1.63	86.80 USD	-0.58 ↓	67.80 - 94.42
⊖ General Electric Co	1.62	24.02 USD	-0.12 ↓	19.87 - 24.95
% Assets in Top 5 Holdings	10.37			

⊕ Increase ⊖ Decrease ☆ New to Portfolio
Portfolio Date :10/04/2013, Price data delayed 15 ~ 30 minutes

Top Sectors SPY More...

	Fund	3 Yr High	3 Yr Low	Cat Avg
Technology	16.70	17.46	16.70	–
Financial Services	15.26	15.26	12.43	–
Healthcare	13.03	13.03	11.68	–
Consumer Cyclical	11.12	11.12	9.35	–
Industrials	10.70	11.68	10.70	–

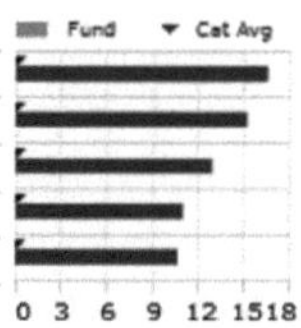

Portfolio Date: 10/04/2013

Latest Distributions SPY More...

Ex Date	Distribution NAV	Income	S/T Cap Gain	L/T Cap Gain	Return Cap	Total
Sep 20,2013	170.71	0.8380	0.0000	0.0000	0.0000	0.8380
Jun 21,2013	158.98	0.8391	0.0000	0.0000	0.0000	0.8391
Mar 15,2013	155.83	0.6937	0.0000	0.0000	0.0000	0.6937
Dec 21,2012	142.74	1.0218	0.0000	0.0000	0.0000	1.0218
Sep 21,2012	145.89	0.7794	0.0000	0.0000	0.0000	0.7794
Jun 15,2012	134.17	0.6883	0.0000	0.0000	0.0000	0.6883
Mar 16,2012	140.29	0.6139	0.0000	0.0000	0.0000	0.6139
Dec 16,2011	121.78	0.7701	0.0000	0.0000	0.0000	0.7701
Sep 16,2011	121.51	0.6250	0.0000	0.0000	0.0000	0.6250
Jun 17,2011	127.05	0.6276	0.0000	0.0000	0.0000	0.6276
Mar 18,2011	127.83	0.5533	0.0000	0.0000	0.0000	0.5533
Dec 17,2010	124.25	0.6528	0.0000	0.0000	0.0000	0.6528

Currency: USD

Figure 8-1. The Morningstar ETF profile of SPDR S&P 500 SPY, 10/08/2013.[1] Reprinted with permission of Morningstar, Inc

[1] `etfs.morningstar.com/quote?ops=clear&T=SPY&region=USA&culture=en-US`

PART

IV

Professionally Managed Assets for High-Net-Worth Investors

CHAPTER

9

Hedge Funds

The global hedge fund industry has historically been known for its lack of transparency. Some call hedge funds a *shadow investment*—meaning that, by and large, the assets held and managed by the funds are out of the public view. Accordingly, this makes hedge funds very attractive to high-net-worth individuals who generally do not like to disclose their investments and the size of their wealth to the broader public. After reading this chapter and coming to appreciate the characteristics of hedge funds, you should understand why this is the case.

In 2013, there were more than 10,000 active hedge funds with assets exceeding $2.4 trillion.[1] The past performance of some of these hedge funds has been outstanding, and the managers of these funds have been rewarded very handsomely for it. In aggregate, however, the story has been quite otherwise for the last decade: since 2003, the Global Hedge Fund Index has underperformed the S&P 500. It will be interesting to observe whether this trend continues in a market of extreme volatility.

What Is a Hedge Fund?

Until 2010, with the passage of the Dodd-Frank Wall Street Reform and Consumer Protection Act (Dodd-Frank Act), there was no formal definition of *hedge fund*. The typical characteristics of such a fund were often cited, such as a largely unregulated private investment fund for high-net-worth investors, but no formal definition was included in any law, including the Investment Company Act of 1940 (ICA). Indeed, the ICA never anticipated the subsequent creation of an investment choice that came to be referred to in the

[1]Hedge Fund Research, Inc. "HFR Global Hedge Fund Industry Report—Second Quarter 2013." `www.hedgefundresearch.com`.

investment world as a *hedge fund*. As discussed in Chapter 2, the term *hedge* in investments means essentially a minimization of investor risk by the taking of opposite *long* and *short* positions. Notwithstanding, many hedge funds historically and presently engage primarily in *speculative* activities, investing assets with more consideration given to the objective of winning a quick and sizeable profit than to the mitigation of investment risk. Whereas hedgers typically strive to avoid an exposure to adverse movements in the price of an asset, speculators take a position in the market and "bet" that the asset price will go either up or down.

According to the Securities and Exchange Commission (SEC), "A hedge fund is defined generally to be any private fund that has the ability to pay a performance fee to its adviser, borrow in excess of a certain amount, or sell assets short."[2]

Note By the SEC's technical definition,[3] a *hedge fund* is:

Any private fund (other than a securitized asset fund):

(a) with respect to which one or more investment advisers (or related persons of investment advisers) may be paid a performance fee or allocation calculated by taking into account unrealized gains (other than a fee or allocation the calculation of which may take into account unrealized gains solely for the purpose of reducing such fee or allocation to reflect net unrealized losses);

(b) that may borrow an amount in excess of one-half of its net asset value (including any committed capital) or may have gross notional exposure in excess of twice its net asset value (including any committed capital); or

(c) that may sell securities or other assets short or enter into similar transactions (other than for the purpose of hedging currency exposure or managing duration).

The three parts of this definition are respectively detailed in the "Advantages of Hedge Funds" and "Disadvantages of Hedge Funds" sections of this chapter, but a cursory reading of it makes it at once clear that a hedge fund is very different from the typical actively managed mutual fund. The typical mutual fund does not engage in borrowing (leverage) or sell assets short; nor do the investors in the fund pay the portfolio manager based on appreciation (the fund's unrealized gains). Mutual funds also have greater transparency than most hedge funds, particularly if the mutual fund does not engage in derivative transactions, which are the focus of many hedge funds.

---

[2]"Form PF: Frequently Asked Questions." `www.sec.gov/divisions/investment/pfrd/pfrdfaq.shtml`.

[3]Glossary of Terms in Form PF (Reporting Form for Investment Advisers to Private Funds). `www.sec.gov/about/forms/formpf.pdf`.

There are many types of hedge funds, but for purposes of tracking performance they are usually sorted into four major categories based on the fund's primary investment strategy: *equity hedge funds*, *relative value funds*, *event-driven funds*, and *global macro funds*. Each category has one or more subcategories. When rating hedge funds, Morningstar delineates funds into seven major categories and adds *debt*, *multi-strategy*, and *fund of funds* to the previous four. (Morningstar also refers to equity hedge funds simply as *equity* and relative value funds as *arbitrage*.)

Brief descriptions of the four major categories follow, together with lists of their subcategories:

- *Equity hedge funds*: These funds buy or *go long on* stocks that the fund manager believes will appreciate in value, while simultaneously selling or *shorting* stocks that the manager believes will decrease in value. The subcategories of this category are:
    - *Dedicated short (pure short) funds*
    - *Equity long/short funds*
    - *Equity market neutral funds*
    - *Emerging market funds*
- *Relative value funds*: These funds are constructed based on differences in market values between related investments. This is known in the investment world as *arbitrage*, which is broadly the achievement of a profit without taking any investment risk. Theoretically, this mispricing of securities should not exist in an efficient market. However, practically and from time to time, mispricing does exist and arbitrage is possible. The subcategories are:
    - *Convertible arbitrage funds*
    - *Fixed income arbitrage funds*
    - *Merger arbitrage funds*
- *Event-driven funds*: These funds seek to profit from significant *market events*, such as the mergers or acquisitions of companies or a company in bankruptcy proceedings or very close to filing for bankruptcy. The managers of these funds buy securities that are offered at deep discounts, often because of specific company distress. As a result, the term *distressed securities fund* is often used interchangeably with *event-driven fund*. The subcategories are:
    - *Distressed debt funds*
    - *Distressed stock funds*

- *Global macro funds*: These funds are invested in the securities of various countries, including the United States, based on macroeconomic conditions. The manager of the fund practices tactical asset allocation and responds very rapidly to changing market conditions within those countries. Any fund with a country or region name in its title is part of this category. Macro fund managers often use leverage and purchase derivative securities (options, futures, and swaps) to increase the impact of market moves. This type of fund typically holds more liquid securities than other types of hedge funds. A subcategory of this type of fund is:
    - *Market timing funds*

As of January 2013, the greatest percentage of hedge fund managers and funds (32.3%) follow a strategy of investing in equities with a long/short orientation and so are categorized as equity hedge funds.[4]

A hedge fund is usually structured with investors in the legal position of limited partners (thus limiting their potential liability only to the extent of their investment), with the investment manager assuming the position of general partner (and its accompanying unlimited liability).

More on the Investment Strategies of Hedge Funds

The various subcategories of hedge funds have different primary investment strategies, as discussed in the following examples.

Equity Long/Short and Equity Market Neutral Funds

As discussed in Chapter 2, when an investor buys a stock or equity, he or she is said to be *long* on that stock. Alternatively, when an investor borrows a stock or equity in anticipation of a price decline, he or she is said to be *short* that stock. As an investment strategy, an investor would be long a stock if anticipating an increase in its price; in other words, the stock is undervalued by the market. An investor would be short a stock if anticipating a decrease in its price; in other words, the stock is overpriced by the market. Ideally, the investor's anticipations with respect to the price movement of both long and short stocks would be correct and he or she would profit in the event of either movement in price.

---

[4]Citi Prime Finance. "Hedge Fund Industry Snapshot." September 2013 (based on August 2013 data); `http://citi.com/icg/global_markets/prime_finance/docs/hf_monthly.pdf`

A hedge fund manager simply does what an investor does in following a long/short equity strategy, but on a bigger scale and sometimes with a view toward hedging (minimizing overall investment risk). For example, suppose a hedge fund manager takes a $10 million long position in Exxon Mobil and a $10 million short position in BP. If there is a market-wide decline in the price of oil, the fund will profit from the short position in BP and will lose from the long position in Exxon Mobil. Therefore the market risk for the fund manager is minimal. So why does the manager adopt such a strategy? Because the manager thinks Exxon Mobil will perform better in the long run and the fund will reap a profit. Stated differently, if the price of Exxon stock does not decline as much as that of BP stock, then the short position will gain more than the long position and the spread trade will be profitable.

The Exxon Mobil and BP example, because the size of the positions is the same, reflects an *equity market neutral* strategy by the hedge fund manager. However, some managers do not practice such a strategy and maintain either a *long bias* or a *short bias*. Accordingly, strategies such as *120/20* are sometimes cited. This means the manager is exposed 120% to long positions in equities and 20% to short positions. Similarly, *130/30* means 130% exposure to long positions and 30% to short positions. Few managers maintain a short bias because almost all managers are "bullish" on the equity markets long-term and expect a general increase in security prices. This is why the first number in the citation means exposures to long positions in equities and why most equity long/short funds have a long bias. Those managers who have total exposure to short positions are said to be managing a *dedicated short fund*.

Arbitrage Funds

The formal definition of *arbitrage* is the simultaneous buying and selling of an asset (such as a currency) in order to profit from a difference in the price. However, the implication of this definition is more profound: arbitrage is the ability to generate a profit *without assuming any investment risk*. This is contrary to a fundamental principle of investing: that a greater reward (return) can only be accomplished by assuming greater risk. An efficient market is designed ideally to prevent arbitrage opportunities. Arbitrage exploits actual inefficiencies, particularly those that a portfolio manager identifies in different markets where the same asset is traded.

Leverage or the borrowing of money can encourage hedge fund managers to engage in arbitrage. Specifically, leverage allows managers to magnify fund returns with only a small amount of the fund's capital at risk. Many hedge fund managers invest with a goal of achieving an *absolute return* (a positive investment performance number regardless of market conditions). When enticing prospective investors to the fund, it is preferable, of course, to quote a higher absolute return percentage than a lower (perhaps more realistic) absolute return percentage. The ability of a hedge fund to leverage investments only adds to the tendency to quote a higher absolute return goal.

The strategy underlying a *convertible arbitrage* hedge fund is that a company's convertible bonds are sometimes underpriced relative to the company's stock. Convertible arbitrage attempts to profit from this mispricing. What is a *convertible bond*? It is a bond that can be converted into a company's common stock at a predetermined time and a predetermined price. It is attractive to an investor because there is now a choice: the investor can either hold on to the bond as is and continue to receive the interest payable from the bond or participate in the company's growth by converting the bond to the company's common stock, usually at a discount to the market value of the stock when converted. In convertible arbitrage, a hedge fund manager buys a company's bonds at the same time the manager shorts its common stock. If the company's stock falls, the hedge fund benefits from its short position. Alternatively, if the company's stock increases in price, the hedge fund converts its convertible bonds into stock and sells that stock at its higher market value, thereby compensating for the fund's losses on its short position.

A second arbitrage strategy is *fixed-income arbitrage*. In this strategy, the hedge fund manager takes opposite long and short positions in fixed-income type vehicles, such as regular (*plain vanilla*) bonds, and attempts to profit from small price discrepancies while limiting the interest-rate risk that is applicable to all fixed-income securities. The most common fixed-income arbitrage strategy is a so-called *swap-spread strategy* whereby the manager takes a long position in a credit default swap instrument and a short position in a U.S. Treasury security (Treasury bond). **Credit default swaps** are very complex financial instruments but basically similar to insurance contracts, protecting the buyer from specific types of investment risk. They are a type of derivative (an asset that takes its value in part from the value of an underlying asset) and are traded over the counter by knowledgeable investors. However, their market value and price are very difficult to determine, and the risks they carry are not transparent to most investors, thereby adding to their risk. When used in a fixed-income arbitrage strategy, credit default swaps typically provide relatively small absolute returns but can lead to huge losses. Thus, a popular saying in the investment marketplace is that a fixed-income arbitrage strategy is like "picking up nickels in front of a steamroller."

A third type of arbitrage strategy is *merger arbitrage*. A hedge fund manager following this strategy executes a trade for a company's securities after a possible merger or acquisition is announced in hopes of turning a profit if the deal actually takes place.

Distressed Securities Funds

Generally, a *distressed* security is one issued by a company that is currently unable to meet its financial obligations. If the security is a bond (debt), it is considered distressed when it is rated CCC or below by a major bond rating agency, such as Standard & Poor's or Moody's. If the security is a stock, there is no formal rating indicating that the stock has entered into a distress category; but if the company issuing stock is likely to subsequently file for bankruptcy, the stock is considered distressed. Because of the fact that bond holders are compensated in a bankruptcy liquidation proceeding before owners of common or preferred stock, most hedge fund managers purchase distressed debt.

When practicing a distressed security investment strategy, the hedge fund manager seeks to purchase the security at a reduced price and, thereby, buy the security at a substantial discount from a "financially healthy" security. Anticipating that the company will not file for bankruptcy, the manager expects the bond's rating and price to improve, rendering the manager and hedge fund investors a significant profit. Of course, this is a risky strategy because the distressed securities may continue to decline in value, and bankruptcy may result, rendering the security (particularly the company's common and preferred stock) worthless. To offset the risk, the hedge fund typically injects new capital into the company, usually in the form of equity. In this manner, the hedge fund is acting like a private equity firm that tries to restructure a privately held company in the hopes of scoring a sizeable gain before taking the company public.

Market Timing (Global Macro) Funds

Managers of market timing global macro funds attempt to identify trends in particular global market sectors or overall global security markets. As a result of this due diligence, managers often take concentrated positions in a certain sector or market and then use leverage to increase the fund's exposure to anticipated movements in price, either upward or downward.

Advantages of Hedge Funds

Unless the investor is willing to assume significant risk and has a substantial amount of capital to invest, the disadvantages of hedge funds often outweigh their advantages. But the advantages of hedge funds include—in addition to the privacy of investments as mentioned at the outset of this chapter—the following:

- An ability to generate a higher-than-average investment return through the implementation of aggressive investment strategies

- An attempt to produce returns with a very low correlation to traditional asset classes, such as stocks, bonds, and cash/cash equivalents
- A highly motivated portfolio manager
- The possibility of investing in a hedge fund **fund of funds**

Ability to Generate a High Investment Return

The preceding sections have already discussed some common investment strategies pursued by hedge fund managers. Generally, the investment practices of short selling, leverage, and the use of derivatives exemplify the hedge fund manager's attempt to generate an abnormally high return for fund investors. All of these practices also carry with them an investor's willingness to assume higher-than-average risk in exchange for a higher-than-average return, an attribute that an investor needs to understand before purchasing an interest in the fund. No single projected annualized return is sought by hedge fund managers as a rule, except an expected return as high as possible as compared to less-risky mutual funds of the same broad style and certainly an excess return to cover the fund's management fee, as discussed later. The highest annual return achieved by any hedge fund style in the period 1995 to 2010 was by an equity long/short funds investment strategy, which returned 69.92% net of fees and expenses in the year 1999.

There is also a detrimental aspect to a hedge fund manager's adoption of aggressive investment strategies to generate a high investment return. Given that hedge funds implement such risky strategies, the orientation of the manager may also encourage the fund to take excessive risk with an investor's money. This is why the selection of a skilled and experienced hedge fund manager is such an important consideration before investing in a hedge fund. Stated another way, if the hedge fund manager does not understand the amount of investment risk inherent in the investment strategies pursued by the fund, the potential for a significant investor loss over time increases dramatically.

Returns with a Low Correlation to Traditional Asset Classes

Correlation measures how an actual return varies relative to its average or expected return. The concept can also be extended to measure how an actual return varies relative to the expected return of other assets or, here, traditional asset classes, such as stocks, bonds, and cash equivalents. The numerical value of the correlation *coefficient* ranges from +1.0 to −1.0. If two assets move exactly together, there is a perfect positive correlation between the two assets, and the relationship is expressed as +1.0. Alternatively, if two assets move exactly opposite of each other, there is a perfect negative correlation, and the relationship is −1.0. As discussed in Chapter 4, because all securities share systematic or *market* risk, when constructing a diversified portfolio managers should seek to acquire securities with as low positive a numerical relationship as possible. The hedge fund structure is optimal when positioning securities with a low correlation to traditional asset classes.

Historically, the average one-year correlation coefficient between equity hedge funds and the S&P 500 index has been about 0.30. In 2012 and 2013, however, this correlation increased to about 0.85.[5] If this trend continues, the supposed advantage of lower positive correlations provided by hedge funds is lessened—so much so that some advisors were advising that the advantage had been lost and a potential investor was better off purchasing a lower-cost index mutual fund.

Nonetheless, the potential for low-correlation investing is inherent in a properly diversified hedge fund. Correlation matrices comparing the movement of one asset to another are available online and in reference journals. During the interval 1970–1999, the correlation between emerging market stocks and the S&P 500 was 0.51, and in 2013 it increased to 0.82.[6] Moreover, the correlation of global bonds, natural resources, and gold to the S&P 500 were all slightly negative (they are now slightly positive). Historically, the negative correlation of derivatives to broad market indexes has made them effective as a portfolio diversification tool, although at the expense of increased risk to the investor.

A Highly Motivated Portfolio Manager

Hedge fund managers are exceedingly well compensated. The standard fees charged by a hedge fund are 2% of the value of the assets under management and 20% of the fund's capital gains (appreciation in share value), although in the wake of the 2008 market decline, these fees decreased by 2013 to an average of 1.6% for management and a take of 18% of gains. If the fund does not generate a positive return, the investors still must pay the management fee.

Safeguards are usually included in the fund's structure to prevent the fund manager from unduly manipulating portfolio performance before being compensated. A common example is the inclusion of a *high-water mark*. This provision operates to preclude a manager from receiving the 20% performance bonus unless the current fund value exceeds its previous highest value. Another example of a constraint on manager compensation is bonus suspension in the event of a loss in portfolio value. For example, the 20% performance bonus

---

[5]Jacob Wolinsky "Hedge Fund Alpha is Negative" July 11, 2013 www.valuewalk.com/2013/07/hedge-fund-alpha-negative/

[6]Elizabeth MacBride "Understanding the Recent Rise in Correlations" *Forbes* 3/09/2011. www.forbes.com/sites/riabiz/2011/03/23/understanding-the-recent-rise-in-correlations-and-turning-it-to-your-advantage/

may not be restored until the fund recoups the portfolio loss in value. Some hedge fund managers, however, have been known to get around this constraint by closing out and liquidating the fund before establishing a new fund.

As in business generally, investors in a hedge fund hope to "get what they pay for." Inasmuch as individuals tend to perform on the basis of how they are compensated, hedge fund managers are highly motivated to grow the fund in value and record annual profits. This can be both a positive and a negative. On the positive side, above-average returns are sought, and the interests of the hedge fund manager and investors are aligned. On the negative side, the fund manager may take unwarranted short-term risk with fund investments to the detriment of the long-term wealth accumulation of the fund's investors.

Possibility of Investing in a Fund of Funds

As discussed in the next section, a hedge fund is not required to report its performance results or correlation between returns, thereby making it very difficult to estimate a meaningful correlation coefficient between asset classes. Essentially, this forces the investor to resort to taking the fund manager at his or her word that the returns and correlations are accurate.

An investor alternative to this lack of transparency by the fund is to acquire shares in a fund that invests in different hedge funds, or a *fund of funds* (FoF). This is also an available alternative in mutual fund investing, but it is much more predominant in the hedge fund marketplace. A FoF offers the potential for even greater portfolio diversification because the fund owns positions in several hedge funds, which, the investor hopes, are the best hedge funds in the marketplace. The manager of a FoF has likely spent considerable time researching the best hedge funds and their managers, so one of the factors that should be taken into account by a potential hedge fund investor has already been considered. But this increased access to information provided by a FoF often comes at an additional cost to the investor. Specifically, because the investor is now purchasing two sets of funds—the FoF and the individual hedge funds acquired by the FoF—the investor pays two sets of management fees, thereby resulting in management fees sometimes as high as 4% of assets.

Disadvantages of Hedge Funds

In addition to increased investor risk and the exceedingly high fees charged by the investment manager in a hedge fund, the disadvantages of a hedge fund investment include the following:

- Very high minimum investment
- No secondary market for trading of shares

- Significant limitation on withdrawals of investor monies
- Lack of transparency in performance reporting
- Lack of government regulation of the industry

Very High Minimum Investment

As mentioned in the "What Is a Hedge Fund?" section, hedge funds are typically organized as *limited partnerships*. As such, they are private organizations and are not publicly traded.[7] Hedge funds also generally limit the number of their investors or limited partners to no more than 100 *accredited investors* as defined in the Securities Act of 1933. Currently, this definition translates to the requirement that the investor have either a minimum net worth of $1.0 million (excluding the value of his or her primary residence) at the time of making the hedge fund investment, or an annual net income of at least $200,000 in each of the two most recent years prior to making the investment and a reasonable expectation of earning this same amount in the current year. An unlimited number of *qualified purchasers* (aka *super-accredited investors*) may invest in a hedge fund. An individual investor is a qualified purchaser if he or she owns at least $5.0 million in investments, not including a primary residence or any property used in a business. Therefore, only a select group of higher-net-worth or higher-net-income individuals and married couples—estimated to constitute about 8% of U.S. households—are eligible as either accredited investors or qualified purchasers for a hedge fund investment. Hedge fund managers are required to verify eligibility of their potential investors by having them complete a required worksheet, but some fall short in fulfilling this responsibility.

The typical minimum initial investment for a hedge fund is $1.0 million. Some hedge funds, commonly referred to as *lite hedge funds*, have lowered this initial investment to as little as $100,000, but that is still a significant amount of money for many investors. Recurring lower investment amounts are then established by the fund, but they are also relatively high. Even if the investor meets the investment criteria for investing in a hedge fund, many do not have the necessary minimum to participate without transferring their IRA or 401(k) account balances to the fund manager. Under existing law, it is possible to invest IRA, 401(k), or any qualified retirement plan monies into a hedge fund, but the plan document may restrict either the amount or the possibility of a hedge fund investment. Therefore, an investor must check with his or her plan administrator before considering making the investment (again, with an informed understanding of the increased investment risk that is inherent in such transfer).

---

[7]A publicly traded limited partnership is referred to as a *master limited partnership (MLP)* and is usually invested in real-estate properties or oil and gas interests. MLPs are discussed in Chapter 12.

No Secondary Market

As noted in the preceding section, hedge funds are privately traded investment vehicles. Therefore, no secondary market exists for the trading of hedge fund shares or interests. Rather, once an individual invests in a hedge fund, that person generally cannot sell the shares. The fund itself may redeem the shares from the investor, but that is relatively rare, particularly given a startup fund's difficulty in raising capital in the first instance. Thus, limited marketability is a real disadvantage of a hedge fund investment, particularly in the first several years of making the investment.

What are the practical implications of the limited marketability of any investment, including hedge funds? First and foremost, limited marketability may place the owner of the investment in a "forced sale" situation when the owner is in need of immediate cash. The result of this situation is typically a sale of an asset at less than its market value—sometimes much less. This is captured in the tax concept of a *lack of marketability discount*, meaning that for tax-valuation purposes (for example, in gift and estate taxation), a reduced value is afforded the taxpayer. But beyond the forced-sale implication, limited marketability can also quickly lead to a lack of asset liquidity. *Liquidity risk*, a close cousin to marketability risk, may be quantified as the difference between an asset's market value and the price at which it can actually be sold. This difference is most pronounced in the case of a thinly traded security, such as the investor's limited-partnership interest in a hedge fund.

Limitation on Withdrawal of Investor Monies

Most hedge funds permit the investor to liquidate his or her money over the course of an investment period, meaning that the investor can convert his or her interest in the fund to cash. However, there are usually significant limitations on the right to liquidate or withdraw. For example, the fund may refuse to repurchase shares until a certain period of time has elapsed, and this time is usually longer than the prohibited redemption period of, say, a mutual fund. A one-year *lockup period* is common in a hedge fund (versus 90 days to 6 months in a mutual fund). In addition, this hedge fund restriction on withdrawal means investors cannot access their money at all during the restricted period, whereas in a mutual fund, the prohibited redemption period does not mean access is not available—only that a percentage penalty is charged on the amount withdrawn. Finally, some hedge funds also limit fund repurchases by the manager to some percentage of the outstanding shares.

These limitations on withdrawal, sometimes referred to as the *exit policies* of the fund, should be clearly detailed in the fund's offering memorandum (the equivalent of a prospectus in a publicly traded mutual fund).

Lack of Transparency in Fund Reporting

Pursuant to the Dodd-Frank Act of 2010, only *large private fund advisers* are required to register with the SEC. Such an adviser is separately defined in the Act as an adviser, including a hedge fund manager, with at least $1.5 billion of assets currently (as of the March 20, 2012 filing date) under management. In addition, *registered investment advisers* (RIAs) with clients who have at least $150 million in hedge fund investments under management are required to register. Therefore, these provisions leave a great many hedge fund managers who do not have to report performance figures to the SEC and who are not subject to their regulations, absent anti-fraud provisions that are applicable to all managers and advisers. A fiduciary duty of the manager and adviser also applies, regardless of the registration requirement.

Those hedge fund managers not required to be registered with the SEC generally self-report their fund's performance results. This provides an incentive for those funds with higher-than-average annual returns to announce those superior results, while simultaneously discouraging those funds with inferior performance to report at all. This lack of reporting also makes it very difficult to verify how properly diversified a fund is, because the correlation coefficients used to construct the portfolio of assets are not public information. Finally, if only funds with superior results report, there is an upward bias on the *average annual return* reported by the hedge fund industry. This fact has been particularly important in recent years when hedge fund returns have, in some instances, lagged those of actively managed mutual funds and passive index funds.

In an attempt to address the *lack of transparency* in fund reporting, the SEC voted in July 2013 to end a decades-old ban on general solicitation by private issuers of securities, including hedge funds and private equity funds (Chapter 11). This means that the past performance of hedge funds can be publicized to prospective investors and is meant to discourage the previous practice of only selective self-reporting of fund performance. However, the ban on general solicitation is not a requirement to report (like mutual fund reporting). Therefore, many funds may elect not to report, particularly if their past fund performance has been below average with respect to their peer funds.

Lack of Government Regulation

The Dodd-Frank Act of 2010 was intended, in part, to improve hedge fund regulation and address hedge fund abuses. It is a matter of debate how successful the legislation has been in achieving these objectives. It is not arguable, however, that before Dodd-Frank there was very little SEC oversight of hedge funds, leading to their rapid expansion as relatively unregulated investment vehicles.

As discussed in the preceding section, only certain hedge funds and hedge fund managers are required to register with the SEC. If they are required to register, they must file a Form PF annually. Managers (and certain RIAs) are subject to *compliance obligations*—including compliance with a *books and records rule*, a *code of ethics rule*, an *advertising rule*, and a general *compliance rule*.

In addition, the manager or adviser must file an annual Form ADV update. Form ADV is the uniform form used by all investment advisers to register with either the SEC or the securities commission in their particular state of business. Form ADV consists of two parts: Part I requires information about the adviser's business, business practices, and types of clients; the more important Part II includes information about the adviser's fees, disciplinary information, conflicts of interest, educational background, and years of experience. Part II of the ADV is known in the financial services industry as the *brochure*. The *brochure rule* under ICA requires that Part II of Form ADV or an equivalent brochure be given to the client both at the time of initial engagement and annually if there are any material changes to the brochure over the course of the past year.

Under the current regulatory system, all investment advisers are regulated by the SEC or a state securities commission, but only a few hedge fund managers are regulated by the SEC. As a result, it is incumbent on investors to educate themselves about the characteristics, returns, and risks of a possible hedge fund investment. The "What Selection Criteria Should Be Used before Purchasing a Hedge Fund?" section of this chapter presents a series of questions provided by the SEC that a potential investor should ask if considering the purchase of a hedge fund. As in so much of professionally managed investing, the proper evaluation of the character and experience of the portfolio manager is critical to investor success. This is made more difficult by the lack of government reporting and regulation of a sizeable majority of the hedge fund industry, but it is not impossible!

Who Should Purchase a Hedge Fund?

The answer to the question of who should purchase a hedge fund is largely provided in the previous sections. For example, only individuals who qualify as either accredited investors or qualified purchasers are legally able to purchase a hedge fund interest. But because compliance with this qualification is left up to the hedge fund manager, it might not be strictly enforced. Therefore, "buyer beware" may be more the rule than the exception.

In addition to individual investors, institutions are major purchasers of hedge fund interests. The largest institutional investors are pension funds, which historically have assumed a sometimes unrealistic discount rate (performance rate) for participants' funds. If the assumed performance rate of investments is not achieved, it adds to the future unfunded liability due retiree/participants in the fund. Accordingly, pension funds have stretched participant accrual of benefits to the absolute maximum allowed under law, sometimes unreasonably so. Institutions that do invest in hedge funds pursue what is known as a *diversified alpha* strategy. As discussed in Chapter 5, *alpha* or the *Jensen ratio* is the actual, annualized return of a fund in excess of the expected, risk-adjusted return of the fund as predicted by use of the *capital asset pricing model* (CAPM). The strategy encompasses a practical, dedicated allocation of a portion of the fund to higher-alpha investments (typically, derivatives) as an alternative to traditional stocks, bonds, and actively managed mutual funds.

Other institutional investors in hedge funds are life insurance companies, securities firms, and investment companies (open-end and closed-end funds). Life insurance companies, given the time horizon and investment needs of their clients, are likely to invest in hedge funds concentrating in debt or high-income equities, whereas securities firms and investment companies, depending on their investment objectives, are more likely to be in equities and leveraged investments.

What Selection Criteria Should Be Used before Purchasing a Hedge Fund?

To educate those considering investing in a hedge fund, the SEC issued a bulletin listing the following items of information to gather and consider before investing in a hedge fund.[8] Subsequent sections add commentary to items of information not been previously addressed in this chapter:

- Read a fund's offering memorandum and related materials.
- Understand the fund's investment strategy.
- Determine if the fund is using leverage.
- Evaluate potential conflicts of interest disclosed by hedge fund managers.

  There are several potential issues to consider here. First, given the lack of regulation by the SEC with respect to hedge funds, the hedge fund manager might not disclose potential conflicts of interest. For example, he or she may serve on the board of directors of a company in which the fund is investing. In addition, the manager might be

[8]SEC Office of Investor Education and Advocacy *Investor Bulletin: Hedge Funds* 10/03/2012. http://sec.gov/investor/alerts

receiving an incentive from a company or industry association to invest in certain stocks. Finally, there might be a conflict of interest on the part of your investment adviser. As an example, your adviser might earn higher fees from the investments in the hedge fund than he or she might earn from other potential investments. This should be disclosed in the investment adviser's ADV Part II, which is required to be given to the investor at the time of engagement of the relationship.

- Understand how a fund's assets are valued.

  As mentioned repeatedly in this chapter, derivatives are often heavily used in a hedge fund's investment strategies. The very name *hedge* fund is derived from the use of derivatives. The valuation of derivatives is exceedingly difficult. Because a derivative takes its value at least in part from the value of an underlying asset, the valuation process of derivatives means investors have to value not only one asset, but two assets. It is often difficult to intrinsically value one asset, particularly an asset such as a stock whose future cash flows are not predictable. When you add to this a traded stock option (another type of popular derivative), the process becomes very complex.

  It is not the purpose of this chapter or book to explain how to value derivatives; the point here is that a prospective hedge fund investor needs to be knowledgeable about the fact that derivative valuation and, by extension hedge fund valuation, is an imperfect science! It is important that investors use independent valuation and reference services, such as Morningstar or a publication or online service that specializes in hedge funds.

- Understand how a fund's performance is determined.
- Understand any limitations on your right to redeem shares.
- Research the backgrounds of hedge fund managers.

  It cannot be emphasized enough that before investing in a hedge fund, you should research the background and qualifications of the hedge fund manager or managers. As mentioned, if the manager is required to register with the SEC, you can obtain this information by reviewing the manager's Form ADV. The SEC Investment Bulletin notes that the Form may be accessed online at the SEC's *Investment Adviser Public Disclosure (IAPD)* website, www.secadvisorsearch.com/. The process of checking for any possible SEC disciplinary procedures with respect to the manager is also particularly important.

If the manager is not required to be registered, the inquiry into his or her background and qualifications is more difficult. You might begin by asking your investment adviser to recommend a hedge fund manager or if the adviser is familiar with the manager you are considering. In addition, google the name of the manager. Finally, ask around and see if you can locate another hedge fund investor, particularly one invested in the fund you are considering, and inquire why they chose a specific fund and its manager. Unfortunately, the fund itself will likely not assist you in this endeavor, because they are loath to disclose investor names without the investor's permission.

- Understand the fees and expenses charged by the fund and fund manager.
- Determine how the fund's assets are safeguarded.

A hedge fund manager's ability to access and transfer fund assets may be misused. The implosion of MF Global Inc. in 2011 is a relatively recent example of the misuse of hedge fund assets. To guard against fund abuses, many hedge funds undergo an annual financial audit, although by law, some are not required to do so. However, as the MF Global scandal revealed, even an annual audit may not be sufficient in some instances.

As part of your due diligence, ask the fund manager where the assets are held and in what form (for example, in a custodial account or trust). If the assets are held by an independent custodian, and this custodian can verify the existence of the assets, you should feel somewhat more comfortable than if this was not the case. Also ask about the fund's internal audit procedure; for example, does it take the signature of more than one person to access the fund assets?

- Ask about others that perform services for the fund.

As the *Investment Bulletin* notes, a hedge fund typically has third parties who provide various services to it, such as an outside adviser who directs investors to the fund, an outside accountant, or outside legal services. You should consider contacting these individuals before you invest in the fund and as part of your due-diligence process. Ask these sources about the accuracy of the fund's offering memorandum and other information provided to you by the fund.

Subsequently, should you choose to invest in the fund, monitor the performance of the hedge fund, and compare the manager's realized return to that of the fund's investment-strategy peers. The purpose of the next and final section of this chapter is to assist you in that process.

How to Evaluate the Performance of a Hedge Fund

Although self-reporting makes the actual performance of many hedge funds difficult to ascertain, some measures for evaluating their performance can be applied. These metrics are discussed in the following sections, together with a review of hedge fund performance during the period 1996–2012.

Risk-Adjusted Return

Given the degree of leverage used by most hedge fund managers, and the corresponding increase in investor risk, computing and measuring a risk-adjusted return for the fund are critical in the evaluation of the fund's performance. In comparing two hedge funds, to *risk-adjust* the returns means to equalize their risk levels, considering the extent of leverage used by each fund. Morningstar does this in its computation of the risk-adjusted return of a hedge fund.

Three other well-known ratios do the same. One is the *Sharpe ratio*, discussed in Chapter 5 in relation to evaluating the performance of mutual funds. The Sharpe ratio has advantages over other risk-adjusted metrics: the computation of a fund's beta is not necessary, and a fund's standard deviation, as used in the denominator of the ratio, is readily observable by checking any investment reference service. As noted by Morningstar in its discussion of how it rates hedge funds, however, the significance of the Sharpe ratio is not easily understood by many investors. For example, if the average excess return of two funds less their risk-free rate (as included in the numerator of the ratio) is equal and negative, the fund with the higher volatility receives the higher score, because it experienced fewer losses per unit of risk. Practically, the total risk of a fund (as measured by standard deviation) is not what really matters to a hedge fund investor.

The relevant risk for any investor, but particularly a hedge fund investor, is likely the fund's downside risk. This is because most investors are risk-averse and fear downside volatility more than they value upside reward. The *Sortino ratio*, discussed in Chapter 5, differentiates between upside and downside volatility by providing a risk-adjusted measure of the fund's performance without rewarding the fund for the upward price changes. In the denominator of the ratio, only the standard deviation of the fund's negative asset returns is taken into account. Thus, the lower the resulting ratio number, the greater the risk of the fund experiencing large losses in its future performance. Alternatively, the higher the resulting ratio number, the less the risk of the fund experiencing potentially large future losses.

The third ratio commonly used in evaluating the risk-adjusted return of a hedge fund is the *Calmar ratio*. Like the Sortino ratio, the Calmar ratio measures the downside risk-adjusted performance of a fund. Unlike the Sortino ratio, however, the Calmar ratio uses a denominator of the maximum drawdown from the fund to penalize the assumption of unnecessary risk. The formula for this ratio is:

$$\text{Calmar ratio} = \frac{\text{Compounded Annual Return of the Fund}}{\text{Maximum Drawdown}}$$

The *maximum drawdown* is the maximum peak-to-trough of the returns and is typically measured over a three-year investment period. Conceptually, the drawdown metric indicates the greatest loss an investor could suffer if a fund is bought at its highest price per share and is sold at the lowest price per share.

Example An investor in hedge fund A makes a minimum investment of $1.0 million. The fund could generate a profit of $500,000 over a period of one year for a compounded annual return of 50%. Alternatively, the fund could lose $250,000 over this same period for a maximum drawdown of 25%. This results in a Calmar ratio of 2, considered to be a good ratio by hedge fund analysts.

The higher the Calmar ratio, the better the risk-adjusted performance of the fund. A Calmar ratio of 1 or higher is considered good; 3 or higher is considered excellent; and 5 or higher is considered outstanding.

Morningstar's Computation of Risk-Adjusted Performance

Morningstar, Inc., describes its computation of the risk-adjusted return of a hedge fund as a four-step process[9]:

1. Calculate the monthly total returns for the fund.
2. Unsmooth the reported monthly returns over a period of at least 3 years (and also for 5 and 10 years if data is available).
3. Adjust the unsmooth returns for the risk-free rate for the same period or periods; the *Morningstar return* is then reported as the *annualized geometric mean excess return* for the period.
4. Calculate the *Morningstar risk-adjusted return* for the same period or periods as *the annualized certainty equivalent excess return* for the period (using statistical techniques).

Thus, the amount of risk reported by Morningstar is the difference between the Morningstar return and the Morningstar risk-adjusted return.

Many hedge funds own illiquid securities. An *illiquid security* in investment terminology means an asset that takes an inordinately long period to sell and convert to cash. There is generally a lack of demand for a thinly traded security. Accordingly, an illiquid security is very difficult to properly price, given the lack of readily available market prices. This leads to the hedge fund manager being largely able to establish the fund's price and manipulate the fund's reported returns. As a result, owning illiquid securities means a fund suffers from *smoothed returns* where all the reported returns have a high degree of correlation (little variation) and do not reflect the proper amount of risk assumed by the investor. To deal with this problem, Morningstar uses a series of *unsmoothed returns* to estimate risk-adjusted return.

The manner in which Morningstar unsmooths or adjusts the total return reported to it monthly by hedge fund managers is complex and involves differential calculus. The reference service uses *expected utility theory* in this adjustment, as first developed by mathematicians John Okenuv and Derek White. Expected utility theory posits that it is possible to quantify how investors feel (and then behave) by comparing one distribution of risk-adjusted returns to another distribution of these same returns. Specifically, a return distribution with a high expected return and a low risk is preferable to one with a low

[9] *Morningstar Rating Methodology for Hedge Funds*. December 2011. https://corporate.morningstar.com/us/documents/MethodologyDocuments/MethodologyPapers/HF_RatingMethodology.pdf.

expected return and a high risk. However, at some point (as measured by the *optimal portfolio along the efficient frontier* in MPT language), the level of risk becomes too great and the investor is willing to settle for a lower expected return to reduce risk. Morningstar uses expected utility theory to determine how much return a typical hedge fund investor is willing to forego in order to reduce risk. This is the *annualized geometric mean excess return* for the period referred to in step 3 of their risk-adjusted return computation.

Example Investor M has demonstrated no preference between one moderately risky hedge fund generating an observable annual return of 10% and a second, riskless fund generating a 4% return (conforming thereby to expected utility theory). In other words, Investor M is willing to give up 6%—the annualized geometric mean excess return—in exchange for the removal of risk.

Note Most hedge fund investors are moderately aggressive to aggressive investors as characterized in a standard risk profile. Thus, the typical hedge fund investor is usually unwilling to sacrifice much expected return in exchange for reduced risk.

When converting all series of reported total returns by hedge fund managers, Morningstar is then able to compare one hedge fund to another on a risk-adjusted basis.

Finally, to be reported by Morningstar and receive one of its star ratings, a hedge fund must have at least 38 continuous months of total returns. All funds in one of Morningstar's seven hedge fund categories are ranked in accordance with its risk-adjusted return computation and given a score. The funds with the highest score receive the most stars, with 5 stars being the maximum rating.

Hedge Fund Performance 1996–2011

A 2012 Bernstein Global Wealth Management research report found an annualized return of 7.3% for all hedge funds from 1996–2011 compared to an annualized return of 5.2% for stocks and 6.2% for bonds over the same period.[10] Most of the variability of return of hedge funds, or 60% of the annualized return quoted in the report, came from hedge fund managers attempting

[10] Bernstein Global Wealth Management and AllianceBernstein Global Wealth Management, "Demystifying Hedge Funds: Taking a Rigorous Research Approach." October 2012. `https://www.alliancebernstein.com/abcom/Perspectives_Web/Current/PrivateClient/DemystifyingHedgeFunds.pdf?uuid=67914af8-170a-11e2-91e8-d2f83f806d28`

to pursue a diversified alpha strategy (versus only 13% from this same source in an actively managed mutual fund). Finally, the report estimated that hedge fund managers achieved a median annualized alpha after fees in the analyzed period of 3.3% (versus only 0.4% for an active stock manager).

The Bernstein data shows that the higher portion of a hedge fund manager's return from his or her alpha decisions makes them a potentially useful portfolio diversifier for high-net-worth investors and institutions. Because alpha theoretically measures the contribution of manager expertise in a professionally managed asset, it is arguable that hedge fund managers from 1996–2011 also "earned their fee" in terms of generating excess performance compared to the stock market as a whole. However, as hedge funds have become larger in size, the probability of a fund maintaining a positive alpha has decreased. Just as with large, actively managed mutual funds, this inverse correlation occurs because the number of profitable opportunities for putting the hedge fund money to work is much less than before. For example, a large fund of any type that attempts to buy an undervalued stock will drive up the price of that stock simply because of the significant one-time demand for that stock caused by a large purchase. This speaks to the possibility of the need for smaller hedge funds and, by extension, a smaller industry, if hedge funds are to prosper in the future.

The next section reviews hedge fund performance during the interval 2008–2012 and identifies which hedge fund category performed best during this period of severe recession and subsequent very slow growth for the economy.

Recent Hedge Fund Performance 2008–2012

I researched the performance of hedge funds for the last five years of market performance (2008–2012), thereby including the pronounced market downturn and economic recession. The researched period also included the slow recovery of all major market indexes such as the S&P 500. I conclude that the HFRX Global Hedge Fund Index, a broad-based measure of the performance of all types of hedge funds, reflected a cumulative loss of all hedge funds of 13.6% over the five-year period. This was compared to a cumulative gain of the S&P 500 of 8.6% over the same period. Moreover, those funds with a stated investment objective of generating an *absolute return* regardless of market conditions suffered a cumulative loss of 18.7% from 2008–2012, equivalent to an annualized loss of -4.1%. This is significant because the term *hedge fund* implies protection against a loss in market value of the fund assets, with the objective of a positive absolute return further reinforcing this implication.

Which category of hedge fund produced the highest annual returns? The specific answer—as should be expected for a period of considerable decline in the value of the dollar and economic growth abroad—is the emerging market hedge fund. More generally, the global macro fund category also performed relatively well. According to the DJ/Credit Suisse Hedge Fund Index reporting the average return of all hedge fund categories from January 2007 to December 2012 (or one year preceding the start of the HFRX data), the S&P 500 was down a cumulative percentage of 2.9% during the period. The top-performing hedge fund style category during the same time frame—emerging markets—was up a total of 2.4%. Global macro was only slightly behind emerging markets during the same period with a total positive return of approximately 2%, but it was up a cumulative 11.3% over the most recent two years of 2011 and 2012. Remember, though, that the S&P 500, although flat in performance for 2011, increased 16.3% in 2012 when considering the reinvestment of all dividends and capital gains of the stocks in the index. Thus, hedge funds did not outperform the broader market in 2012.

My conclusion: A high-net-worth individual should carefully consider alternative forms of professionally managed assets before deciding to invest in a hedge fund or any of its widely accepted categories. Hedge funds generally have not proven their worth in the investment marketplace in terms of actual realized annual performance and—particularly given their high-cost structure—will likely have trouble outperforming broader-based stock and bond indexes in the future. There will be exceptionally performing funds, of course, and this chapter was designed to help the prospective investor identify proper criteria to use in selecting those funds.

The next chapter discusses another possible investment for accredited high-net-worth and high-income investors which also uses hedging techniques to minimize the risk of a substantial loss: *managed futures programs*.

CHAPTER

10

Managed Futures

Some investment advisors and reference services include managed futures as a type of hedge fund and report its performance along with other hedge fund strategies. There are, however, important differences between a managed futures fund or program and a traditional hedge fund. First, managed futures are generally proprietary and offered as an optional service by broker-dealer firms; whereas hedge funds are independently operated by a professional money manager.

Second, the trading of futures contracts in managed futures must be done by a professional holding the *commodity trading advisor* (CTA) designation and passing a certain examination (the Series 3 examination) required by the National Futures Association (NFA), a self-regulatory watchdog organization. The CTA makes all trading decisions on a client/investor's behalf by means of a revocable power of attorney. Most hedge fund managers do not hold or maintain the CTA designation.

Third, investors can usually trade in and out of managed futures once a month, usually with five business days' notice to the fund or program. In a hedge fund, the investor's power to withdraw money from the fund is much more limited and typically includes a *lock-up period*.

Preliminary to a discussion of managed futures, a basic understanding of futures, futures contracts, and futures markets is necessary.

Futures, Futures Contracts, and Futures Markets

Futures are a type of derivative or an asset that derives its value from another asset known as the *underlying*. They are sometimes referred to as an *alternative* investment because they not part of the three major asset classes (stocks, bonds, and cash). As a type of derivative, futures have no intrinsic value of their own, as stocks and bonds do. As discussed in Chapter 4, the intrinsic value of a security or an asset is defined as the present value of that security as determined using a *discounted cash flow* (DCF) approach to valuation. Intrinsic value has an advantage over a *relative valuation* method (such as the P/E of a stock) inasmuch as it does not rely on a comparison of its value to another marketplace security whereby market factors may distort the "true" value of the subject security. Intrinsic value depends only on information derived from the issuing company's financial statements and the proper analysis of this information by the investor or fundamental security analyst.

There are three broad types of futures and futures contracts: those involving commodities, such as agricultural products or precious metals; financial instruments, such as Treasury bills; and currencies, such as a country's currency (for example, the British pound). A *futures contract* is an agreement for the future delivery of a commodity or financial instrument at a specified date for a specified price. Such a contract often expires monthly; therefore, to maintain a constant presence in the market, futures traders must renew or *roll* the old futures contract by purchasing a new contract. The contract details the quality and quantity of the asset to be delivered and is standardized to facilitate trading on a futures exchange (or in the futures market). A contract similar to a futures contract is a *forward agreement*, which is entered into privately by two individuals or institutions and is not standardized for trading among buyers and sellers (the public). The majority of futures contracts historically have been for commodities, although recently financial futures and currency contracts have become much more prevalent.

There are two primary participants in the futures market: *speculators*, who establish positions in anticipation of price changes of the commodity or financial instrument; and *hedgers*, who use futures contracts and other types of derivative assets, such as options, to reduce risk.

Note A third type of participant in the futures markets—*arbitrageurs*—attempt to take advantage of mispricing of the contracts entered into by speculators and hedgers. Because in practice only very small arbitrage opportunities are observed in the futures markets, this discussion is limited to only the two primary participants.

Managed futures programs at the proprietary level are typically designed to hedge and not to speculate. The market price for a particular futures contract depends on the supply and demand for these contracts by speculators and hedgers. Speculators buy or sell futures contracts when there is an excess or insufficient supply. They are essential in erasing the imbalance of supply and demand resulting from the hedgers' inability to agree on prices for future delivery of the subject matter of the contracts (for example, commodities). Speculators are also essential in the marketplace to assume the transfer of risk from hedgers.

CTAs making the investment decisions in a managed futures program typically operate as hedgers in the futures market. As such, they reduce the risk of loss in a commodity, financial, or currency futures transaction by simultaneously taking the long and short positions in a particular transaction. Buying a futures contract is referred to as *going long* or *taking a long position*, whereas selling a futures contract is called *being short* or *taking a short position*.

An individual is *long* if he or she is in possession of the subject matter of the futures contract (for example, a farmer with the commodity wheat in the ground). Conversely, an individual is *short* if he or she wants or needs to possess the subject matter of the contract in the future (for example, a user of wheat). When an individual hedges, he or she takes the opposite position from the position in which they currently are in. For example, if the farmer is long and concerned about the possibility of a price decline of the wheat in the ground before he can harvest it and get it to market, he can go short and sell a futures contract to lock in the current higher price. This transaction is referred to as a *short hedge*. Because the user of wheat is short and is concerned about the possibility of a price increase before she needs the wheat, she would go long and buy a futures contract to establish a specified lower price or enter into a *long hedge*.

Example of a short hedge Assume that in June of a given year, a farmer has wheat in the ground that cost him $6.00 per bushel to produce. The price for delivery of that wheat in September (after harvesting) is $6.75 per bushel. Because the farmer is long, to hedge he takes the opposite position (or short) by selling a futures contract in June to lock in the price of $6.75 per bushel of wheat for September delivery. The buyer of that contract is likely a speculator in the futures market. If the price of wheat declines to $5.90 in September, the farmer suffers a potential price loss of $0.10 per bushel. However, because he sold a futures contract on this same wheat, the farmer receives $6.75 per bushel for his wheat, making a total profit of $.75 per bushel.

What if the price of wheat increases to $7.50 per bushel in September? The farmer still receives the price of $6.75 and makes a profit of $0.75 per bushel. Who gets the remaining profit of $0.75 per bushel ($1.50 total price increase in wheat less sales price profit of $0.75)? The buyer of the futures contract or speculator to whom the risk of loss was transferred by the farmer/hedger.

In a managed futures program, the CTA essentially takes the place of the farmer if engaging in a short hedge. If engaging in a long hedge, the CTA hedges in the opposite direction and takes the place of the user of wheat by purchasing a futures contract to lock in a lower price for delivery of the wheat. In either position, the CTA puts up very little of the purchase price of the contract as cash collateral and thus extensively uses margin.

Why is a speculator interested in the futures market? Because of the possibility of **leverage**. In a futures transaction, the individual (either on the buy or sell side of the transaction) provides an amount of money to guarantee the contract's execution. This amount of money, referred to as **margin**, is very small in relation to the size of the transaction or contract—sometimes as small as 5% of the total. It is rarely higher than 10%, although in times of high market volatility, the initial margin requirement may increase to 15%. Because the amount of margin is so small, the possibility of a significant percentage gain is increased beyond that which is possible with more of the individual's money at risk.

Example of leverage in the futures market (continuing the previous example of a short hedge) Assume that the speculator's contract controls 10,000 bushels of wheat harvested by the farmer or $67,500 in total (10,000 times $6.75 per bushel). The contract has a margin requirement of 5%, meaning the speculator must deposit $3,375 to the farmer's broker, who maintains the margin account on behalf of the farmer. Then assume that, as in the previous example, the price per bushel of wheat for September delivery increases to $7.50. This means the speculator's profit is $0.75 per bushel (after the farmer's price received) or a total of $7,500, for a total percentage profit of 222% ($7,500 divided by $3,375 times 100).

Of course, the price could also go *against* the speculator by September (the September price of wheat could decline rather than increase), thereby magnifying the percentage loss to the speculator. This is why, as the amount of leverage increases, so does the risk of investment to the investor!

The futures market is regulated by the Commodity Futures Trading Commission (CFTC). CTAs must also register with the CFTC before they can manage public money. As with mutual funds and mutual fund trading, which are regulated by the SEC, the CFTC does not protect market participants from a loss in value. Rather, the regulation is limited to enforcing uniform standards for trading on the futures exchange. The primary commodity futures exchange is the Chicago Mercantile Exchange (CME), which merged with the Chicago Board of Trade in 2008 to form the CME Group. Financial and currency futures are traded on various exchanges throughout the world, including New York City and London. A clearing house acts as an intermediary in futures transactions. One of the functions of the clearing house is to guarantee that no default of the contract entered into by the parties occurs. Thus, no default risk is inherent in futures trading.

What Is a Managed Futures Fund or Program?

A *managed futures fund* is an open-ended investment company (or mutual fund) managed by CTAs or, sometimes, by a registered individual known as a *commodity pool operator* (CPO). A *managed futures program* is typically proprietary and is structured as a limited partnership with the securities firm serving as the general partner in the program. Such a program is offered as an additional service of broker-dealers for interested clients, who tend to be higher-net-worth, relatively aggressive investors. The program is also managed by a CTA or CPO. These advisors select the specific futures contracts to be bought and sold in lieu of an individual investor, who typically does not have either the time or the expertise to engage in futures trading. Alternatives to managed future funds and programs are exchange-traded funds (ETFs) and exchange-traded notes (ETNs) with portfolios based on a commodity index. (Chapter 8 discusses ETFs and ETNs.)

As of 2013, there are about 50 managed futures mutual funds, up from only one such fund in the year 2009. Investments in such funds can be made with a relatively low initial investment of $500, whereas minimum investments in managed futures programs are much larger, sometimes as much as $250,000. Managed futures mutual funds introduced the concept of **momentum-based** investment trading strategies to investors; they feature, as do the portfolio assets of a managed futures proprietary program, an extremely low long-term correlation to traditional stocks and bonds. Thus, managed futures mutual funds, ETFs, and proprietary programs serve as effective diversifiers in the overall investment portfolios of knowledgeable clients.

CTA managers of managed futures accounts follow two main types of investment approaches or strategies. The first is *trend following,* whereby managers use proprietary or fundamental methods to determine the direction of a trade—that is, whether to pursue a long or a short hedge. The second strategy is *market neutral,* whereby managers look to generate a profit from futures trading among many different global markets or among different futures contracts in the same market. Those who practice market-neutral strategies to profit from nondirectional trading in future markets are known as *spreaders.* These approaches are not mutually exclusive, and some CTA managers simultaneously pursue both strategies.

Advantages of Managed Futures

A managed futures program or fund offers several advantages. Among these are the following:

- Greater transparency and liquidity
- Unique income tax advantages

- Enhanced returns
- Reduced portfolio volatility risk
- Participation in global markets

The following sections examine each of these possible advantages in turn.

Greater Transparency and Liquidity

The term *transparency* is used a great deal in investments and essentially means that there are no impediments in the disclosure of market activity undertaken by the portfolio manager and the investor. In the case of managed futures, *transparency* means that investors in the program or fund see every trade made by the fund's manager. The investors also receive confirmations of each trade, with respect to either the buy or sell side of the transaction. Typically, online access to trades is also available. Although transparency is also usually afforded the investor in mutual fund transactions, the lack of transparency is a definite disadvantage in traditional hedge fund and funds-of-funds investing, because trading there occurs largely in private markets.

Another advantage of managed futures is their relatively greater liquidity. Futures contracts trade every market day and can usually be bought or sold very quickly—generally in a matter of seconds. They can usually be *offset* or closed out quickly by means of a reverse trade. As discussed in the "Futures, Futures Contracts, and Futures Markets" section, one of the requirements of futures contracts and futures trading is that the party that is long (that is, the party that is in possession of the commodity or financial instrument) *delivers* the subject matter of the contract. For commodity futures, delivery normally consists of sending a warehouse receipt for the appropriate quantity of the underlying commodity. For financial futures, delivery is most often accomplished by a transfer of registered ownership to the buyer. However, delivery as a means of closing out a futures contract is not as frequent as offsetting a futures position.

When a futures position is offset or closed out, the position holder (typically a speculator) simply takes a position opposite from the position that he or she occupies in the market. For example, suppose a speculator is short the commodity of wheat and has a contract to buy wheat in September. If the speculator wishes to close her position, she can go long and sell a contract for the delivery of wheat in September. Therefore, the two contracts cancel or offset each other, because one is a purchase and the other is a sale of the wheat. This also makes the delivery of wheat to the speculator unnecessary. However, just because the contracts are canceled and delivery does not take place, that does not mean profits or losses on the contracts do not occur. Quite the contrary: because the speculator can enter into a contract for the purchase of wheat at any reasonable price, and because gains and losses for each margin account are **marked-to-the-market** at the end of each futures trading day, there may be a realized profit or loss.

Example Assume that a speculator enters into a contract to buy wheat at $6.00 per bushel for September delivery (the speculator goes long). If the price of wheat rises to $6.10 per bushel for September delivery, the speculator makes a profit of $0.10 per bushel (times however many bushels are the subject of the contract).

Operationally, funds are transferred into the speculator's margin account and withdrawn from the margin account of the farmer or other speculator who is short. If, as a result of the transfer of funds, the losing party's margin account does not meet the maintenance margin requirement established by the brokerage firm, the broker issues a margin call. The losing party must meet the margin call (deposit the requisite amount of money in the account to bring the account equity up to the maintenance margin requirement), or the broker closes out the loser's position.

Of course, the long speculator in the previous example might see the price of wheat decline for September delivery and thereby sustain a loss at the end of the futures trading day. But as a practical matter, speculators are very aware of their risky position and typically close out their position to limit losses. An experienced managed futures manager who is hedging in the same manner as the speculator will do the same to limit the client's exposure to losses in the account.

Unique Income Tax Advantages

There is a capital gains tax preference for investments that are held for a certain period of time. Currently, this period of time, otherwise referred to as the *long-term capital gains preference*, applies to most investments that are owned for a period of more than one year before they are sold. This preference awards a tax rate of only 15% for most investors and no tax rate whatsoever for investors in the lowest 10% and 15% marginal income tax brackets (the rate is 15% for taxpayers in the 25% or above brackets and reaches 20% for those in the highest tax bracket of 39.6%). However, this required holding period to achieve a capital gains preference does not apply in the case of futures and managed futures transactions.

Per the Economic Recovery and Tax Act of 1981 (ERTA), short-term profits (those resulting from futures contracts of one year or less in duration) are treated as 60% long term and 40% short term. Thus, 60% of the profit is eligible for the lower capital gains preference rate of 15% (or zero or 20% in some cases). This is in marked contrast to short-term trading profits in stock that are taxed as 100% short term. The ability to have more than half of potential profits taxed as a long-term gains in futures transactions is a considerable tax advantage to participants in a managed future fund or program. Why does the government provide for such tax advantage for futures? Presumably because the government recognizes the importance of providing liquidity to a market that may potentially suffer from a lack of liquidity, thereby rewarding those participants assuming the risk of an otherwise-risky investment.

An additional tax planning strategy arises from the capital gains preference awarded to all futures markets participants. If a managed futures investor includes his or her account in a self-directed IRA or retirement plan, the compounding power of tax-advantaged gains increases. As an example, if a managed futures investment is made in a tax-deferred account, such as a retirement plan, the profits from the account grow entirely tax-free until distributed. Moreover, investing with futures in a retirement account broadens the markets in which the investor participates, thereby spreading investment risk.

Enhanced Returns

The advantage of enhanced returns by means of the percentage-rewarding effects of leverage in futures contracts was touched on in the "Futures, Futures Contracts, and Futures Markets" section. But to a CTA managing a managed futures fund or program who is most interested in hedging, the possibility of an enhanced return is not as important as the risk-reduction potential of the fund. Remember, hedging is focused on minimizing price losses more than maximizing price increases of the fund, which is the primary concern of speculators participating in the futures market.

The type of return that is of interest to both hedgers and speculators is a **risk-adjusted return**. This involves the computation of a fund's *drawdown*—the maximum peak-to-valley drop in the fund's performance. A ratio used to measure the extent of a managed future's fund drawdown is the Calmar ratio, discussed in Chapter 9 in relation to evaluating the performance of a hedge fund manager. This ratio and drawdown percentage may also be used in comparing the performance and return of managed futures to major stock indexes, such as the S&P 500. In this regard, it is interesting to note that, during the period of January 1980 to 2003 (a period that encompassed several bear markets, including a severe bear market from 2001–2002), managed futures had a maximum drawdown rate of only −15.7% compared to the S&P 500's drawdown rate of −44.7%. More recent managed futures performance is discussed in the final section, which demonstrates that managed futures managers have been hedging effectively for a long time.

Reduced Portfolio Volatility Risk

As discussed in Chapter 4, the diversification of a portfolio is best accomplished by combining assets with a negative correlation to one another or assets with as low as positive correlation as possible. As an asset class, managed futures may be inversely or negatively correlated with other asset classes such as stocks or bonds. A study, for example, found that the returns on long positions in commodity index futures are negatively correlated with the returns from comparable equity portfolios.[1] Largely this is because most worldwide commodities are traded in U.S. dollars; therefore, as the dollar falls in value, commodities tend to rise. Gold also shows some negative correlation with stocks and bonds. This fact of negative correlation between assets leads to hedging opportunities for managed futures portfolio managers.

If two asset classes have a perfect negative correlation of −1.0, then when one asset class has a higher than expected return, the other asset class has a lower than expected return. The exact reason for this is beyond the scope of discussion in this book. Nevertheless, this fact means that it is possible to weight a portfolio's assets so that all total risk of the portfolio (as measured by standard deviation) is eliminated. Moreover, such a portfolio would have a positive expected return equal to the weighted average of the asset classes' expected returns. Essentially, the higher expected return of one asset class would predominate over the lower expected return of the other asset class. The appropriate weighting of the asset classes (for example, futures with equities) and the optimization of the investor's allocated capital are the goal of the CTA portfolio manager.

If the CTA is successful in asset allocation and optimal minimization of risk, the volatility (ups and downs) that most stock investors experience is smoothed out. The negative correlation between futures and traditional asset classes also means that managed futures can potentially profit in any market environment. As an example, if the stock market is declining, the inclusion of managed futures in an investor's portfolio may offset the severity of the decline by exhibiting a positive return. Alternatively, if the stock market is rising, most of the upside potential of the increase in stock prices is still realized with a managed futures component.

Participation in Global Markets

Managed futures are traded on many regulated commodities and financial futures markets around the world. Some 150 futures markets are available to CTA managers through improved technology and electronic networks.

---

[1]Gary Gorton and K. Geert Rouwenhurst. "Facts and Fantasies about Commodity Futures." *Financial Analysts Journal*, 62, no. 2 (2006): 47–68.

After the CME Group in Chicago, the Latin American exchanges handle the greatest volume of trading, with Asia following. Interestingly, the City of London exchanges are down the list with respect to the volume of futures contracts traded.

The growth of futures markets around the world offers CTAs the opportunity to diversify funds and programs not only by product, but also by geography. Each of these markets exhibits some negative correlation to the others. (Note that one of the advantages of investing in international or global mutual funds is the negative or lower positive correlation among the respective countries' economies and resident companies.) Finally, investing in managed futures on a global scale affords the investor some protection against the political risk of some countries by spreading the risk among more stable countries. Political or country risk, like currency risk, can affect the value of commodities and financial futures similarly.

Disadvantages of Managed Futures

As mentioned at the beginning of this chapter, some reference services treat managed futures programs as a type of hedge fund. Therefore, the disadvantages of managed futures are very similar to those of hedge funds (Chapter 9). Three disadvantages that are partially or fully unique to managed futures funds or programs warrant additional discussion. These three disadvantages are as follow:

- Futures are an extremely risky investment, due not only to the amount of leverage used by traders but also to the unique characteristics of the futures market.
- Futures are very difficult to explain to a new, potential investor.
- Management fees associated with managed futures programs are high.

Futures Are Extremely Risky

The extent of leverage employed by futures traders (hedgers and speculators) was discussed in the first section. Nevertheless, two conditions unique to futures markets—*contango* and its opposite, *normal backwardation*—can significantly increase volatility and lead to *roll losses* by traders.

In futures trading and futures markets, it is important to understand that as a futures contract approaches its maturity or expiration date, the futures price must converge toward the spot price. (See Chapter 1 for a discussion of futures and futures prices.) This is because at the date of maturity, the futures price must equal the spot price; otherwise, arbitrage—the making of a risk-free profit—would be possible. Traders monitor the relationship of the spot price to the future price through a futures yield curve. If conditions in the futures market are normal or positive, the shape of this curve is upward-sloping—meaning futures prices are rising and the futures price is below the expected future spot price. This is called *normal backwardation* and results in the making of a profit when traders roll futures contracts from one month to the next. In other words, the *roll return* is positive when traders can sell last month's futures contracts for more than it costs them to buy next month's contract.

However, futures markets and the shape of the futures yield curve can be the opposite of the normal backwardation condition. That is, the futures market scenario known as *contango* can arise. In this condition or scenario, futures prices are falling and the future prices is above the expected future spot price. Thus, the roll return of traders, particularly speculators, turns negative, and traders now have to buy next month's contract for more than the amount for which they can sell last month's contract. This leads to trading losses, which, given the extent of leverage used, are multiplied in percentage. An experienced CTA can anticipate the shape of the futures yield curve changing and contango arising—but those who do not add to the losses incurred by a client.

Regardless of the shape of the futures yield curve, normal backwardation and contango increase the volatility of the futures market and futures trading. A method for reducing this volatility is to invest in a managed futures fund that tracks an index (a managed futures index fund) and returns only a small *roll yield*. Such a fund takes into account normal backwardation and contango and reduces the volatility of the futures market. In practical effect, the investor in a managed futures index fund is sacrificing the possibility of a sizeable positive return for limiting the amount of potential losses that may be incurred in futures trading. A managed futures program manager or CTA who is hedging and not speculating has this same objective.

Futures Are Difficult to Explain

A major precept of Warren Buffett in describing how he invests (and how others should invest) is, "Never invest in something you do not understand!" Futures and futures markets exemplify the truth of that statement for most investors. Moreover, derivatives generally are not well understood by many, including some investment advisors, and therefore they should be avoided unless you take the time to educate yourself about what they are, how they are traded, and how to make an informed decision about whether to make such an investment and at what price. Although managed futures by definition transfer much of this responsibility to an expert, investors still need to have a basic understanding of futures and alternative investments to select the correct expert to manage what is often a significant initial minimum sum to establish an account. Of course, these minimums can be significantly reduced by investing in a managed futures mutual fund or ETF alternative.

It is not easy to find information about futures or to monitor their performance. Although the CFTC does provide extensive market reports about futures to industry participants and the public, major financial newspapers like the *Wall Street Journal* gives only broad information (although it is provided daily). In addition, futures price information and quotes, even when given, are not easy to understand. For example, there is a category of information entitled *open interest*—which means the total of all futures contracts entered into and not yet offset by transaction (taking an opposite position to close out the contract) or delivery of the underlying asset. Should this number be high or low? Experts in futures can divine that a large amount of open interest means new money is flowing into the futures marketplace and the present price trend will continue. A declining open interest number implies that the prevailing present price trend is coming to an end. Thus, major market moves (up, down, or sideways) can be anticipated. However, this can only be done in conjunction with an understanding of past prices for the contract and the volume of buying and selling. In summary, futures trading is extremely complex and should only be conducted by an investor or market professional who knows what they are doing!

Management Fees Are High

Unless you are investing in a managed futures index fund, or sometimes a managed futures mutual fund that is passively managed, management fees in managed futures programs can be equivalent to those of hedge funds. For example, just as hedge funds do, managed futures programs usually charge an annual management fee and a performance fee, with both fees based on a net (or after-commission) profit. The standard management fee is 2%, and the standard performance fee is 20% of net profit. The management fee is assessed even in the event of a loss in value of the account for the investor. Moreover, when trading in the account occurs, a typical broker's commission of 6% on the amount of the trade is passed along to the account holder. The broker may also charge an introductory fee when the investor first invests in the account.

The positive news is that operating expenses in a managed futures account generally are not as high as those of hedge funds, owing to a lower cost of compliance with legal, accounting, auditing, and other management expenses.

Who Should Participate in a Managed Futures Fund or Program?

Since the mid-1980s, institutions have been heavy investors in managed futures. Such institutions include pension funds, insurance companies, endowments, and private foundations. More recently, however, individual investors have opened accounts either with managed futures funds or as part of managed futures programs. Individuals invested in a fund, particularly an index-based fund, can enjoy the benefits of the fund with a small opening deposit, whereas individuals participating in a program tend to be accredited investors with a high minimum net worth or income. It is estimated that approximately $200 billion of assets are under management in managed fund programs. This can be expected to increase as long as the stock markets continue to be volatile and hedge fund returns underperform, as discussed in Chapter 9.

Why should an individual include managed futures as a part of his or her portfolio? To the reasons discussed in the "Advantages of Managed Futures" section, the following five reasons may be added:

- Managed futures permit an investor to diversify beyond the traditional asset classes.
- Overall portfolio volatility is reduced.
- Potential returns may be increased.
- Enhanced returns are possible in any kind of market environment.
- Strong performance is likely even in a down market.

As mentioned, futures as an asset class, and specifically gold futures or futures that track a gold index, are negatively correlated with stocks and only slightly positively correlated with bonds. Between 1994 and 2012, futures had a negative 0.09 correlation to the S&P 500 index of large-cap stocks. (This is not perfect negative correlation, but nevertheless, there is inverse movement between the asset classes.) During the same period, futures had only a positive 0.19 correlation with the Barclay's Aggregate Bond Index. Therefore, in an inflationary environment, which is not good for either the stock or bond market, futures can serve as a significant hedge against losses. As a result, risk-averse investors should include a percentage of their portfolio in managed futures. The appropriate percentage varies among knowledgeable investment advisors, but a core holding of 10–15% of total assets is probably beneficial.

What Selection Criteria Should Be Used before Including Managed Futures in a Portfolio?

Selection criteria to consider before including managed futures as part of your portfolio include the following:

- Decide if futures are right for you.
- Decide what type of trading style pursued by the CTA manager is right for you.
- Compare the return of one managed futures fund or program to another on a risk-adjusted basis.
- Study the disclosure document provided by the fund or program for the applicable fee structure.
- Find a CTA with whom you are comfortable.

Decide if Futures Are Right for You

If you were to look at a risk pyramid measuring the expected return of an investment with the investment risk assumed by the investor, you would find futures at the very top of the pyramid. This means that futures are extremely risky and only for the very risk-aggressive, particularly if you are in the market as a speculator. Futures prices can change very rapidly and generate sudden losses or considerable profits. Thus, you should be comfortable with this volatility if participating in a managed futures proprietary program or investing in a managed futures fund. The risk is magnified by the degree of leverage inherent in futures trading. Brokers opening a margin account, which is necessary to participate in the futures program, assist the investor in determining whether futures trading is feasible. This is the case because brokers open such an account only if the investor has proven they can withstand the potential losses from futures trading.

Whereas managed futures portfolio managers are usually in the futures market to hedge, investors who are *bona fide hedgers*—in the market only to hedge—make up only about 2% of the overall futures market. Thus, speculators predominate! Although the presence of speculators is critical in the operation of the futures market, such individuals are there for only one reason: to make a sizeable profit by taking advantage of leverage. When a bear market is anticipated, speculators can add to the downward pressure on prices by going short and selling futures contracts. The average investor needs to be aware of this possibility. In addition, like a hedge fund manager, a managed futures portfolio manager is under extreme pressure to perform—to achieve a sizeable positive, absolute return for investors. To this pressure is added the incentive of the manager's performance reward of 20% receipt of profits. Before allocating a percentage of his or her portfolio to managed futures, the investor also needs to be aware that the managed futures manager is under pressure to assume the position of speculator rather than hedger.

Decide What Type of Trading Style Is Right for You

As noted in the "What Is a Managed Fund or Program?" section, CTA managers of a managed futures fund or program tend to follow either a *trend-following* or *market-neutral* strategy when trading futures. Trend followers try to discern price trends in the futures markets as signals as to when to go long or short. This is similar to what a technical analyst does more broadly in advising clients when to buy or sell in the stock market. Alternatively, market-neutral managers aim to profit from nondirectional trading strategies. Their goal is to arbitrage market mispricing by betting on the convergence of spreads—the difference between the increase in value from a long position and the decrease in value from a short position. Although probably oversimplified, because market-neutral strategies do not use past or current market trends to dictate trading, the approach is similar to that of a traditional fundamental analyst. Which is best? There is no definitive answer to this question; but if you believe in any form of market efficiency (including futures markets), trend following or technical analysis is likely to be of little use to you as an investor. Therefore, you may wish to diversify your portfolio with a managed futures fund or program manager following more of a market-neutral strategy.

Efficient markets and the efficient-market hypothesis (EMH) were discussed in Chapters 4 and 6. As first developed by Eugene Fama, winner of the Nobel Prize in Economics, and subsequently refined by others, the efficient-market hypothesis does not analyze efficiency in the futures markets. However, a basic assumption of efficient markets is that prices correct very quickly to prevent arbitrage from occurring.

In the futures market, a relationship known as **spot-futures parity** must hold in the absence of arbitrage opportunities. The spot-futures parity formula is:

$$F = S(1 + r)^T$$

where

F is the futures price

S is the spot or cash price

r is the risk-free rate of interest per period

T is the number of periods (maturity date of the futures contract)

By using this formula, an investor or a CTA manager can determine what the futures price *should be* relative to the spot price. If the futures price derived by the formula is not the same as the futures price established by the futures exchange, then an opportunity for arbitrage exists (although probably only for an instantaneous period of time and with a very slim profit margin).

Example Assume that you are engaged in a financial futures transaction and speculating on the futures price of a non-dividend-paying stock, such as a technology stock. The price of this stock is currently $50 per share. The risk-free rate is 4% per year, and the futures contract on the stock matures in six months. When using the spot-futures parity formula, you find that the futures price should be $ 51.00, determined as follows:

$$S(1 + r)^{T}$$

$$= \$50\ (1 + .04)^{.50} = \$50\ (1.0198) = \$50.99 \approx \$51.00 \text{ per share}$$

If the futures price of this stock was below $51.00—let's say $50.50—you would short 100 shares of stock (a round lot) at $50 per share and invest the $5,000 proceeds at 4% annually. You would then buy a futures contract (go long because you are shorting the stock) and make a risk-free profit of $50 as follows:

At the end of the six months, you would have ($5,000 × 1.02) = $5,100.

You would then use $5,050 to buy the stock to fulfill your obligation on the futures contract and return the stock to close out the short position. Thus, you pocket the $50 without taking any risk—the definition of *arbitrage*.

Of course, if an arbitrage condition were to exist, you could make even more risk-free profit by buying more shares or round lots of stock and then shorting them. However, this example does indicate the slim profit margin associated with arbitrage in the futures market—a margin that is even slimmer with a low risk-free rate, such as currently exists in the marketplace.

Compare Return on a Risk-Adjusted Basis

You should compare the risk-adjusted returns of several managed futures funds or programs. In the case of managed futures, as with hedge funds, a ratio measuring the average drawdown or dispersion of returns from that of an average level may be used as an appropriate metric. For hedge funds, the Calmar ratio divides the *maximum drawdown* into the compounded annual return of the fund. The *average drawdown* is a variation of the Calmar denominator suited to managed futures: instead of the maximum dispersion from the peak to trough of returns over a three-year period, it is an average dispersion.

Example Managed futures Fund A has a quoted annualized return of 20%, and Fund B has a return of 12%, but Fund A has an average drawdown of –20% and Fund B has an average drawdown of –4%. Therefore, the return-to-average-drawdown ratio of Fund A is 1, whereas the return-to-average-drawdown ratio of Fund B is 3. This means that Fund B, although exhibiting a lower quoted annualized return, has a better risk-adjusted return. Said another way, the investor in Fund B is receiving a higher annualized return per unit of risk assumed.

There are, of course, other risk-adjusted metrics, such as the Sharpe ratio and alpha (the Jensen ratio). These may also be used for purposes of comparison, and many CTA-tracking services provide them to a prospective investor. The NFA requires that CTAs use standardized performance measures in their disclosure document, which is the managed futures equivalent of a mutual fund prospectus.

Study the Disclosure Document for the Fee Structure

There is a general understanding among prospective investors that managed futures program managers (CTAs) are compensated very similarly to hedge fund managers—that is, they receive an incentive performance fee of 20% of generated profits. Specifically, you should review the disclosure document provided by the managed futures program or fund to determine if there is a front-end service charge (*load*) to participate in the program or fund. If it is a program, there probably is not, because performance fees predominate along with an annual management fee of 2%. But a managed futures fund may have a load. Mutual funds, including managed futures funds, are generally prohibited from charging a performance fee. However, some managed futures program have gotten around this by taking advantage of a loophole known as the *commodity-trading-advisor structure*. In such a structure, CTA managers use multiple hedge fund managers through offshore entities, which are not considered subadvisors to the fund and can charge performance-based fees. This structure is extremely difficult to ascertain from the disclosure document and from the actual operation of the fund because any performance fees are deducted from the fund's NAV. As of the year 2012, 11 managed futures funds were using the structure, holding 35% of all fund assets estimated at $7 billion.

In 2012, the CFTC voted to have all managed futures mutual funds that invest in commodity futures register with it, along with the previously required SEC. Thus, two regulatory bodies now have jurisdiction over the majority of managed futures funds (versus programs). Generally, the CFTC requires more extensive disclosure than does the SEC, including the monthly reporting of any performance fees charged by the fund. In addition, the new CFTC oversight requires funds to include a break-even analysis showing how much the fund needs to earn on an annual basis to compensate for the performance fees being charged.

What about maintenance fees and initial minimums disclosed in the disclosure document? Typically, managed futures fund maintenance fees are somewhat higher than those of the typical, actively managed mutual fund, but these fees have been coming down in recent years. As stated, managed futures programs usually charge a 2% standard maintenance fee. Although the initial minimums are lower for managed futures funds than for programs, some funds essentially trade off lower-than-average maintenance fees for a higher minimum investment. For example, one fund may charge a 1.25% maintenance fee but require a $1.0 million initial investment.

Find a CTA with Whom You Are Comfortable

Because a CTA is trading for you in a *discretionary account*, such that he or she does not have to seek your prior approval for any trade that is made in it, the selection of a proper CTA is particularly important in managed futures. In the final analysis, your selection is a judgment call, but there are certain items to consider in making this call:

- In a proprietary program, start by interviewing all brokers who are considered futures specialists by the brokerage firm. Typically, the firm assists in this process by prescreening brokers with whom you may feel comfortable.
- Consider the CTA's past track record. Although "past results are no guarantee of future performance," they do give you a place to begin; and if the past results are favorable (and are relatively longer in time), that is of course preferable to a negative record over a short period of time.
- Ask about the CTA's investment trading style, and determine whether it aligns with your preferred style or strategies with respect to a managed futures fund or program.
- Ask the CTA how he or she is compensated. Some managers may take excessive and unnecessary risk if they reap a reward in the form of a performance fee and think more short-term when you are (and should be) a long-term investor in managed futures.
- Check the NFA website for any possible disciplinary action that may have been imposed on the advisor (and how this action was settled with the NFA).

Remember, you should only be investing in managed futures if you are an experienced investor with a history of mutual fund or other types of PMA investing. Follow the same procedure and account for the same basic considerations you used in selecting a manager for that previous share and allocation of your portfolio.

How to Evaluate the Performance of a Managed Futures Fund or Program

The trading of futures contracts on margin makes the performance history of managed futures funds or programs unique. Specifically, managed futures programs often use at most 15% of their assets for margin or an initial good-faith deposit on a futures contract—and most of the time only 5% of the total (*notional*) value of the contract. This small deposit leaves the remainder of the assets in the fund or program to be reinvested, usually in cash equivalents such as U. S. Treasury securities. These cash equivalents, in turn, generate interest for the fund or program, adding to its total return.

Many academic studies have been done examining the performance of managed futures funds and programs (although the latter more than the former, because the first managed futures fund did not debut until late 2009). Many of these studies neglect to include the portion of return that comes from interest on the cash collateral or cash equivalents held among the assets of the fund or program. In other words, they focus only on the returns that are derived from the trading of futures contracts and understate the total return. Although the interest generated on cash-equivalent assets has been at historically low levels since the financial market meltdown of 2008–2009, some of these studies go back well before that event. The Barclays CTA Index, which tracks the performance of managed futures programs, returned more than 6% on an annualized basis from 1994 to 2009, some of which consisted of higher interest rates earned on cash collateral assets.[2]

Morningstar Advisor cites its own data in analyzing the part that cash collateral interest contributed to the total return of managed futures programs.[3] Between January 1994 and December 2012, the Morningstar MSCI Systematic Trading Index returned an annualized 8.6% return. During the same period, U.S. Treasury securities returned an annualized 3.1%. Assuming an 85%/15% split between the return from futures trading and cash collateral, the cash portion contributed 2.6% of the total return over the same time period. Subtracting the cash portion return yields the same 6% return of the Barclay's

[2]Barclay CTA Index, BarclayHedge, www.barclayhedge.com.

[3]*Morningstar Advisor* magazine. Morningstar Inc. www.Morningstar.com.

CTA index from 1994–2009. Therefore, it is safe to say that managed futures programs and funds returned at least a 6% annualized return since 1994 to date—not a bad return considering the extreme volatility of the stock market during this period, particularly since the year 2000. Moreover, managed futures programs and funds generated this return by smoothing out the stock market's volatility.

How did managed futures programs perform in 2008, when the S&P 500 declined by 37%—the worst stock market year since 1937? According to the Credit Suisse/Tremont Managed Futures Index, managed futures strategies resulted in a gain of 17.59%, not accounting for fees and other expenses.[4] It is also interesting to note that bonds as an asset class exhibited a positive return in 2008 but increased only 2.93% when using Vanguard's Total Bond Market Index ETF as a proxy. (Note also that hedge funds generated a negative return of 20% in 2008.) Thus, the negative correlation power of managed futures to stocks and low positive correlation to bonds proved true in 2008 and dispelled any doubts overall as to their importance as an effective diversifier in an investor's portfolio.

As a prospective investor, you should ascertain the following metrics used to evaluate the historical performance of managed futures funds and programs:

- Annualized return (in both bullish and bearish markets)
- Risk-adjusted return and average drawdown
- Sharpe and Calmar ratios
- Alpha coefficients
- Performance in relation to certain relevant benchmark indexes

Respecting the future of managed futures funds and programs, investors should be aware that managed future strategies that are based on interest-rate declines, such as shorting currencies of nations that are attempting to stimulate their economies, will probably no longer thrive. As interest rates rise, however, managed futures funds and programs may be expected to receive a greater return on their allocations to cash and cash equivalents, returning them to more normal levels. In addition, traditional hedging strategies used to lower overall portfolio risk should continue to be of value.

The next chapter takes up the third and last topic in professionally managed assets for high-net-worth investors: a potential investment in the growth of private businesses via a private equity fund.

---

[4]Credit Suisse Tremont Managed Futures Index, Credit Suisse Group, www.hedgeindex.com.

CHAPTER

11

Private Equity Funds

The world of private equity and private equity funds is potentially very lucrative (offering the potential for extremely high returns) but extremely risky (not for the faint of heart). Private equity generally buys distressed private (non-publicly traded) businesses, positions them in a fund available to wealthy investors, and attempts to turn those businesses around financially before "taking the business public"—that is, engaging in an *initial public offering* (IPO) of the shares. A segment of private equity firms also invests in start-up businesses and are known as *venture capitalists*. Because individual investors in private equity funds are primarily *accredited investors* (investors with a net worth of at least $1.0 million, excluding primary residence), it is appropriate that private equity and private equity funds constitute the third and final chapter in this section on professionally managed assets for high-net-worth investors. Because of the paucity of individual investors with the requisite capital to fund private equity and private equity funds, the industry primarily depends on institutional investors, such as pension funds, to provide capital.

Before branching into a detailed discussion of private equity funds, a broader look at the world of private equity is required.

Private Equity

Private equity is, fundamentally, an investment in a non-publicly traded business. Because the equity is directed to private firms, most of the capital provided is afforded to an *unincorporated* entity (unlike public businesses, which are almost exclusively *incorporated*). The most common form of unincorporated entity in private business today is the *sole proprietorship*. A major disadvantage of organizing a business in the sole proprietorship form is its inability to secure much capital from the public. Indeed, there is a maxim that the primary investors in a sole proprietorship (beyond the founder) are "friends, families, and fools"! However, private equity firms, in their role as venture capitalists, are not among the "fools" investing in a sole-proprietorship private business or the proprietorship's cousin, a one-member *limited liability company* (LLC).

Private equity firms undertake considerable time and resources in performing **due diligence** with respect to potential private businesses in which they invest, so much so that the actual funding of startup businesses by private equity/venture capital firms is less than 2%.

Why does private equity fund such a small percentage of startup businesses? The answer in short is the "lack of sufficient growth" inherent in most private businesses. The notable exceptions to this limitation are technology and bio-technology (pharmaceutical) firms, which do exhibit the type of growth curve desired by private equity firms. The preferred annualized growth rate of a private business (before the private equity firm takes the business public) is 50–70%—a financial impossibility for most businesses that are not on the cutting edge of technology or developing a new product or service sought after by a broad swath of the public. In exchange for this cash infusion in a startup business, the private equity firm receives equity (common stock), or sometimes convertible preferred stock, in the business with a future goal of an IPO of the equity and a (hopefully) sizeable return on its money. The terms of the private equity stake or investment in the business is presented to its management team and founders through a **term sheet**. Issues that are addressed in the term sheet vary among firms, but in all sheets the present value of the private business must be determined prior to investment by the firm or outside investors.

Private equity firms are also in the business of turning around and stabilizing the cash flow of public businesses that are experiencing so-called "financial distress" (on the road to possible insolvency and/or bankruptcy). To that end, a private equity firm may take a public company *private*. This means that the firm, usually with capital from outside investors in the form of a private equity fund, typically places directors on the now-private firm's board of directors and arranges for the financing needed to purchase the publicly held stock. When the financing requires substantial borrowing or debt, as is typical in reorganizing the public business into a private entity, a transaction referred to as a *leveraged buyout* (LBO) occurs. These buyouts are very risky to the investor, because the purchased company's balance sheet is now burdened with a significant amount of long-term debt, the interest on which must be "serviced" by the private firm. As a result, if the cash flow from the previously structured public business is not stabilized before the LBO transaction, or the future cash flow from the now-private business does not increase, the private business will fail over time and the investor loses all or most of his or her invested funds. To minimize this risk, a distressed firm is usually included as a part of a portfolio of private or soon-to-be-private businesses in a private equity fund.

A distinguishing characteristic of a private equity/venture capital firm is that not only have they raised funds from others to grow businesses in the form of a private equity fund or *financial intermediary*, but they also take a considerable financial stake in the success or failure of the private business. This financial intermediary function differentiates the private equity/venture capital firm from another major player in the funding of start-up businesses, a so-called *business angel* or wealthy individual (not a firm) who invests *directly* in the business and lends his or her expertise to the business.

What Is a Private Equity Fund?

A *private equity fund*, usually structured as a limited partnership entity, owns the stock of a business that is not publicly traded. Because this stock is not traded in the public market, it is referred to as *private equity*. The general partner of the fund, the private equity firm, manages the fund and usually places one or more representatives on the private business's board of directors. Typically, if the private business is an unincorporated entity, the private equity firm/general partner of the fund requires incorporation of the business as a necessary condition for being included among the fund's holdings.

A private equity fund is similar to a hedge fund or mutual fund but with several major differences. Unlike a hedge fund, which usually owns many different types of securities, a private equity fund owns stock in only a few companies and controls these companies (that is, the company's founder has ceded control of the private business to the private equity firm). In contrast to a mutual fund, which might own only a small percentage of the publicly held company's stock, a private equity fund owns all or almost all of the private company's stock. Finally, the motivation of a private equity fund manager is much different from that of a hedge fund manager. A private equity fund manager is interested in making a profit from a business when it is sold or does an IPO at some point in the future, whereas a hedge fund manager focuses on the profit potential of a business *now* and applies complex trading strategies to ensure a maximum immediate return. However, both types of funds usually employ leverage to meet their profit goals.

Private equity fund managers follow several investment strategies, and a particular fund is often organized to benefit from the selected strategy. Among the strategies funds focus on are (1) venture capital or startup businesses, (2) growth of a more mature business, and (3) leveraged buyouts. A definite advantage of the private business world and investments in it is that the universe of potential businesses is quite large. Thus, a private equity fund can invest in private businesses that are just beginning their business life, invest in distressed businesses, or take public companies private in an effort to sustain their business life and grow the balance sheet. Like hedge funds, private equity funds can also adopt a "fund of funds" approach and make investments in a fund whose primary objective is to invest in other private equity funds.

The type of targeted investor in a private equity fund is discussed in the "Who Should Invest in Private Equity Funds?" section of this chapter. As with a hedge fund, individual investors must typically be accredited. This means the individual must have a net worth in excess of $1.0 million (excluding primary residence) or have an annual income in excess of $200,000. Institutional investors have their own requirements; but because private equity funds can generate a large potential annualized and total return, institutions have historically been a major contributor to private equity funds. This is particularly true if the institution includes a money manager with a background in private companies, either as an investor or actual entrepreneur, who is therefore comfortable with the high risk of private equity.

How is a private equity fund formed? First, the fund's objective, fee structure, and governance are established. As mentioned, usually the fund is structured as a limited partnership, with the private equity firm acting as the fund's general or managing partner. Money from targeted investors is then solicited through a *private placement memorandum* (PPM) disclosing all relevant information to the investors. Among the elements of the PPM are the private equity firm's (general partner's) capital contributions and the limited partner's capital contributions. It is very common to stage or stagger the limited partner's investments in the fund in the form of a *capital call policy* or *drawdowns*. For example, a sample capital call policy may read:

> *Installments are to be paid within 30 days of a call notice; each call is to consist of no more than 20 percent of the total committed capital of the investor; and the investor should expect all calls within the first five years of the term of the fund.*

These installments are in addition to an initial minimum contribution (capital subscription) of varying amounts depending on whether the investor is an individual or institution. (The initial minimum contribution is usually *larger* for the institutional investor.) The total amount of money to be contributed by the investor to the fund is known as *committed capital*. The first year that the private equity fund draws down committed capital is referred to as the fund's *vintage year*. *Paid-in capital* is the cumulative amount of capital that has been drawn down.

The PPM also references the number of private companies to be included in the fund. Usually, this is in the range of 15 to 18 companies. From experience, out of every ten private companies in which the private equity/venture capital firm invests, only one is expected to achieve the sought-after annualized return of 50–70%. This extremely rewarding business is sometimes referred to as a *venture utopia firm*. Four of every ten private companies survive but do not generate the sought-after annualized return (these companies are referred to as the *living dead*). Finally, the remaining five private companies will likely fail, although their date of failure may exceed the term of the fund. These failing companies are referred to as *black hole investments*. In total, the private equity/venture capital firm plans for a portfolio annualized return of 20–25%, or about double the percentage return that may be expected from large-capitalization public stocks, or 5–10 percentage points in excess of small capitalization public stocks. Of course, this excess return is necessary to compensate for the additional risk inherent in private equity investing.

Once the fund has obtained the necessary capital contributions for the size of the fund (also quoted in the PPM), the actual investments in the private companies can begin. It is at this point that the private equity/venture capital firm enters into due diligence on what private companies should be included in the fund. Commonly, the private equity firm also borrows a percentage of its capital contribution, thereby using leverage to magnify its potential return. As discussed in Chapter 4, the use of leverage also increases the risk of investment to potential equity holders in the fund. Most private equity firms use some form of screening criteria to determine which private companies will be funded. Chief among these is the potential for growth of the business and industry, as well as the founder and management team that will operate the business.

Advantages of Private Equity Funds

There are numerous advantages to private equity and private equity funds. Among the most notable are the following:

- Private equity money helps to ensure the success of a private business.
- Incentive structures can directly link growth of the business to rewarding management and employees.
- Accountability of the business to the owners of the fund is enhanced.
- Little if any disclosure to public regulators is required.
- Private equity firms tend to be patient investors, not demanding short-term results from a business.

Let's consider each of these advantages separately.

Private Equity Money Can Lead to the Success of the Private Business

Private equity can take the form of startup capital (*seed money*), focusing on the growth and improvement of the business or on exit strategies from the business, either by sale to another business or by an IPO. However, the overriding concern of any private equity firm (and fund in which private businesses are included) is the *creation of value* for the private business. To that end, the firm employs tried-and-true management strategies to ensure the business's success.

One of the most common methods of contributing to the success of the business is for the private equity/venture capitalist firm to designate a representative to sit on the business's board of directors, usually chairing the board. This typically means that the day-to-day control of the business remains with the entrepreneurial team and founding member(s), but overall governance and strategic planning are shaped by the private equity firm. Moreover, the private equity fund investors (of which the private equity firm is the majority shareholder) often control the business's voting stock. If the business is not incorporated at the time it is included in the private equity fund, a necessary condition of participating in the fund is to convert from an unincorporated to incorporated form. This form of incorporation is almost always the regular or C corporation form of business, although the LLC entity is also sometimes used.

In addition to chairing or participating on the board of directors of the private business, private equity firms may become directly involved by recruiting talent for the business's management team. Empirical studies have shown that of the factors that contribute to the eventual success of a business, the management team is foremost in importance. Said another way, the differentiating factor between the success and possible failure of any business is the *quality of its management team*. An astute entrepreneur (business founder) recognizes his or her limitations as a manager and, sometimes, will cede control early in the development cycle of the business to others; if not, the private equity firm can assist in communicating this recognition to the entrepreneur.

With the private equity firm's help, is the success of the private business guaranteed? The answer to this question is a most definite no. (Remember that five out of every ten private businesses fail, often within about four years of the startup date.) Nevertheless, given the small percentage of private businesses that are even included in a private equity fund, the overall percentage of businesses is narrowed; and, with the assistance of private equity expertise, their chances of success are likely greater than they would otherwise be outside of the fund. The intrusion of private equity and the structuring of a private equity fund can help to minimize the likelihood of a total failure of the business.

Incentive Structures Can Link Growth of the Business to Reward of Employees

In a publicly traded business, incentive compensation techniques such as **equity-based stock options** and **restricted stock plans** have been common for years. However, a business whose stock is traded on a public exchange has an inherent advantage over a private business: the value of the business as determined by the market is reflected in the market value of a share of its stock. The value of a *private* business is much more difficult to determine. Nevertheless, the term sheet presented to all private businesses participating in a private equity fund includes the ascertained *fair market value* (FMV) of the business as arrived at by the private equity firm. This process also encourages the business to structure as a corporation with its easily divisible per-share value.

Capital raised in the form of equity (common stock) is by far the most common type of capital used by a private business. In part, this is because the granting of common stock costs the business nothing in the form of expended cash—that is, other than the expense of printing up stock certificates for the recipient owner. Moreover, the granting of common stock avoids the issuance of debt in a small business and its accompanying creditor relationship assumed by the bond holder or owner. This creditor relationship means that the bond holder is entitled to the legal payment of interest on the debt (*debt servicing* on the part of the business) and, if not paid on a timely basis, can enforce payment, including the filing of bankruptcy proceedings for the business. Thus, startup businesses without a predictable cash flow avoid the use of debt in their capital structure if at all possible.

However, the entrepreneur/business founder needs to be judicious in the use of equity capital. This is because the entrepreneur ultimately bears the disadvantage of *diluting* his or her shares, resulting in a lower percentage of overall ownership than if equity capital had not been "spread around" in lieu of cash compensation for management and employees. Of course, this is less of a concern for an entrepreneur who accepts funding from a private equity firm or investor, because loss of control will likely be the end result anyway. Still, the entrepreneur needs to recognize that he or she suffers from dilution in granting incentive compensation in the form of common stock; no dilution is suffered by the *ultimate recipient of that stock.*

Once a present value for the business has been determined, it is relatively simple to express a percentage of this value in the form of a stock share. Stock can then be granted to management and employees in the form of an equity-based option or restricted stock with little expense. A stock option must generally be granted at its then current FMV, although restricted stock can be, and usually is, granted at a discount to FMV. This process ties the performance of management and employees to growth in the value of the business. As a result, managers and workers should become more efficient and hardworking. The most obvious extension of an incentive compensation technique is an *employee stock ownership plan* (ESOP), which not only serves to reward employees through their hard work by vesting in them ownership of the company, but also serves as a potential market for otherwise-difficult-to-sell stock of a closely held business owner.

Enhanced Accountability

As a side benefit to providing incentive ownership to employees in the form of stock, private investors can now directly link their investment to parties responsible for creating value or growth of the business. This is particularly the case with the business's management/employees. Stated simply, if the management of the business does not create value, the private investors know who to hold accountable. As such, evaluation of management and their contribution to the business is much more straightforward.

In recent years, an evaluation technique used to evaluate the performance of managers known as **economic value added** (EVA) has become predominant in both private and public businesses. The formula for EVA is:

EVA = NOPAT – (after-tax dollar cost of financial capital used)

To compute the *net operating profit after taxes* (NOPAT), a firm takes its *earnings before interest and taxes* (EBIT) from its income statement and multiplies it by (1 minus the marginal tax rate of the unincorporated business or corporation).

Example ABC Corporation (a privately held business) reports an EBIT of $500,000 for the current fiscal year and is in a 25% marginal income tax bracket. Therefore, its NOPAT is $375,000 [$500,000 * (1- 0.25)]. If ABC's after-tax dollar cost of financial capital used was $100,000 for the current year, its resulting EVA is $275,000 ($375,000 less $100,000).

There are two major advantages in using EVA as a management-evaluation technique. The first is the disconnect between the stock price of the business, as determined solely by internal factors, and the market's determination of stock price (if a public business). In other words, any market noise that is adding to or detracting from the price of the company's stock as determined only by management decision is removed. Second, for any business, EVA separates business operation from its financing. Finally, because a private business is unlikely to pursue significant debt financing, the EVA method is a more direct metric to use in determining how much value management has added—and, thus, to what extent they should be held accountable by private investors.

Little-to-No Required Public Disclosure

One of the reasons that a private business is private is likely because it does not care to register its stock with the SEC or file the necessary public reports. Moreover, a private business's owner desires to keep its finances and financial results hidden from the public; the financial statements of a private business are not open to the public. (This may not be the case with private businesses in a regulated specific industry where providing information to state regulators is required.) Of course, this changes when a private business is considered for inclusion as part of a private equity fund because the private equity firm must review the business's financials beforehand and then monitor its performance as part of the fund's holdings.

What public disclosure is required of a private business? First, if incorporated or organized as a LLC, the business must file its formation documents with the Secretary of State for the state in which it is incorporated or organized. Historically, filing formation documents with the State of Delaware has been a popular choice because of its lenient debtor laws and restrictions on creditor rights. After formation, private businesses are not required to report any information to the public other than amendments to initial formation documents, such as the corporate charter or bylaws. However, if the private business is sold or made a part of a private equity fund, additional disclosure of this fact to the Secretary of State is required in most states. Finally, the closure of a private business, usually by liquidation proceedings under Chapter 7 of the federal Bankruptcy Code, would need to be open to the public through a review of court records.

Historically, there have been many political arguments with respect to the amount and extent of regulation of private businesses. As a result, those businesses that are involved in the provision of a public service, such as banking, tend to be more heavily regulated than other, more proprietary businesses. But, as a well-established rule, for a private business to most effectively operate, such business should be free of the expensive mandated disclosure requirements applying to publicly traded corporations.

Private Equity Firms as Patient Investors

Private equity firms invest in a private business to make it more valuable, thus aligning the interests of private equity investors and those of private business management. As a rule, private equity firms *sequence* these investments over a period of time and do not make one lump-sum cash infusion. For example, a second-round investment may not be made until certain benchmark performance has been achieved, most notably in the form of a prescribed annualized rate of return. Thus, private equity firms tend to be more patient investors than a public shareholder and are relatively unconcerned about a one-year aberration in profits or net income.

Nevertheless, when a private business is made a part of a private equity fund, the business's exit strategy becomes more pronounced. There is a maxim among entrepreneurs, at least among those willing to cede control to others, that "You hope for a sale and pray for an IPO" of a startup business. If a private business is included among the holdings of a private equity firm, this maxim is now actualized by the private equity firm. Typically, a sale of the business for a profit is the intermediate to long-term goal of the private equity firm, although for those venture utopia businesses (businesses experiencing a 50–70% annualized growth rate), an IPO may be the more likely exit strategy. Sale of the assets of a private business to outside buyers includes both the tangible and intangible assets of the business. Among the most valuable of intangible business assets is any intellectual property of the business, such as any copyrights or patents. These assets are often separately valued from the buildings and real property (tangible assets) owned by the business.

The considerations involved in the sale of a family business to others are much different than those for a non-family business. For instance, a family business and its stock are much less likely to end up as part of a private equity fund on account of the preference of many family business owners to engage in business continuation planning in an attempt to keep the business within the family. Most family businesses remain in either unincorporated or LLC entity form with the interest sold during the lifetime of or bequeathed to a family member successor at the death of the senior family member/owner.

Disadvantages of Private Equity Funds

Most private equity funds are structured as *limited partnerships* (LPs). This form of entity and its disadvantages are discussed further in Chapter 12. Among the disadvantages of private equity funds are those inherent in LPs, such as restricted access and relative illiquidity.

In addition to these two disadvantages, a considerable disadvantage of investing in a private equity fund is its higher cost and minimum initial investment. Finally, private equity firms increasingly are adding debt to private businesses included in a private equity fund, to fund dividend payouts to the firm, potentially endangering the business's financial success.

Let's examine each of these four disadvantages in more detail.

Restricted Access

The traditional way of investing in private equity and structuring a private equity fund is through an LP. (Note that some funds are structured as S corporations.) LPs are generally open only to institutional investors and accredited investors. A very limited number of non-accredited investors—no more than 35—may generally be solicited by a PPM issued by private companies seeking financing, although this is changing with the rapid ascent of **crowdfunding**.

In addition to being generally restricted in solicitation to accredited investors, funds previously could not solicit investments from anyone with whom they did not have a preexisting personal or business relationship. It is estimated by the SEC that only 7.4% of U.S. households meet the accredited-investor net worth definition. However, since September 2013, the limitation of a previously established relationship no longer applies. Specifically, as long as the fund is sold to accredited investors, there is no need for the preexisting relationship, thereby opening up the fund for restricted mass marketing to the public. This is consistent with the Jumpstart Our Business Startups (JOBS) Act signed by President Barack Obama in April 2012.

Relative Illiquidity

As noted in the "Advantages of Private Equity Funds" section, private equity firms do not tend to be short-term investors. This putative advantage may alternatively be perceived as a disadvantage inasmuch as there is no interest in selling the private business interest, thereby making it a relatively illiquid investment. (Remember that *liquidity* means the ability to convert the asset or investment to cash without a significant potential loss to the asset's value; it is closely related to the *marketability* of an asset or the ability to sell it quickly.) For this reason, when structuring the private equity fund in a LP form, the LP usually has a term of at least ten years before the investor can withdraw an amount equal to their initial investment. Some LPs have provisions whereby investors can offer their interest for sale to other investors (or the private equity firm general partner), but there is no guarantee of either receptivity to the sale or an amount that may be paid.

In Chapter 12, you learn about a type of LP known as a *master limited partnership* (MLP), which combines the tax benefits of the entity with the liquidity of publicly traded securities. Nonetheless, most private equity funds are structured as private limited partnerships so as to avoid registration with the SEC. In turn, this means that generally only accredited investors and institutions may participate as investors in the fund.

High Costs

The fee structure of a private equity fund varies with the reputation and expertise of the private equity firm, as well as what the market will bear as of the point in time the fund is organized. A management fee of 2% of committed capital is not unusual, and the percentage fee can be even higher in times of aggressive market environments. A 20% share of any profits made by the fund manager is also not uncommon. Like hedge funds, the fee structure of a private equity fund is referred to as a *two and twenty shop*, meaning a 2% ongoing annual management fee and a 20% "take" of realized profits. Also as for hedge funds, this 20% profit share is taxed under current tax law as carried interest, making it eligible to be taxed under preferential tax rules as a long-term capital gain. Politically, this tax treatment has been the subject of much controversy, with some arguing that the profit share is conceptually the same as a fee for services rendered and should be taxed as such.

Often, private equity firms employ placement agents (external fundraising teams or firms) to raise capital from potential investors in the fund. These placement agents typically take a fee of 1% of the funds they raise. The normal number of investors in the fund, including the private equity firm/general partner, is around 40–50, with the placement agents reaching out to considerably more than this number to achieve a "fully subscribed to" fund.

Addition of Debt to Fund Dividend Payouts

As mentioned in the first section of this chapter, a private equity firm may finance its acquisition of a private business in part with debt (leverage). The private business then aims to service this debt with its future earnings. In *dividend deals*, private businesses that add more debt do so to pay dividends to their private-equity-firm owners. In turn, the dividend payouts are distributed to the owners of the private equity fund, including institutions and accredited investors. This added debt, referred to in the business as a *private recapitalization*, can increase the business's risk of default and lead to its financial decline if not properly managed.

Although the concept of private recapitalization is controversial, the technique has been used in recent years to provide yield to fund investors in a period of historically low interest rates. In essence, the technique is a substitute for a purchase of high-yield bonds, but with the added risk of an investment in stocks. According to the *Wall Street Journal*, private equity firms are helping to encourage dividend deals and private recapitalizations because they are currently holding large amounts of cash and pursue relatively few buyouts of private businesses. Fewer buyouts means fewer issuances of the traditional high-yield bond financing alternative.

Potential investors in private-equity funds should be aware of this trend and mandate disclosure of the practice by the private equity fund/general partner. If they do not, investors will be accepting a rate of return more indicative of a bond yield than the higher rate of return required of a stock or equity investment.

Who Should Invest in Private Equity Funds?

Private equity funds are generally limited to accredited investors and institutional investors, such as pension funds, insurance companies, endowments, and securities firms. Some funds structured as private limited partnerships may attract up to 35 non-accredited investors as limited partners. This number is established by the Securities Act of 1933 and subsequent amendments so as to allow the fund to avoid registration of its securities with the SEC. It is part of the Regulation D safe-harbor transaction exemptions that took effect on April 15, 1982. The definition of an **accredited investor** is also included in Rule 501 of Regulation D.

An investment in a private equity fund is indicated when an investor wishes to invest in a private business (and participate in its growth) but lacks the knowledge, time, or expertise to take an active role in the business. In addition, a limited-partnership investment is warranted in cases in which the investor does not want the unlimited liability or the responsibility of a general partner. The investor's investment time horizon should be approximately ten years in length, because the fund typically has a ten-year life, with the possibility of extension for up to three years. Finally, recognizing the inherent risks of combining an investment in private business with the general illiquidity of the limited partnership form, an investor can take advantage of the investment diversification provided by a private equity fund. The type of individual best suited to this form of investment is one who is or has been actually involved in the management and strategic planning of a closely held (non-publicly traded) business.

What Selection Criteria Should Be Considered before Investing in a Private Equity Fund?

The selection criteria to be used in making a decision whether to invest in private equity are both internal (fund-specific) and external (performance-related). Internal considerations, as for professionally managed assets generally, include the costs of the fund and the expertise and track record of the fund manager. External considerations, or primary performance measures used by most reporting services providing private equity data, are the fund's *internal rate of return* (IRR) and its investment multiple.

These four criteria are discussed in turn in the following sections.

Costs of the Fund

As mentioned in the "High Cost" section of this chapter, the typical fee structure of a private equity fund is "2/20" (a 2% management fee coupled with the manager's take of 20% of profits made). It is sometimes be higher, such as 2/30.

But as a potential investor, you should be sure to examine (or ask for) the actual terms of the manager's compensation agreement. There should be both a *preferred return clause* in the agreement as well as a *clawback* provision.

The preferred return clause, also known as the *hurdle rate*, specifies the minimum annual (positive) return to which the limited partners are entitled before the general partners receive any portion of the profits made by their investment. Typically, this hurdle rate is around an 8% IRR, but some agreements include a greater rate. IRR is essentially another way of expressing the total percentage return achieved by the private equity fund manager. Of course, you want that rate to be as high as possible, but it also needs to be realistic. As you will see, in the 1990s, some funds achieved an IRR of around 75%; but it is unlikely that we will ever again see market and economic conditions as favorable as they were then, so a hurdle rate that high is *not* realistic and should not be used.

The clawback provision gives the limited partners the right to reclaim (claw back) a portion of the general partner's (private equity fund manager's) carried interest in the event that losses from subsequent investments result in the manager being paid too much carried interest. Such provision is also very common in a hedge fund manager's compensation and, from the standpoint of the limited partner in a private equity fund, should be as restrictive as possible with respect to the general partner. For example, the compensation agreement might have a provision stating that when cumulative profits are computed at the termination of the fund, distributions received by a general partner in excess of 20% will be considered excessive and returned to the limited partners. Of course, 10% is even better if you are a limited partner, but the general partner/private equity manager likely will not agree to such a low percentage.

Expertise of the Fund Manager

Unlike public equity investing, which is much more transparent, investing in private business requires greater expertise on the part of the private equity firm and fund manager. Hence, as a potential investor, you should ask about the due-diligence process undertaken by the firm in deciding on actual private business investment. For example, what is the extent of the due diligence performed? Are placement agents used? And, if so, what amount of experience do these agents have in private equity investing? Is a visit to the actual business conducted? And, if so, was the management team interviewed? What is the outlook of the industry in which the business is situated? All of these are particular issues to be considered before a private equity investment is made. There are many more questions as well, so you may wish to ask the private equity firm for a list of the screening criteria/checklist that it uses to perform the due-diligence function.

As with choosing a hedge fund manager, the number of years of experience is a critical criterion in selecting a private equity fund manager. (The hedge fund manager should be evaluated more broadly in terms of the range of investments, because derivatives and public securities are also in play.) If working with a well-known private equity firm, such as the Blackstone Group or Carlyle Group, you can be assured of many years of experience in the field. However, firms such as these can preselect their own investors by specifying very high minimums to subscribe to the fund or by enforcing very aggressive capital call provisions. Therefore, they tend to work primarily with institutions and not individuals. The firm that is soliciting your participation in a fund may not be nearly as well known. As a result, it is incumbent on you, the potential limited partner investor, to verify both the experience and track record of the firm. Of course, the longer the experience of the private equity manager and the greater the excess performance of the private equity firm to the public market, the better.

There are online and print resources for checking the rankings of private equity firms and managers. Among these are the *Pensions and Investments (PI) Databook List* and *Thomson ONE Banker/Venture Expert*. In addition, a search of private equity firms yields a multitude of firms in the business of investing in private businesses and forming funds. But, as an investor, you should first decide on the type of fund in which you wish to invest, because there are different stages of funding by the private equity firm. For example, some firms specialize in startup businesses (*venture capital funds*), whereas others concentrate on the growth stage of the business and/or the exit stage. Firms that concentrate on the sale of private businesses to another firm or taking the company private are referred to as *buyout funds*. The performance of both venture capital and buyout funds is discussed in the "How to Evaluate the Performance of a Private Equity Fund" section of this chapter.

Internal Rate of Return (IRR) of the Fund

The IRR of any asset or fund measures the fund's rate of return by assuming that all cash inflows generated by the fund and returned to the investor are reinvested at the IRR rate. The method uses a discount rate that equates the present value of the expected future cash inflows with that of its outflows. As applied to private equity funds, the method measures the limited partnership's annualized IRR based on fund contributions and distributions, net of fees and the profit shares (carried interest) paid to the private equity firm/general partner. Because most reporting services analyze a fund's performance at a particular point in time when it is likely that all cash has not yet been returned to the investor, the estimated value of any unrealized fund investments (the *residual net asset value* of the fund) as of the last reporting date is used as a final cash inflow. The method of computing IRR is essentially a trial-and-error process, but it is made much easier with the use of either a financial function calculator or a spreadsheet solution.

Example Assume that a private equity fund requires an initial minimum investment of $1.0 million and generates a dollar return of $530,000; $430,000; $187,400; and $150,000 for investors over a four-year period. (Note that the typical life of a fund is ten years, but four years is used here for purposes of simplicity.) Applying the IRR function to these five values entered in an HP 10 B II financial function calculator yields an IRR of 14.69% annually.

Investment Multiple of the Fund

The *investment multiple* of a private equity fund compares the sum of all fund contributions by investors to the sum of all fund distributions and the value of any unrealized investments, net of fees and carried interest. Specifically, it is the ratio of the total value of the fund to its paid-in capital. The total value of the fund is the sum of cash returned to investors and the remaining net asset value (NAV) as estimated by the private equity fund manager. It gives the potential investor insight into the fund's performance by showing the fund's total value as a multiple of its cost basis. A *higher* investment multiple indicates *better* fund performance.

Three other private equity ratios, similar to the investment multiple, are required to be reported to potential investors by the Global Investment Performance Standards (GIPS). The first of these is the *realization multiple*, also known as the *distributions to paid-in (DPI) multiple*. It is calculated by dividing the cumulative distributions by paid-in capital and gives the potential investor an appreciation of how much of the fund's return has actually been paid out to date to all current investors. The second ratio required by GIPS is the *residual value to paid-in (RVPI) multiple* or the fund's residual NAV divided by paid-in capital. This ratio provides a measurement of how much of the fund's return is dependent on the market value of the investments. Finally, the *paid-in capital (PIC) multiple* is computed by dividing paid-in capital by committed capital and reflects the percentage of the fund's committed capital that has actually been drawn on by the fund.

How to Evaluate the Performance of a Private Equity Fund

There are several methods to evaluate the performance of private equity funds, but keep in mind that the underlying data used in this evaluation is not as readily available as it is with publicly traded funds, such as mutual funds. For example, Morningstar, Inc., only follows publicly traded funds and not those structured with private (non-publicly traded) businesses. This is also the case with other well-known reporting services such as Thomson-Reuters and Value Line Investments.

A study by Harris, Jenkinson, and Kaplan uses the metrics of a fund's IRR and investment multiple to evaluate the performance of a private equity fund.[1] The study segregates funds into those that are primarily structured as *buyout* funds versus *venture capital (VC)* funds. Finally, it compares the returns of *private* equity funds to those of *public* equity or equity mutual funds.

In the period studied by the authors (1984–2008), the earlier-year funds reflect a return of cash to the investors (with no remaining NAV), whereas the later-year funds are still operating, with little cash returned to investors and the multiples therefore primarily consisting of residual NAV. The average number of funds studied in a given year was 24, with a high of 74 in 2007. The study reported a mean, median, and weighted average for the investment multiple (as well as for IRR) as of each year and averages for each decade of the study's time span.

The study found that, for private equity *buyout* funds, the IRR averaged around 14% annually and the average investment multiple was approximately 2. Average IRR performance of a fund structured to achieve a buyout of an existing private business peaked in the mid-1990s with a weighted average of 19.3% annually, but with a greater investment multiple average of 2.81 throughout the latter half of the 1980s. The weighted average IRR of such fund declined considerably beginning in 2005 and continued its downward trajectory to the end of 2008, as did the investment multiple weighted average over the same timeframe. Respectively, the weighted-average IRR of a typical private equity buyout fund was only 3.38% from 2005–2008, and the investment multiple average was 1.10. The single greatest performance year in terms of both weighted-average IRR and investment multiple was 1990, when the average buyout fund returned 52.9% with a multiple of 3.37.

The result for private equity *venture capital* funds was more varied over the time period of 1984–2008. Specifically, the weighted-average IRR of such fund was 38.6% for the 1990s with an investment multiple of 3.76. This compared to a weighted-average IRR of 15.8% for the 1980s and an investment multiple of 2.37. The single greatest performance year of a typical venture capital private equity fund was 76.7% in 1996, with an extremely high investment multiple of 6.33 (the single greatest investment multiple year was 1994, when such fund averaged 6.58). However, unlike buyout funds in the early 2000s, which did not experience a

---

[1]Robert S. Harris, Tim Jenkinson, and Steven N. Kaplan, "Private Equity Performance: What Do We Know?" Fama-Miller Working Paper; Chicago Booth Research Paper No. 11-44; Darden Business School Working Paper No. 1932316; NBER Working Paper No. 17874. Available at SSRN `http://ssrn.com/abstract=1932316` or `http://dx.doi.org/10.2139/ssrn.1932316`.

considerable decline in performance until 2005, venture capital funds suffered greatly from the dot-com bust beginning in 2000 and predicted the bust in exhibiting negative IRRs from the years 1998–2000. Similarly, the weighted-average IRR of a venture capital private equity fund was only 0.3% in the decade of the 2000s compared to that of 11% for a fund structured for buyout purposes. The corresponding data for weighted-average investment multiples was only 1.07 for a venture capital fund versus that of 1.46 for its buyout fund comparison.

The more interesting question is how the performance of private equity funds compares to that of *public* markets throughout the time period of 1984–2008 that was the subject of the study. Here are the conclusions of the authors:

- The average private equity fund outperformed the S&P 500 Index of large-cap stocks by a factor of 20–27% over the life of the fund (generally 10 to 13 years). This works out to an excess performance of at least 3% per year, net of fees and carried interest.
- Venture capital private equity funds outperformed public markets substantially until the late 1990s, but they have underperformed public markets since then. Since the year 2000, the average venture capital fund has underperformed public markets by about 5% over the life of the fund.
- Annual performance for buyout and venture capital funds decreases with the amount of total capital committed to each type of fund. In other words, a greater influx of capital invested in each type of fund is associated with lower subsequent performance. Why this occurs is unknown, but it does suggest that a contrarian investment strategy may have been more successful in private equity investing versus public markets.
- IRR and investment multiples explain at least 90% of the variation in performance of private equity funds versus that of public markets, with investment multiples explaining substantially more of the variation than do IRRs.
- There is greater risk associated with private equity funds related to the long-term capital commitment required of investors, the uncertainty of future cash flows, and the liquidity of holdings that differ from public markets. However, the extent of the return premium required by investors to assume this risk requires further research.

Now let's look at the more recent performance of private equity funds from 2008–2013.

Recent Private Equity Fund Performance

Preqin provides performance data for all private equity funds over a one-, three-, five-, and ten-year period ending with the first quarter of 2013 or March 31, 2013.[2] It compares this performance to standard public market indexes and, most notably, the S&P 500 index of large-cap stocks. Because the more comprehensive Harris et al. study (op. cit.) provides the same basic information over the period of time up until the end of 2008, I review only the one- and three-year information for all funds, with the exception of comparing the performance of private equity funds to the S&P 500 from the end of first quarter 2008 to 2013. This permits evaluation of private versus public fund performance during the severe recession and subsequent slow economic recovery.

Here is a summary of the Preqin data:

- Over the one-year period ending 3/31/2013 (or 3/31/2012–3/31/2013), all private equity funds generated an average IRR of 11.3% annually with buyout funds generating the greatest average IRR of 13.4% annually.
- Over the three-year period ending 3/31/13 (or 3/31/2010–3/31/2013), all private equity funds generated an average IRR of approximately 14.0% annually (buyout funds did 16.0% annually).
- Compared to the S&P 500 Index of public stocks over the one-year period, private equity funds underperformed by 2.7 percentage points or an IRR of 11.3% annually versus 14.0% annually for the S&P 500 Index.
- Compared to the S&P 500 Index of public stocks over the three-year period, private equity funds slightly outperformed the S&P 500 Index by approximately 1 percentage point or an IRR of 14% annually versus 13% annually for the S& P 500 Index.
- Compared to the S&P 500 Index of public stocks over the five-year period ending 3/31/2013 (or 3/31/2008–3/31/2013), private equity funds again slightly outperformed by approximately one half of one point or an IRR of approximately 7.0% annually versus approximately 6.5% annually for the S&P 500 Index. (Note: Approximate figures are necessary because the data is presented in graphical and not numerical form.)

[2]"The Preqin Quarterly Update: Private Equity, Q1 2013," 2013, www.preqin.com/docs/quarterly/PE/Preqin_Quarterly_Private_Equity_Update_Q1_2013.pdf.

Over shorter time frames (such as one year), private equity funds underperformed the public market during the time of market recovery (as in the first item in the preceding list), whereas over longer time frames including the severe market downturn (such as five years) they slightly outperformed the public market. It can be inferred that private equity may exhibit some negative correlation with public markets in times of economic challenge and provide an effective diversifier to a high-net-worth investor's overall portfolio.

This concludes the part of this book concerned with pooled assets available primarily to high-net-worth individuals and institutions: hedge funds, managed futures funds or programs, and private equity funds. The next part examines alternative PMAs "for the masses": *limited partnerships* (LPs) and *real estate investment trusts* (REITs) in Chapter 12 and *individually and separately managed accounts* in Chapter 13.

PART

V

Alternative Professionally Managed Assets

CHAPTER

12

Limited Partnerships and Real Estate Investment Trusts

Limited partnerships (LPs) were a heavily used form of investment vehicle prior to 1987, when their attractiveness was restricted by the Tax Reform Act of 1986 (TRA 86). Specifically, a series of tax statutes known as the *passive loss rules* significantly curtailed the use of limited partnerships to pass through tax losses to investors in excess of their amount of capital invested in the partnership. As a result, such terms as a *10-to-1 tax writeoff* appeared in investment terminology, meaning that a limited partnership received $10 of tax losses for every $1 of capital invested in the limited partnership. Obviously, this was a tax abuse (not to mention a distortion of investment principles), so Congress acted to correct the situation in TRA 86. Since that time, investors in limited partnerships have been investing in LPs based on the economic potential of the assets positioned in the partnership entity. Typically, these assets consist of either real estate, energy, or natural resources.

The focus of this chapter is on *master limited partnerships* (MLPs), arguably the most well-known of LPs since TRA 86, and their primary investment alternative, *real estate investment trusts* (REITs). Preliminary to discussing MLPs, the next section identifies and distinguishes several other types of limited partnerships under the rubrics of *private limited partnerships* and *public limited partnerships*.

Private Limited Partnerships

The most common example of a *private limited partnership* is the private equity fund. As discussed in the preceding chapter, a private equity fund is typically available only to accredited investors or institutional investors, such as pension funds or university endowment funds, through an offering known as a *private placement*. Private equity funds can also be offered to no more than 35 non-accredited investors and still avoid registration of the fund with the SEC. However, most non-accredited investors are not comfortable with the inherent risk of a private equity fund; nor do they have the necessary funds to satisfy the fund's investment minimums. Thus the inclusion of private equity funds (and private limited partnerships) in the "Professionally Managed Assets for High-Net-Worth Investors" part of this book (Chapters 9–11).

As you learned in the preceding part, private limited partnerships/private equity funds are typically segregated into those focusing on investing in startup businesses (venture capital funds) and those concentrating on more mature businesses, up to and including the exit stage of the business (buyout funds).

Public Limited Partnerships

A *public limited partnership* is an LP that is registered with the SEC and publicly traded on an exchange but not as a corporation. This type of LP is offered to the general public through the investor's broker and by a broker-dealership securities firm. Unlike an MLP, a public LP is *not* treated as a corporation for income tax purposes and therefore "passes through" the income or loss of the partnership entity to the general and limited partners. The most common example of a public limited partnership is a *real estate limited partnership* (RELP), with the real estate developer serving as the *general partner* (GP) and subsequently soliciting capital from individual investors in the capacity of *limited partners* (LPs). The partnership agreement between the GP and LPs generally provides for the allocation of income and losses generated by the partnership assets through a "special allocation" provision. Normally, the agreement provides for an allocation to the LPs of a certain increased percentage until the capital contribution of the LP is recovered and, then, for a reduced and fixed percentage thereafter. For example, the agreement may provide for an allocation of 90%/10% income (and loss) split to the LP and GP, respectively, until the LPs' capital contribution is recovered, with a 50/50 split thereafter.

One of the major disadvantages of the public limited partnership (and the MLP to be subsequently discussed) is the probable inability of the LP to recognize a loss from the public limited partnership for income tax purposes. As noted, a public limited partnership allocates a certain dollar amount of loss to the LP based on his or her percentage contribution. However, at the LP's level (on his or her income tax return), he or she is limited by a series of three tax provisions:

1. The LP cannot deduct a loss allocated by the partnership entity in excess of the LP's basis (or adjusted capital contribution) in the partnership. This is an extremely complicated computation, but usually the basis of an LP in any publicly limited partnership is relatively low. Thus, a large loss allocated by the partnership generally cannot be fully deducted in any one year by the LP.
2. The LP cannot deduct a loss in excess of the amount that he or she is "at risk" in the partnership investment. Again, to compute the actual amount that an LP is at risk is very complicated, but generally the LP must have cash invested; and if leverage is used by the partnership, the LP must also have personal liability in the event that the note is not repaid by the partnership (or the LP must be obligated on a so-called *recourse note*).
3. The LP cannot deduct a loss if he or she is only a *passive investor* in the limited partnership entity. This means that the LP must *materially participate* in the activities of the limited partnership and meet a separate definition of what is necessary to do so under the U.S. Treasury Regulations. For most LPs, the satisfaction of this definition is very difficult to meet.

In summary, these three limitations result in a deferral (*suspension*) of any tax loss allocated to the LP by the partnership until the asset generating the loss is actually sold. For instance, let's say that LP/Taxpayer A is allocated a loss of $10,000 by public limited partnership XYZ, but that Taxpayer A has a basis of only $2,000. However, Taxpayer A is only a passive investor in partnership XYZ. As a result, Taxpayer A cannot deduct *any* portion of the loss, even though he or she has contributed capital of $2,000, until partnership XYZ sells the asset and disposes of it as a part of its portfolio. There is one major exception to this deferral treatment: if partnership XYZ subsequently generates $10,000 of income from its activities and makes this distribution to Taxpayer A to the extent of his or her partnership interest, Taxpayer A can offset the income by the loss. But from a practical standpoint, this occurrence may be extremely unlikely without some major new asset acquisitions or restructuring by partnership XYZ; that is, once losses begin from an investment, they are likely to continue for some period of time before reversing and generating income to the investors.

The differences between the major type of publicly traded limited partnership—the RELP—and a REIT are explored in the "REITs vs. RELPs" section of this chapter.

What Is a Master Limited Partnership (MLP)?

A *master limited partnership* (MLP) is a publicly traded partnership consisting of corporate assets that are spun off from the corporate entity (known as a *rollout* of assets) and/or from a private limited partnership (known as a *rollup* of assets). The MLP combines the tax benefits of a limited partnership with the liquidity of publicly traded securities or *units* offered to the public. The buying of MLP units makes an investor a limited partner in the MLP, the units of which are then bought and sold on the New York Stock Exchange, NASDAQ, and other public exchanges.

A difference between the MLP and the generic public limited partnership is that an MLP is generally a partnership entity operating an *active business*, whereas the public limited partnership may simply be (and often is) only an investment fund. Nevertheless, keep in mind that even though the MLP may be operating an active business (and thereby materially participating), the limited partner in the MLP is typically "passive" and, therefore, subject to passive-loss rule limitations. There are also mutual funds or ETFs that own a number of MLP units; although the passive-loss rule restrictions are avoided with these funds, the typical MLP ETF charges a fee of 0.82% annually, much higher than the conventional stock-based ETF with a management fee of only 0.14% or 0.15% annually.

Because of tax code requirements, MLPs are structured primarily by real estate, energy, and natural resource (commodity) businesses. These businesses may be relied on to pay a regular quarterly cash distribution and generate a higher-than-average yield to income-seeking investors. Moreover, investors do not have to pay taxes on the distribution in the same manner as a corporate dividend. In many cases, this means that the distribution is "only 20% taxable," as the sales literature promoting MLPs is fond of proclaiming to prospective investors. An LP in an MLP is allocated a proportionate share of the MLP's income and capital gain via an annual Schedule K-1 report and is subsequently responsible for paying income tax on the same. However, the LP is also allocated a proportionate share of the MLP's deductions, losses, and tax credits. As a result, it is likely that the LP will pay tax equal to only about 20% of his or her total taxable distributions. Along with the higher yield, this tax treatment is a major attraction of the MLP to the investor/limited partner.

Like a hedge fund or private equity fund, an MLP can use leverage to enhance the return of an investor/limited partner (of course, also at the risk of magnifying his or her potential losses). As a pooled asset, the MLP is usually able to borrow more money than could any single investor. Whether the investor/limited partner qualifies to deduct his or her proportionate share of losses from the MLP that has engaged in leverage depends on the investor's tax status of the investor: if he or she is *at recourse* for the loan (are personally liable for its repayment in the event of the MLP's default), the loss is permitted under the *at-risk rules,* as long as the investor also materially participates in the activities of the MLP. However, if he or she is *not* personally liable for the debt's repayment (*non-recourse debt*), the loss is disallowed regardless of any material participation by the investor in the activities of the MLP. There is a limited exception from this rule for a LP who invests in an MLP owning *real property* assets: in this instance: the investor is at risk for the share of debt secured by the real property even if he or she is *not* personally liable for the debt (otherwise known as *qualified non-recourse financing*).

Historically, MLPs have not moved in concert with the Standard & Poor's 500 Index of large-cap stocks, thereby providing some diversification benefits from an all-stock portfolio. But as with any primarily fixed-income investment, MLPs are vulnerable to interest-rate risk. This is especially true of smaller MLPs that are leveraged and thus vulnerable to rising interest rates and borrowing costs. Said simply, as interest rates increase, the valuation of MLPs declines, leading to losses for the investor, such that the greater the leverage, the greater the amount of potential loss.

Advantages and Disadvantages of MLPs

Besides access to professional management, MLPs offer the following advantages:

- High income yields
- Favorable taxation of distributions
- Greater liquidity and marketability than a private limited partnership

These advantages are considered in turn in the following sections.

High Income Yields

The income yield on an MLP is the income generated by the MLP divided by its price. In 2013, that yield is approximately *double* than the yield on 10-year Treasury notes and *triple* the dividends paid on S&P 500 stocks. Moreover, because that yield is generated primarily by investments in energy and commodities, it could increase even further as that sector and asset class grow. Thus, MLPs provide an alternative to historically low current yields on bonds and other fixed-income type investments. However, as you will see, this is accomplished at the notable cost of a deferred tax liability that is passed along to investors.

The total return on MLPs has also been strong over the past decade. From 2003 to mid-2013, MLPs generated an average annualized total return—income yield plus any changes in the price of the asset—of 16%. This compares to U.S. large-cap stocks' overall average annualized return of 7.3% for the same period. The total return on U.S. long-term corporate bonds averaged 6.18% for 2003 to mid-2013, and the return for U.S. long-term treasuries was even lower at 6.08%.

Favorable Taxation of Distributions

Distributions made from an MLP are generally only 20% taxable. But when is such a distribution actually taxable? The answer is that it is taxable in one of two situations:

- When the investor/limited partner's adjusted basis in the units reaches zero. The adjusted basis of a partnership interest is usually dynamic at any point in time, but it begins with the original price paid for the units of the MLP. This original *cost basis* is then adjusted downward with each distribution and each allocation of deductions and upward with each allocation of income. This process means that at least some of the distribution made by the MLP may not be taxed at all in a given year (or until the investor's basis in the MLP units is fully recovered for tax purposes).
- When the investor/limited partner sells units at a gain from his or her adjusted basis. Operationally, because the distributions have decreased investor basis, they have increased the potential amount of taxable gain. Some of this gain may be taxed at lower capital-gain rates, but some of the gain is also recaptured at higher ordinary income rates. The portion of the gain recaptured is equal to the amount of depreciation passed through to the investor as part of the distribution made by the MLP.

The distribution that is made to the investor is payable out of the MLP's **distributable cash flow**. This is not the same as the taxable income of a corporation or investment company, such as a mutual fund. Thus, the actual distribution made is not classified (or taxed) like a dividend; rather, it may be treated as a reduction in the investor's basis and not taxed until one of the previous two taxable events occurs.

The taxable distribution is reported to the investor on a Schedule K-1 by the MLP. The schedule reflects the investor's share of each item of income and loss that has been experienced by the MLP. In addition to the reporting of income and loss, the schedule directs the investor where to report the item on his or her income tax form for that year. The transfer of income tax record-keeping to the MLP sponsor is considered by some to be an additional advantage of the investment.

Greater Liquidity and Marketability

Unlike stocks, bonds, or mutual funds, an interest in a private limited partnership may be extremely difficult to sell. This is because of the very limited market for the partnership interest. Some private partnerships may allow the interest to be sold to other partners or even back to the general partner (usually at a stated discount), but there is no guarantee of interest. There may also be a prohibition on the sale of the interest by the terms of the partnership agreement. Whatever the restriction, this lack of marketability also typically leads to a lack of liquidity of the partnership interest. Often, the illiquidity of the interest results in a reduced sales price, if the interest can be sold at all.

An MLP has the same partnership structure as the private limited partnership but issues investment units that trade on an exchange like common stock. Thus, there is ready marketability of the units and, hopefully, increased liquidity as well. For example, according to the National Association of Publicly Traded Partnerships (the trade association for MLP sponsors), there are currently more than 100 energy-related MLPs alone. These MLPs provide a tax-favored alternative to investing in the individual common stock of energy businesses. This is not to mention the inherent advantages of investing in pooled or professionally managed assets, as discussed in Chapter 2 of this book.

Disadvantages of MLPs

Now let's consider the disadvantages of an investment in the MLP form of professionally managed asset. The most considerable drawback is likely the inability to deduct losses generated by the MLP in a given taxable year because of the passive-loss rule limitations, but there are other drawbacks, including the following:

- The loss of investor control
- The relatively high risk of the investment
- The lack of an optimal investment vehicle in which to own the MLP

Passive Loss Rules

A net loss from an MLP (a distribution of a negative amount for tax purposes) is considered a **passive loss** under Internal Revenue Code Section 469. As a result, if a net loss is reflected on the Schedule K-1 furnished to the taxpayer/limited partner by the MLP, this loss cannot generally be *recognized* (claimed as a deduction) by the taxpayer for that year. Instead, it is carried forward into future taxable years and used to reduce taxable income from that same MLP in a year in which the MLP has income from its overall portfolio of assets. Moreover, any loss that remains (after the netting of income by the previous loss) cannot be deducted from the taxpayer's other income until the MLP units are sold in their entirety (or there is enough income in the future year to absorb the loss).

Example Taxpayer A purchases an interest in an MLP and receives a Schedule K-1 reflecting a loss of $15,000 for taxable year 2012. In 2013, the MLP generates income of $20,000 attributable to Taxpayer A's interest. For 2012, Taxpayer A cannot claim any of the $15,000 loss as a deduction under the passive-loss rule limitations; rather, the loss must be carried over until a year in which the MLP generates income. Thus, in 2013, Taxpayer A can offset $15,000 of taxable income by utilizing the 2012 loss. The remaining $5,000 of loss cannot be deducted until either Taxpayer A's units in the MLP are sold or another $5,000 of taxable income attributable to Taxpayer A's percentage interest in the MLP is generated by the MLP.

In addition, income from an MLP cannot be used to offset losses either from a private limited partnership or another public limited partnership. Accordingly, the loss sustained by the MLP may only be used to offset income from the *same* MLP. In practice, it may be difficult for an MLP that is currently suffering losses to generate income in future years. This is another consideration that you should keep in mind before deciding whether to actually purchase the units of an MLP or engage in the trading of units in the secondary market for the asset.

Loss of Investor Control

As with any professionally managed asset, an investor who purchases MLP units loses investment control. Specifically, the LP must now rely on the management expertise and investment acumen of the GP responsible for the partnership. If investors do not like the cumulative performance or management practices of the GP, they can band together with other disgruntled LP investors in an attempt to remove the GP. However, this may prove to be both a very costly and lengthy legal undertaking.

High Risk of the Investment

In general, limited partnership investments tend to be relatively risky because of their inherent lack of liquidity. This disadvantage is somewhat minimized by the purchase of MLP units, but even there the subject matter of the partnership's investment (for example, real estate) may make the purchase unsuitable for the average investor. Of course, this is particularly the case if the investor either has not taken the time to understand the risks of a possible purchase of MLP units or does not understand the investment even after researching it.

The risk of the investment is increased if the manager of the MLP takes advantage of leverage to make purchases for the partnership's portfolio. More importantly, under the terms of the partnership agreement, the LPs may be liable for their proportionate share of any loans taken out in the name of the partnership. As mentioned, this occurs when the LP is "at risk" for the liability in the capacity of an "at-recourse" investor.

Lack of an Optimal Investment Vehicle in Which to Hold the MLP Units

Like all investments, there are essentially only two choices for positioning MLP units: a taxable or a tax-deferred account. Let's take the second choice first.

Some investors wish to hold MLP units in a tax-deferred account, such as an IRA. This is possible, but there are several important limitations. First, an investment in MLP units by an IRA is considered to be an *unrelated business*. As such, income generated by the MLP and allocated to the IRA owner is subject to the **unrelated business income tax** (UBIT). It is not taxed as long as the income from the MLP, plus all other unrelated business income, does not exceed $1,000 in any taxable year. But, as a potential investor, you should be aware that it is the IRA's share of the partnership's *taxable income* (and *not* its distributable cash flow) subjected to imposition of the UBIT. Typically, the partnership's income is a different amount than its distributable cash flow, and it may be difficult for the investor to determine without access to the partnership's financial statements.

The other choice is a taxable account. As discussed, the purchase of MLP units and positioning in a taxable account can be a highly tax-efficient option for an individual investor, but extensive record-keeping is often required. Fortunately, most MLP sponsors do most of these record-keeping for you. Another tax-efficient option to hold in a taxable account is an MLP I-Unit. These publicly traded corporations hold MLP units and, subsequently, make distributions to investors in the form of more units rather than cash. Because the distributions are made in the form of units or shares, this permits the investor to postpone the recognition of any taxable event until the sale of the shares, similar to any other stock.

There are also MLP funds that may be held in a taxable or tax-deferred account. The first of these funds are those taxed as regular corporations and include ETFs, mutual funds, and closed-end funds. Such funds pay out distributions in the form of qualified dividends (rather than distributable cash flow like the typical MLP) and report such dividends to investors on an IRS Form 1099 and not Schedule K-1. However, they incur a corporate-level tax of 35% on net income, a cost that is passed along to investors and reduces their amount of dividends received. This practice also makes the annual expenses charged by the fund extremely hard to predict.

The second type of MLP fund is *not* taxed the same as a regular corporation, meaning no double taxation occurs (that is, taxation of income at the MLP level and then again at the shareholder level). To maintain this tax-favored status, no more than 25% of the fund's assets may consist of direct MLP holdings. Therefore, the fund is invested heavily in non-MLP holdings, which may deter potential investors interested in the enhanced yield offered by MLPs. Some funds have dealt with this limitation on MLP holdings by establishing wholly owned subsidiaries that subsequently make additional MLP investments, but this "indirect holding" strategy is currently being challenged by the IRS and may prove impossible in the future.

Finally, there are MLP *exchange-traded notes* (ETNs). These products, which may be owned either in a taxable or tax-deferred account, consist of unsecured debt instruments designed to replicate the return of an MLP index. Like other MLP funds, they report to shareholders via an IRS 1099 form and not a Schedule K-1. However, they are generally not income-tax-efficient. The payouts are taxed as ordinary income (and not as a qualified dividend) for federal income tax purposes and are also subject to state income taxes. In 2013, the ordinary income tax rate could be as high as 43.4% for individuals making in excess of $400,000 annually. This rate consists of a top marginal income tax rate of 39.6% plus 3.8% Patient Protection and Affordable Care Act of 2010 (Obamacare) surtax. Hence, if an investor is to invest in MLP ETNs, they should be held in a tax-deferred account like an IRA.

Who Should Invest in MLPs?

Unlike hedge funds and private equity funds, where institutional ownership predominates, individual investors are the primary owners of MLPs. What type of individual investor should purchase MLP units? The answer to this question is an individual who understands the advantages and disadvantages of the investment before making it, has limited capital, and desires the income tax efficiency that is provided by an MLP. An individual who is looking to stretch the yield of a fixed-income investment and is also interested in the potential growth of the real-estate and energy sectors of the economy should also find MLPs attractive.

Generally, tax-exempt institutional investors, such as pension funds and university endowments, shy away from MLPs. This is because any cash distributions received from an MLP are considered *unrelated business taxable income* and create taxable events on any distribution of more than $1,000. This is also true for individuals who own MLPs in an IRA account. Therefore, the best way to own MLPs is in a taxable account where distributions are made by the MLP out of its distributable cash flow and reported to the investor on IRS Form Schedule K-1.

What Selection Criteria Should Be Considered before Investing in an MLP or MLP Fund?

The following questions should be asked before purchasing an MLP or MLP (some of which have already been discussed and will not be repeated):[1]

- How will annual payouts be taxed?
- What portion of these payouts is expected to be tax-deferred until I sell my MLP units or shares?
- Will the investment raise my tax-preparation costs?
- Will I receive an annual IRS Form 1099 or Schedule K-1?
- Could this investment generate taxable income if held in a tax-deferred account?
- Does this MLP fund owe corporate-level taxes (is there double taxation)? And, if so, how can I estimate my potential dividend?
- Will my investment return be subject to the 3.8% Obamacare surtax?
- What happens if I die owning this investment?

---

[1] Laura Sanders and Jason Zweig, "The Dark Side of Higher Yields," *Wall Street Journal*, August 9, 2013, `http://online.wsj.com/news/articles/SB10001424127887323838204579000631768402564`.

Will My Investment Return Be Subject to the 3.8-Percent Obamacare Surtax?

As is now generally well understood by most investors, beginning in 2013, a surtax of 3.8% is imposed on the net investment income of certain higher-income taxpayers to fund the implementation of the Patient Protection and Affordable Care Act of 2010 (Obamacare). This tax is imposed on individuals whose modified adjusted gross income (MAGI) is above $200,000 annually for a single-filer taxpayer or above $250,000 annually for a married-filing-jointly taxpayer. If a taxpayer's MAGI is above those levels, their share of net partnership income from the MLP as reported on IRS Schedule K-1 is taxable for purposes of the surtax. However, quarterly distributions made by the MLP are *not* treated as net investment income and may still be treated as a tax-deferred return of capital until the taxpayer/investor sells the MLP units. This is in contrast to the taxation of corporate dividends made by an MLP fund and reported to the taxpayer on IRS Form 1099, which *are always* subject to the surtax. Again, this is a reason the taxpayer/investor is better off with an MLP that makes distributions via a Schedule K-1 and not Form 1099.

Said another way, an MLP that is not part of a mutual fund is more tax-efficient than one that is included in the fund's portfolio.

What Happens If I Die Owning This Investment?

The basis of any MLP units or MLP fund shares held by the investor at his or her date of death is *stepped up* (or *stepped down*) to the market value of the units on the date of death. In the case of MLP units or fund shares, this market value is easily ascertained by checking with the general partner/sponsor or referencing a financial newspaper or journal. In the case of a private limited partnership, such as a private equity fund, the determination of value is more difficult because there is no readily observable market value. Rather, the services of a qualified appraiser should be solicited to perform an analysis that takes into account possible discounts for lack of marketability and/or minority ownership of the interest.

Finally, in addition to seeking answers to the standard questions listed at the beginning of this section, you should inquire as to the track record of the general partner/manager of the MLP. Typically, limited partners only contribute capital to the MLP and do not materially participate in the partnership's activities (thus the term *passive investors*). As such, the ultimate success of the MLP depends almost entirely on the expertise of the GP. As a potential investor, you should investigate the background of the GP, what experience he or she has in similar ventures, and how any previous MLPs have been offered have performed. You should also compare the performance of the MLP against that of a common benchmark or index used in the industry. In part, this is the purpose of the next section.

How to Evaluate the Performance of MLPs

When evaluating the performance of an MLP, you should pay close attention to the amount of discounted cash flow (DCF) that is generated by the assets of the partnership. DCF is the amount of cash that an MLP *could* pay out to its investors in a given period. Just as for any business deciding how to distribute its net income, a well-managed MLP parcels out a portion of that income to investors as a return on investment (a *dividend*) and retains a portion of that income for future business growth (*retained earnings*). The allocation of the percentage of net income—including the decision whether to pay a dividend at all—depends on the objectives of the business. For example, technology businesses sometimes do not pay out dividends but instead retain all earnings to spur future development and growth of the business. Alternatively, financial businesses have historically paid out a larger percentage of income in the form of dividends.

Because one of the features of an MLP is a higher-than-average income yield, investors are very concerned with how much cash the business is generating. (Note that cash generation is also extremely important to a private business and thus to a private equity fund, as discussed in Chapter 11.) Specifically, investors want to ascertain how much cash is potentially distributable by the MLP in the form of income to unitholders or to fund growth. The computation of DCF is conceptually simple and begins with the net income on a business's income statement; from that figure, certain non-cash items, such as depreciation, are added back. These non-cash items are usually shown as expenses on the income statement but are for tax purposes only and do not involve the expenditure of any cash by the business. Thus, you add them back and subtract any capital expenditures to arrive at DCF.

Example A business reports $500 million in net income at the end of the fiscal year. It also reports $100 million in depreciation, depletion, or amortization entries on its income statement, all of which are non-cash items. Finally, the business's capital expenditures are $160 million. Thus, the DCF for the business is $440 million ($500M + $100M – $160M). This amount may be used either to provide income to unit holders in the MLP or to fund the future growth of the business or both.

So, how do you use DCF to evaluate the performance of an MLP? First, you can reference the amount of DCF as a stand-alone computation such that the more the DCF, the better the performance. Second, and more importantly, you can include DCF as the numerator in a ratio unique to MLPs known as the *coverage ratio*, given by this formula:

$$\text{Coverage ratio} = \frac{\text{Distributable Cash Flow (DCF)}}{\text{Actual Cash Distribution}}$$

Generally, investors want to see a coverage ratio of between 1.2 and 1.5, in addition to growing quarterly distribution payments made by the MLP. Therefore, in the previous example where the business generated $440 million of DCF, it should distribute no more than $367 million to arrive at a coverage ratio of 1.2. In turn, this means you want the DCF to be 1.2 times the amount of actual cash distribution, thereby allowing $73 million for future growth of the business. When applying this metric to the MLP in its entirety, you simply use the same coverage ratio of 1.2 for all businesses that are included in the partnership's portfolio.

You can also use the coverage-ratio metric in comparing the performance of one MLP against another. Other metrics used in evaluating the performance of MLPs are the income yield and annualized total return. As discussed in the "High Income Yield" section, MLPs have performed quite well over the last decade, generating an annualized total return of approximately 16% with a current income yield in excess of 5%. Whether MLPs can sustain this performance is open to question, but the fact of such superior returns during a severe bear market, an economic recession, and a subsequent tepid economic recovery bodes well for the future. Nevertheless, it is up to the investor to conduct appropriate due diligence before making a purchase of MLP units and/or a fund which includes MLPs in its portfolio.

The next section moves on to the major alternative to an MLP, particularly in the real estate portion of the economy: the real estate investment trust (REIT).

What Is a Real Estate Investment Trust?

REITs are usually structured as corporations rather than as partnerships. This is a major distinction between a REIT and an MLP, meaning there are also major differences in the taxation of the two investment vehicles, both at the entity and shareholder (or unitholder) level. Another distinction between the two entities is that a board of directors elected by investors governs and operates the REIT, whereas the MLP is managed and operated by a GP. Finally, although the majority of REITs are publicly traded, some are not ; but all MLPs are publicly traded by definition.

A REIT is a publicly or privately traded closed-end investment company that invests in a managed, diversified portfolio of operating real-estate properties or real-estate mortgages and construction loans. If it invests in operating properties, the REIT is categorized as an *equity REIT;* if it specializes in lending funds for construction or investing in real-estate mortgages, the REIT is known as a *mortgage REIT*. Equity REITs invest mainly in income-producing commercial properties, such as apartment buildings and shopping centers, which lease space to others. Mortgage REITs typically invest in real estate indirectly by lending funds that are used to build properties. There are also *hybrid REITs*, which combine the features of both equity and mortgage REITs, and *office REITs*, which invest in commercial real estate (offices) in larger U.S. cities. Office REITs are further categorized into *high-barrier market* REITs and *low-barrier market* REITs. *High barrier* typically refers to coastal central business markets, such as New York and Boston, whereas *low barrier* means suburban markets where it is easier to construct new office buildings, such as in suburban Atlanta and Dallas.

Most REITs are publicly traded and are equity REITs, but there are also non-traded REITs (private REITs). Private REITs are not as popular with investors as publicly traded REITs because they are typically sold with high upfront charges and are difficult to sell if the investor wants to dispose of his or her interest in the REIT. Another problem with a private REIT, just like any private asset or business, is that the intrinsic value of the REIT is extremely difficult to determine. The share price/net asset value (NAV) of the private REIT is established by the REITs board of directors, but there is typically a question whether those shares are undervalued or overvalued in relation to their intrinsic value. Finally, a private REIT can be leveraged to fund payouts to the investors if the portfolio of the REIT does not earn enough, thus increasing the risk to the investor without a commensurate increase in the rate of return. (Note that whenever the generic term *REIT* is used throughout the rest of this chapter, it refers to a *publicly traded* REIT unless otherwise specified.)

Publicly traded REITs may be purchased by investors in a number of ways, including through dedicated mutual funds, closed-end funds, and ETFs. Among the most popular ETFs that focus on REITS are the SPDR Dow Jones REIT and iShares Dow Jones U.S. Real Estate. Investors can also include REITs in a taxable or tax-deferred account by purchasing individual REITs directly or with the assistance of a broker or an investment advisor. Finally, there are REITs that focus on international real-estate markets. The largest ETF currently focusing on non-U.S. properties is the SPDR Dow Jones International Real Estate ETF.

REITs vs. RELPs

A major alternative to the publicly traded REIT is the *real estate limited partnership* (RELP). As is evident from its name, a RELP is organized as a partnership and not as a corporation or investment company. There are other differences between it and a REIT, as summarized here:

Feature	REIT	RELP
Organization	Corporation	Partnership
Publicly traded	Generally, yes	Generally, no*
Liquidity	More	Less
Taxation investor level	Like a stockholder	Like a limited partner
Investor return	Primarily income	Primarily growth
Investor risk**	Less	More

*Exception for a small number of publicly traded partnerships
**Increased for both in the event of leverage

Advantages of REITs

The advantages of a REIT include the following:

- Limited liability
- No double taxation of income
- Ability to leverage investments
- Discounts from book value (increased leverage)
- Inflation protection
- Diversification benefits

Limited Liability

REIT shareholders are treated the same as mutual fund shareholders or as individual shareholders of common stock in a corporation. As such, their liability is limited to the extent of their investment in the REIT. They are also taxed accordingly; they pay taxes on the distributions from the earnings of a REIT in the form of a dividend. This means that the distributed income is taxable as ordinary income similar to salaries and wages earned by the shareholder/taxpayer. However, because REITs do not typically pay corporate taxes, most dividends payable from the REIT do *not* qualify for favorable long-term capital-gains treatment (that is, taxed at a maximum rate of 20%). A small portion of dividends paid by REITs may constitute **qualified dividend income** (and qualify for the tax preference), but this is the exception and not the general rule.

Also, because REIT shareholders are treated the same as mutual fund shareholders (absent the dividend tax preference), most REITs feature a purchase of their shares in small denominations, sometimes as low as $50. Moreover, there is no minimum number of shares that an investor must buy, although *round lot* purchases (100 shares) predominate in the marketplace.

No Double Taxation of Income

As long as the REIT distributes at least 90% of its income to shareholders, no corporate-level tax is imposed on that income. Thus, as with mutual funds, the **conduit principle** applies, and double taxation of the REIT's income is avoided. But unlike some stock mutual funds that pay a low dividend yield, the fact that a REIT must distribute almost all of its income to maintain its tax status means that a *higher* dividend yield is almost always paid. As a result, REITs may be an attractive investment for yield-hungry investors, particularly those suffering from the historically low yield payable from individual bonds or bond mutual funds. However, note the difference in the taxation of REIT dividends versus dividends received from a mutual fund or closed-end investment company as described in the preceding section. This should be a major tax consideration for any investor who is considering the purchase of REIT shares.

Several other requirements must be met before the REIT avoids the double taxation of its income. The first is that at least 75% of the REIT's portfolio must be invested in real-estate properties or in loans secured by real property or mortgages on real estate. Similarly, at least 75% of the REIT's *gross income* must be derived from real-estate rents, mortgage interest, or gains generated from the sale of real estate owned. There must also be at least 100 shareholders of the REIT with no more than half the total outstanding shares of the REIT owned by 5 or fewer individuals at any time during the second half of each taxable year. Finally, the REIT must be managed by one or more directors.

Ability to Leverage Investments

The ability to leverage investments in a REIT is both a shield and a sword. Borrowed money can be used to significantly increase the percentage return on an investment and value of the REIT shares if the return on the REIT's investments exceeds the interest paid on the debt. Conversely, the use of this money can increase the risk of investment to the shareholder by adding too much debt to the REIT's balance sheet, thereby driving down its return and resulting in financial-distress costs. As with any professionally managed asset investment vehicle that uses leverage, a potential investor needs to analyze the amount of debt used by the vehicle to determine if it is sustainable based on future-cash-flow projections for the vehicle and the companies or real-estate properties in which it is investing.

Equity REITs tend to incur more leverage than mortgage REITs. Indeed, equity REITs generate income to their shareholders based on the difference between the net rental income generated by their property purchases and the interest that is paid to finance the purchase of those properties. If equity REITs incur too much leverage and then see the vacancy rate in properties owned increase, the cash flow from the REIT is threatened, driving down the NAV of its shares. Therefore, on balance, an equity REIT should be thought of as having more risk than a mortgage REIT.

Discounts from Book Value (Increased Leverage)

The *book value* of a corporation is also its accounting value and is computed by subtracting the corporation's total liabilities from its total assets to arrive at shareholder equity. Similarly, the book value of a REIT is its remaining NAV after subtracting liabilities from assets.

Historically, REITs have sold at a discount from their book value, thereby in effect increasing the amount of positive leverage utilized on behalf of the investor. This discount has ranged from 5% to 20% less than an investor would have to pay if buying a proportionate share of the assets in the REIT directly. For example, let's say that an equity REIT is selling at a 5% discount from book value, and the commercial real properties purchased by the REIT are yielding 5% inside the REIT. Thus, the investor is purchasing an interest in the REIT for 95 cents on the dollar, with a corresponding proportionate interest of 5 cents for every 95 cents invested. This works out to an increased yield of 5.26% versus 5% if he or she had invested directly in the commercial real properties outside of the REIT.

Inflation Protection

Prior to the Great Recession of 2007–2009, the purchase of real estate served historically as a hedge against inflation. This was particularly the case with equity REITs, in which some appreciation (growth) in the value of the underlying commercial properties could be anticipated. Alternatively, mortgage REITs may suffer from a loss of purchasing power given their fixed-interest rate orientation. In other words, if inflation accelerates and interest rates rise, the value of a mortgage REIT's underlying mortgage investments will fall, thus causing a reduction in the NAV of its shares. This is less likely to occur with an equity REIT, where the concentration of investments is in income-producing properties.

Mortgage REITs have investment characteristics similar to those of mortgage-backed securities. This begs the question for an investor interested in real-estate mortgages: why not just purchase a bond mutual fund investing in conventional mortgages? The answer to this question is primarily one of income security. An investor making an investment in a mortgage-backed security mutual fund must be concerned about reinvestment rate risk as mortgages within that fund are refinanced. More precisely, as mortgages are refinanced because of declining market interest rates, the value of the pool of mortgages from which their investment income is derived falls, generating less future income for the shareholders. The mortgage principal that is paid off as a result of refinancing is passed through to the fund investor, but now he or she must reinvest at a lower interest rate than before (hence, the term "reinvestment rate risk").

Diversification Benefits

REITs tend to have a low positive correlation with that of the broader stock and bond markets. This means that they can provide an effective diversifier for an investor when constructing a portfolio of assets. A small allocation to REITs can assist in reducing the overall volatility of the investor's portfolio while at the same time increasing its dividend yield. Moreover, unlike bonds, REITs (particularly, equity REITs) have the potential for significant growth of underlying assets and an increase in share price during periods of inflation.

As discussed in Chapter 4, active portfolio management means a percentage allocation of contributions to traditional asset classes, such as stocks, bonds, and cash/cash equivalents. An often used fourth asset class is "alternatives", in which real estate is sometimes positioned. Alternatively, some portfolio managers consider real estate as a separate asset class entirely. This is because of the diversification benefits shown throughout market cycles. For instance, in those years when stocks and bonds (financial assets) have performed poorly, real estate (real assets) have tended to do well (or less badly). The opposite is also the case. As of December 31, 2012, REITs invested in U.S. real-estate properties and mortgages produced an annualized average total return of 11.6% over the previous 10-year period. This compared to an average total return of 7.1% for stocks in the S&P 500 Index.

Disadvantages of REITs

Like any investment, REITs also have disadvantages. The most important of these are the following:

- Interest rate risk
- No pass-through of tax losses
- Discounts from book values
- Management fees and costs

Interest-Rate Risk

REITs have the potential to produce *negative* total returns during a time of high market interest rates. This occurs for reasons specific to the two REIT types. With respect to mortgage REITs, investors tend to gravitate toward safer assets with less default risk, such as U.S. Treasury securities (that technically have no default risk) and/or investment-grade corporate bonds. Also, loss of purchasing power of generated income from a mortgage REIT occurs with high or increasing interest rates, which follow inflation and inflationary expectations. With respect to equity REITs that employ leverage, higher interest rates mean that it is more expensive for the REIT to borrow the funds necessary to make additional purchases of property, therefore compromising growth and, potentially, cash flow.

Some equity REITs, particularly those that do not use much leverage, try to counter interest-rate risk by pursuing a "buy and hold" philosophy and not selling properties until they are rented to capacity. However, remember that at least 90% of the REIT's net income, *including capital gains*, must be distributed to investors. When the portfolio properties are sold, the REIT may realize a substantial capital gain from the appreciation of the properties. So, although the net effect to the investors is a greater before-tax cash flow, there is now less potential future appreciation of their share value as well as increased cash-flow volatility (that is, the income from that property is now removed). You should be aware of this effect when appreciated properties are disposed of by equity REIT management.

No Pass-Through of Tax Losses

Unlike RELPs, which are a *pass-through* type of tax entity, REITs cannot pass through losses to the investor/shareholder. Rather, these losses are trapped at the corporate level, which takes the losses before distributing income to the shareholder. In contrast, if the investor were to invest in real-estate properties directly, the losses would be passed through; presuming certain rules are met with respect to active participation in real-estate activities, those losses may be partially or fully deductible.

Some trustee/managers of REITs attempt to get around this restriction of passing-through of losses by distributing cash flow in excess of the REIT's income and treating this excess as a nontaxable return of the investor's capital contributions. But this characterization is misleading because the investor's cost basis in the REIT is *reduced* by the amount of the non-taxable distribution. As a result, the reduction in cost basis may lead to *higher* capital-gains taxes in the future. You need to closely analyze the IRS Form 1099 issued by the REIT to determine what portion of the distribution is taxable as ordinary income (dividends), capital gains, and a nontaxable return of capital.

Discounts from Book Value

There is also a disadvantageous aspect of the discount-from-book-value feature of a REIT, previously considered in its advantageous aspect. Specifically, once

REIT shares are purchased at a discount from book value, there is a possibility that an even greater discount percentage may result from future market activity. Stated colloquially, it may be difficult to "keep the rock [the value of the REIT shares] from sliding even further downhill"! If this is the case, and investors purchase the shares at a lesser discount from a lower price where the shares ultimately settle, they will suffer a capital *loss* when they sell their shares. Under current tax law, investors must first use any capital loss to offset any capital gain and then are limited to an offset of other income (such as salary and wages) of only $3,000 in any one taxable year. The remaining unused capital loss may be carried forward indefinitely until used up—but once again, only in an amount of $3,000 against other income in any future year.

Management Fees

With respect to management fees, a distinction needs to be drawn between non-publicly traded (private) REITs and publicly traded REITs. Private REITs have a higher amount of initial charges than publicly traded REITs, including commissions to the broker/salesperson that may run as high as 15% of the offering price. A commission may also be paid to a broker when purchasing a publicly traded REIT, but is not as high as that payable for a private REIT. As a result of these higher up-front costs, a private REIT must take more risk to earn back the investor's initial investment and achieve the desired return. You need to keep this in mind when deciding between a private and publicly traded REIT and reconcile it with your tolerance for risk.

The management fees of publicly traded REITs are generally similar to those of mutual funds and range from about 0.50% to 1.50% of assets managed. Of course, there may be an additional advisory fee for the investment advisor or financial planner who is working directly with the investor. But the more accurate comparison between applicable fees is between an indirect investment in real estate (usually via the purchase of REIT shares) and a direct investment in real estate. Accordingly, if you were to directly purchase a real-estate property, there would typically be no management fee charged or stock broker's commission. (There may be a real-estate commission cost if using a real estate broker or agent.) The tradeoff for this is the management expertise brought to bear by the REIT trustee and the extra time that may be incurred if you invest directly. Therefore, you first need to make the decision whether to invest directly or indirectly in real estate and, subsequently, if opting for indirect ownership, whether to invest in the form of a REIT, a RELP, or a real-estate mutual fund.

Who Should Invest in REITs?

An investor who has a limited amount of capital, does not wish to purchase real-estate properties directly, and yet desires some participation in real estate should consider the purchase of REIT shares. In addition, an investor who wishes to diversify his or her portfolio beyond financial assets should investigate the purchase of a REIT. Finally, unless the investor thoroughly understands the risks and costs associated with a non-traded REIT, he or she should purchase only shares of a publicly traded REIT, which are much easier to buy and sell.

With respect to specific types of REITs, an investor who is interested primarily in income should purchase shares of a *mortgage REIT*. Alternatively, where some capital appreciation in addition to income is the goal, an investor will find the purchase of shares of an *equity REIT* to be more suitable. This is also the case if the investor wants to take more risk and invest in a vehicle that may employ leverage to magnify gains. When an investor wishes to combine purchases of both real-estate properties and mortgages, the purchase of a *hybrid REIT* is preferable.

What Selection Criteria Should Be Considered before Investing in a REIT?

Some of the criteria to be taken into account before the purchase of a REIT have been mentioned in the discussion on advantages and disadvantages. Specifically, here are some important considerations in the decision whether to invest in a REIT and, if so, in what type of REIT:

- The types of assets in which the REIT invests
- Whether leverage will be employed
- If the purchase of real-estate properties is in the REIT's prospectus, whether the trust will geographically diversify its purchases
- The projection of the REIT's future performance
- The quality of the REIT's management

A discussion of each consideration follows.

Types of Assets in Which REITs Invest

From a broad perspective, the investor should ascertain whether the REIT is investing in real-estate properties, mortgages and construction loans, or a combination. You should also consider the risk involved in investing in each form of asset, as well as the overall objective of the REIT—whether it is emphasizing the generation of income or capital appreciation or both.

Although the investment risk assumed with an equity REIT is likely more than that of an mortgage REIT (particularly if the equity REIT is employing leverage), the risk of the underlying assets may be increased with the purchase of some mortgage REITs. For instance, a mortgage REIT that is investing in construction loans is considerably riskier than a mortgage REIT that is purchasing government-backed securities, such as pass-through certificates issued by the Government National Mortgage Association (Ginnie Mae). The income from a mortgage REIT concentrated in construction loans is also less stable than that of a mortgage-backed security REIT. Alternatively, equity REITs focusing on proven real-estate properties have greater income stability than those concentrating on new construction. Both of these types of properties in equity REITs should experience capital appreciation, depending on local market conditions, although proven properties may have less potential for future growth.

Will Leverage Be Employed?

Many investors were caught unaware by the magnitude of the downturn in real-estate properties beginning in late 2006 and continuing into 2012. They also were surprised that commercial real estate probably suffered more than residential properties, even though the commercial industry had experienced several boom-and-bust cycles prior to late 2006. If the equity REIT purchasing these types of properties employed leverage, it only made an already bad situation even worse! Accordingly, potential investors should first consider whether the REIT uses leverage when making purchases of real-estate properties, and then, if so, to what degree leverage is used. If your risk tolerance does not permit the increased risk evidenced by leveraged investing, you should not be purchasing shares of a REIT using leverage.

Will the REIT Geographically Diversify Its Purchases?

Unlike the marketplace for financial assets, the market for real estate is almost exclusively local. As has been said many times by a knowledgeable real-estate professional, there are only three factors to be considered in the purchase of commercial or residential real estate: "location, location, and location!" Therefore, you want to know *where* the REIT will be purchasing properties or investing in construction loans. It stands to reason that REIT managers who invest only in a part of the country or geographic region that they extensively follow and know very well are less likely to make poor investments. However, this is easier said than done. You may be better off investing in a REIT that makes purchases in as broad a geographic area as possible, although not in those areas with a considerable amount of political or real-estate market risk.

An interesting analogy to the geographic reach of REITs is an investment in an emerging-markets mutual fund. Historically, countries such as Brazil, Mexico, China, and Indonesia have proven the positive value of an investment not only in financial assets there, but also in real-estate properties. For example, China has a currency (the yuan) that is not convertible into foreign currencies, including the U.S. dollar. This forces Chinese investors to invest only in Chinese assets and particularly tangible assets, such as real estate. Thus, there is considerable pressure on the buy side for real-estate properties in China, driving up their prices. This phenomenon is expected to continue in the future, although, as happened in Japan, investors need to be wary of the possibility of an overheating of the Chinese real-estate market, leading to a rapid decline in value.

Projection of Future Performance

As with any potential investment, projection of future performance is probably the most difficult consideration to determine. An increase in the value of REIT shares depends on the future income from the properties owned by the REIT, which in turn depends on the amount of rent from and vacancy rate of the properties. Generally, a potential investor desires REIT properties generating as high a rent as the local market allows, as well as little to no vacancy rate. Moreover, you should seek out REITs owning properties that can be sold at an appreciated value, thereby producing sizeable capital gains. Therefore, it is helpful if you understand the process by which the REIT selects its properties for purchase.

Most REITs rely on the expertise of professional real-estate appraisers to determine which properties to purchase. These appraisers may be delineated into ones pursuing a specialty in commercial versus residential real properties. Generally, REITs employ commercial real-estate appraisers, usually those with the Member of the Appraisal Institute (MAI) designation. Such an appraiser typically uses an income approach when determining the current fair market value of a property. This approach uses assumptions such as rent multipliers and **capitalization rates**. As can be easily understood just by a definition of how to derive a capitalization rate, one appraiser's assumption of the growth rate of real property is likely not the same as another's, thereby potentially leading to a difference not only in the current value of the targeted property but also in the future value. Moreover, this does not take into account any unexpected declines in the broader economy, as occurred in 2007–2009. All this makes the projection of future performance of REITs very difficult. Some common metrics used to analyze the historical performance of REITs are provided in the upcoming evaluation section; but from this discussion, you should realize that the more familiar you become with the real-estate market in which the REIT is planning to invest, the better you will be able to project its future performance.

Quality of the REIT Management

The question of management quality is, of course, a recurring theme in the analysis of whether to invest in *any* professionally managed asset, including the possible purchase of REIT shares. Unfortunately, there is no single, reliable source to evaluate the quality of REIT management. The National Association of Real Estate Investment Trusts (NAREIT) provides a web site, `www/reit.com/`, that covers many aspects of REIT investing, but the site does not evaluate any particular REITs or their managers. Thus, it is left to the investor to determine the experience of the REIT manager, including how long he or she has been with the REIT under consideration for investment, their educational and professional credentials, and their track record. With respect to any past performance, the prospectus of the REIT will be quick to point out that past performance is no guarantee of future returns. However, if a manager has consistently underperformed his or her peers, it is likely that future performance will not be significantly different.

How to Evaluate the Performance of REITs

Certain additional metrics can be used to evaluate the performance of REITs that are different than the traditional metrics—such as dividend yield and annualized total return—used to evaluate stock mutual funds. Among these REIT-specific metrics are

- Vacancy rates
- The quality of the real-estate properties or mortgages in which the REIT invests
- The percentage of trustee or management ownership in the properties owned by the trust

Like hedge funds and private equity funds, the percentage of ownership owned by the trustee of the REIT is a valuable indication of how much he or she believes in the future growth and income of the properties they have chosen to purchase. However, unlike a hedge fund or private equity fund, the REIT trustee usually is not compensated in the form of carried interest or a percentage of the value of the trust properties. This may be a disincentive for the trustee in generating profits for the investor.

The NAREIT website reports on the performance of various types of REITs over a long period of time. The two metrics of performance that it uses are dividend yield and the annualized total percentage return. The dividend yield for a stock or any income generating non-debt asset is derived by dividing the dividend per share by the current share price. For example, if the dividend per share on REIT A was declared to be $1.50 per share and the current share price of REIT A is $30, the dividend yield for the REIT is 5%. As of July 31, 2013, the average annual dividend yield for all REITs was 4.3% according to the FTSE NAREIT All REITs index. However, for mortgage

REITs, which primarily generate income, the average annual dividend yield was much higher at 12.6%.[2] The all-equity REIT yield was 3.5% as of July 31, 2013. This compares to the S&P 500 index of stocks' average 2.1% dividend yield over the same period of time.

The annualized total percentage return of a REIT includes the dividend yield plus the capital gains (or loss) yield. It is computed as follows:

1. Calculate the total gain factor by dividing the final value of the REIT by the initial value of your investment. For example, let's say that you purchased shares of a REIT for $50 and sold those shares for $70. This results in a factor of 1.4 and is a total percentage return (or *holding-period return*) of 40%. Of course, the problem with holding-period return is that the time frame over which you owned the stock is not taken into account.
2. Divide 1 by the number of years you owned the REIT. For example, if you owned it for 3 years, you divide 1 by 3 to get 0.33.
3. Raise the result from step 1 (here, 1.4) to the exponent of the result from step 2. In this example, you raise 1.4 to the 0.33 power. The result is 1.1174. Then subtract 1 from this number to derive 0.1174.
4. At this point, you can perform one of two processes. First, you can multiply 0.1174 times 100 to get an annualized total return of 11.74%. Alternatively, move the decimal place in the result 0.1174 two places to the right to reflect a percentage of 1/100th of the total. This also results in an annualized total return of 11.74%.

Note that an annualized total percentage return is really a form of *geometric* return, because it considers compounding of interest. This is in contrast to the *arithmetic* return of 13.33% in the example (40 divided by 3), determined by dividing the holding-period return by the number of years you owned the investment.

Recall that as of December 31, 2012, all U.S. REITs had generated an annualized percentage return of 11.6% in the previous 10-year period. This compares to an annualized return of 7.1% for all large-cap stocks and approximately 4.5% for all bonds. This is an excess performance for REITs of 4.5 percentage points and 7.1% respectively.

The next chapter focuses on the *retail* side of PMAs— specifically, *individually and separately managed accounts*, both of which are alternatives to traditional mutual-fund investing.

---

[2]FTSE NAREIT Mortgage REIT index.

CHAPTER

13

Individually and Separately Managed Accounts

Many investors do not know the difference between a *fee-based advisory account*, an *individually managed account*, and a *separately managed account* as offered to them by their investment advisor or financial planner. Moreover, they likely do not really care to know the difference, as long as the costs of each type of account to them are reasonable. The focus of this chapter is on *separately managed accounts* and, then, in how they differ from traditional mutual funds. However, first, I need to review the discussion from Chapter 1 of the characteristics of a fee-based advisory account and the distinction between individually managed and separately managed accounts.

Fee-Based Advisory Account

An *advisory account* is a type of account established by an investment advisor or financial planner that permits access to a wide range of investment options, but with the investment guidance of a retail expert. The term *fee-based* is often replaced with the term *asset-based* (or, sometimes, neither is used), but both terms mean that the investment advisor is paid a percentage fee by the client/investor based on the amount of *assets under management* (AUM) for the client. This fee varies among investment advisors, but it usually declines in percentage the greater the amount of assets managed for an individual investor, such as $1.0 million. The major type of advisory account managed by investment advisors is a tax-deferred account, such as retirement accounts consisting of **defined contribution plan** assets. The most prevalent type of retirement account managed is a traditional IRA, which can be further titled as a *participant IRA* (meaning additional contributions can be made by the client to the IRA as initially established by the advisor) or *rollover IRA* (meaning proceeds are transferred on a tax-free basis from one employer-sponsored plan to the IRA).

A major structural alternative to the advisory account is a brokerage account established by a (stock) broker. A broker may or may not be an investment advisor (more about that shortly), but he or she is paid in a brokerage account in the form of commissions. Technically, a commission is paid to the broker by the product sponsor and is not a fee paid by the client. However, this distinction is largely irrelevant to the client because the money paid to the broker or investment advisor reduces the amount of investment that goes to work for the client or to which the client is entitled. Nonetheless, it is easy to understand that a broker, at least more so than the investment advisor, is perceived to have a conflict of interest in establishing a brokerage account and trading securities; that is, the more trades the broker makes, the more he or she is compensated. This same problem is not as apparent in an advisory account because the investment advisor only makes more in the form of a fee if the account increases in value for the client.

Still, there are also certain incentive problems with the advisory account. Whereas a brokerage account rewards brokers for transactions (*churning* the account), the advisory account may encourage the investment advisor *not* to engage in transactions, even when these transactions may be for the benefit of the client. This is particularly the case when, pursuant to the terms of some advisory accounts, the investment advisor pays for the transactions out of his or her percentage fee, and the trading charges are not separately billed to the client. In addition, the investment advisor may be too slow to rebalance the client's portfolio, as based on a previously agreed asset allocation, for fear of losses to the account value. Stated differently, the investment advisor may be too cautious when action is warranted given future market and economic conditions.

In recent years, the distinction between brokerage activities (the sale of securities) and investment advice has become blurred. The *Investment Advisors Act of 1940* (IAA) carved out an exception for brokers to be licensed as investment advisors where such investment advice to a client is "incidental" to their brokerage activities. But the IAA never envisioned brokers establishing fee-based brokerage accounts in addition to the traditional type of brokerage account. Why is this important? Because a broker's legal obligation to the client in the recommendation of securities is not the same as that of an investment advisor, presumably regardless of the type of brokerage account. Specifically, a broker only must sell a security to the client that is suitable in meeting his or her financial goals, whereas an investment advisor must at all times act for the exclusive benefit of that client.

Let's look at an example. Assume that a broker has two mutual funds A and B, both of which are suitable for meeting the financial goals or objectives of the client to increase the client's net worth. However, mutual fund A is a *load* fund and pays the broker a service charge (commission) of 5.5%; mutual fund B is a *no-load* fund and does not pay the broker a service charge. The expense ratio charged by mutual fund A is 1.5% of assets managed, whereas mutual fund B's expense ratio is only 1.0% of assets managed. Under the suitability standard relevant to the brokerage activities, a broker can legally buy mutual fund A for the client even though it has a higher expense ratio. On the other hand, an investment advisor could not do this; under his or her legal obligation of acting at all for in the exclusive benefit of the client, the advisor must buy mutual fund B for the client because it has a lower expense ratio, thus saving the client money in the future and not reducing the account value as much as mutual fund A.

Because many investment advisors are also financial planners, the *Financial Planning Association* (FPA) in July 2004 initiated a lawsuit in the U.S. District Court for the Washington DC Circuit on behalf of its members to level the playing field between brokers and investment advisors. Specifically, the FPA sued the SEC for overreaching its authority in passing a temporary broker-dealer rule in 1999 exempting brokers from also operating under the same exclusive-benefit standard (known in the law as a *fiduciary obligation*) when operating fee-based brokerage accounts. In May 2007, the FPA prevailed in that lawsuit; however, action was delayed by the SEC in implementing the standard. This delay was essentially codified in the Dodd-Frank Wall Street Reform and Consumer Protection Act of 2010, where a committee of the SEC was directed to study the issue and make a recommendation to the SEC Board with respect to how to proceed. In 2013, the SEC committee completed its work and recommended that there be a uniform fiduciary standard adopted for brokers as well as investment advisors. This is so regardless of the type of brokerage account offered, whether fee-based or one generating commissions for the broker. (As mentioned in Chapter 2, note that fee-based brokerage accounts were banned effective October 1, 2007, in favor of non-discretionary advisory accounts.) The SEC Board had not yet acted on this recommendation as of late 2013.

Individually Managed Account

An *individually managed account* (IMA) is a customized portfolio of securities that is developed to meet the financial goals of an investor. An IMA is similar to a *separately managed account* (SMA), which is the major focus of this chapter; however, an IMA tends to be for higher-net-worth clients with substantial discretionary income to invest. Also, an IMA is more structured individually to achieve an investment objective of income or capital appreciation (growth) of the underlying securities or a combination of both of these objectives. Both IMAs and SMAs are designed to be as income tax-efficient as possible, with investors receiving direct ownership of the underlying securities and not a proportionate percentage as with mutual-fund investing.

In addition to these differences, IMAs also vary in structure from SMAs as follows:

- An IMA offers an investor enhanced direct access to an expert portfolio manager, in contrast to an SMA. The maxim that "money buys access" definitely is operative with an IMA portfolio.
- Because an IMA offers enhanced access, investors in such an account have more input into investment decisions made by the portfolio manager. In contrast, an SMA tends to be constructed more on a model portfolio or one-size-fits-all basis.
- Institutional investors are also permitted more direction with an IMA than an SMA. This is an extension of the greater service level provided by IMAs for investors with more money to invest.

Regardless of the differences, some investment advisors equate the terms *IMA* and *SMA*. Indeed, when either term is googled, both types of accounts appear among the search hits. Investment advisors offering either type of account are paid on an AUM basis with no initial transaction costs (commissions) incurred by the client/investor when purchasing the initial securities for either account. There is also full transparency in both accounts, so that you can observe and review the actions of the portfolio manager at all times. This is typically provided in an online manner to clients.

I now move on the primary focus of the chapter: SMAs.

What Is a Separately Managed Account?

A *separately managed account* (SMA) is an account that is owned by an individual investor and looked after by a hired professional money manager, such as an investment advisor or third-party money-management firm. If this sounds like a fee-based advisory account (advisory account) structured and monitored by an investment advisor, that is because they are many similarities between an SMA and an advisory account. If the advisory account includes individual stocks and bonds (and not mutual funds), it could be argued that the two types of accounts are the same. Specifically, in both accounts, the investor owns the investments directly, often in a custodial arrangement registered in the investor's name.

Therefore, the real distinction to be made is between separate and commingled accounts, such as mutual funds. In an advisory account owning mutual funds, investors in the account own shares of a commingled investment vehicle, which in turn owns individual securities, such as stocks, bonds, or derivatives. This distinction is important for the following reason: if an investor in a commingled account wants to change the allocation of one security in relation to another security (that is, to effect overweighting or underweighted of one security in the portfolio), the commingled account manager (mutual-fund portfolio manager) does not make this change. In contrast, the SMA money manager makes any investment decision and changes based on the individual's financial goals.

In an SMA, who is this money manager? Usually, it is the **investment advisor** (IA) working directly with the client. This IA could be representing a broker-dealer (also sometimes serving in the capacity of *registered representative*) or, more likely, is a *registered investment advisor* (RIA) or working with a RIA and a separate custodian of the funds. Notable fund custodians in the marketplace today are Charles Schwab & Co. and TD Ameritrade Institutional, but there are others. You should be aware that the custodian of an SMA may or may not be a broker-dealer, just as the IA may or may not be a registered representative. Confused? As a typical investor, you are not alone; however, from the preceding discussion, it may be important to you to work with an IA because they are currently under a higher legal obligation (a fiduciary standard) to represent your best interests. By the way, an IA has the same legal standard to act only in your exclusive benefit as does any other professional, such as an attorney, a CPA, or a CFP handling your money.

Usually, the IA works on a discretionary basis with respect to making investments in an SMA. Of course, this means that they actually choose the investments to make up the SMA. Most, however, do not choose the investments without input from the client. Most IAs also usually work on the basis of a minimum level of money that must be under their management before they will accept the engagement of responsibility from the client ("take the case," in legal lingo). As a general rule of thumb, this price of entry begins at $100,000, but very experienced and in-demand IAs have a much higher minimum, such as $1.0 or $2.0 million. For money management customized for institutional clients, such as pension funds or insurance companies, the minimum account size may range from $10.0 to $100.00 million. Regardless, the client is paying for essentially two important attributes inherent in any SMA: the ability to customize the portfolio, usually in an extremely tax-efficient manner; and the expertise of the IA/money manager at the retail level.

Recently, still another term is being used with respect to SMAs and sometimes used by investment advisors: *unified managed account* (UMA). The UMA is an evolution of an SMA and means a professionally managed private account that is rebalanced regularly and includes individual stocks, bonds, mutual funds, ETFs, and other securities in one account. In addition, multiple investment managers are frequently used in a UMA instead of only one as is the norm in an SMA. Alternatively, if all of these securities were not in a single account, and the investor wanted to diversify into each investment vehicle, he or she would need to open multiple accounts and pay multiple fees. For purposes of simplicity, I will equate UMAs with SMAs and discuss only SMAs throughout the remainder of this chapter.

Advantages of SMAs

The primary advantages of SMAs are as follows:

- Customized risk management
- Income and capital-gains (tax) management
- Freedom from the market pressures of commingled assets
- Higher return potential
- Transparency in reporting

Let's look at each of these individually.

Customized Risk Management

Every investor is unique and faces unique circumstances in his or her financial life. For example, an investor may want investments that generate both income and growth, while also being concerned about possible *downside risk* (safety of the investment). On the other hand, a commingled asset, such as a mutual fund, usually is structured around a single investment objective. If you want income and safety, you may be interested in a bond mutual fund; but if growth is a priority, a stock mutual fund may be of interest. Regardless, more than one commingled asset will need to be purchased. In an SMA, individual stock and bond purchases can be tailored to the growth and income/safety objectives and perhaps supplemented with a single growth-and-income type of mutual fund. Other investment strategies such as *emerging market equity* and *global fixed income* may also be pursued by the SMA manager.

Also, in an SMA, an investor can establish specific guidelines with respect to investments, such as maturity dates, concentration limits, bond rating requirements, and the extent of liquidity. All of these are risk-control considerations that may be taken into account by the investment advisor. Other metrics that can be used to manage risk are industry diversification and benchmark selection. Finally, prohibited transactions, such as the inability to leverage investments or the use of derivatives, can be specified. The risk-control mechanisms and list of prohibited transactions may be included in the **investment policy statement** (IPS), which is the guideline for asset allocation and security selection by the investment advisor in his or her agreement with the client/investor.

Income and Capital Gains Management

Unlike mutual funds and REITs, which operate as a conduit in distributing income and capital gains to an investor, an SMA allows for tax management. For example, an investor in a high marginal income tax bracket probably wants to recognize as little interest or dividend income as possible. As a result, the investment advisor can structure the SMA with low-yield investment vehicles, such as growth stocks, which pay a very small dividend, if any. Alternatively, if an investor has generated sizeable capital gains from portfolio assets, the investment advisor managing the SMA may recommend selling some assets that have declined in value and harvesting those tax losses in applying the losses against gains. Finally, an SMA avoids the possibility of a late-year mutual-fund investor's paying income taxes on gains of fund assets that he or she did not actually earn. These tax-management techniques generally are not available with commingled assets.

Income-tax efficiency is also sought by corporate client/investors. In practice, corporate financial managers are equally focused on the income potential and accounting gains generated by their investments. This is particularly the case for larger, publicly traded corporations that report a great deal of investment income among their longer-term assets on the balance sheet. (A privately held company likely is concentrated on cash acquisition and maintenance to a greater degree than a publicly traded corporation.) Moreover, a holding company—as contrasted with a going concern—that owns the stock of several underlying corporations depends very heavily on the amount of income generated by its investments.

Freedom from Market Pressures of Commingled Assets

A significant reality faced by a mutual fund portfolio manager is volatile cash flows. Specifically, this means that the portfolio manager cannot control fund inflows and outflows. As discussed in Chapter 5, a mutual-fund portfolio manager must keep an unproductive cash reserve in the fund at all times to fulfill investor redemptions. If the manager does not estimate the amount of redemptions properly, the fund may be left with too much idle cash in the portfolio (*cash drag*). An SMA avoids this problem by customizing the amount of cash to individual investor needs and, typically, uses cash (money market) accounts only as a temporary depository between investments made by the investment advisor.

There is another consequence of volatile cash flows associated with mutual funds. If the market trends downward rapidly, such as in 2008, the mutual fund may experience an unexpected excessive demand for cash redemptions. Although this demand is likely a reflection of investor emotion rather than reason, the herd effect of many investors cashing out at the same time may force the mutual-fund manager to sell some portfolio assets at a loss—and sometimes before he or she wants. Of course, this results in a loss of share value for the remaining investors, thus encouraging them to redeem shares as well.

Alternatively, separate-account investing is not impacted by cash-flow implications resulting from the actions of other investors. Rather, investors in an SMA can and do work much more closely with their investment advisor to try to anticipate upcoming market events and react accordingly (buy or sell without the interference of herd-effect pressures).

Higher Return Potential

The higher return potential of SMAs is primarily with reference to the money market and money-market mutual funds. To be part of the money market (versus the longer-term capital market), generally obligations with maturities longer than 13 months are not permitted. See SEC Regulation 2a-7. This means that potentially higher-yielding income securities, which typically are represented by capital market securities, cannot be purchased by a **money market mutual fund** (MMMF). Indeed, MMMF returns are generally expected to be in line with the 90-day or 3-month U.S. Treasury Bill security. Alternatively, an SMA may keep only a limited amount of funds in lower-yielding securities, such as those exhibited by a MMMF and the money market generally.

There is also another way that SMAs can generate higher income yields: by using the purchasing power of large institutions to purchase individual, longer-term bonds. For example, when interest rates are stable, most investors purchase longer-term debt obligations (individual bonds or bond mutual funds) to generate a higher yield. Similarly, when interest rates are declining, investors may invest in bonds and bond mutual funds with longer maturity dates to lock in higher yields if they expect future interest rates to continue to decline. Because an SMA offers the possibility of an investment advisor's selecting high-quality individual bond issues, the higher yield of longer-term maturity obligations is assured. When interest rates are expected to increase, the investment advisor can also purchase short-term maturity obligations/ individual bonds, whose prices will not decline as much as those issued longer-term. This is at the expense of sacrificing yield in favor of minimizing interest rate risk.

Transparency in Reporting

An often-cited advantage of SMAs is the ability of the client/investor to receive customized reporting that is unavailable from commingled investment vehicles. The extent of the available information is essentially limited only by investor preferences and the investment advisor's technological capabilities. In an online program, the investor also may be able to audit the investment advisor's activities on a real-time basis, sometimes for no additional fee. Largely for this reason, an SMA has been described as "your own private mutual fund."

Public mutual funds generally release performance information on a quarterly or semi-annual basis, but even then with a 30- to 45-day lag. This makes it difficult for investors who are not following daily market movements to decide on tactical investment strategies. This problem can be somewhat minimized by the personal relationship with the retail investment advisor but is not completely mitigated. Moreover, as discussed in Chapter 5, an individual's cost-basis information with respect to a mutual fund is not easily determinable. The recent rule requiring the tracking and furnishing of this basis to the investor has assisted in this determination, but the rule applies only to new fund shares and stocks acquired through **dividend reinvestment plans** (DRIPs) beginning January 1, 2012. The IRS began receiving a reporting of this basis in the 2012 taxable year.

Disadvantages of SMAs

Among the disadvantages of SMAs are

- High management and transaction costs
- Possible lack of attention to the investor's account by the investment advisor
- Possible expertise of an experienced investor, making it appear that management fees for accounts are unnecessary
- Possible increased tax management with an alternative mutual-fund purchase

High Management and Transaction Costs

Two costs may be greater in an SMA than in, for example, a commingled account such as a mutual fund.

The first is the AUM annual percentage fee charged by the investment advisor. This cost is typically 1–1.5% of AUM by the investment advisor for a particular client; however, the fee can be as high as 3% of AUM. It is also typically adjusted downward as the amount of assets managed for the client by the investment advisor increases (a common breakpoint is $1.0 million of AUM). The fee is usually deducted from the client's account quarterly or four times per year and agreed to by the client and the investment advisor via an upfront investment advisory agreement.

The second potentially high cost in an SMA is that of transactions occurring within the account. Sometimes trading costs are passed along to the client, meaning that an advisor who engages in a lot of trades (buying and selling of individual stocks and bonds) incurs higher expenses for the client. In addition to the trading fee, the investment advisor, if also a broker licensed to buy and sell securities, makes money from a spread in the price paid for the stocks and bonds and the price at which the securities are resold to the client. Specifically, the investment advisor/broker buys the stocks at a lower *bid price* and then resells them to the client at a higher *ask price*. For the most part, unlike the AUM fee, which is shown on a quarterly statement, this spread between the bid and ask price is not transparent to the client.

Possible Lack of Attention to the Client's Account

The performance of a customized portfolio, such as an SMA, is difficult to track—particularly so if your portfolio is one of hundreds or even thousands that the investment advisor must maintain and operate on a daily basis. Of course, technology has assisted considerably in this regard; still, the amount of information that needs to be monitored and tracked may be overwhelming for any one individual. Therefore, it may be helpful to limit the selection of an investment advisor to customize your SMA to an individual or firm that has a smaller number of assets under management to increase the likelihood that personalized attention will paid to your particular account. This concern is most acute in times of extreme market volatility.

Possible Expertise by an Experienced Investor

There are several consequences when an experienced investor structures an SMA. First, if the investor is truly educated and experienced in the intricacies of investments, it is probably unnecessary for him or her to work with (and pay) an investment advisor. However, be very careful here! Any number of individuals believe that they can more properly manage their investments than an investment advisor; in other words, they fall prey to not recognizing their own limitations. As a result, they sell in a down market and buy in an up market, thereby reversing the age-old advice of "buy low and sell high." If nothing else, sometimes the cold analytics of an experienced investment advisor—one who has invested throughout a number of market cycles—can keep the individual from acting on emotion rather than reason.

Second, if an experienced investor does seek out the advice of an investment advisor, why would this investor now want to overrule the decision of an expert whom they are paying to customize and manage an SMA? Stated another way, if the investor has recognized the value of an investment advisor and SMA, he or she should not try to limit the value of the professional relationship and thus not get his or her "money's worth. Again, this is really part of the investment decision: initially whether to invest by means of an SMA, and then determining who the best investment advisor is to help the client reach his or her financial goals.

Possible Increased Tax Management with the Alternative Purchase of a Mutual Fund

Alternatively, an investor may be better off purchasing an index mutual fund with a *low turnover ratio* than structuring an SMA. A low turnover ratio, defined as the number of times a security in a mutual fund has been replaced with another security in comparison to the total holdings of the fund, leads to more efficient income-tax management. Low turnover also results in lower transaction costs incurred by the fund and passed on the investor in the form of higher returns. Alternatively, if the mutual fund has a higher turnover ratio, transaction costs increase as well as the probable tax liability of the investor. As an example, the more turnover in a fund, the more likely it is to generate **short-term capital gains**, thus resulting in the gain being taxed to the investor at higher ordinary income tax rates.

In the year 2013, the top marginal income tax rate for an individual is 39.6%, which beginning in 2013 is augmented by another 3.8% for tax on unearned income (like mutual-fund dividends) to fund the upcoming implementation of Obamacare. This is a total top federal marginal rate of 43.4% payable on so-called *ordinary income*, such as salaries and wages. However, gains from assets that are held for one year or less—or *short-term capital gains*, are taxed at the same rates as salaries and wages. This is in contrast to gains from assets sold after one year, which are taxed according to a long-term capital gains preferential tax rate, with a maximum rate of 20% (23.8% when adding in the Obamacare surtax).

Who Should Invest by Means of an SMA?

The straightforward answer to the question of who should invest by means of an SMA is a buy-and-hold investor who wants the assistance of an investment advisor or third-party manager when structuring a customized portfolio. Investors with a greater amount of discretionary income to invest may be best suited for an SMA so as to spread money among various investment objectives or strategies. In addition, although the inclusion of selected mutual funds may be helpful in diversifying the account, an investor who also wants to purchase individual stocks and bonds likely should investigate an SMA. As discussed in the following selection criteria section of this chapter, the excess performance of an SMA is best ensured by choosing a skilled and experienced investment advisor or third-party manager. This is very similar to the selection of a portfolio manager at the mutual fund level if proceeding alone and without the assistance of a broker or investment advisor. Thus rereading the criteria in choosing a mutual fund portfolio manager, as first discussed in Chapters 4 and 5 of this book, may also assist you in selecting an investment advisor to customize and maintain an SMA on your behalf.

What Selection Criteria Should Be Used in Structuring an SMA?

Because an SMA is a customized portfolio consisting of specific securities selected by an IA, the selection criteria to be considered are broadly based around, first, the services provided by the IA and, second, the features of the SMA.

With respect to the services provided by the IA, it is first incumbent on you, the client/investor, to clearly understand and communicate your financial goals to the IA. Then, make sure the IA is providing at least the following services to you in exchange for his or her asset-based percentage fee:

- Assisting in defining your financial goals
- Establishing an IPS and working with you to structure an appropriate asset allocation
- Evaluating and recommending specific securities as part of the agreed-on asset allocation
- Monitoring the account and performing periodic rebalancing of the assets as necessary to comply with IPS allocations
- Measuring investment performance and the effectiveness of his or her investment activities on an ongoing basis

Additional services may be rendered by the IA, such as constant availability by phone or e-mail to discuss the investment trends and market conditions. This availability should not be separately charged back to the client in lieu of the asset-based percentage fee.

An SMA should include the following account features:

- As low as possible initial account minimum. It is unlikely that the account minimum will be lower than $100,000, but if you can find a lower minimum, you should take advantage of it.
- Unlimited withdrawals and redemptions of securities if possible. Note that as a buy-and-hold investor, you likely will not wish to redeem securities frequently; but if the need arises, you should be permitted to do so on an unlimited basis.
- Account statements reporting the value of your account holdings should be sent to you at least monthly.
- There should be one asset-based percentage fee that also includes all trading expenses, if possible.
- The more assets (and asset value) you position (own) in the account, the lower an asset-based percentage fee should apply. This means that a sliding-scale schedule of fees should be offered.

Again, the experience and background of the IA in structuring and managing the SMA cannot be overstated. Some IAs have been excused from taking and passing the Financial Industry Regulatory Authority (FINRA) licensing exam for IAs (known in the trade as a *Series 65 exam*) because they previously passed a much more rigorous financial-planning examination, such as the Certified Financial Planner (CFP) examination. After passing this ten-hour examination and meeting the requisite education and ethics requirements of the CFP Board of Standards, an individual is awarded the highly-regarded CFP license. This means that the individual has been certified as meeting certain minimum standards to provide comprehensive financial planning advice, including that of investment management.

How to Evaluate the Performance of SMAs

The primary alternative to an SMA is a traditional mutual-fund investment. Therefore, the metrics used to evaluate the performance of a mutual fund, as discussed in Chapter 5 of this book, also apply to evaluating SMAs, most particularly the annualized total return achieved by an SMA compared to the mutual-fund alternative. However, SMAs also consist of what are known in the financial marketplace as *composites*, so a definition and evaluation of such a term is relevant to this discussion.

According to the *Global Information Performance Standards Handbook*, a composite is "an aggregation of one or more portfolios into a single group that represents a particular investment objective or strategy." An example of a composite objective or strategy is global equity or emerging-market income. The former strategy is executed by investing in U.S. and international stocks, whereas the latter strategy concentrates on debt issues of companies in emerging markets, such as China, India, and Mexico. An important measure of evaluation of a composite or SMA is whether it complies with the *Global Information Performance Standards* (GIPS) and whether a third-party auditor has issued an opinion that the SMA is in accordance with these standards. This is similar to a CPA issuing an opinion that a publicly traded company's financial statements are in compliance with *Generally Accepted Accounting Principles* (GAAP) standards.

What are the GIPS, and who developed them? They are a set of ethical standards that apply to the way in which investment performance is presented to potential and existing client/investors. They were first developed in 1999 by the Association for Investment Management and Research, now known as the Chartered Financial Analyst (CFA) Institute. Many mutual-fund portfolio managers hold the CFA designation, as well as some investment advisors. GIPS ensures that these managers and investment advisors have structured an SMA in accordance with certain widely recognized and accepted global standards, which then allows for a uniform evaluation of performance. Such standards also permit a standard analysis across global markets, including not only the U.S. market but foreign markets as well.

The provisions of GIPS include several prerequisites with respect to the presentations and disclosures of SMAs, but they also include computational measures. For example, time-weighted or geometric rates of return are required. This means that the annualized return of an SMA, taking compounding into account, is usually lower than the traditional arithmetic method of computation. However, geometric returns are not dependent on inflows and outflows of funds from a mutual fund over which the portfolio manager has no control. As such, geometric returns are a better performance measure than the oft-quoted arithmetic used by most mutual funds. The standards also require SMAs to initially show a minimum of at least five years of GIPS-compliant history. After meeting this minimum, the SMA must evolve to a track record of 10 years. If the SMA has been in existence for less than five years, it must provide its entire history since inception to a potential investor.

The rigorous requirements that must be met for a CFA charter holder have been previously discussed in Chapter 2 of this book. When selecting an investment advisor or third-party company to manage an SMA, the CFA credential may be an important differentiator.

Recent Performance History of SMAs

Aggregate SMA performance history is difficult to obtain because the performance of most SMAs is only reported for that composite or single account. For example, Morningstar, Inc. provides performance information on more than 6,300 U.S.-domiciled separate account composites, as well as an increasing number of UK-domiciled SMAs. However, this data is available only to certain premium subscribers for a fee and as part of a specific product, such as Morningstar Direct or Morningstar Principia. Usually, institutional representatives or financial planners are the major users of these services.

In 2008, during the depths of the Great Recession, SMAs outperformed traditional mutual funds in 25 of 36 stock and bond market categories.[1] Table 13-1 summarizes the average 2008 SMA performance as compared to mutual funds.

Table 13-1. Average SMA's Performance Compared to Average Mutual Fund's Performance, 2008

Category	SMA Annual	Mutual Funds	+/- Percent
Large Cap Stock	-34.79 %	-37.9%	+3.11%
Large Cap Value	-38.44%	-40.9%	+2.46%
Large Cap Growth	-34.94%	-37.38%	+2.44%
Mid Cap Stock	-37.13%	-39.68%	+2.55%
Small Cap Stock	-34.77%	-36.88%	+2.11%
Foreign Large Stock	-42.30%	-44.06%	+1.76%
Intermediate Bond	+0.73%	-5.07%	+5.80%

Data are scarce with respect to SMA composites (exacerbated by the fact that the annualized return is arithmetic rather than geometric), but what data there are indicate that SMAs outperformed traditional mutual funds in the period 2006–2008. But notice the percentage difference in performance in the year 2008. With the exception of intermediate bonds, where SMA managers recognized the impact of falling interest rates in 2008 more rapidly than did mutual-fund investors and managers, the excess performance on an after-fee basis was approximately the same between the two investment alternatives. The result is thus consistent with the overall statement made in Chapter 5 that actively managed mutual funds (and probably SMAs) have a difficult time outperforming broader market indexes over the longer term .

This concludes this book's look at alternative PMAs for the average investor, which followed a detailed examination of PMAs primarily for high-net-worth investors. The final part of this book examines PMAs of insurance-company-managed pooled assets, such as variable life insurance and variable annuities.

---

[1]Morningstar data as reported by Ian Salisbury, "SMAs Beat Funds in 2008," *Wall Street Journal*, March 12, 2009, `http://online.wsj.com/news/articles/SB123679669243098151`.

PART

VI

Managed Assets and Life Insurance Companies

CHAPTER

14

Variable and Variable Universal Life Insurance

Life insurance company-managed products are a large part of the *professionally managed assets* (PMA) universe of options. This chapter and the next examine variable life products (including variable universal life) and variable annuities, respectively. Both variable life products and variable annuities are products in which the cash value (in the case of variable life options) or accumulation units (in the case of variable annuities) are invested in mutual fund–type investments. A life insurance policy is purchased to protect survivors from the risk of premature death of the insured, whereas an annuity is purchased to protect the annuitant from the risk of *superannuation* (the risk of outliving his or her income during his or her lifetime).

Variable universal life (VUL) is a hybrid policy including characteristics of both universal life and variable life policies. This chapter looks first at the latter two policy types as background to its focus on VUL.

Universal Life Insurance

Universal life (UL) is a variation of the traditional *whole life* insurance policies historically sold by life insurance companies. A **whole life** policy is an insurance contract that is designed to provide protection over the insured's whole or entire life. This is in contrast to *term* insurance, which provides protection only for a temporary or specified period or term. A distinguishing characteristic of whole life insurance is the accumulation or buildup of a specific amount of the insured's premiums for the policy into a cash value available to the insured in the form of loans or withdrawals as long as the policy protection does not lapse. The most typical cause for the policy lapsing is that the insured (who is also usually the owner of the policy) simply does not pay the requisite premiums due to keep the policy in force. At that point in time, the owner/insured is considered to have terminated the policy and is entitled to any cash surrender value under the policy.

A whole life policy typically requires the payment of an ordinary level premium. In addition, the policy's cash value is normally invested in very conservative assets, including those in the money market. Some whole life policies are *interest-sensitive*, meaning the rate of guaranteed interest on the cash value varies based on a market benchmark rate and is reflected in an increasing dividend payment to the owner/insured of the policy. However, this connection is not immediately transparent to most owners. Alternatively, the annual UL statements explicitly reflect the amount of credited interest, with a rate normally tracked to rates paid on investment-grade corporate and municipal bonds (a so-called *current assumption rate*). Historically, UL policies have paid a rate of interest on the policy's cash value a percentage point or two higher than municipal bonds.

A distinguishing feature of UL from whole life is that the UL premium is flexible instead of fixed. A *flexible premium* means that the policy owner is given the option to pay whatever amount of premium he or she wishes, as long as a minimum mortality expense is paid. Moreover, the death benefit payable from a UL policy adjusts (*adjustable death benefit*) based on the amount of premium that is chosen to be paid by the policy owner. This death benefit may be increased or lowered over time, although sometimes increases in the benefit may require evidence of continued insurability by the owner/insured.

Most UL policies offer two death-benefit options, normally referred to as Option A and Option B under the terms of the policy. Option A provides for a fixed or level death benefit. Thus, as the cash value accumulated within the UL policy increases, the pure insurance portion (mortality protection) of the policy is reduced to keep the total death benefit constant. Alternatively, Option B provides for a death benefit equal to a specified level of pure insurance protection plus the policy's cash value at the time of death. Thus, the death benefit increases as the cash-value portion of the UL policy grows or increases.

Option B of a UL policy can be thought of as combining a traditional whole life policy death benefit with a term insurance addition or *rider* equal to a dynamic, current cash value.

Variable Life

Variable life insurance marries whole life insurance with investments. Specifically, in variable life, the policy owner directs the investment of cash values among various securities, usually mutual funds. This is in contrast to universal life, where the investments are made by the insurance company. Like whole life, variable life requires a level premium payment and has a guaranteed death benefit of a specified minimum amount. But variable life differs from whole life in three important respects.

First, the death benefit is variable. The death benefit or *face value* of the policy may increase or decrease, but not below a guaranteed minimum. Insurance companies use several methods to determine the adjustment to the death benefit, but all are tied to the performance of the policy's cash value, which is in turn dependent on the market performance of the directed securities.

Second, there is no guaranteed minimum cash value. This, of course, can be both good and bad. In an ascending market, the cash-value return percentage may be significant, which is further aided by the fact that the cash value builds up income-tax-free. Variable life insurance must qualify as insurance and not as a disguised investment, or the cash-value tax shelter provision does not apply. This means that certain complex tests must be met by any variable life product, as discussed in the next section.

Finally, in a variable life product, the policy owner's funds are placed in separate accounts that are not part of the insurance company's general reserve. As a result, if the insurance company should financially fail, the creditors of the company cannot attach the separate accounts held on behalf of a variable life insurance policy owner. Although an argument can be made that this feature is of limited value to a policy owner who should be investing only with a highly rated insurance company, to some owners this may be of critical importance.

Given the characteristics of variable life insurance and a variable life product, a potential policy owner should understand that the investment risk of performance of the underlying securities contributing to the growth of the policy's cash-value element is entirely assumed by the owner. This is why it is often said that variable life and VUL insurance are only appropriate for experienced, relatively risk-aggressive owners/investors.

The remainder of this chapter focuses on VUL insurance, which is the most commonly purchased form of variable life insurance. It is sold by investment advisors who are licensed at the state level as insurance *producers*, as well as holding a Series 65 securities license at the federal level (or substituting an appropriate financial-planning designation in lieu of the securities license).

What Is a Variable Universal Life Insurance Policy?

A **variable universal life** (VUL) insurance policy) is a flexible-premium variable life policy. As such, it combines a basic feature of a universal life policy (a flexible premium) with a basic feature of variable life (a variable death benefit). With respect to the first feature, the policy owner is entitled to skip a premium payment on a VUL policy as long as the cash value in the policy is sufficient to cover the mortality expense (pure insurance) portion of the policy. Of course, this means excess premium payments should be made in the first several years of coverage, so as to build up a sufficient cash value.

With respect to the second feature, the VUL owner is given the ability to choose between two death-benefit options similar to Options A and B for universal life policies. Under the provisions of Option A of a VUL policy, the death benefit remains level, whereas under Option B, the death benefit varies directly with changes in the policy's cash value. Under Option B, the most popular choice of VUL death-benefit options, the total death benefit is equal to a level pure insurance amount plus a dynamic cash-value amount.

It is sometimes recommended by investment advisors that an individual in good health in advancing years of age should consider reducing the amount of a VUL death benefit, thereby saving on premium costs. However, it is important for a VUL policy owner to understand the income tax consequences of the **modified endowment contract** (MEC) rules when decreasing the amount of the death benefit payable under the policy. The triggering of these rules can occur if the policy owner reduces the death benefits within the first seven years of issue and fails the *seven-pay test*. If this results, the policy becomes an MEC, resulting in distributions under the policy taxed as *interest first* rather than the usual recovery of *capital first* rule applying to a non-MEC (normal) insurance policy. Distributions under the policy for this purpose include withdrawals of the cash value as well as loans taken by the policy owner that are secured by the policy's cash value.

Example Suppose that the guideline annual premium under a VUL policy, to avoid application of the MEC rules, is $12,000 annually based on the original death benefit payable from the policy. The policy owner pays $10,000 each year for the first four years, or a total of $40,000. In year five, the owner withdraws cash value of $50,000 from the policy, which also reduces the death benefit by the same amount. The recomputed guideline annual premium is now $9,000. Thus, the policy in year five becomes an MEC and fails the seven-pay test because the cumulative premiums paid to year five ($40,000) exceed the sum of the seven-pay recomputed guideline annual premiums of $36,000 ($9,000 × 4). This test is applied retroactively as of the original issue date of the policy and as if the policy had been issued at the reduced death benefit. The consequence of this failure to meet the seven-pay test requires that ordinary income tax be paid by the owner on the withdrawal of $50,000 in year five.

As a practical matter, most required VUL policy illustrations show the maximum amount that must be paid within the first seven years the policy is in force, so that the policy is not treated as an MEC.

Advantages of VUL

A major advantage of a VUL policy is that the purchaser obtains life insurance protection as well as making an investment in mutual funds. Therefore, as discussed in the "What Selection Criteria Should Be Used in Purchasing a VUL policy?" section, the real choice to be made is whether to invest in mutual funds directly (likely, as part of an advisory account) or with the life insurance overlay. Life insurance as an investment affords certain tax advantages to the investor/policyowner that an investment outside of life insurance does not. The next sections discuss these tax advantages and others, including in turn:

- Discretion in the timing and amount of premium payments
- The ability to change the level of death benefits
- The ability to withdraw a significant portion of the cash value of the policy without surrendering the policy
- Transparency in reporting

Tax Advantages of a Life Insurance Product

Any permanent life insurance product, such as a VUL policy, has two inherent tax advantages. The first is the ability of the policy's cash value to grow free of an annual income-tax event or without current taxation. This does not, however, mean that the increase in the policy's cash value may never be taxed. Rather, any taxable event may only be deferred. For example, if the policy owner surrenders the policy for its cash value, and the amount of this cash value at the time of surrender is greater than the policy premiums paid at such time, the difference or excess between the two amounts is taxable to the owner as ordinary income. Moreover, although there is no income taxation at the time of death, if the policy owner dies without accessing the cash value during his or her lifetime, the insurance company retains the cash value and does not pay the beneficiary that additional amount as part of the death proceeds. (Note that in a VUL policy, if the owner selects the Option B death benefit, the beneficiary is paid this cash value in the form of, essentially, a term-insurance rider.)

The second tax advantage of a life insurance product is the non-taxability of the death proceeds when received by the beneficiaries. The only exception to this tax treatment is if the **transfer-for-value rule** is triggered for income tax purposes. Under this rule, if the insurance policy is sold (not gifted) to a third party during the owner's lifetime, a portion of the death proceeds is income-taxable to the purchaser as ordinary income on receipt of the proceeds.

Example Suppose that B purchases a $250,000 VUL policy from owner A for $125,000. (Of course, after purchasing the policy, B changes the beneficiary to himself and pays the annual premiums to keep the policy in force.) The annual premium for this policy is $10,000, and A dies two years after she sells the policy to B. Thus, B has a cost basis in the policy of $145,000 at the time of A's death. Because the transfer-for-value rule has been triggered, B must pay income tax on $105,000 of the death proceeds or the difference between the face value of $250,000 and his cost basis of $145,000 (his $125,000 original purchase price plus the $20,000 of additional premiums paid).

Before 1997, the transfer-for-value rule was triggered in a viatical settlement between a *viatication company* (usually the insurance company provider) and an individual/policy owner who was expected to die within a short period of time, such as from cancer or AIDS. Normally, the insurance company bought back the VUL policy (or any other cash-value-type policy) for at least its cash value from the insured, who then used the proceeds received for his or her final medical expenses. The same result occurs with a policy that is issued with an accelerated death-benefits rider. In 1997, Congress changed the tax law so that proceeds from viatical settlements and accelerated death benefits are tax-exempt as long as the insured's life expectancy is less than two years at the time of viatical sale or receipt of the accelerated death benefit. In addition, the viatical settlement company must be licensed to do business in the insured's state of residence. Most states, but not all, have followed the federal lead in exempting such payments from income tax. Therefore, it is best to consult a tax advisor in your state before proceeding with either a viatical settlement or the purchase of an accelerated death-benefits rider.

Discretion in the Amount and Timing of Premium Payments

A major advantage of a VUL policy is the ability of the owner to vary the amount and timing of premium payments. This advantage is limited only by the requirement that there be enough cash value in the policy to cover the mortality and expense charges associated with insuring against the insured/owner's risk or premature death (the primary purpose of any life insurance policy). The owner can add to the premium payments at any time, thereby taking advantage of the tax preference given to the buildup of insurance cash value, or forego making a premium payment altogether, as long as mortality and expense charges are satisfied. In contrast to a traditional whole life policy, should a premium payment not be made, the creation of a policy loan in a VUL policy does not occur.

The Ability to Change the Level of Death Benefits

A VUL also permits the owner of the policy to vary the amount of death benefit that is payable from the policy. As discussed in the "What Is a Variable Universal Life Insurance Policy?" section, if the death benefit is decreased within the first seven years that the policy is in force, the disadvantageous MEC taxation rules may apply. These rules may also be triggered if the death benefit is increased, although this is rarely the result. Instead, most VUL policies require evidence of continued insurability in the event of a voluntary increase in the death benefit. This is to be contrasted to an increase in the death benefit resulting from the policy's favorable investment performance.

VUL death benefits generally depend on the investment performance of the underlying assets selected by the insured/owner. Most VUL policies offer a wide array of possible investment choices, typically consisting of mutual funds. Among the mutual funds offered are stock and bond funds, both domestic and foreign. Stock funds usually include index funds as well as more aggressive small cap stocks and even real estate funds. Bond funds include GNMA (Ginnie Mae funds) as well as corporate and municipal securities. A money market fund is almost always offered for those investor/owners who wish to be very conservative. Finally, policyowners are given the right to switch among funds usually once per policy year.

The Ability to Withdraw the Policy's Cash Value

A cash-value withdrawal from a VUL policy is an example of a **living benefit** available under the policy. Other types of common living benefits are policy dividends, lump-sum receipts of cash value when the policy is surrendered, and any amount received on partial surrender of the policy. Such benefits are taxed under a specific tax rule included in Internal Revenue Code (IRC) Section 72, commonly referred to as the *cost recovery rule* or *first-in first-out* (FIFO) *rule*. This rule treats amounts received as a living benefit as a nontaxable recovery of the policy owner's *investment in the contract* or *basis*, generally defined as the total premiums that have been paid by the owner less any prior nontaxable distributions such as a policy dividend. Only after the owner's investment in the contract has been recovered is any additional withdrawal amount received treated as taxable interest in the policy. Assuming that the contract is a regular or non-MEC contract, the FIFO rule provides a huge tax advantage over the typical securities investment.

A major exception to the FIFO rule is if the policy is considered to be an MEC. Technically, an MEC is a life insurance policy that meets the IRC Section 7702 definition of life insurance and is funded more rapidly than permitted under a seven-pay level annual premium test. The result of MEC tax treatment is that a living benefit under a VUL, such as a cash-value withdrawal, becomes a distribution under the policy and is taxed the same as an annuity distribution. In other words, the cost recovery rule does *not* apply. Thus, the first distributions (withdrawal of cash value) from a MEC are not considered a nontaxable recovery of the policy owner's basis, but rather the investment earnings on the contract. The earnings are considered withdrawn first (not last as under the cost recovery rule) and are taxable before the policy owner's basis is recovered. In addition to the ordinary income tax on distributions under an MEC, a 10% penalty tax may be applied to a distribution made before the taxpayer attains age 59.5.

Although a cash-value withdrawal from a VUL issued after June 20, 1988, (the effective date of the MEC rules) is not generally taxed as a distribution, it can become taxable if made within the first 15 years after the policy issue date. In such case, all income or earnings growth in the amount of the cash surrender value under the VUL are considered as having been received by the owner and taxable to the extent of the gain. The actual amount that is taxable depends on when the withdrawal is made during the 15-year period, subject to a statutory ceiling.

Transparency in Reporting

Because a VUL policy is considered to be within the definition of a security under the Securities Act of 1933 and amendments thereto, a prospective purchaser must be given a prospectus. This is typically in addition to a policy illustration reflecting the possible growth of the policy's cash value and death benefit given certain assumptions. The prospectus includes not only important financial information about the insurance provider, but also the investment characteristics of the insurance product and the fees associated with the product. As is well understood by most prospective purchasers, the expenses of a VUL are generally greater than those of a traditional mutual fund purchase, because the cost of life insurance protection must be assumed by the purchaser.

Once the owner receives the prospectus and obtains coverage under the policy, he or she receives annual reports on the performance of the underlying mutual funds in which the policy contributions are invested. Each of the policy elements, such as cash value and death benefits, is broken down separately. This unbundling permits the policy owner to track actual performance of the elements against the policy illustration provided to him or her at the time of purchase. It also permits decisions to be made about possible changes in the underlying funds or portfolio rebalancing to be accomplished in the future.

Disadvantages of VUL

As mentioned in the preceding section, the cost of a VUL policy is greater than that of a mutual fund investment, even after factoring in the fee charged by an investment advisor in a fee-based advisory account. Consumer Federation of America maintains that VUL costs can reduce the policy's annualized return by as much as three percentage points.

Other major disadvantages of a VUL policy include the following:

- The policy owner (not the insurance company) bears all investment risk of the policy.
- The policy owner must accept responsibility for making the premium payments to keep the policy in force.
- Surrender of the policy in the early years of issuance may result in a considerable loss.
- Capital gains on the underlying assets when taking withdrawals are converted into and taxed as ordinary income.

The following discussion examines each of these disadvantages in detail.

Policy Owner Bears All Investment Risk

Unlike with a traditional whole life insurance policy, there is no minimum schedule of guaranteed cash values with VUL. Instead, cash values vary with the investment performance of the underlying assets (usually, mutual funds) and are equal to the market value of the assets in a separate account set aside for the policy owner. Moreover, if the investment performance of the VUL policy is poor or the cash-value portion is declining, the policy owner may be required to pay additional premiums to maintain the policy's mortality protection.

VUL policies are a form of *defined-contribution* account. Similar to that concept found in retirement accounts, most notably 401(k) retirement plans, the risk of investment performance is shifted from the company (here, the insurance company provider) to the participant (here, the owner of the VUL policy). Thus, the term *self-directed*, as first discussed in Chapter 1 of this book, also applies to VUL policies. If an insured/owner of a VUL policy directs investment purchases for the policy, it is incumbent on the owner to become as knowledgeable and experienced in sound investment practices and portfolio management as possible. Yet too many purchasers of VUL are unfamiliar with investments and portfolio management. Although most purchasers of VUL policies direct investments only in concert with an investment advisor (IA), this fact again speaks to the necessity of selecting and working with a competent and experienced IA.

Policy Owner Must Accept Responsibility for Premium Payments

At first inspection, the requirement of a VUL policy owner to make premium payments may appear unexceptionable, inasmuch as premium payments need to be made on all types of life insurance to maintain coverage. But an additional concern arises in a variable life type of policy. In a traditional whole life policy, policy premiums can be taken from the policy's existing cash value if so elected by the policy owner. Further, because the premium amount in a whole life policy is fixed and must be made, there is a forced savings element inherent in such a policy. This also means that a whole life policy is extremely unlikely to lapse unless the owner chooses to cease premium payments altogether and exercise the policy's **non-forfeiture options**. In a VUL policy, by contrast, the forced savings element is lacking.

As discussed in the "What Is a Variable Universal Life Insurance Policy?" section, premium payments are not required to be made in a VUL policy as long as there is sufficient cash value to maintain the policy coverage. But this apparent advantage may also be a disadvantage, because VUL policy owners can very easily choose to skip too many premium payments, thus resulting in an unintentional lapse of coverage. To reduce this likelihood, most companies specify and assess a target monthly, quarterly, or semiannual premium payable by the policy owner. Usually the policy owner is aware of the need to make this target premium amount when he or she is approved for coverage. However, remember that the policy owner in a VUL policy can change the amount of the death benefit through subsequent actions, including cash withdrawals and policy loans. Therefore, the target premium amount can vary, a fact that should be communicated to a prospective policy owner by the insurance company provider.

Surrender of the Policy May Result in Considerable Loss

Insurance companies must include a surrender charge in any insurance product to recover sales commissions and initial expenses incurred when issuing a policy or annuity. (See Chapter 15 for a discussion of types of annuities and, most notably, a deferred variable annuity.) This charge is imposed if the policy owner surrenders the policy in exchange for any accumulated cash value. Usually, such charge is only in effect for the first five to ten years of the policy's life and, in later years within this stipulated period, declines by about a percentage point annually. Typically, such charge begins at 10% of the cash value accumulated in the policy; but in some cases, it can be as high as 15% of the cash value. As would be anticipated, if an insured/owner surrenders the policy in the early years of coverage, the overall dollar loss can be substantial because of the surrender penalty.

In a VUL policy, the surrender charge may be ascertained by reviewing the policy illustration provided to the prospective purchaser during the sales process. It is also on the annual statement provided by the insurance company provider to the owner. The illustration or statement shows both a cash-value amount and a net cash-value amount for a given policy year. The *cash-value amount* is the amount on which investment performance is based; the *net cash value* is the amount that the company will pay if the policy is surrendered by the owner. The difference between these two amounts (cash value and net cash value) is, accordingly, the *surrender charge*.

Capital Gains on Underlying Policy Assets Are Taxed as Ordinary Income

The taxation of capital gains on policy assets as ordinary income is a major difference between a VUL policy (or any insurance policy) and a traditional mutual fund. More precisely, appreciation in value on sales of mutual-funds shares is treated as capital gains and, if such shares are held by the shareholder for at least a year subsequent to purchase, may qualify for a long-term capital-gains tax preference. The maximum rate applicable to long-term capital-gains transactions is currently 20% for individuals with a taxable income in excess of $400,000 annually; this is to be contrasted to a maximum rate of 39.6% annually if taxed as ordinary income. (Note: in 2013, a surtax of an additional 3.8% is added to both rates to fund the implementation in 2014 of the provisions of the Patient Protection and Affordable Care Act of 2010, a.k.a. Obamacare.) In addition, capital gains may only be used to offset capital losses, and not the ordinary losses that may result from the underlying assets of an insurance policy.

A basic rule of income-tax management is to convert ordinary income into long-term capital gains, thereby ensuring a lower marginal tax rate and taking advantage of the nearly 20% difference between the two rates. As explained, this rule is violated in the case of certain withdrawals or surrender of the cash value in a VUL policy. But remember, there is favorable tax treatment of the build-up of cash value in a life insurance policy; that is, in the absence of surrender for more than the owner's basis in the policy, the increase in value may never be taxed at all during an insured/owner's lifetime. Moreover, in many VUL policies, owners may withdraw a sizeable portion of the cash surrender value income-tax-free. Finally, the tax exemption afforded to a payout of most death proceeds from a VUL policy may more than compensate for the tax-rule-management violation.

Who Should Purchase a VUL Policy?

It should be self-evident that a VUL policy is, first and foremost, most suitable for an individual who requires initial or additional life insurance protection. Given the inherent investment risk and potential decrease in both the cash value and death benefit, a VUL policy is probably more feasible for supplemental life insurance coverage, with the initial protection of the insured's earning power and risk of premature death being covered by either a term or traditional whole life policy. Securing coverage via the purchase of a universal life policy as basic coverage is also a possibility.

Second, a VUL policy should only be considered by a relatively sophisticated investor, because of the need to self-direct the investments of the underlying assets. You should be of the belief that you can make prudent investment decisions and, preferably, also possess considerable investment experience. You should work as closely as possible with an IA whose judgment is not clouded by the attractiveness of a sizeable commission payment on the sale of an insurance product. In this transaction, the IA is held to the legal standard of a fiduciary, which may help to dispel investor fears of a possible conflict of interest. Finally, you must be willing to assume the risk of investment and the lack of a guaranteed cash value inherent in any VUL policy.

In the small business context, VUL may be especially appropriate where there is a need for the growth of cash value and/or increasing death benefits. For example, in a traditional **split-dollar life insurance** arrangement used in executive compensation where the business-as-policy-beneficiary receives the death-benefit portion equal to the amount of accumulated cash value, VUL may be a very effective funding mechanism. Similarly, the use of **key-person life insurance**, where the business is the sole beneficiary of death proceeds to substitute for the loss of temporary cash flow due to the death of a key-person owner or employee, may also effectively include a VUL policy as the primary funding vehicle.

What Selection Criteria Should Be Used in Purchasing a VUL policy?

Because the underlying assets consist of mutual funds, the same criteria, with several exceptions, may be used in purchasing an appropriate VUL policy as in selecting open-end investment companies (mutual funds). These criteria—as recited in Chapter 5 and as employed by Morningstar, Inc., in making recommendations to its subscribers—are as follows:

- Process
- Performance

- People
- Parent
- Price

Although all of these are important in selecting the best VUL policy to meet an investor/owner's financial goals, mutual-fund performance deserves special mention.

Of the many ways to evaluate the performance of a mutual fund, the one most commonly cited is total annualized return. The computational process in deriving total annualized return has been discussed several times in this book, but it is important to realize that such return is quoted on an arithmetic basis and, therefore, does not account for the effects of annual compounding. In addition, total return implies a combination of both the income yield and capital gains yield from stock or bond mutual funds in arriving at the return quoted. In the case of a stock mutual fund, the income yield is dividends paid from the composite stocks in the fund, whereas in a bond mutual fund, such yield is derived from interest paid on the composite bonds in the fund. (In the case of a balanced mutual fund, the income yield consists of both dividend and interest payments on the underlying securities.) Investors purchase a stock mutual fund primarily for its capital-gains yield, in contrast to bond-fund purchasers, who are most interested in the income yield.

Total return can be quoted in terms of both a dollar return and a percentage. Usually, total percentage return is the accepted metric. However, total return lacks the element of time that the investor has owned the particular mutual fund; thus, it must be annualized for a more effective evaluation measure. The prospective investor also needs to know whether the total annualized return quoted is on a before-tax or after-tax basis and whether the return takes into account ongoing fund expenses. Most reference services, including Morningstar, quote total return on a percentage basis before any taxes on the disposition of fund securities are considered and after accounting for ongoing fund maintenance expenses.

Of course, no return can be properly evaluated without considering the amount of risk assumed by the investor. As discussed in Chapter 4, a proper understanding of the relationship between return and risk has been the major contribution of modern portfolio theory (MPT) in investments. Of the several types of risk—among them total, unsystematic, and systematic risk—MPT ranks systematic risk as measured by the security's beta coefficient (beta) as most important. MPT also propounds the famous capital asset pricing model (CAPM) in determining the investor's required or risk-adjusted return. This model is used as a benchmark in reflecting what the expected return of an investment in an efficient market should be. Thus, if the actual portfolio total annualized return (Rp in the Jensen or alpha model) exceeds the return expected under CAPM, the fund is said to have *overperformed* and to have a positive alpha. This metric provides a measure by which to evaluate the performance of mutual-fund portfolio managers and leads to a search generally for mutual funds with as much return as possible while assuming as little systematic risk as possible ("more alpha for less beta").

The first of the several exceptions or qualifications to the primacy of investment performance in selecting a VUL policy is policy expenses. Such expenses include front-end sales loads (commissions paid to the insurance producer), premium tax loads, surrender charges, and administrative fees associated with maintaining the policy. Generally, VUL policies have higher expenses than traditional whole life or universal life policies because of the need to prepare an investment prospectus, register the policy as a security with the SEC, and provide a wide array of mutual-fund investment choices. Also, remember that VUL is life insurance, thereby requiring a charge for mortality expense. A typical total breakdown between mortality expense charges and the cost of investment management of the mutual funds underlying the policy's cash-value accumulation is 1.65% or 0.80% (80 basis points) for mortality expense and 0.85% (85 basis points) for investment management. Depending on the company and the age of the insured/owner when the VUL policy is underwritten, however, charges can be as high as 2% for the combined expenses.

The second exception or qualification to the primacy of investment performance of the underlying assets in a VUL policy concerns policy loans. You should not consider a VUL policy unless it provides for the ability to access the cash value of the policy in the form of a nontaxable loan. Loans are permitted from a VUL policy, but they are not the same as those from a traditional whole life policy. This is because a loan in a VUL policy equal to the full, accumulated cash value could potentially leave the insurance company provider with less than complete protection for the debt if the value of the underlying mutual funds declined after the loan was made. Accordingly, most insurance company providers restrict loans on VUL policies to approximately 75% of the policy's cash value. (This is in contrast to an accessible amount of approximately 90% on traditional whole life.) Thus, the prospective purchaser of a VUL policy should recognize the need for a policy loan option but also understand that the nature of the policy restricts what cash value could otherwise normally be accessed.

How to Evaluate the Performance of VUL Policies

Unlike traditional mutual funds, a prospective owner of a VUL policy must be provided with a policy illustration or ledger statement. The typical components of this illustration are as follow:

- Amount of insurance coverage and type of insurance (here, VUL).
- Current age and gender of insured.
- Annual premium and monthly premium if paid by automatic deduction.
- Premiums accumulated at a specific compounded annual percentage interest rate. (Note: This component reflects the amount of premium accumulated at a compounded interest rate if not used to purchase the VUL policy.)
- Death-benefit increase due to the projected dividends payable under the policy purchasing additional paid-up insurance at a specified, assumed investment return. (Note: A 0% investment return is among the specified returns.)
- Cash-value projected value based on a specified net investment return after expenses and deductions. (Note: A 0% investment return is among the specified returns.)
- Insurability status, such as smoker or nonsmoker, rated or non-rated.

It is important for the prospective owner to establish that the assumed investment returns shown on the illustration are not unreasonable in light of current and future market environments. The assumed investment return should, ideally, be provided for each year that the policy is expected to be in force. Ideally, the illustration also should show what items constitute expenses and deductions that will be charged against the separate account making up the VUL policy and whether these expenses and deductions are contractually guaranteed not to increase. If this information is not shown on the illustration, it is important for you to ask for it verbally.

Once you purchase the VUL policy, you should track the actual performance of the underlying mutual funds and compare it to the policy illustration or ledger statement. The most valuable measure of performance to use here is the total annualized return of the underlying mutual funds net of ongoing fund-maintenance expenses. If you are not satisfied with the investment performance, you should direct a reallocation of assets among other funds consistent with your risk tolerance.

Finally, you must remember not to surrender the policy for the period of time during which a surrender charge applies, or a considerable dollar loss from the initial purchase price will occur. A rate of return on surrender should be provided either in the policy illustration or verbally by the life insurance producer. When this rate of return is a positive percentage, or the projected cash surrender value—even after the surrender penalty—is greater than the premiums paid to the date of surrender, it means that income taxes will also be due on surrender. During the surrender-penalty years of the policy, it is difficult to envision an actual rate of return high enough to compensate for both the loss of cash value due to penalty and the amount of taxes due on surrender.

As discussed in Chapter 5, several reference services are available to monitor and evaluate the investment performance of traditional mutual funds. Historically, information on the investment performance of variable life policies, including VUL, was lacking. This is changing, however. In 2003, Morningstar, Inc., announced the creation of the "most comprehensive variable product universe in the industry" with the enlargement of its database to include complete coverage of 975 variable life policies, 2,800 underlying insurance funds, and 30,500 subaccounts.[1] Morningstar has been providing data on variable annuities since the 1990s. The data, which is included in various Morningstar products, and notably its Principia version for investment advisors, permits the comparison of VUL underlying mutual fund performance against that of traditional mutual funds.

Prior to the Morningstar announcement of a comprehensive database to track VUL performance, few academic studies assessed the performance of separate accounts within a VUL policy. One study that analyzed the performance of the stock portfolios maintained by insurance companies as an institutional investment as an alternative to mutual funds concluded that, on the basis of risk-adjusted performance such as that expected using modern portfolio theory, life insurance stock and mutual fund portfolios yielded similar returns.[2] This speaks to the investment acumen of portfolio managers employed by insurance companies and other institutions, who are well-trained to consider investment risk as a critical component of effective management.

This chapter has considered variable life and VUL as professionally managed assets. The next chapter takes up the annuity form of life insurance product. One such form, the deferred variable annuity, often sold to and purchased by pre-retirees, has been the subject of much discussion, both positive and negative, in recent years.

---

[1]Morningstar, Inc., "Morningstar Enhances Variable Annuity Data to Create Most Complete Database in Industry," July 8, 2003, `http://corporate.morningstar.com/us/asp/subject.aspx?xmlfile=174.xml&filter=PR4063`.

[2]Robert T. Kleiman and Anandi P. Sahu, "Life Insurance Companies as Investment Managers: New Implications for Consumers," *Financial Services Review: The Journal of Individual Financial Management*, 1, no. 1 (1991): 23-24.

CHAPTER

15

Variable Annuities

No book taking up the subject of professionally managed assets (PMAs) could be complete without a detailed examination of annuities and, most notably, the deferred variable annuity. Such is the purpose of this chapter.

Annuities are a product issued and backed by a life insurance company. They are a risk-management tool purchased primarily by retirees to ensure against the risk of *superannuation* (outliving one's accumulated retirement funds). In exchange for a cash (premium) payment to an insurance company, which then invests the payment, the owner (aka *annuitant*) receives a systematic liquidation of the principal and interest over his or her lifetime or other specified period. In common usage, the term *annuity* refers only to the payout stage of the product. Nonetheless, there can be, and frequently is, an accumulation stage that may last for a significant period of time.

Annuities can be categorized in a number of ways, but most commonly they are classified according to either the date the benefits begin—whether immediately or in the future—or the type of benefit payment—whether fixed, variable, or indexed. If the benefit does not begin immediately, defined in the annuity contract as within a year from the date of the first premium payment, the benefit is *deferred* and, thus, will be paid only after an accumulation stage. During the accumulation stage, the annuity grows income-tax-deferred with components of earnings or growth and of principal (the owner's *investment in the contract*). If withdrawals are made by the owner during the accumulation stage, they are taxed as withdrawals of earnings first (meaning that such portion is fully taxable as ordinary income) and non-taxable return of principal second. In addition, certain withdrawals before the owner attains age 59.5 are subject to a 10% penalty, just as for a life insurance policy that is considered to be a modified endowment contract (MEC), as discussed in Chapter 14.

In the payout or distribution stage of the annuity, the owner's monthly or annual (annuitized) payment is divided into two portions: the first portion is considered to be the nontaxable return of principal (investment in the contract), and the second portion is treated as taxable earnings. The amount of each payment that is considered non-taxable is determined by a tax concept known as the *exclusion ratio*, written in formula format as follows:

$$\textit{Excluded portion of payment} = \frac{\textit{(Investment in Contract)}}{\textit{(Expected Return of Contract)}}$$

where

- *Investment in Contract* is the amount paid for the annuity by the owner/annuitant.
- *Expected Return of Contract* is the total amount that the owner/annuitant should receive over the life of the annuity, which in turn is equal to the amount of monthly or other periodic payment multiplied by the specified term or owner's life expectancy as determined by the IRS annuity tables.

Example A single individual owner/annuitant of XYZ deferred fixed annuity is receiving a payment of $1,000 per month over his lifetime and has an investment in the annuity contract of $160,000. He is currently age 65 and, therefore, under the IRS Table V actuarial table has a life expectancy of 20 years. This means the expected return of the contract is $240,000 ($1,000 per month times 12 times 20 years). Accordingly, the amount of monthly payment that may be excluded from income taxation (considered as the portion of the payment representing the non-taxable investment in the contract) is $667 ($160,000 divided by $240,000, equal to 66.7%). The remaining $333 portion of the $1,000 total monthly payment is treated as taxable earnings growth.

Once an owner/annuitant has fully recovered his or her investment in the contract, all of each subsequent annuity payment is taxable. Full recovery occurs at the end of the expected payout term, meaning that an owner/annuitant who outlives the expected term will pay income taxes on the entire amount of payment. Similarly, should the owner/annuitant not make an investment in the contract, which happens in the event of a before-tax lump-sum contribution to the annuity, all of the payment is taxable, and the exclusion-ratio computation does not apply. A before-tax contribution, whereby the owner/annuitant is said not to have a basis in the contract, normally occurs with the purchase of an annuity using a lump-sum payout from a **qualified retirement plan** in which the owner/annuitant no longer participates. An annuity in which the owner/annuitant has no basis in the form of after-tax contributions is called a *qualified annuity* for tax purposes.

There is considerable debate with respect to whether an owner/annuitant should ever *annuitize* the annuity over his or her lifetime. *Annuitization* means receiving the payments over a period prescribed by a lifetime actuarial table used by the insurance company. Several disadvantages are associated with this technique. First and foremost, if you, the owner/annuitant, die before the time projected by the insurance company, you will have made a losing bet. That is, the insurance company will not have to pay you as much income as they projected; and, in turn, you will not receive the actuarial equivalent of your expected return on the contract. Second, what happens if you need more in the future than the annuity payment you are currently receiving? Typically, the amount cannot be adjusted, and you lose access to the principal remaining in the annuity account balance. Finally, when annuitization is chosen, during the first several years of the annuity distribution period, you are receiving back only your own money. Thus, no investment risk or any other risk is assumed by the insurance company, which is one of the reasons you presumably bought the annuity in the first place!

So who should annuitize an annuity? The answer to this question is generally any individual in reasonably good health and with a favorable family history of longer-than-normal life expectancy. In such a situation, the owner/annuitant may very well win the bet of outliving the insurance company's projected life expectancy for him or her and receive more than the company expects to pay as an actuarial lump sum. However, even in this situation, you should be aware that the annual investment return assumed by the insurance company during the accumulation stage of the annuity is relatively low, so that you incur an opportunity cost.

Finally, most annuities have a surrender charge if the annuity is surrendered during the early years of the contract. This charge is usually 7% of the annuity's account value for the first year, declining one percentage point until the charge reaches zero for the eighth and later years. The charge is assessed to help compensate the insurance company for the commission paid to the annuity salesperson or broker. Most variable annuities permit a withdrawal of up to 10% of the account value without imposition of a surrender charge.

Preliminary to the major PMA subject matter of this chapter—the deferred *variable annuity* (VA)—the next four sections describe several historically popular types of annuity, as well as several other recently introduced annuities designed to provide the comfort of guaranteed retirement income.

Immediate Fixed Annuity

An *immediate annuity* is an annuity whose annuity payment to the owner/annuitant begins no later than one year after all premiums are made as required under the annuity contract. Typically, the premium payment for an immediate annuity is a *single-premium* lump-sum payment, usually consisting of accumulated amounts from an individual's IRA or a lump-sum distribution from a qualified retirement plan, such as a Section 401(k) plan. An individual in or close to retirement hands over this lump sum to an insurance company in return for a specified monthly payment as long as the individual lives. Although the concept of an immediate annuity is relatively simple, investment advisors caution about several potential pitfalls. First, if the payout is fixed in amount (as is the case with most immediate annuities), the monthly payment to the owner/annuitant usually is not adjusted for inflation, so the annuitant loses purchasing power. Second, once you commit to receiving an annuity payout from the insurance company, there is no going back. In other words, you cannot reclaim the money you previously invested in the contract. Finally, the historically low interest rates in today's market environment work against the owner/annuitant; locking in a very low internal rate of return on a fixed annuity could be disadvantageous if interest rates rise in the future, resulting in a considerable opportunity cost associated with the annuity.

As a result of these potential pitfalls, most immediate fixed annuity purchasers are advised by IAs and financial planners to invest only a portion of their retirement savings in such product. Typical advice given is to estimate an amount equal to your fixed monthly expenses, such as mortgage, rent, and transportation, and leave the remainder in higher-interest-bearing accounts or mutual funds. Given the increasing chance of sizeable healthcare expenses as an individual ages, planners also recommend a side account of cash (outside of any contributions made to an immediate annuity) of approximately $200,000 to cover such expenses during retirement.

Equity-Indexed Annuity

An *equity-indexed annuity* (EIA) is an annuity with a rate of return on its accumulated cash value tied to a market index, such as the S&P 500. The annuity contract specifies that the owner/annuitant will be credited some percentage of the amount by which the underlying index has increased, subject to an annual maximum percentage or *cap*. Alternatively, if the index declines, the owner/annuitant's losses are restricted to zero; in other words, the owner/annuitant cannot lose money on his or her investment. With an EIA, the investor essentially agrees to cap his or her potential gain from the annuity contract in exchange for a guarantee that he or she cannot suffer a loss from what they have invested in the contract.

However, there are problems with this approach to cash-value accumulation. The primary issue is that the gain on the index does not include any dividends paid by the companies making up the index. In addition, placing a limit on the capital gains achieved by the stock in the index can prove disadvantageous in wealth accumulation, particularly in a rapidly rising market. Finally, although the no-loss guarantee of an EIA is intuitively attractive, you are still taking a risk and are not being properly compensated for it, because gains are capped and dividends are not credited to your account. For all these reasons, many potential annuity purchasers conclude that the real choice to be made is between a VA and an EIA. Usually, unless your investment time horizon before retirement is relatively short so that you cannot recover from a down market, the conclusion is that a VA is the preferable alternative.

Longevity Insurance Annuity

In recent years, a new type of annuity referred to as *longevity insurance* has been offered by many insurance companies. A longevity insurance annuity is a contract designed to pay the owner/annuitant a benefit if he or she survives to a pre-established age, usually 85. At that time, the benefit is usually paid in the form of a guaranteed income stream for the remainder of the owner's life and permits the insurance company to pay higher-than-normal investment returns for the relatively small percentage of owners who live to receive a benefit. The term *longevity insurance* is used to characterize the annuity as a means of ensuring against the risk of the owner's unusually long life.

The problem with the longevity insurance type of annuity is obvious: not many owners live to the age of prescribed payout. As a result, the promise of a high-investment-return payout is illusory for most, yet the requirement of a higher-than-normal premium payment still exists. Relatively few individuals are willing to take the risk of paying more money for a future benefit that they are likely not to receive. Thus, some insurance companies have revised the product to allow owners to begin receiving income much earlier in a renamed longevity insurance form known as a *deferred income annuity*.

Deferred Income Annuity

A *deferred income annuity*, first introduced in 2011 by several well-known insurance companies, is a hybrid product offering some of the benefits associated with a deferred variable annuity and some associated with an immediate fixed annuity. As with the deferred annuity, the owner/annuitant may choose to defer the payments until the future, normally from 2 to 40 years, permitting the money invested to grow income-tax-free. As with the immediate annuity, the monthly payout is fixed and generally does not increase, as a variable annuity does. The product has been very popular since the market downturn in 2008, when insurance companies offering deferred variable annuities with a relatively high **guaranteed minimum income benefit** (GMIB) found themselves unable to maintain the guaranteed rate.

In a deferred income annuity, you structurally trade off the flexibility of withdrawing the annuity in a lump sum (as a variable annuity provides) to achieve a higher income payout at the time of distribution. A deferred income annuity investor also does not get to self-direct the underlying investments of the annuity, as he or she can with a VA. For example, an owner/annuitant who waits for nine years before receiving an annuity payout may achieve a return on investment of 8% on a $100,000 contract versus a guarantee of 5% on a variable annuity. In most deferred income annuity contracts, the longer the owner/annuitant waits before receiving a payout, the greater is the potential return on investment. In addition, as for any annuity product, if the owner/annuitant dies before receiving a payout, the product will pay a death benefit to his or her named beneficiaries.

There is one notable advantage of a VA compared to the deferred-income annuity: the VA has the potential for growth of the account value and thus greater wealth accumulation. Accordingly, investors who are most concerned about growth and wealth accumulation typically choose the VA, particularly if it is offered with guaranteed benefits with respect to income and/or withdrawals, whereas investors most interested in a predictable income stream opt for the deferred-income annuity form.

The remainder of this chapter examines the deferred VA.

What Is a Deferred Variable Annuity?

A VA may or may not defer income payouts, but given its primary attractiveness to a pre-retiree who is looking for a guaranteed income source during retirement, deferral is almost always chosen. Conceptually, VAs are mutual funds wrapped in the annuity tax-deferral investment vehicle. Like any annuity, VAs feature a death benefit or life insurance protection, but because they are not life insurance as defined by the tax law, the death benefit is typically taxable. (Note: There are some forms of annuities used for executive compensation purposes that may not have a taxable death benefit, but they are beyond the scope of this book.) If the payouts from a VA are annuitized (most are not, but rather are withdrawn), the payout/distribution is taxed according to the exclusion ratio rule formulated at the beginning of this chapter.

As the name suggest, VAs provide for a variable payment that may be used as an inflation hedge to keep the purchasing power of the owner/annuitant stable in times of increasing prices or market values. This is in distinct contrast to the behavior of a fixed annuity payout, which loses purchasing power over time if inflation persists. At the time of distribution or payout, the *units of credit* accumulated in a separate cash-value account in the name of the owner (also known as *accumulation units*) purchase an amount of *retirement income units*. The value of each of these retirement income units depends on its dollar value when the payment is made, which is in turn based on the investment results of the accumulation units. For example, let's say that the annuitant from a variable annuity is entitled to a payment based on 100 annuity units each month. If the dollar value of the retirement income units varies from $12 to $13 to $14 over a three-month period, the annuitant is entitled to $1,200; $1,300; and $1,400 per month, respectively.

The investment options available to the owner of a VA are many (just as for variable life insurance products) and typically include diversified stock, bond, money market mutual funds and alternative investments such as commodities and precious metals. Foreign stock and bond funds are also usually part of the VA investment choices, which can be self-directed and allocated among asset classes as chosen by the owner. Although it is important to note that the owner cannot select funds external to those provided by the insurance company, normally the possible options are so vast and diversified that there is no need to invest elsewhere. Thus, the question for you as the investor becomes how much of your retirement savings to direct into the purchase of a VA and not where to direct the allocated investments. As a practical matter, to implement good diversification strategies, an investment advisor usually recommends that a retiree investor (or soon-to-be retired investor) not allocate all of his or her retirement funds into one or more VAs.

VAs normally provide a guaranteed death benefit that protects the owner/annuitant against a loss in principal if the market declines. The terms of the typical death benefit state that if you die during the accumulation period of the annuity, the amount paid to the named beneficiary of the annuity will be the greater of the amount invested in the contract or the account value at the time of your death. Some VAs also provide an *enhanced death benefit* that periodically adjusts the value of the account to lock in any investment gains and then resets this benefit at the adjusted amount. For example, a 5% enhanced death-benefit provision resets the amount received by the beneficiary at the annuitant's death to the principal plus 5% interest.

VAs have become extremely popular in recent years because of the so-called *living benefit* riders that have been offered to potential investors on a guaranteed basis. Among these riders, available for an additional percentage-of-investment charge of around 1%, are two often-purchased guarantees, ensuring a minimum income benefit from the annuity regardless of how the markets perform—a *guaranteed minimum income benefit* (GMIB) rider)—and the ability to withdraw a guaranteed amount during lifetime even if the investor's initial investment is exhausted—a *guaranteed lifetime withdrawal benefit* (GLWB) rider). If you purchase the GMIB rider, usually for around a 1% additional charge, you are guaranteed that a hypothetical account, known as your **benefit base**, will grow at a minimum *step-up rate* each year—say, 5%—even if the underlying mutual-fund investments of the annuity lose money. Most annuity contracts then allow you at the distribution stage to access the higher of either the benefit base or the account value, if the underlying asset performance exceeds that of the step-up rate compounded on the benefit base. In addition, the benefit base resets at the higher of these two amounts for the purposes of future distributions. The GLWB rider, usually also available for another 1% expense charge, permits withdrawal amounts of 4% to 5% per year of the original amount of money invested in the annuity.

An important distinction between the GMIB and GLWB riders occurs in the distribution or payout stage. A GLWB rider guarantees that you will receive a percentage of your original investment for the duration of your life in the form of an **income withdrawal benefit**. A GMIB rider, on the other hand, carries a greater degree of risk that an income payout will be made to you. For example, assume that an owner/annuitant elects a 10-year-term certain benefit. This means that if he or she should die during the term certain of 10 years, the policy's benefits will be paid to the owner's designated or named beneficiaries (usually the spouse or other family members) for the remainder of the specified period. However, should the owner outlive the term certain—say, he or she dies in the eleventh year—the payments will be discontinued immediately. Most married owner/annuitants elect a joint-and-survivor payout, meaning that the income benefits are payable over a period of two lives instead of only the annuitant's life, but this type of payout in turn reduces the amount of monthly payout to the annuitant.

Since the 2007–2009 Great Recession and financial market meltdown, many insurance companies that sell VAs with living benefits have significantly scaled back guarantees offered on new contracts, while simultaneously increasing fees. Other companies have limited or prohibited additional investments in already-existing contracts, posing a dilemma for investors who already have purchased a VA-rider combination of benefits. Specific steps to take if you are one of these previous owners are discussed later in this chapter, but new investors who purchase currently offered riders offering guaranteed minimum income or withdrawal benefits will find that they are not nearly as generous as those sold before the Great Recession. A few insurance companies have even offered cash buyouts to existing investors willing to cancel the GMIB and/or GLWB riders. Whether an existing owner should accept or reject this cash buyout is not discussed in this book. Such a decision is based on **time-value-of-money** (TVM) principles, of which any knowledgeable investor should be aware.

Advantages of a Variable Annuity

The main advantage of a VA is as a hedge against the potential loss of purchasing power that arises from many other fixed-income products, such as a fixed annuity. Although the inflation hedge advantage is why many individuals purchase a VA, other advantages include the following, which are considered in turn in the following sections:

- The guarantee that the annuitant cannot outlive his or her money (that is, protection from the risk of superannuation)
- The ability to invest in the stock or bond market but with a guarantee of minimizing systematic risk
- The possibility of assuming more risk (and, therefore, potentially higher returns) because of living-benefit guarantees
- A higher effective yield on the annuity's underlying investments because of the tax-deferral feature of the annuity

Guarantee of Not Outliving Money

Any annuity is the opposite of any type of life insurance. A life insurance policy provides protection against the risk of dying too soon (the risk of premature death) before sufficient financial assets can be accumulated to ensure the security of the named beneficiaries. An annuity provides protection against the risk of living too long and outliving whatever financial assets have been accumulated during the annuitant's lifetime (the risk of superannuation). Thus, an annuity protects primarily against the loss of lifetime income because the annuitant outlives his or her projected life expectancy. The term *primarily* is used in the preceding sentence because an annuity, like life insurance, does provide a death benefit to the named beneficiaries on the contract. But unlike life insurance, where the death benefit is usually non-taxable to the beneficiaries, the death benefit under an annuity is usually taxable to the heirs or beneficiaries of the owner/annuitant.

Annuitants tend to be relatively healthy individuals who expect to live longer than most individuals. An individual with a family history of longevity is a good candidate for the purchase of an annuity. Moreover, if this individual is concerned about the impact of inflation on the potential purchasing power of his or her future income, the purchase of a VA may be advisable. In calculating the premiums to be paid for annuity contracts, actuaries use special mortality tables reflecting the potentially longer life of the typical annuitant.

Ability to Invest in the Market While Minimizing Risk

As has been discussed throughout this book, stock and bond investors assume what is referred to as *systematic* or *market risk* when investing in the stock or bond market. Systematic risk is one of two components of total risk, with the other component being unsystematic risk. Good diversification practices, however, can essentially diversify away unsystematic risk, leaving the investor to assume and manage only systematic risk. Also, as you have learned under the principles of modern portfolio theory (MPT), systematic risk can only be minimized; in other words, it is not possible to mostly diversify away systematic or non-diversifiable risk.

An effective minimization-of-risk tool now being offered by many VA insurers is living benefits, including lifetime guarantees in the form of riders (contractual additions) to the annuity contract. Among these are the guaranteed minimum income benefits (GMIB) and the guaranteed lifetime withdrawal benefits (GLWB) discussed in the "What Is a Deferred Variable Annuity?" section. Others include

- The *guaranteed minimum withdrawals benefit* (GMWB), which guarantees that the annuitant can annually withdraw a specified percentage of his or her total premiums paid for the annuity until recovering the entire investment
- The *guaranteed minimum accumulation benefit* (GMAB), which guarantees that the account value of the contract will be equal to a specified minimum amount after a certain number of years

Of course, these rider/guarantees come with an additional percentage charge, which is one of the biggest disadvantages of a VA when compared to a traditional mutual fund or other type of pooled asset.

Nevertheless, most if not all of these guarantees provide protection against the volatility of markets, particularly that of a declining market. This makes a VA with living benefits most attractive to an investor in or nearing retirement who wants to minimize the risk of excessive volatility. For example, it has been statistically shown that an individual just entering into retirement in a declining market environment cannot follow the typical **4 percent plus inflation annual withdrawal rule** used by most investment advisors and financial planners when informing clients of an annual withdrawal percentage from their retirement funds. Indeed, if a client just retiring and entering into a bad market environment attempts to withdraw 4% or slightly more from his or her retirement plan account balance, they will likely not outlive their accumulated funds. Rather, such clients either need to adjust their annual withdrawal amount to a lower percentage amount, thereby potentially impacting their standard of living throughout their retirement years, or simply continue (or return to) gainful employment.

Possibility of Assuming More Risk

Some investment advisors argue that there is no reason for a VA annuitant to invest conservatively when he or she has paid for the GMIB living-benefit rider offered as an addition to the contract. In other words, you should invest to exceed or outperform that percentage by which the benefit base of the contract is guaranteed to increase and thereby obtain the advantage of the higher reset amount for income withdrawals going forward.

However, there is a caveat with respect to the reset amount possibility. Some VA insurers increase the fee or percentage charged for taking advantage of the reset. This can create a decline or drag in the overall investment performance of the VA. Thus, the annuitant experiencing only a small increase in his or her benefit base, and less than the reset amount, encounters a dilemma. Specifically, the annuitant in this case may be better off in sticking with his or her current benefit base (and at the lower fee charged) than resetting the benefit base to the higher amount and incurring the greater fee. Better yet, of course, is not to purchase a VA with this provision; however, that is becoming more difficult given the restructuring of many VAs today to make up for the too-generous offerings of insurers before the 2008 market meltdown.

As mentioned earlier in this chapter, the mutual fund offerings available to most owner/annuitants in a VA are varied and vast. Some insurers are also putting in place contract terms whereby, unless the owner specifies otherwise, he or she will be invested in funds where the account's portfolio managers can minimize, for example, exposure to stocks when markets become extremely volatile. Still other insurers are moving in the direction of offering more index mutual funds as a possible investment choice within VAs. Both of these run counter to the "stay aggressive" stance promoted by some advisors, but each does try to implement the basic MPT objective of achieving the greatest amount of expected return for the minimum amount of systematic risk assumed by the investor.

Higher Effective Yield on Tax-Deferred Investments

Because the interest on any annuity payouts not taken immediately is deferred for income-tax purposes, this results in a higher effective yield for the owner/annuitant. For example, let's say that a taxable fixed annuity features an annual interest rate of 5% and that the owner/annuitant is in a 33% marginal income-tax bracket. Accordingly, the after-tax yield received by the owner/annuitant is 3.35%, computed by taking the nominal rate of 5% times (1 minus the marginal tax rate of 0.33). In contrast, the deferred annuity owner earns the nominal and before-tax return of 5% annually.

How much of a difference in total wealth accumulation can the difference between an annual 5% and 3.35% return make at the time of an investor's retirement?

Example Assume a $300,000 initial lump-sum investment in an annuity with an investor having a work-life expectancy of 10 years remaining until his retirement (and initial withdrawal from the annuity). The investor with the 5% effective yield would have a total of $71,582 more accumulated in the account value of the annuity than the investor with the 3.35% effective yield. The time-value-of-money computation, using an HP 10 B II financial function calculator, is as follows:

Assuming the 5% effective yield:

PV = -$300,000 N= 10 I/YR= 5 FV= $488,668

Assuming the 3.35% effective yield:

PV= - $300,000 N= 10 I/YR= 3.35 FV= $417,086

Because there is a direct or positive relationship between the time that a single lump-sum amount is invested and its accumulated future value, the dollar difference between the two effective yields increases in amount, the greater the number of years that the after-tax impact is deferred.

Disadvantages of a Variable Annuity

There are disadvantages associated with a VA, most notably its cost in comparison with alternative investments. As discussed in the "What Selection Criteria Should Be Used in Purchasing (or Maintaining) a VA?" section of this chapter, some investment advisors and financial planners maintain that you should consider purchasing an immediate fixed annuity to cover your basic fixed expenses and then invest the remainder of your savings in a mutual fund. The reason for this recommendation is the cost of the VA and all of its offered living-benefit riders.

In addition to their high costs, VAs have the following disadvantages:

- Investment earnings are taxed at ordinary income, rather than capital gain, tax rates.
- Not all VAs are created equal (offer the same contract terms and living benefits).
- The flexibility of individuals who previously purchased VAs is currently restricted, given all the recent changes to the contract by VA insurers.

Cost, Cost, and More Cost

In addition to the surrender charge if an owner/annuitant surrenders the VA for its cash value, VAs typically contain the following fees and expenses:

- *A mortality and expense risk charge*: This is the insurance component charge of an annuity and pays for the following:
  - The mortality risk associated with the guaranteed death benefit and excessive longevity
  - A guarantee that annual expenses associated with maintaining the annuity contract will not exceed a certain percent of assets after issuance
  - An allowance for the insurer's profit
- *An administrative charge*: This charge covers paperwork, recordkeeping, and periodic performance reports (usually provided on a quarterly basis) to the owner/ annuitant.
- *An investment management charge*: This charge is a payment to the portfolio manager and mutual fund for the services provided in the management of the separate account investment portfolio.

There may also be additional charges for distributions from the annuity contract, an annual contract fee (normally a flat $50 or $100), and an upfront sales charge similar to the load fee on a mutual fund. In total, all the charges, before the addition of possible living-benefit riders, is usually around 1.50–2.00% of the account value of the contract.

Living-benefit guarantee riders are usually each around 1% of assets of the annuity's benefit base, although depending on the insurer, they can be less than 1%. In total, therefore, the usual cost of a VA with several of the most heavily utilized living-benefit riders (for example, the GMIB and GLWB) easily exceeds 3% of the account value or benefit base, and approaching 3.5-3.6% of the same. Of course, this means that the subaccount mutual fund underlying investments in the VA must outperform the typical mutual fund by slightly more than 2% annually to provide a commensurate return. (As mentioned in Chapter 2, the average expense charge for an actively managed mutual fund is approximately 1.4% of assets managed.)

Low-cost VAs are available from such well-known mutual-fund companies as Fidelity Investments and Vanguard Investments, whose *all in* (total) cost is 0.60% (or slightly higher) of the account value. In addition, certain insurers such as Jefferson Pilot offer low-cost VAs for approximately 0.40% of the account value. This low cost is before the addition of any living-benefit riders, which, depending on the product, may or may not be available to the prospective purchaser. A small number of low-cost annuity providers also do not impose a contract-surrender charge.

Investment Earnings Are Taxed as Ordinary Income

The earnings (unearned income) generated from the underlying securities of the VA are taxed at the annuitant's ordinary income tax rate applying to earned salary and/or wages. This is the taxable result regardless of the source of these earnings, such as stocks that are held long term and would otherwise qualify for preferential capital-gains treatment.

Currently, long-term capital gain income is taxed at a rate of 20% for those in the highest 39.6% marginal income-tax bracket and 15% for those in the 25% or higher marginal bracket. However, for those annuitants in the lowest marginal income tax brackets of 10% and 15%, there is no tax on long-term capital income. Therefore, some annuitants in the lowest tax brackets, which include some retirees, are deliberately electing to pay income tax on annuity distributions when, if held outside the annuity form, there would be no tax. This disadvantage is somewhat offset by the fact that dividends from mutual funds, if held in the deferred annuity form, are not taxed until later distribution. Nevertheless, VAs in which the owner/annuitant is invested in stock mutual funds are less attractive tax-wise than if the owner invested outside of the annuity form and directly in the mutual fund.

Not All VAs Are Created Equal

Although some insurers/VA sponsors have discontinued their annuity offerings since the 2008 market meltdown, there are still numerous VA products in the marketplace. Some of these products offer no living-benefit guarantees, some offer only one, and others offer one or more. In addition, some insurers guarantee a minimum payment in the GMIB rider only if the owner annuitizes payments, whereas others do not. Still others do not impose a surrender charge on withdrawals, whereas others do. The point is that not all VAs are the same and it is up to the prospective purchaser to work closely with his or her IA to understand the conceptual basis and purpose of an annuity and to differentiate VA products based on the features and possible living benefit guarantees that are most important to him or her.

Also, you must be aware of the source and tax implications of the money that is contributed to the annuity. For example, contributed funds that derive from the rollover of proceeds from a fully tax-deductible IRA or qualified retirement plan are taxed in full at the time of distribution. This is because, for income-tax purposes, you are considered as not possessing a tax basis in any part of the annuity distribution. Such a qualified annuity also requires that distributions begin to be made no later than April 1 of the year following the year in which you turn age 70.5. Alternatively, a nonqualified annuity for tax purposes is the standard commercial annuity that is purchased. In such an annuity, contributed funds consist of primarily after-tax monies, thus creating a tax basis in the annuity and constituting an investment in the contract for purposes of the exclusion-ratio computation. At the time of distribution, only contributed funds that have not been previously taxed to you are taxable. As a result, usually only the earnings generated from the annuity during its accumulation stage are taxable as ordinary income to you.

Restricted Flexibility in Recently Issued VAs

As mentioned, some VA product providers/sponsors have gotten out of the business entirely. Many of those sponsors that have not have nevertheless severely restricted their fund or investment choices and/or future contributions. Others have cut back on income guarantees. This leaves the previous VA owner/annuitant in a somewhat precarious position. Specifically, if offered an annuity replacement by an IA or financial planner, you should ensure that the replacement product has the same income guarantees as your existing annuity contract. Moreover, with respect to an existing contract, should you (the owner/annuitant) receive a letter from the annuity sponsor about changing terms of the contract, read the letter carefully and direct any questions about its impact to your IA. If this is not the same advisor who sold you the annuity, ask your new advisor to review the letter and explain its potential consequences with respect to future benefits paid from the annuity contract.

Finally, consider any changes to the death benefit payable from an existing VA and what happens if you make future withdrawals from the contract. In some contracts, the death benefit is terminated if the owner/annuitant withdraws too much from the cash value of the annuity. If this is the case, you want to know how much you can withdraw without impacting either the existence or amount of death benefit that is payable, and you may want to add additional monies (if the existing VA permits it) to protect the death benefit payable to your named beneficiaries.

Who Should Purchase a VA?

The primary purchaser of a VA is an investor approaching or near retirement, with an optimal age of purchase probably around 55. This allows for the tax-free deferral of earnings accumulated on the cash-value portion of the annuity. Specifically, a VA is most appropriate for a pre-retiree who wants more control over his or her investment choices and is looking for a hedge against the potential purchasing power loss associated with a fixed-income investment such as a fixed annuity. Such investors can also take advantage of the risk-management tools typically offered by the VA product in the form of living-benefit guarantees with respect to both income and withdrawals from the product. Finally, as an insurance-based product, a VA includes a death benefit similar to life insurance, although the death benefit is taxed to the product's beneficiaries in the same manner as if the annuitant had received the benefit of a lifetime payout.

Again, it is important that only a portion of an investor's retirement savings be positioned in a VA. A VA should be viewed as a supplement to a traditional IRA or other taxable investment. Because annual contributions to an IRA are limited, a VA may be an effective after-tax choice for at least some of your savings. In this case, a non-qualified annuity would be funded with after-tax dollars up to the amount chosen by the owner/annuitant. (There are no limits on annual contributions to a non-qualified annuity.) However, you should also consider other taxable alternatives—most notably the possibility of investing in traditional mutual funds or ETFs with after-tax dollars using the investment strategy of dollar-cost averaging.

What Selection Criteria Should Be Used in Purchasing (or Maintaining) a VA?

Before purchasing a VA, here is a series of questions to consider:

- What are its annual fees and expenses, including the charges for any living-benefit riders that are added to the annuity contract?
- Are you willing to be locked in to the annuity for at least the period necessary to not incur a surrender charge, usually seven to ten years? (This is typically a declining charge, with the highest percentage of the account value imposed in the early years of ownership.)
- Do you understand your tolerance for risk?
- Are you willing to tolerate potential fluctuations in monthly income? (VA monthly payouts fluctuate with the investment experience of the underlying mutual funds or subaccounts.)
- Have you evaluated the total return performance for the VA subaccounts over a period of time? (The upcoming section on evaluation of VA performance includes the quote page from Morningstar, Inc. on a sample type of VA currently available in the marketplace.)
- Have you evaluated the financial strength of the VA insurer/sponsor by reviewing its rating from a credible insurance rating service, such as A.M. Best? (Try to purchase a VA only from an insurer rated A+ or better. The highest Best rating is A ++.)
- Do you need the monies invested in the VA before age 59.5? (Cash withdrawals from a VA made before the owner attains age 59.5 are generally subject to a 10% penalty in addition to income tax payable at ordinary income rates.)

- Are you aware that, if you should die, earnings on the VA death benefits are taxable to your beneficiaries in the same manner as if you had received them during your lifetime? (This results in a choice for an owner/annuitant of whether the owner pays taxes on the lifetime earnings or shifts that responsibility to the VA beneficiaries.)

Given all the recent changes to existing VA contracts, here is also a series of questions for an existing VA owner/annuitant:

- Should you accept the new terms of the contract or cancel the contract and invest in an alternative professionally managed asset? (A general rule of thumb in answering this question is: if the benefit base in the VA is currently at least 15% higher than the account value, you should probably keep the existing contract and accept its new terms.)
- What is your withdrawal-rate percentage using the GLWB rider as compared to a percentage of the account value in the contract?

Example Your withdrawal-rate percentage is 5%, and you have a benefit base under the contract of $500,000. Thus, you can withdraw $25,000 per year. If your account balance is only $450,000, the withdrawal amount of $25,000 represents a percentage of 5.56% per year. This is higher than the 5% withdrawal rate and more than the 4% that is typically recommended by investment advisors and financial planners to maintain a reasonable standard of living during the annuitant's retirement period without a significant chance of outliving his or her money.

- If offered cash of a sizeable amount by the insurer to drop a given rider on an existing VA contract, should you accept the offer? (The general answer to this question is "No." If an insurer wants to offer you cash of a sizeable amount, it is likely because the rider has economic value to you and the insurer, which value the insurer is probably trying to obtain at a discount.)
- If you keep the annuity and own a GMIB rider, when should you begin to take the minimum income benefit? (The general answer to this question is "As soon as possible." If you are age 65 or older, the income from taking the payments now outweighs any increase that might be achieved by step-ups and a reset of the account value in the future. This is because you want to begin receiving income payments out of the insurer's money and not yours!)

- If you are intent on surrendering the annuity, when should you do so? (As discussed earlier, the answer here is "Not until the surrender charge period expires." However, if you have to surrender, wait until the percentage owed if you surrender the contract falls below the annual expenses of the contract so as to also avoid losing a portion of your value invested in the contract.)

Finally, before purchasing a VA and investing a portion of your hard-earned money, consider what else you could do with the money. If investing with after-tax dollars, you should maximize all available before-tax investment vehicles first. This means that you should fully fund any tax-deductible options, such as a 401(k) plan or traditional deductible IRA, before purchasing a VA from a highly rated insurer.

The real alternative to a VA is a direct investment in traditional mutual funds or ETFs. During the accumulation period, VAs offer investment options that are essentially the same as mutual funds or ETFs. Moreover, they enjoy the advantage of tax-deferral. However, tax on the appreciation of mutual fund shares is deferred until the shares are sold by the owner. Once this occurs, the realized gains are taxed at preferential capital gains rates if the owner has held the shares for more than a year. VAs do not enjoy this advantage because all appreciation is taxed at ordinary income rates. Mutual fund shares also receive a step-up in basis to their fair-market value at the owner's date of death. Conversely, there is no step-up in value in the hands of the beneficiary when the owner/annuitant dies.

The final section of this chapter explains how to evaluate the performance of a VA.

How to Evaluate VA Performance

Though not as exhaustive as its databases for mutual funds or ETFs, an active database tracking the performance of selected VAs and their individual subaccounts is maintained by Morningstar, Inc. An example of the pages of a Morningstar information for a sample VA—Perspective Advisors II, as underwritten by Jackson National Life Insurance Co. (JNL VA)—is reproduced in Figure 15-1.[1]

[1]The full Morningstar quote for the Jackson National Life Perspective II Variable Annuity (JNL VA) includes four additional pages, which list the names of the 98 subaccounts, the advisor and subadvisor for each account, the category of fund (for example, large growth or large blend), and the fixed-expense charges, as well as the Morningstar star rating for each subaccount and its percentage total return. In turn, the total returns are provided for year to date (YTD), one-year return, and a five- and ten-year return if the fund has been in existence for at least that period from the policy inception date.

Release date 09-30-2013 | FINRA Members: For internal use or client reporting purposes only. Page 1 of 5

Perspective Advisors II

Policy Inception	Policy Type	Net Assets	Subaccounts
08-29-11	VA	0.03	98

Insurance Company Information

Jackson Natl Life Insurance Co
Jackson Natl Life Insurance Co
Lansing, MI 48909-7889
—

Policy Ratings	
A.M.Best Rating	A+

Purchase Information

Premium Type	Flexible
Maximum allowable subaccounts	—
Maximum owner age	—
Closed to New Investors	Yes

Policy Features

Free Withdrawals	
Maximum % of Account Value	100.00
Minimum Withdrawal $	500.00
Transfer	
Free Transfers Per Year	—
Minimum Transfer $	—

General Features	
Dollar Cost Averaging	Yes
Rebalancing	Yes
Asset Allocation	Yes
Standard Death Benefit	PR,RF

Annuity Options	
Annuitization Type	—
Maximum Annuitant Age	—
Payment Options	
Period Certain	No
Single Life	Yes
Single Life w/Period Cert	No
Single Life w/Full Ref	Yes
Joint + Survivor w/Period Cert	No
Joint + Survivor	Yes

Minimum Initial Purchase $	
Non-Qualified	25000
Qualified	25000
Minimum Additional Purchase $	
Non-Qualified	5000
Qualified	2000
Qualification Availability	
Non-Qualified	—
Qualified	No

Fees and Expenses

Policy Charges	
Annual Contract Fee $	50
Annual Contract Fee %	—
Maximum Front Load %	0.00
M&E Risk %	1.60
Administration Charge %	0.15
Distribution Charge %	0.00
Total Insurance Expense	1.75

Surrender Charges	%
Year 0-1	—
Year 1-2	—
Year 2-3	—
Year 3-4	—
Year 4-5	—
Year 5-6	—
Year 6-7	—
Year 7-8	—
Year 8-9	—
Year 9-10	—

Subaccount Information

Equity Style

	Value	Core	Growth
Large	26	17	24
Mid	1	7	5
Small	3	2	2

Total # of Equity Subaccounts 87

Fixed-Income

	Ltd	Mod	Ext
High		5	
Mid	1	7	1
Low	4	12	

Total # of Fixed-Income Subaccounts 30

Star Ratings	
★★★★★	6
★★★★	12
★★★	28
★★	29
★	12
Not Rated	11
Total Subaccounts	98

Asset Distribution %	
Fixed	—
Variable	—
Variable Breakdown %	
Domestic Stock	—
International Stock	—
Taxable Bond	—
Money Market	—

MORNINGSTAR®

Figure 15-1. Morningstar quote and policy investment options for Jackson National Life Perspective II Variable Annuity (JNL VA), September 30, 2013

With respect to the included information for JNL VA, first note the policy rating of A+ for the particular annuity and its sponsor, Jackson National Life Insurance Co., Lansing, MI. Next, the Policy Features section provides info about:

- What, if any, percentage of the account value can be withdrawn, and what the minimum amount for any one withdrawal is
- How many transfers can be made each year, and the amount of the minimum transfer
- The annuity options and maximum owner age, if applicable
- Payment options (such as a period certain, single-life payout, and other forms of possible benefit payouts)
- General features of the policy

Next, notice the Purchase Information section and, particularly, the minimum initial purchase for non-qualified and qualified annuity forms. As with mutual funds, the "closed to new investors" notation is very important; here, the JNL VA is closed to new investors, meaning that the VA is not being sold to any new prospective purchasers. This is consistent with the practices of many insurers who have determined that they were likely too generous to past purchasers with respect to policy features and benefits. Now look at the very important Fees and Expenses section. The JNL VA is showing a total insurance expense charge of 1.75% (of the account value)—this is before additional expenses or fees charged for any guaranteed living-benefit riders offered by the insurer/sponsor. Finally, aggregate subaccount information is included, breaking down the total number of equity and fixed-income subaccounts, as well as indicating the number of Morningstar star ratings for each subaccount/mutual fund and the number of subaccounts that are not rated.

The Morningstar quote does not comment on the quality of the JNL VA, leaving it to the prospective owner/annuitant to observe that the Perspective II product is underwritten by a highly rated insurer and has total insurance expenses that are consistent in percentage amount with many other VAs. There is also a wide range of investment options offered in the form of subaccount/mutual funds, thereby ensuring the opportunity of appropriate diversification. A supplement to the Morningside quote, not reproduced in Figure 15-1, shows that many funds are offered in each asset class: domestic stock, international stock, taxable bond, and money market. Of course, the percentage breakdown of each class, and included funds, is self-directed by the individual owner/annuitant and therefore cannot be shown on an aggregate basis.

Comparison of VA Performance with Mutual Funds

As can be expected, a reliable comparison of VA to mutual fund historical performance is extremely difficult to obtain because of the exceedingly large number of products and long time period. However, academic studies, using a number of underlying assumptions, have generally arrived at the following conclusions:

- Given the increased fees, drag on historical VA performance, and its comparison to the lower fees associated with a direct mutual-fund purchase, the accumulation period of the VA should be as long as possible.
- If a lower total annualized rate of return is assumed for a VA, the number of years of accumulation period to break even with the performance of a direct mutual fund purchase becomes even longer.
- The VA purchase becomes relatively more advantageous when the continuing benefits of tax deferral are considered in the comparison to a direct mutual fund purchase.

Finally, remember that the comparison of VA performance to a direct mutual fund purchase may not really be fair, given the respective primary reasons for each purchase. A prospective purchaser of a VA is most interested in such a product for income: more precisely, to provide an income that cannot be outlived during the retirement period. A prospective purchaser of a mutual fund is probably most interested in the growth potential of the vehicle and is much less concerned about the risk of superannuation and how to prevent it.

This chapter concludes the "Managed Assets and Life Insurance Companies" part and, with it, this book's survey of the universe of PMAs. It is now time to summarize what has been covered in this book and to compare one PMA to another in tabular form in the next and final chapter.

PART

VII

Summary

CHAPTER

16

Summary of the Present and Future of Professionally Managed Assets

This book has considered the broad subject of professionally managed assets (PMAs) in several contexts. The first part discussed the "how and why" of PMAs, including basic investment concepts and the prevailing investment theory of **modern portfolio theory** (MPT) in explaining market movements and asset pricing. The book then took up individual PMAs, beginning with the most popular type: the open-ended investment company, more popularly known as a mutual fund. Three chapters were dedicated to the growth of mutual funds, long-term investing in mutual funds, and how to evaluate their performance.

Parts 3 through 6 covered in detail the following PMAs, their advantages and disadvantages, how to select them (among often multiple offerings), and how to evaluate their performance:

- Closed-end funds (CEFs)
- Unit investment trusts (UITs)
- Exchange-traded funds (ETFs)
- Hedge funds
- Managed futures funds and programs
- Private equity funds
- Master limited partnerships (MLPs)
- Real estate investment trusts (REITs)
- Separately managed accounts (SMAs)
- Variable universal life (VUL)
- Variable annuities (VAs)

Discussions along the way touched on similarities and contrasts of each of these PMAs with other products designed to accomplish the same basic investment objectives.

Tables 16-1, 16-2, and 16-3 summarize and compare each of the listed PMAs across three groups of four types each. Table 16-1 tabulates the characteristics of the four PMAs defined and regulated by the Investment Company Act of 1940 and subsequent amendments: mutual funds, CEFs, UITs, and ETFs.

Table 16-1. Comparison of 1940 ICA Managed Assets

Factors to Consider	Open-End Fund (Mutual Fund)	Closed-End Fund	Unit Investment Trust (UIT)	Exchange-Traded Fund (ETF)
Type of investor	Small (direct)	Small (broker)	Small (broker)	Small (direct)
Primary investment objective	Income and/or growth (depends on fund)	Primarily income (depends on fund)	Primarily income (depends on trust)	Income and/or growth (depends on fund)
Primary asset advantage	Diversification of assets	Ability to purchase at NAV discount	Stable income stream	Diversification of assets
Primary asset disadvantage	Sales and mgmt. expenses	High mgmt. expenses	Self-liquidating/fixed term	Transaction costs (like an individual stock)
Primary selection criteria	Quality asset manager	Quality asset manager	Low as possible expense ratio	Very low mgmt. expenses
Primary evaluation metric	Risk-adjusted return (beta)	Total distribution rate	Annualized total return (ATR)	Index benchmark ATR

Table 16-2. Comparison of Managed Assets for High-Net-Worth Individuals

Factors to Consider	Hedge Fund	Managed Futures Fund or Program	Private Equity Fund	Master Limited Partnership (MLP)
Type of investor	Accredited or qualified purchaser	Small (if fund); accredited (if program)	Accredited or institution	Tax-oriented or tax-motivated
Primary investment objective	Four categories (most common: equity hedge)	Hedging with futures	Rapid growth of private business	Real estate and oil and gas
Primary asset advantage	Possible high invest. return	Negative correlation	Creation of business value	High income yield
Primary asset disadvantage	Increased risk (use of derivatives)	Increased risk (use of leverage)	High risk of private business	Lack of liquidity of partnership interest
Primary selection criteria	Background of fund manager	Fund or program (different criteria)	Experience of private equity manager	Tax-efficiency of MLP
Primary evaluation metric	Diversified alpha	Risk-adjusted return and average drawdown	IRR and investment multiple	Distributable cash flow

Table 16-3. Comparison of Alternative and Insurance-Based Managed Assets

Factors to Consider	Real Estate Investment Trust (REIT)	Separately Managed Account (SMA)	Variable Universal Life (VUL)	Variable Annuity (VA)
Type of investor	Small (if publicly traded)	Larger individual investor	Insurance owner/investor	Annuity owner/investor
Primary investment objective	Real estate income or gains	Depends on investment policy statement	Growth of death benefit	Growth of cash value or benefit base
Primary asset advantage	Diversification of real estate assets	Custom risk management	Flexibility in premiums	Tax-deferral of growth
Primary asset disadvantage	Management fees (if non-public)	High management cost	High relative cost	High relative cost
Primary selection criteria	Types of real estate assets	Services provided by invest. advisor	Policy features and insurer	Living benefit guarantees
Primary evaluation metric	Dividend yield	Composite ATR	ATR of underlying funds	ATR of underlying funds

Table 16-2 tabulates the characteristics of managed assets that are marketed exclusively or primarily to high-net-worth investors (mostly accredited investors as that term is defined in Regulation D to the Securities Act of 1933): hedge funds, managed futures funds and programs, private equity funds, and MLPs.

Table 16-3 tabulates the characteristics of four types of alternative and insurance-based PMAs: REITs, SMAs, VULs, and VAs.[1]

The Future of Professionally Managed Assets

The future of PMAs is exceedingly bright! Most if not all PMAs share the common characteristic of providing instant diversification of assets, an attribute that most small investors cannot achieve with the purchase of individual stocks or bonds. Certain PMAs, such as hedge funds, offer the ability to hedge investor risk by taking advantage of opposite positions in the market. Finally, other PMAs, such as managed futures, exhibit negative correlation with the majority of market assets, which can prove valuable in a declining market.

With respect to specific PMAs, expect the tremendous growth of ETFs to continue. Similarly, index or passively managed mutual funds will likely increase in importance. The primary reason for the growth of these PMAs is directly related to their cost advantage; both are able to provide diversification for the small investor at a much lower cost than other PMAs that depend on active management strategies. A 2012 study found an approximate 1% cost advantage, translated into actual long-term performance, of ETFs in comparison to actively managed mutual funds.[2] Such cost savings can add up to a tremendous total-dollars-accumulated advantage for ETFs. How much of an advantage? Assume that an investor invests a lump sum of $100,000 in both an actively managed fund and ETF at age 25. Both PMAs achieve an annualized total return of 8% over the typical 40-year work-life expectancy of an investor, or until the investor attains the age of 65. ETF A's management fee is 0.20%, and actively managed mutual fund B's management fee is 1.20%. Thus, the investor in the ETF obtains a 1% overall (after-fee) performance advantage. At the time of the investor's retirement at age 65, the investor will have $627,734 more in the ETF than in the actively managed mutual fund. To be precise, the ETF will accumulate a future value of $2,017,207 (with an after-fee return of 7.8%), whereas the mutual fund will accumulate to $1,389,473 (with an after-fee return of 6.8%).

[1]Derivative assets are mentioned only sporadically in this book. I urge you to seek out additional information on derivatives, because they are much in the financial news these days, both in a positive and negative light. Such information is available both in academic textbook and practical treatise form.

[2]Lubos Pastor and Robert F. Stambaugh, "On the Size of the Active Management Industry," *Journal of Political Economy*, University of Chicago Press, vol. 120(4), (2012): pp 740–781.

Conversely, expect the attractiveness of relatively high-cost PMAs to decline. As mentioned in Chapter 9, the combined asset management-carried interest fee charged by hedge fund managers has already been driven down since 2008 by the institutional investors that make up a large percentage of that PMA's client base. A similar phenomenon has occurred in the corporate world, where "pay for performance" continues to undergo revisions, usually resulting in a lower bonus or incentive award for the corporate executive. Other PMAs that may decline in importance owing to their relatively high cost are VUL policies and VAs. However, other motives for the purchase of these assets, such as life insurance and retirement income protection, may act to somewhat offset the cost disadvantage.

I hope this book has, if nothing else, given you an appreciation for the use of PMAs in your investment portfolio as well as an understanding of the advantages and disadvantages of each treated asset. As investors' financial goals continue to be better defined by investment professionals, it is likely that additional PMAs will be developed to fulfill them. The likelihood of a profitable financial future depends on your staying abreast of the PMA choices available in the marketplace and their particular suitability to the achievement of your financial goals.

Glossary

A

accredited investor. A permissible—or sometimes exclusive—investor in certain professionally managed assets, such as a hedge fund or a private equity fund. A formal definition is found in Rule 501 of Regulation D of Securities Act of 1933 and includes both institutions and specified individuals. For an individual to be considered as an accredited investor, they must have: (1) a net worth, or joint net worth with the individual's spouse, in excess of $1.0 million at the time of the purchase of the asset, excluding the value of the primary residence of such individual; or (2) income exceeding $200,000 in each of the two most recent years, or joint income with a spouse in excess of $300,000 for those years, and a reasonable expectation of the same income level in the current year.

actively managed (active management). A form of portfolio management that requires the manager to make specific investment decisions with respect to asset allocation and security selection using various analytical tools, such as intrinsic-value models of valuation. The goal of this form of management is to achieve a return in excess of previously specified market indexes. This type of portfolio management is to be contrasted to *passive management* in which the manager attempts only to replicate a market index return.

Alternative Minimum Tax (AMT). A separate form of individual or corporate taxation in which the individual or corporation pays the higher of this separately computed tax or the regular income tax. The AMT form of computation includes the adding back of specified *tax preferences*, such as the inclusion of (otherwise) tax-exempt interest payable from municipal bonds.

annualized return (a.k.a. effective annual return). Effective annual return = $(1+HPR)^m - 1$, where HPR is the *holding period return* and m is the number of holding periods in a single calendar year.

arbitrage. The simultaneous purchase and sale of identical assets and currencies to take advantage of price differences in different markets, including international asset and currency markets. Effectively, the making of a risk-free profit by an investor.

B

benefit base. An amount used in a variable annuity with *living benefits* to calculate the amount of funds on which the annuitant can draw income annually. Typically, the amount is calculated based on the amount of annuity principal and grows each year by a guaranteed rate, such as 5%. The annuitant receives this rate of return in each year for which a withdrawal is not taken and for a specified time period or until a specified maximum age is reached.

beta (or beta coefficient). A measure of the systematic (market) risk associated with a particular stock or stock mutual fund. The measure is also part of the *capital asset pricing model* (CAPM) used to determine the required return of a stock or portfolio. The formula for beta is

$$\beta_i = (\rho_{im} * \sigma_i)/\sigma_m$$

Where β_i is the beta coefficient of a sample asset, ρ_{im} is the correlation coefficient between the asset and the market, and σ_i and σ_m are the *standard deviation* of the asset and market, respectively.

broker (or stock broker). An individual who serves as an intermediary in bringing together market participants, owing a duty of suitability (or finding suitable investments) to the investor/client.

C

capital asset pricing model (CAPM). A model as developed by William Sharpe and others based on the proposition that a stock's expected rate of return is equal to the risk-free rate of return plus risk premiums for market and stock, assuming a diversified portfolio. The model permits computation of an investor's required rate of return given these assumptions by the formula

$$r_i = r_f + (r_m - r_f)\beta_i$$

Where r_i is the expected return of the stock (or required rate of return of the investor), r_f is the risk-free rate of return, r_m is the return of the market, and β_i is the *beta* coefficient of the stock.

capitalization rate. A rate of return on real estate or a small, private business based on the amount of income that the real estate or business will generate in the future. Such rate is often used to estimate an investor's potential rate of return on an investment. It is the reciprocal of the earnings multiplier or price-earnings ratio.

commodity. A tangible or intangible asset whose price is determined by supply and demand. An example of a tangible commodity is an agricultural product, such as wheat, and an example of an intangible asset is a currency.

conduit principle. A principle under tax law specifying that the entity's income is passed through to the individual owner (or owners), included in the individual's taxable income, and taxed at the individual's top marginal rate. Alternatively, the entity serves only as a "conduit" or shell for purposes of transferring the entity's taxable liability to its individual owner.

conglomerate. A business that has expanded into areas of operation different and distinct from its original purpose. An example of such a business is General Electric.

correlation. The tendency of two variables to move together, expressed in a standardized manner with a number ranging between –1.0 (for perfect negative correlation) and +1.0 (for perfect positive correlation). Zero expresses no identifiable linear relationship.

coupon rate. The stated rate of interest on a fixed-income obligation, such as a bond. Specifically, the dollar amount of interest paid to a bondholder annually (or coupon payment) divided by the bond's *par* value, usually $1,000.

credit default swap. A transaction that is designed to transfer the risk of fixed-income products, such as a collateralized debt obligation, between parties. The transaction is considered insurance against non-payment by the underlying obligor or debtor.

crowdfunding. Effectively, the use of small amounts of investor capital or cash infusions to finance a new business venture. Recently, the term has come to be equated with the financing of a new business through Internet solicitations.

custodian. A financial institution, such as Charles Schwab & Co. or TD Ameritrade Institutional, responsible for the safekeeping of an investor's market assets; typically used by an *investment advisor* or financial planner in the management of a client's funds.

D

defined contribution plan. A category of tax-*qualified retirement plan*, such as a 401(k) plan, in which the amount of employer and employee contributions is "defined" (limited) by tax law. More generally, **a defined contribution plan** is a retirement plan that adopts a profit-sharing orientation to structuring and funding a participant's individual account balance, as contrasted to a pension plan or defined-benefit type of tax-*qualified retirement plan*.

distributable cash flow. A metric used in the evaluation of master limited partnerships (MLPs), among other assets, that measures the amount of cash available to limited partners. Specifically, the metric is computed by adding back non-cash items to the net income generated by the MLP and subtracting capital expenditures made in the year or period evaluated.

dividend reinvestment plan (DRIP). A type of automatic reinvestment offered by many stocks and mutual funds whereby declared dividends are reinvested (rather than being distributed to the shareholder) to purchase additional shares of stock. The major advantage of the plan is cost-effectiveness, including the avoidance of brokerage commissions on the share purchases.

dividend yield. The portion of cash flow from a stock that is represented by the payment of a dividend. The yield is computed by dividing the end-of-period dividend by the beginning-of-period price of the stock on a per-share basis.

dollar cost averaging. An investment strategy that involves the purchase of a fixed value of securities at regular periods to reduce the impact of price fluctuations. The goal of the strategy is to purchase as many securities as possible regardless of price and market conditions.

due diligence. An investigation of all the material facts related to the possible purchase of an investment. Commonly used to describe the process of selecting private companies to include among the positions of a private equity fund.

duration. A measure of a bond's interest-rate sensitivity. Specifically, the weighted average time it takes to collect a bond's interest and principal repayment on a present-value basis.

E

economic value added (EVA). A method used to compute a firm's profitability as generated only by internal operations. Specifically, EVA is computed by taking the firm's net operating profit after taxes (NOPAT) and subtracting the annual cost of all the capital that is expended by the firm. If the firm has generated a positive EVA, value has been created for the shareholder/owners.

effective annual rate (EAR). The rate that, under annual compounding, would have generated the same future value at the end of the first year as was provided by more frequent compounding, such as monthly or quarterly. The rate is different from the annual percentage rate (APR) quoted on an asset or liability unless the returns on an annual basis are equivalent (that is, each return is compounded only annually).

Efficient Market Hypothesis (EMH). An underlying theory of market behavior that posits that all important information with respect to securities is reflected in the price of that asset as determined by market participants. The logical conclusion of the theory is that it is impossible for an investor to consistently outperform a market basket of securities or a market index adjusted for risk and trading costs.

equity-based stock option. A right to acquire employer stock (an option on the stock) at some predetermined time in the future at a predetermined price; typically, granted to executives of a firm as incentive compensation to perform well and thereby substantially increase the market price of the underlying stock.

exchange-traded note (ETN). A type of debt security that is traded on a major securities exchange, such as the New York Stock Exchange. However, unlike stocks of an exchange-traded fund (ETF), which have no maturity date, purchasers of an ETN can hold the security until maturity, at which time the purchaser receives a cash amount equal to the principal amount as based on the performance of a market index.

F

formula investing. A broad form of investment strategy where an investor does not actively trade or manage their portfolio, but instead follows a certain set of automatic rules regardless of market conditions. An example of the form includes *dollar cost averaging*.

4% plus annual inflation withdrawal rate. A popular rule of retirement income planning enunciated by financial planners, positing that a retiree has a high probability of not outliving their accumulated retirement funds by withdrawing an annual amount equal to 4% of principal, subsequently increasing the amount by the rate of annual inflation.

fund family. A number of mutual funds offered by the same investment company, such as Fidelity Investments or Vanguard Funds. The advantage of the approach is increased flexibility for the investor with the offering of multiple funds to meet their investment objectives.

fund of funds. Historically, mutual funds that invest in the shares of mutual funds. More recently, an investment strategy followed by hedge funds and private equity funds, among others.

G

guaranteed investment contract (GIC). A debt security offered by an insurance company, where the interest rate paid is guaranteed but the principal of the security is not (although the risk of default is, nonetheless, very small). The security is usually issued in large denominations and is heavily used in both defined-benefit and defined-contribution types of retirement plans, particularly where a pension benefit is promised by the employer/sponsor.

guaranteed minimum income benefit (GMIB). A type of additional benefit (rider) available in a variable annuity contract ensuring that an annuitant will receive an income payment from the annuity regardless of market conditions. The benefit option is primarily advantageous for those annuitant/owners who plan to annuitize their annuity during the distribution stage.

H

hedging. The taking of opposite positions (long and short) in an asset at the same time to reduce the risk of loss through price fluctuations. An example of hedging is a hedge fund or a managed futures program or fund.

holding company depository receipt (HOLDR). A basket of approximately 20 stocks selected by Bank of America Merrill Lynch to represent a market sector, a subsector, or an industry. Similar to ETFs, HOLDRs may be bought and sold throughout the day (like a stock) and have lower-than-average expenses.

I

income withdrawal benefit. A popular *living benefit* offered by a variable annuity that allows the annuitant the right to withdraw a maximum percentage of their investment each year until the initial contribution amount is fully recovered. An example is the guaranteed minimum withdrawal benefit (GMWB).

Individual Alternative Minimum Tax. One of the two forms of the *Alternative Minimum Tax* system; the other form applies to corporations.

initial public offering (IPO). The first or initial sale of common stock to the general public, usually with the assistance of an investment banking firm. In the private market, the sale of common stock to private investors (and functional equivalent of an IPO) is a private placement.

interest yield. The portion of cash flow from a bond that is represented by the payment of interest, usually semi-annually. More broadly, the yield of a bond reflects the true rate of return for investors who purchase the bond at a variable price (that is, at *par* value, at a discount from par, or at a premium to par).

investment advisor (IA). An individual licensed to provide investment advice to investors, who may or may not also be a *broker* licensed to sell securities to the general public. An investment advisor assumes a fiduciary duty to act in the exclusive benefit of clients at all times.

investment policy statement (IPS). A written document or agreement between the *investment advisor* and investor/client specifying such items as the optimal asset allocation for the investor. Such a statement is required by law if the investment advisor is providing investment advice with respect to a *qualified retirement plan*, but it is also recommended in investment activities generally.

K

key person life insurance. A type of life insurance policy purchased by a business insuring the life of a key member of the business, such as the owner or manager, with the business as policy beneficiary and the death proceeds from the policy serving as income replacement for the business.

L

leverage. Broadly, the use of debt in the capital structure of a firm; however, the term is commonly used to describe the use of borrowed money in investing. The effect of leverage is to magnify the potential gain from an investment, but it also increases the risk of an investment through the magnifying effect of any loss.

living benefit. A term used in a life insurance product, such as an annuity, to describe the use of a policy or contract feature during the lifetime of the insured or annuitant/owner. Such benefit is usually available to the purchaser of the product in the form of an additional policy feature at an additional premium or percentage charge (otherwise referred to as a policy rider).

M

Marcus study. An empirical study ("The Magellan Fund and Market Efficiency," *Journal of Portfolio Management*, 1990) by A. J. Marcus exploring the reasons for the success of Fidelity Investment's Magellan Fund as then managed by Peter Lynch.

margin. The amount that an investor/purchaser must contribute from their own money when buying securities on credit. The initial margin amount is established by the Federal Reserve Board, with the subsequent maintenance margin amount to be maintained established by the brokerage firm/lender.

mark-to-market. An accounting practice recording the price of a security or account to reflect its current market value rather than its book (or accounting) value. The practice is commonly done in the futures market to ensure that *margin* requirements are satisfied daily, with the possible result that the future participant will be faced with a margin call if the current market value causes the margin account to fall below the required maintenance margin amount.

market capitalization. The market value of the company's stock as determined by multiplying the current price per share of the stock times the number of outstanding shares. Commonly, market capitalization is differentiated into large, medium or mid, and small types of stock.

modern portfolio theory (MPT). A theory first developed by Harry Markowitz, premised on a risk-averse investor constructing a diversified portfolio establishing the investor's satisfaction or utility by maximizing portfolio returns for a given level of risk. A hallmark of the theory is the creation of an efficient frontier of all portfolios that offer the highest amount of expected return for a given amount of risk as measured by the portfolio's *standard deviation*.

modified endowment contract (MEC). A term in tax law that classifies as an investment an insurance policy that does not satisfy certain rules, thus resulting in the taxable earnings from a cash-value life insurance policy being recovered first before the non-taxable return of capital invested in the policy. Effectively, it results in a "last-in-first-out" tax treatment of loans or withdrawals of a life insurance policy's cash value, constituting a reversal of the normal rule of taxation that applies to regular or non-MEC life insurance policies.

momentum-based. A type of *active management* investment strategy with an investor goal of capitalizing on the continuance of existing market trends. Specifically, the strategy seeks to purchase stocks that are currently much in favor with market investors ("hot" stocks) while selling stocks that are out of favor ("cold" stocks).

money market mutual fund (MMMF). A type of mutual fund that specializes in the purchase of short-term or money market securities, such as Treasury bills, negotiable certificates of deposit, commercial paper, or bankers' acceptances.

N

net asset value (NAV). The asset value of a share in an investment company, such as a mutual fund. Such value is determined by subtracting the total liabilities of the investment company from its total assets and then dividing the result by the number of shares outstanding in the company.

non-forfeiture options. A series of choices or options offered to the owner of a life insurance policy that is allowed to lapse or terminate. Specifically, such options provide the owner with the ability to use any accumulated cash value in the policy to surrender the policy for cash, purchase additional paid-up protection, or purchase extended term protection.

P

passive loss. A term in tax law that is used to generally prohibit the deduction of a loss in value from a property or security in which the investor does not materially participate. The provision operates to generally deny the deduction of the loss in value (suspends the loss) until the property or security generating the loss is sold. It commonly applies in *master limited partnership* (MLP) and limited partnership investments.

passively managed (or passive management). A form of portfolio management where the manager seeks to earn a return for investors equal only to a broad-based market index, such as the Standard & Poor's 500 index. This type of portfolio management is to be contrasted with *active management*, which requires the portfolio manager to practice investment strategies and employ investment tools designed to achieve a return for investors in excess of the benchmark market index. Passive management is employed by most ETF and index fund managers.

prospectus. The formal legal document filed with the Securities and Exchange Commission by a company engaged in an *IPO* (or other subsequent solicitation of capital) that details important facts about a securities offering, such as a mutual fund. The equivalent of a prospectus in a private market solicitation of funds is the *private placement memorandum* (PPM).

Q

qualified dividend. A tax term that permits the recipient of the dividend to take advantage of a preferential tax rate (currently the same as that afforded long-term capital gain income) in the payment of taxes on dividend income. A dividend is considered qualified if it is declared and paid by a domestic corporation or a qualified foreign corporation and the stock is held by the investor for at least 60 days prior to the ex-dividend date of the stock.

qualified retirement plan. A tax term describing a retirement plan that meets a number of requirements under I.R.C. Section 401(a), most notably a non-discrimination requirement making the plan benefits available to all eligible employees. A common example of a qualified retirement plan is a Section 401(k) retirement plan, named after the Internal Revenue Code section and subsection authorizing the same.

R

R-squared (a.k.a. coefficient of determination). A statistical measure derived by squaring the correlation coefficient between two variables. In investments, R-squared tells a prospective investor how much of the movement of a security, such as a mutual fund, is determined by the movement of the overall market. The higher the fund's R-squared, the more likely the fund is well-diversified.

regulated investment company. A company that is regulated or qualified under Regulation M of the U.S. Treasury Regulations to pass taxes on investment gains or losses made at the company level through to investors at the individual level. Examples include an open-end investment company (mutual fund), a closed-end fund (CEF), or a unit investment trust (UIT).

restricted stock plan. A type of non-qualified compensation plan typically afforded to executives by employers, but which restricts the transferability of the stock until a specified "substantial risk of forfeiture" terminates or lapses. An example of such a restriction is a prohibition with respect to sale of the stock until the executive has performed a specified number of years of service with the employer.

risk-adjusted return. Any type of investor return that includes a quantification of investor risk or the uncertainty of future returns. An example of a risk-adjusted return is the required rate of return of the investor used in *modern portfolio theory.*

S

semivariance. In investments, a measure of the dispersion of actual or expected returns that occur below the average or mean return. The measure is also used to statistically quantify the possibility of a below-average annual return or downside volatility. An alternative measure of risk as compared to *standard deviation*, which measures total volatility.

short-term capital gains. A tax term specifying the taxation of an investment that is held (owned) by an investor for one year or less before it is sold at an appreciated value. Specifically, an appreciated investment that is held short term is taxed at the same marginal rate as investor salary and wages, also referred to as ordinary income.

speculation. An investment that offers a potentially large investment return but is also very risky (may experience considerable volatility or excessive price movements up or down). More broadly, term implies a reasonable probability that the investment will experience a significant loss. In the future markets, a speculator takes the opposite position of a hedger and is transferred the price risk that the hedger is trying to avoid.

split-dollar life insurance. A contractual agreement under which the costs and benefits of a life insurance policy are shared between the employer and employee/executive. There are several types of split-dollar insurance and methods of payment, but all afford a fringe or work-related benefit to the employee/executive.

spot-futures parity. A relationship in the futures market that reflects, by use of a formula, the appropriate futures price of a *commodity* or financial instrument as compared to its current (spot) rate. Spot-futures parity is an example of the "law of one price," by which parity between the two prices should hold or opportunities for *arbitrage* will occur.

spread. Used in a number of references to investments and financial markets, most commonly refers to the difference between the bid and ask prices when purchasing or selling a security.

standard deviation. A statistical measure of the volatility of a set of observations. In investments, standard deviation is used to quantitatively measure the amount of total risk of an asset or portfolio and is derived by computing the square root of the variance.

systematic risk. One of two components of the total risk of an asset or portfolio, with the other component reflecting unsystematic or company-specific risk. Also known as non-diversifiable risk or market risk, systematic risk is the risk from fluctuations in securities prices as measured by a stock's or portfolio's *beta* or *beta coefficient*.

T

target (date) fund. A type of mutual fund that automatically resets its asset allocation based on a selected time frame for the investor. Commonly, the date used for resetting the asset allocation in the portfolio is the investor's planned or estimated retirement year.

tax-deferred account. An investor account where taxes on the income from investments in the account are deferred until some point in time occurring in the future. The most notable example of a tax-deferred account is a retirement plan established by the investor.

tax-exempt account. An investor account in which there is no taxation now or in the future on the income from investments that are part of the account. The most notable example of a tax-exempt account is an account or portfolio consisting entirely of municipal bonds.

term sheet. A non-binding agreement used in private equity transactions, specifying the terms under which an investment will be made. Typically, the term sheet specifies an investor's rights and obligations when making an investment in a private equity fund.

time value of money (a.k.a. discounted cash flow analysis). Generally, the concept that a dollar received tomorrow (its future value) is not equal in value to a dollar received today (its present value). A critical concept in finance, time value of money computations use the process of compounding and discounting to determine the future value and present value of a single sum, respectively, and payments of an equal amount to determine the future and present value of an annuity.

transfer-for-value rule. A tax rule specifying that if a life insurance policy is transferred for value (sold) to a third party, a portion of the death proceeds payable from the policy is taxable to the third-party purchaser. If an exception to the rule applies, the proceeds are nontaxable to the purchaser or the normal rule of income taxation of death proceeds applies.

turnover ratio. In investments, the portion or percentage of a mutual fund's holdings or positions that have been replaced with other holdings. Effectively, the higher the turnover ratio, the less tax-efficient is the fund and the greater is the taxable pass-through of gains and losses to the mutual fund shareholder.

12b-1 fee. A fee charged by some mutual funds to cover marketing expenses and promotional distributions of the fund. Usually, a 12b-1 fee is charged in addition to fund-management expenses, service charges, and *load fees*.

U

universal life. A type of cash-value life insurance policy that features flexible premium payments and an adjustable death benefit. The cash-value accumulation is uncertain, but the policy offers a minimum cash-value guarantee. Unlike a traditional whole life insurance policy, universal life separates the death-benefit element from the accumulation element of the policy.

unrelated business taxable income (UBTI). Income generated usually by a *qualified retirement plan* trust that is unrelated to the trust's tax-exempt purpose and is, therefore, subject to tax. An example of UBTI is any investment made by the tax-exempt trust using borrowed money (*leverage*), which is generally categorized as a prohibited transaction engaged in by the trust.

V

variable life. A type of cash-value life insurance policy that provides a guaranteed minimum death benefit, but a benefit that generally fluctuates based on the market value of investments in the separate account within the policy. In addition, the cash-surrender value of the policy fluctuates depending on the market value of the underlying investments, usually mutual funds.

variable universal life (VUL). A type of cash-value life insurance policy featuring flexible premiums and separate cash-value investment accounts. Effectively, a combination of the features and benefits of the *universal life* and *variable life* types of life insurance policy.

W

whole life. A type of cash-value life insurance policy providing protection for the entire or "whole" life of the insured. It is the most historically common type of life insurance and requires premium payments under a continuous payment arrangement or on a limited payment basis. The cash value is usually invested in conservative-type investments, such as bonds, and is part of the insurer's general reserves.

Y

yield to maturity (YTM). The compound average annual rate of interest earned on a bond if it is held to maturity. If the bond is bought at *par* and held until maturity, the YTM is equal to the *coupon rate* on the bond; whereas if the bond is selling at a discount (or premium) to par, the YTM is more (or less) than the coupon rate, respectively.

I

Index

F

G

H

N

O

P

Q

R

S

T

U

V

W, X

Y, Z

MIX
Papier aus verantwortungsvollen Quellen
Paper from responsible sources
FSC® C105338

If you have any concerns about our products,
you can contact us on
ProductSafety@springernature.com

In case Publisher is established outside the EU,
the EU authorized representative is:
Springer Nature Customer Service Center GmbH
Europaplatz 3, 69115 Heidelberg, Germany

Printed by Libri Plureos GmbH
in Hamburg, Germany